Colonial and Postcolonial Incarceration

COLONIAL AND POSTCOLONIAL INCARCERATION

Edited by

Graeme Harper

continuum
LONDON • NEW YORK

Continuum
The Tower Building, 11 York Road, London SE1 7NX
370 Lexington Avenue, New York, NY 10017-6503

First published 2001

British Library Cataloguing-in-Publication Data

A catalogue record for this book is available from the British Library.

ISBN 0-8264-4865-8 (hardback)
  0-8264-4918-2 (paperback)

Library of Congress Cataloging-in-Publication Data

Colonial and post-colonial incarceration / edited by Graeme Harper.
    p.   cm.
  Includes bibliographical references and index.
  ISBN 0–8264–4865–8 — ISBN 0–8264–4918–2 (pbk.)
  1. Imprisonment—History. 2. Slavery—History. 3. Colonization—History.
  4. Postcolonialism—History. 5. Imprisonment in literature. 6. Imperialism in literature.
  I. Harper, Graeme.

HV8705 .C65 2001
364.6—dc21

                                                                    2001017324

Typeset by CentraServe Ltd, Saffron Walden, Essex
Printed and bound in Great Britain by Creative Print & Design Wales

Contents

Contributors

John Brannigan is Research Fellow at the Institute of Irish Studies, The Queen's University of Belfast. He is the author of *New Historicism and Cultural Materialism* (Macmillan, 1998) and *Beyond the Angry Young Men: Literature and Culture in England, 1945–1965* (forthcoming, 2001). He has also published essays on postcolonial literature, literary theory and contemporary English writing. He is currently working on a book-length study of the writings of Brendan Behan.

Di Gan was born in China and educated there before she came to the United States for graduate study. She received her MA in American Studies from Baylor University in 1997 and is currently working on her dissertation for a doctoral degree in American Literature. She is married to Marcelo Blackburn.

Shane Graham is a doctoral candidate in English and African Studies at Indiana University, Bloomington. He is currently writing a dissertation entitled 'Trauma, Memory, and Representation in South African Prison Writing and the Truth Commission'.

Emily A. Haddad is Associate Professor of English and Coordinator of Graduate Studies in English at the University of South Dakota. Her book, *Orientalist Poetics: The Islamic Middle East in Nineteenth-Century British and French Poetry*, is forthcoming from Ashgate Publishing. She is also author of an article on Florence Nightingale's travels in Egypt, which appeared in *The Journal of African Travel Writing*, and she has contributed a chapter to *Borders, Exiles, Diasporas*, a volume published by Stanford University Press. She received her PhD in Comparative Literature from Harvard University.

Graeme Harper is Director of the Development Centre for the Creative and Performing Arts at the University of Wales, Bangor. His publications include *Black Cat, Green Field* (Transworld), *Swallowing Film* (Q) and a range of work in various anthologies, books and journals, including *Ariel, Dalhousie Review, Sight and Sound, CineAction, Southerly* and *Outrider*, as well as biographical studies in the *Dictionary of Literary Biography* and *New*

Dictionary of National Biography and original works of fiction and film. He holds doctorates from the University of Technology, Sydney, and from the University of East Anglia. His awards include the Australian National Book Council Award for New Writing, the Premier's Award for Writing, a Commonwealth Universities' scholarship and a European Union fellowship.

John C. Hawley is Associate Professor of English at Santa Clara University, California. He has edited ten books, including *Christian Encounters with the Other* (New York University Press, 1997) and *The Postcolonial Crescent* (Peter Lang, 1997). His research interests are Victorian and postcolonial literature, gender studies and the intersection between religion and literature. He currently serves on the executive committee of the Pacific Ancient and Modern Language Association, and is past Chair of the MLA's Executive Committee on Literature and Religion.

James D. Le Sueur is Assistant Professor of History at the University of Nebraska-Lincoln. He received his PhD from the University of Chicago in 1996. He is the author of *Uncivil War: Intellectuals and Identity Politics During the French–Algerian War* (University of Pennsylvania Press, 2001) and is editor of the English translation of Mouloud Feraoun's *Journal, 1955–1962: Reflections on the French–Algerian War* (University of Nebraska Press, 2000), *The Decolonization Reader* (Routledge, forthcoming), and the *Decolonization Sourcebook* (Routledge, forthcoming). He is the editor of the republication of *Assassination! July 14* (University of Nebraska Press, 2001) for which he has written 'Before the Jackal', a monographic essay of the novel's publishing history. His current research focuses on immigration, popular cultural and right-wing radicalism in France in the aftermath of decolonization.

Susan K. Martin is a Senior Lecturer in the School of English, La Trobe University, Melbourne. She has written extensively on nineteenth-century Australian women's writing and on representations of Australian space. She is currently working on a study of the understanding of space in Australia, and a jointly authored project on the cultural meaning of gardens and gardening in nineteenth- and twentieth-century Australia, called 'The Culture of Gardens in Australia'.

Cynthia L. Ragland is an Assistant Professor, teaching early American and Native American literature in the English Department at Central Connecticut State University in New Britain, Connecticut. She formerly taught at the University of Wisconsin–Oshkosh, where she first became interested in both early American epidemics and Indian captivity narratives. Presently, she is researching the factual and fictional Indian captivity narratives of the nineteenth century and also the narratives of Native

American children who attended federal, off-reservation boarding schools in the late nineteenth and early twentieth centuries.

D'Arcy Randall worked as Senior Editor at the University of Queensland Press in Brisbane, Australia and is now a doctoral candidate in the Department of English at the University of Texas at Austin. She taught a comparative course in Australian and Texas film and literature, co-founded the journal *Borderlands: Texas Poetry Review*, and has published articles, essays and poetry in a variety of journals in Australia, Canada and the USA.

Mary Ross is undertaking postgraduate studies at La Trobe University, Melbourne, specializing in international prison narratives. She has presented papers at the African Studies Association of Australia biannual postgraduate conference and the Australian and Iberian Latin American Association annual conference, both focusing on literary themes in prison writing.

Kay Schaffer is an Associate Professor in the Department of Social Inquiry at Adelaide University, where she teaches on the Gender Studies and Cultural Studies programmes. Her books include *Women and the Bush: Forces of Desire in the Australian Cultural Tradition* (Cambridge University Press, 1988/89), and *In the Wake of First Contact: the Eliza Fraser Stories* (Cambridge University Press, 1995). She has edited *The Olympics at the Millennium: Power, Politics and the Games* with Sidonie Smith (Rutger University Press, 2000), *Constructions of Colonialism: Perspectives on Eliza Fraser's Shipwreck*, with Ian McNiven and Lynette Russell (Cassell/Leicester University Press, 1998), and *Indigenous Australian Voices: a Reader* with Jennifer Sabbioni and Sidonie Smith (Rutgers University Press, 1998).

Kerry Sinanan is completing her doctoral thesis at Trinity College Dublin. Her primary area of research investigates the eighteenth-century British slave trade to the Caribbean, reading texts by slavers, ex-slaves, planters and abolitionists. She teaches a wide range of courses in Trinity College Dublin, and in University College Dublin, including Postcolonial Studies, Gender Studies, and literature from the Renaissance to the nineteenth century.

Daniel J. Vitkus is Assistant Professor of English at Florida State University and specializes in Shakespeare, Renaissance drama and the culture of early modern England. Dr Vitkus taught for six years at the American University in Cairo, Egypt, before moving to Florida. He has edited *Three Turk Plays from Early Modern England* (Columbia University Press, 2000) and *Piracy, Slavery and Redemption: Barbary Captivity Narratives from Early Modern England* (Columbia University Press, 2001) and is currently completing a book-length study titled *Turning Turk: English Theater and the Multicultural Mediterranean.*

James Whitlark is Professor of English at Texas Tech University, where he has won the New Professor Excellence in Teaching Award and the President's Excellence in Teaching Award. He is the author of *Illuminated Fantasy: From Blake's Visions to Recent Graphic Fiction* (Fairleigh Dickinson University Press, 1988) and *Behind the Great: A Post-Jungian Approach to Kafkaesque Literature* (Fairleigh Dickinson University Press, 1991).

Acknowledgements

A book on colonial incarceration and its narratives has been brewing in my mind since my first doctoral work, beginning in 1990 under the supervision of Professor Stephen Muecke at the University of Technology, Sydney. Stephen, whose work on Australian indigenous culture, its languages and philosophies, is rightly renowned, was a good sounding-board for my early research on colonial incarceration – those trips to former colonial outposts around the world; time spent in the prison houses of America, Australia, Africa, the visit to what was, perhaps, the final days of a configuration known as 'Eastern Europe'. I thank him for this early encouragement.

I wish also to acknowledge, formally, the obvious and essential contribution made by Continuum Publishers in commissioning this book, in particular Janet Joyce for following the project through to completion and, with her assistant, Valerie Hall, ensuring that it reached its audience. My heartfelt thanks, Janet, for your ongoing support.

In addition, and very importantly, I owe a great debt of gratitude to Linda Jones, our departmental Research Administrator. As assistant, supportive reader of my editorial changes, checker of copy, chaser of references, fixer of format, she has been absolutely superb. This book owes much to her energy, thoroughness and attention to detail.

I also thank my wife Louise and our two boys, Myles and Tyler – Louise who accompanied me on those prison trips, not always to the most pleasant of situations (being caught in two national revolutions was hardly my plan!), and the boys who have had to listen to talk about things which, in the majority of families, have no place in casual conversations over coffee.

Finally, sincere thanks go to the contributors. It is the intention of this book to show as wide a range of cultural and stylistic approaches to what 'colonial incarceration' involves, how it has appeared and how its history can be discussed. The writers have come from different backgrounds, different discourses and different thematic positions, but they have equally applied themselves to their work with great vigour and support. Thanks to each, and all, of you.

*For all those who remain, through political
oppression, or cultural and economic subjugation,
incarcerated – even here in our 'advanced' twenty-first century!*

Introduction

GRAEME HARPER

Has the non-West ever subjected the West to as many, or as brutal, a set of instances of incarceration as that imposed in the name of Western imperialism? The question is a moot one. It would be wrong, of course, to think that imperialism, and its counterpart colonialism, have been restricted to the wants and desires of Westerners. Colonial ambition, imperial politics and, more broadly, cultural and economic hegemony are part of human life; certainly, they are an integral part of the human discourses of modernity. That this modernity has often been branded as Western is, perhaps, one reason that colonial incarceration seems to be linked most strongly with the rise of Western cultural and economic hegemony. But this simple equation should not be taken for granted.

Colonial and Postcolonial Incarceration considers the narratives of incarceration as they are generated through the discourses of imperialism and colonialism, charts instances of colonial incarceration – the historical, personal and cultural narratives that have sprung up in and around it – and the ways in which 'incarceration' (I put the word in quotation marks here to emphasize that it has both a literal and a metaphoric dimension) has been part and parcel of the making of *post*colonial societies. Showing the sometimes ill-defined boundaries between 'warders' and 'prisoners' is one way of recognizing that some general aspects of incarceration have been integral to the making of colonized societies; likewise, that the reach of carceral discourse goes well beyond the physical appearance of the prison and its bars. In this regard, many of the functional traces of the carceral identified by Michel Foucault in *Discipline and Punish: The Birth of the Prison* stand up to examination in this study of colonial incarceration. However, Foucault's thesis also quickly reveals its Eurocentric roots. Where the elements of cultural and personal evolution (which colonization by definition imposes) can be located in Foucault's ode to the panopticon is difficult to imagine. Likewise, where Foucault's discussion of the artifice of justice can be placed in such a cultural, economic and societal mêlée that is colonialism is highly debatable. Not least, it has been important to acknowledge here the full extent of what can be called the 'the colonization of freedom' – the situation by which a day-to-day life becomes an exemplar for a form of colonial subjugation or subservience – and to consider the role of individual experience in exposing the conditions of a subjugated yet often vibrant colonized culture.

When Ignatius Sancho, born on board a slave ship sailing from Guinea to the West Indies, wrote in 1776 to the great English writer Laurence Sterne that he was 'one of those people whom the vulgar and illiberal call *"Negurs"*'[1] he was not only declaring, literally, his 'lowly' place in the white imperial world, but also his relative sense of closeness to a *meta-physical* understanding of his captivity in Britain. A protégé of the Duke of Montagu (bequeathed, on the Duke and Duchess's death, enough wealth to give an outward appearance equal to the inward British 'education' his employers had provided), Sancho's case is unique enough in its personal history. Yet, it is hardly unfamiliar in its relegation of the colonized to the position of the exotic and quaint *within* imperial discourse.

Nor is Sancho's eventual move from servant to shop owner necessarily a further exemplification of his inclusion in white British culture, as Caryl Phillips seems almost to intimate in *Extravagant Strangers*. Rather, Sancho's affectation, the lightness of his criticism of the colonial culture, his preoccupation with his own rollicking domestic life, reveal most power-fully that he was neither an integrated member of British culture nor far enough removed from it to be considered either independent or free. Such also is the established role of the 'integrated' general prisoner who, through their labour, helps maintain the very prison in which he or she is incarcerated and who provides, through their 'criminality', a moral foil by which the incarcerators can define their 'superior' selves, yet is required to aim to reach the ideals prescribed by these same incarcerators.

This act of endeavouring to meet an imperially imposed ideal is, in itself, a return to the beginning of the colonial carceral cycle. Whether, in the 'modern' Western world, this is the product of a Protestant work ethic identified by Max Weber as the grounding for Western capitalism; whether it is the product of the psychology of the id, in which meeting the ideals of others, for their pleasure, places the pleasure-provider in a cyclical carceral (an interesting thought in light of the history of Western entertainment or, indeed, of the enthusiastic critical reception of much postcolonial literature published in the West); or whether the cyclical nature of this kind of carceral enterprise could perhaps have relevance to some wider Existentialist philosophy is not the point.

Colonial incarceration presents a meeting of personal and public histories; it finds its way into the creation of texts and records based on a distinctive and sometimes brutally uncomfortable set of human interac-tions, and it calls to mind the kinds of multi-layered and multitudinous life experiences that only the very best social and cultural historiography can ever hope to reach.

Norval Morris and David J. Rothman, writing in their introduction to *The Oxford History of the Prison: The Practice of Punishment in Western Societies*, note that 'it is apparent that Western societies typically carry expectations of the prison that are unreal and contradictory'.[2] There could, likewise, be no better description of the carceral consequences of imperialism. Expectations, the clash of one 'real' against another, the contradictory nature of the experience, are all part of any discussion here.

Although 'Who is really free?' and 'Who is *truly* imprisoned?' are hardly new calls, they do reflect on our own expectations (my own, in fact, in writing this from within the modern West) as to the true nature of colonial incarceration. The aim of *Colonial and Postcolonial Incarceration* is to investigate and consider this nature.

Outlining the link between maritime commerce, early modern mercantilism and religious affiliation, Daniel Vitkus discusses in 'The circulation of bodies: slavery, maritime commerce and English captivity narratives in the early modern period' the meeting of Ottoman and English empires. This clash of mercantile wills highlights many of the economic imperatives by which colonial incarceration identifies itself with imperial ambition. The comparison here between Christian and Muslim confirms that 'geographic' or 'territorial' definitions hardly touch the surface of how we can view the parameters of the colonial carceral. That the metaphysics of the act of incarcerating are underpinned by other than a 'bricks-and-mortar' identity, a religious ideal in this case, is an important starting point in the study of the prisons of colonialism.

Susan Martin's chapter follows this line, considering captivity fiction from late nineteenth- and early twentieth-century Tasmania. The question is not one of physicality but of the appropriation of Aboriginal cultural history by white Australian authors. This form of imperial *re*-creation is a well-established mode of celebrating the indigenous Other and ranks alongside those gloriously inaccurate works of romantic visual art which Western travellers brought back from the Pacific in the eighteenth and nineteenth centuries. This distinctive Tasmanian captivity fiction becomes in this sense, Martin suggests, a kind of 'tourist guide', a contradictory collection of rarefied sights and experiences at which Anglo readers could marvel. Displacement of the actual Aboriginal population by these fictionalized captivity ideals is an intriguing piece of discourse to say the least. It is difficult not to make comparisons with those wondrous cinematic *re*-creations that have made the site of the Bastille and island of Alcatraz such outstanding tourist attractions – reality not withstanding!

It is the broader literary heritage of colonial imprisonment that John Hawley approaches in 'Colonizing the mind: "Leo Africanus" in the Renaissance and today', most specifically the kind of hybridity which the colonial situation produces. It is important here to consider the role of warders, guards and guardians in maintaining and promoting a division between the captive and the free. A well-known taunt from guards to inmates taking college courses in one particular Californian youth prison is 'use a gun and get a college education'. The similar social backgrounds of the guards and prisoners in the institution works against the social hierarchies needed to promote definitions of innate 'criminality' which separate the incarcerated from the incarcerating. Taunts like these maintain order in a system founded on sometimes dubious political, cultural or economic agendas. Hybridity, like mimicry, sits uncomfortably in this kind of separatist ethos; yet it is hybridity, like synthesis, which is part of the colonial experience. This, in essence, is the crux of Hawley's investigation of concealment and exchange in the 'cages' of colonialism.

Closely reading accounts of slavers and slaves can assist in increasing an understanding of the emotive, dispositional and behavioural context of colonial incarceration, of the reality of the individual carceral experience within the context of a more holistic view of world colonial history. Kerry Sinanan's close reading of the enslavement narratives of John Newton and James Irving affords us this opportunity. The 'traded place' of the slavers is tantamount to their trading of identities and, in keeping with the tropes of incarceration texts, identity is founded here in an outward appearance of superiority. That momentarily lost, the 'trade' undertaken, metaphoric references to a 'journey' from 'trading' to 'traded' individual only reinforce a colonial captive's constant demand for self-definition. That neither Newton nor Irving lose sight of their identities, of their Christian, English origins, further exemplifies the links between a sense of imperial right and the uniqueness, noted by Weber, of our particular modern brand of capitalist enterprise. The mode of production is, indeed, the engine of this particular colonialist regime.

Indeed, national identity has been the product of much of the ages of discovery and imperialism which have typified the rise of the West from the eighteenth century to today. In this regard, Cythnia Ragland's 'Urban captivity narratives: the literature of the yellow fever epidemics of the 1790s' is focal to a discussion of the metaphorics of colonial incarceration. As Ragland points out, 'the eighteenth-century epidemic chronicler found himself caught between the simultaneous desires of decrying the threat posed to the nation from the outside and boasting of the nation's capacity to overcome those threats'. That this was a significant form of promotion for American exceptionalism, presenting it as a *post*colonial republic rather than colonial possession, is important enough; however, it is additionally important that these accounts adopted and transposed the rhetoric and language of Indian captivity narratives, with their emphasis on redemption and aspiration. A paradox, indeed, in light of the living conditions afforded the Native American.

A useful cross-cultural comparison is made between American captivity narratives, of the kind important to Ragland's discussion, and Australian captivity narratives in Kay Schaffer and D'Arcy Randall's chapter 'Trans-global translations: the Eliza Fraser and Rachel Plummer captivity narratives'. In particular, the promotion of racial superiority in popularly consumed literary forms makes notable reading in the recognition of the borders and frontiers which Western imperialism has defined and then celebrated. Not least, it is possible to see between the lines of these comparative tales the role of 'white' discourse in the creation of modern civilization myths and to consider the regulation of the white 'uniform' of superiority as it could be regulated in such widely appealing tales. If such popular culture – which occupies the same ground as the paranoia cinema of America's Cold War 1950s and the 'yoof' TV of Britain's 1980s – can define an attitude and an intention, but somewhat hide the cultural politics of its creation, then the carceral discourse it represents is far from panoptic. More accurately it can be described as determinedly refractive, splitting an image away from a true sighting of itself.

Moving to narratives of Western imperialism in Africa, Emily Haddad investigates the economic imperatives imbued in Mungo Park's *Travels in the Interior Districts of Africa*. Masculinity and whiteness are focal here, as are definitions of property and the body. In fact, it is the emphasis on property which gives due recognition to the paradoxical rhetoric of all carceral discourse. In *The Man Died: The Prison Notes of Wole Soyinka*, Soyinka, 1986 winner of the Nobel Prize for Literature, writes:

> Dreams. More strictly, variations of one dream. I would be on the scaffolding of a building in construction, high up. Cold. Mists. The mist barely reveals the outlines of my co-workers on other parts of the building. They are shadowy forms in blurred contours . . .[3]

Soyinka's body might be incarcerated, but his dream state uses this physical evidence as a bridge on which to paradoxically cross to a form of creative release. The same occurs in Breyten Breytenbach's *The True Confessions of an Albino Terrorist*, as it does in Christopher van Wyk's poem, 'In Detention':

> He fell from the ninth floor
> He hanged himself
> He slipped on a piece of soap while washing
> He hanged himself
> He slipped on a piece of soap while washing
> He fell from the ninth floor
> He hanged himself while washing
> He slipped from the ninth floor
> He slipped on the ninth floor while washing
> He fell from a piece of soap while slipping
> He hung from the ninth floor
> He washed from the ninth floor while slipping
> He hung from a piece of soap while washing[4]

If the body were the only site of freedom or incarceration then colonialism might simply be the possession of visible territorial terrain. Of course, this is not the case. So Park's use of 'feminine-encoded tactics', his own commodity-fetishism, his concerns with material value, only help to emphasize the role of the intangible in the colonial carceral.

How different is it when we shift to the tangible context of an instance of war? Certainly colonial ambition, borne in the actual locking-up of dissenters, the creation of patrolled indigenous 'missions' and 'reservations', the imposing of curfews and pass cards, has brutally tangible results. The incarceration of the Aboriginal population in Australia has been an issue right up to the final decades of the twentieth century – not least because of the peculiarly frequent instances of 'unnatural' Aboriginal deaths in custody. Likewise, recent atrocities in Algeria, founded on political changes and religious determinism, extend back through the Algerian War of Independence, and have produced a set of atrocities which have been as unremitting as they are insupportable.

In this same sense, James Whitlark uses the context of Japanese prisons during the Second World War to consider the binary extremes of Occidentalism and Orientalism, founded on ideals of indigenity which neither one warring side nor the other could easily abandon. Certainly, Whitlark's depiction of 'competing racisms' is an important one for a consideration of the engine of colonial war. The promotion of 'rightness', the imbuing of 'superiority' and, finally, the textual instances of narratives of stereotype and survival against 'immoral' desires of the 'alien' are all components of this state of war and as important to it as the economic imperatives which are so often blamed for territorial ambitions. If in the texts of prisoners of war we find strong evidence of such fuel for colonialism, this is in keeping with the maintenance of walls and bars to divide the prisoner from the warder.

James Le Sueur's 'Torture and the decolonization of French Algeria: nationalism, 'race', and violence during colonial incarceration' is equally a consideration of the prisons of colonial war. Notably, however, Le Sueur concentrates on the act of torture, and it is here that the intellectualization of the conditions of colonialism seem to fall so miserably short of understanding the reality. That Le Seuer's work is, in part, about the infamous case of Djamila Boupacha only makes this inadequacy more profound – Boupacha was tortured and sexually abused, her rape, disfigurement and subsequent dismissal by the colonial authorities all seemingly beyond the scope of any dispassionate academic discussion. Yet, here too, is one of the great ironies of what constitutes an incarcerated state in the colonial sense: it was the intellectuals, Simone de Beauvoir most significantly, who championed Boupacha's case. 'Torture,' Le Seuer says, was a 'logical outcome' of the final years of French imperial rule in Algeria. If so, then the logical outcome of de Beauvoir's involvement should rightly continue to be a recognition of the importance of the politically engaged intellectual in the prevention of such atrocities.

In all this – the physical and metaphysical appearances of the colonial carceral – not yet has the idea of the 'lexical prison', the prison of words, made an appearance. A definition of lexical prisons might be: those language conditions where words themselves fail to approach truth conditions, suggesting their limitation as tools within a particular colonial situation. That is not to say that communication is completely impaired; rather, that the communicative possibilities are other than purely lexical. In colonial situations, words often do not so much fail as act to incarcerate meaning, intention, understanding. Take Rosa Burger's lexical prison of the public self in Nadine Gordimer's *Burger's Daughter*:

> What I say will not be understood.
>
> Once it passes from me, it becomes apologia or accusation. I am talking about neither . . . but you will use my words to make your own meaning. As people pick up letters from the stack between them in word-games. You will say: she said *he* was this or that: Lionel Burger, Dhadhla, James Nyaluza, Fats, even that poor old fellow, Orde Greer. I am considering only ways of trying to take hold; you will say: she is Manichean. You don't understand treason; a flying fish lands on deck from fathoms you glide over. You bend curiously, call the rest of the crew to look, and throw it back.[5]

In her chapter, Mary Ross examines the lexical prison in her study of the language of literary production and detention in Kenya. Not only do these lexical prisons declare themselves in literary fiction and in the diaries of prisoners, but also in versions of the popular press. Ross's consideration of the role of 'news services', the *Manyani Times*, *Waya Times* and *Mukoma Times*, is unique in this regard.

Di Gan, born and educated in China before arriving in the USA to study, picks up on such popular textual foundations of the narratives of colonial incarceration in 'Trapped daughers: American Chinatowns and Chinese American women'. This look at the role of textual enclosure within the context of immigration makes it plain that cultural hegemony has its roots as much in very personal expectations and needs as in the holistic public discourses of national definition and political exclusion. The fact that the Western world has so vigorously engaged the creation of its Chinatowns only helps to emphasise how quickly racial and cultural stereotypes become part of the societal norm. Gan follows the tensions, contrasts and conflicts engendered in this 'separatist' colonialism through four popular novels of 'normalized/colonized Chineseness'. The result is a study of the personal power dynamics of what she calls the 'assigned ethnic cells' of the East within the West.

Not 'within' but 'near to' is the starting point for John Brannigan's study of colonialism in the relationship between Ireland and Britain. Most specifically considering depictions of nationalism in Irish prison literature, Brannigan analyses Brendan Behan's *Borstal Boy* within the historical story of nineteenth-century Irish nationalist literature, such as John Mitchel's *Jail Diary*, John Devoy's *Recollections of an Irish Rebel* and Thomas Clarke's *Glimpses of an Irish Felon's Prison Life*, to investigate 'the sacred myth of heroic struggle'. The difficulties of national liberation are far greater and more complex than is often imagined, as Brannigan shows, and the questions of nationalist resistance produce a set of contradictions which sometimes collapse the boundaries of these opposing cultures. That this collapse can equally reflect the changing nature of colonial evolving to postcolonial is significant indeed.

Finally, to one of the most well known and widely observed recent cases of postcolonial liberation – that of South Africa.

Shane Graham's 'Apartheid prison narratives, the Truth and Reconciliation Commission, and the construction of national (traumatic) memory' considers truth and memory as they effect (or affect, perhaps) the colonial carceral experience. That it touches that raw nerve exposed in the meeting of imperial politics with the aftermath of a brutal colonial history is hardly surprising; nor that such an aftermath involves a degree of *re*-writing and *re*-thinking in order to reinstate what has previously been suppressed or denied. What is striking about Graham's study, however, is the degree to which any formal commission or investigation produces a new round of memoir and documentation (the meta-texts of colonialism, that is, which are often as confusing and ill-defined as the colonial carceral itself).

The *truth*, of course, lies somewhere in the relationship between the discourses of report and revision and that of live, actual, current, colonial experience. The *memory* Graham discusses is, as he points out, as much about raising the experience of surviving the colonial carceral from an unconscious to a conscious state and, simultaneously, seeking affirmation from others as to the character and importance of this experience.

Undoubtedly, identity is one of the overarching thematic concerns in a study of the colonial carceral. The broader reaches of cultural hegemony is another. The intersections between personal and public history is a third. And the functional and structural dimensions of the movement between the evidence of the colonial carceral in the form of texts, and the actual conditions which produce those texts, is a fourth.

That these themes provide both physical and metaphysical insight into the colonial carceral is undeniable. What is even more striking, however, is that colonial incarceration has distinct and important dimensions which general studies of incarceration have not often acknowledged or incorporated. It is these which *Colonial and Postcolonial Incarceration* seeks to readdress.

Notes

1. Ignatius Sancho, 'Letter to Mr Sterne', in Caryl Phillips (ed.), *Extravagant Strangers* (London, Faber, 1997).
2. Norval Morris and David J. Rothman (eds), *The Oxford History of the Prison: The Practice of Punishment in Western Societies* (Oxford, Oxford University Press, 1995), p. xi.
3. Wole Soyinka, *The Man Died: The Prison Notes of Wole Soyinka* (Harmondsworth, Penguin, 1975), p. 85.
4. Christopher van Wyk, 'In detention', in Andre Brink and J. M. Coetzee (eds), *A Land Apart: A South African Reader* (London, Faber, 1987), p. 50.
5. Nadine Gordimer, *Burger's Daughter* (London, Cape, 1979), p. 171.

CHAPTER ONE

Criminal minds and felonious nations: colonial and postcolonial incarceration

GRAEME HARPER

Building the colonial prison

Such were the 'convicts' whom tradition has described as fearsome 'criminals'. *Even today* the inhabitants of Adelaide who arrived later and of their free will are wont to recall Southern Australia 'is not a convict country'. But if they were not criminal at the outset, they became criminal without realizing it, that is, by the massacre of aborigines. Sensitive only to what had been their misfortune they strove to transform New South Wales into the *land of justice* which their motherland failed to be for them. A large number of their descendants hate England.[1] (my italics)

Despite a now considerable history of academic study of colonialism, the colonial carceral remains, in intellectual circles, a largely untheorized *site of difference*. In fact, so very little has been written by scholars about the colonial carceral that it would not be facetious to suggest it has become almost invisible in the ongoing project of defining a *post*colonialism.

Perhaps the directness of such a study has prevented it being given the attention it warrants (i.e. to deal with sites of incarceration under colonialism, in a way which leaves no doubt as to the effects of imperialism, might appear to be lacking intellectual subtlety). Perhaps the place of incarceration studies within the wider tenets of literary, historical or cultural studies has not been strong enough to draw scholars to the subject (i.e. the study of incarceration, being an amalgam of social history, textual analysis, sociology and politics, might appear, at first glance, to be merely some kind of architectural history – 'bricks and chains' history, the history of the prison block). Yet it seems likely the reason for the lack of attention given to the colonial carceral is more disturbing than either of these.

There is certainly a failure by scholars based in the West to locate in the broader tenets of colonial theory a set of criteria for considering the difference between colonial incarceration and incarceration generally. But this appears to be backed by what Stephen Slemon has rightly pointed out is the 'neo-colonialism of Western academic institutions themselves',[2] the industry of academic postcolonialism beyond, but contiguous to, the urgent politics of the enterprise. Suffice it to say, the significance of the prison as an instrument of discipline and punishment is based in part on empirical fact and in part on myth, on explicitness and mystery, on reality and unreality, on knowledge and ignorance, on past and present, on success and failure. It is the paradoxical nature of prison, its metaphoric as well as its physical identity, which made Jeremy Bentham's panopticon such an ominous development.

Bentham's panopticon did not simply attack the bricks-and-mortar design of the prison; it sought to remove the metaphoric substance of the prison's identity by substituting for the imaginative paradoxical dimension the product of a morally charged scientism. The panopticon was, after all, far more than an architectural design; it carried with it Bentham's rigorous social, political and economic philosophy.

What, after all, is the philosophy of imprisonment? To speak colloquially: it is the site of ethical trepidation, a useful Other for gauging the moral actions of the free, an enclosure to keep the evil from the good, the location of the dangerous in a world we would otherwise believe to be largely safe, a place of judgement and legal definition, something to do with retribution but also rehabilitation, an arena for the modelling of better citizens, a cyclical enterprise like an ancient waterwheel (i.e. prisoners being released to dry out, only to return to the dark water from which they came). And so it goes on.

The prison is so imbued with such condemnatory significance that to suggest whole societies, whole nations, as well as the most innocent of imaginable individuals, have been (and still are) *actually* incarcerated by colonialism is to cut a dark swathe through what has been the steady intellectual spread of postcolonial theory into such traditionalist discourses as the study of literature in English Literature departments, as well as into more vibrantly contemporary ones such as Gender Studies.

To say that such postcolonial enterprises have, in themselves, been 'neo-colonial' is not to deny that they have been essential in raising to the fore issues about individual and societal subjugation; nor that without the still burgeoning intellectual enterprise of postcolonialism it would be possible to find scholars who have made colonial incarceration the subject of their investigations. But the fact remains: the specific study of the colonial incarceration carries with it what Foucault calls in a slightly different context 'the extreme solidity of the prison'.[3]

Incarceration is not, and cannot be, simply another trick in a bag of postmodern intellectual voice tricks (i.e. announcing the emergence of the multiple, formerly suppressed, voices of the modern world). The colonial carceral is – and excuse the rhetorical listing here: the point is best made by the 'sound' of the march of evidence! – a set of literal, metaphoric, lexical, physical, metaphysical, public and personal artefacts which are as current as they are historical, and which have previously been included only in generic discussions of colonialism. They are, by any definition, distinct – both in their wider condition within colonialism, and in terms of their 'bricks and chains' identity.

Mis-reading colonial history

The quotation from Marc Ferro which opens this chapter is an intriguing one. He is talking, of course, of the convict history of Australia. Debates within Australian historiography concerned with the motivation behind Britain's decision to 'convictize' *Terra Australis* revolve largely around two axes. On the one side, the question of whether the Empire was mostly serving its economic and strategic needs (i.e. sending convicts to the Pacific in order to stake claim to *Terra Australis* before French colonial enterprise became too enamoured of this idea itself). On the other, the argument that Britain was seeking simply to rid itself of a pressing social problem (i.e. the overcrowding of its gaols). More sophisticated versions of these axes exist, but the directions are largely the same.

Undoubtedly, weighing up the evidence, the middle ground is easiest to argue (i.e. the combination of economic and strategic imperatives with pressing social needs at the imperial core). We could see this as the driving motivation behind the creation of colonial carcerals generally. For example, why the French felt so strongly about the potential loss of their Algerian territory was not simply a matter of prestige and the 'charm of North Africa' (a fact often listed in terms of the cultural importance to France of the Algerian training ground for many of its soon-to-be-elite commercial and intellectual class). The importance of Algeria as 'birth-place' of a generation of notable Paris-based intellectuals (from Albert Camus to Hélène Cixous and Jacques Derrida) is not coincidental. Equally, however, the economic potential of Algeria (in oil and gas production particularly) carried strategic political implications. The decision not to give up colonial territory, to fight so brutally to retain it, finds logical form not *just* in the cultural, or *just* in the strategic. Both come into play.

Add to this, then, the personal narratives, the youthful conscripted military assignments, the place of the 'North African charm' in the minds of the French, holidays on the Mediterranean's south shore, the exoticism of the relatively nearby Sahara. Follow the paths of intellectuals north from Oran and Algiers to Paris, and it is possible to see in the very personal life histories of French colonials the kind of emotive, behaviourist motivations which help further to explain even the grossest elements of the Algerian carceral. Better to imprison a nation, after all, than lose sight of the self.

If this seems too simplistic an assessment, consider the effect of the Indian wars on the psyche of ordinary nineteenth-century American settlers (such a strong pioneering ethos as theirs was not only created by a steady, simple movement across welcoming territory); or the racist arguments of eighteenth-century slavers (fear-driven in unfamiliar Africa and personally threatened by the numbers of slaves they culled and the 'alien' language, ideals and attitudes of their captives); or the importance of a Muslim-free Kosovo in the minds of ordinary Serbs (history, after all, is never monologic and the emphasis on one moment can easily negate the importance of another); or the place of that other, real India, the India of Tagore and the Tamil writer Rajam Krishnan, in the ideas of the imperial British – so well depicted here in Salman Rushdie's *Midnight's Children*:

> Methwold's Estate was sold on two conditions: that the houses be bought complete with every last thing in them, that the contents be retained by the new owners; and that the actual transfer should not take place until midnight on August 15th.
>
> 'Everything?' Amina Sinai asked. 'I can't even throw away a spoon? Allah, that lampshade . . . I can't get rid of one *comb*?'
>
> 'Lock, stock and barrel,' Methwold said, 'Those are my terms. A whim, Mr Sinai . . . you'll permit a departing colonial his little game? We don't have much left to do, we British, except to play our games.'[4]

Games and pastimes are located at the very crux of a social identity. That Australia is a rugby league nation, England a soccer one, America the home of gridiron football – these are no throwaway facts. Methwold's game is the game of retention, of imprinting. What Rushdie is depicting is the continuation of colonialism, not its dissolution. And so the Sinai home becomes an enclosure rather than a site of release. Hardly surprising that Saleem Sinai struggles with the label 'Anglo-Indian', the hybrid state of the colonized. No great leap either to acknowledge that Rushdie himself has been subject to accusations of being somehow 'non-authentic', an Indian in England, as if this negates his Indian cultural integrity.

> '. . . It's all worked out excellently,' William Methwold says. 'Did you know my ancestor was the chap who had the idea of building this whole city? Sort of Raffles of Bombay. As his descendant, at this important juncture, I feel the, I don't know, need to play my part. Yes, excellently . . . when d'you move in? Say the word and I'll move off to the Taj hotel. Tomorrow? Excellent. Sabkuch ticktock hai.'[5]

The personal cages of colonialism hold equal sway with colonialism's holistic history. The carceral is always a combination of the individual cell, the personal experience of the prisoner, and the function and structure of the institution of incarceration. Thus Foucault's mistake in *Discipline and Punish*. A largely functionalist historiographer, Foucault misses the point about the individualization of history, about its evolutionary characteristics. In the situation of the colonial carceral, this is tantamount to denying a large part of the experience. The character of the colonial carceral is as much the interpretative and evolutionary reach of colonial rules and regulations as it is the wider function and structure of the rules themselves.

'I understand you have matriculated, your name is Nathanial, isn't it?' says the magistrate in William Modisane's first short story, *The Dignity of Begging*, published in South Africa in 1951:

> He turns a page of the report prepared by a worker in the non-European Affairs Department. 'Yes, here we are. Nathanial Mokgomare, the department recommends that you be sent to a place where you will be taught some useful trade. I want you to report to Room 14 at the department's building tomorrow morning.'
>
> This is not what I had bargained for; my brilliant idea has boomeranged. Why must I take a job when I can earn twice a normal wage begging? After all, what will horses do if I take a job. I *must* uphold the dignity of begging. Professional ethics prevent all beggars from working.[6]

Heavy with irony, the narrator's loss of his ability to control his own life represents one of the primary tropes of imprisonment discourse: the regimentation of life; the buzzers and bells of the prison; the neat cellular structure; the routine of eat, exercise and sleep.

Most importantly, the colonial carceral imposes one set of temporal and spatial orders on another, and it does so *across* cultures. Thus the terrible mismatch of indigenous Australians to the pastoral mindsets of European settlers. Not only were settlers imposing time and space priorities on the nomad, but also a European work ethic out of step with the religio-economic pattern of Aboriginal life. Add to this the exceptional spiritual significance attached to the shape and location of indigenous geographic space in Australia, and European scepticism concerning this spiritual significance (no better exemplified than in the land rights battles of the 1970s and 1980s), and some sense of the degree of temporal and spatial subjugation is plain.

Not that the regimentation of these wider social movements and structures is the end of this fact of colonial incarceration. Chains, the chaining or tethering of slaves, servants and the indentured, the production of passes and the imposition of curfews: all of these represent, in addition to their obvious signification of control, a temporal and spatial ordering out of keeping with the natural evolutionary character of a meeting of cultures. They are, in this sense, instruments of temporal and spatial hegemony used so that the philosophy, the aesthetics even, of one culture's dealings with time and space preclude the existence of alternatives offered by another.

It is interesting to follow the European's reception of the indigenous Australian's concept of 'The dreamtime'. In fact, even the settler translation of the concept itself is a kind of proto-Freudian label and seems so far removed from the metaphysics of the ideal – like converting the Christian 'God' into 'Supreme Being', it misses much of the meaning. The Native American, likewise, has often been reduced to a kind of

nature-loving child or tragic victim; the Native American philosophical
views of time and space are seen largely as *appropriatable* alternative
lifestyles in an otherwise sceptical Western society. Similarly, despite the
illogic of the exercise, the vast tribal differences on the African continent
have often been amalgamated into one Western view, as Nadine Gordimer
has pointed out. 'Africa has many images,' she writes. 'To speak of the
"image" of Africa is perhaps to fall into the very trap I'm hoping to
dismantle: acceptance that there is a total *signification* which stands for our
continent.'[7]

Which is why, indeed, Marc Ferro's interpretation of Australian history
is both intriguing and inaccurate. *'Even today,'* he writes, 'the inhabitants
of Adelaide who arrived later and of their free will are wont to recall
Southern Australia "is not a convict country".' This, in part, is true. But
such calls are not based on a repudiation of criminality. In fact, in the
white Australian sense, criminality has been everything from a mark of
disdain, to a declaration of solidarity, to (particularly in the 1980s in the
approach to the bicentenary of white Australian settlement) a statement
of national identity and separateness from Britain.

Ferro continues: 'But if they were not criminal at the outset, they
became criminal without realizing it, that is, by the massacre of aborigines.' This, too, has some truth to it. Yet discussion of the slaughter of
indigenous Australians can be undertaken neither in a wholesale nor in a
simplistic fashion. It is true to say that where indigenous and settler
Australians met, and confrontations occurred, it was the indigenous
Australian who mostly lost out. The unfortunate consequence of following
this line of reasoning slavishly, however, is that it presents a picture of a
purist ethnography, a sense of loss of culture rather than of its evolution.

The colonial carceral, like all situations of incarceration, is an evolutionist site of difference. Here, one culture imposed upon by another, one
made subservient to another, one imprisoned by another, does not negate
the movement of culture along a continuous timeline of change. To say
that a non-European culture disappears as the result of European
hegemony is a denial of the colonial carceral's general condition, and of
the resilience of the indigenous culture itself – that is (again like all
carcerals) to impose change at a more rapid rate, to place it within a
discourse of retribution for moral, ethical or even political difference, and
to tie this incarceration to some sense of rehabilitation.

In the colonial carceral, in other words, one culture is seen to be in
negotiation with the principles of change imposed by another. Thus the
wider carceral of colonialism, paradoxically, is a 'zone of cultural negotiation', whereas the general carceral, the prison as it is known generically,
is not. Prisoners might enter the generic prison with a personal or legal
agreement to rehabilitate, but the system itself provides only for meeting
the conditions laid down by incarcerators, and no cultural evolution can
take place. The condition of the colonial carceral is more complex.

John Kadiba, writing of his life in colonial New Guinea, says this:

My parents had no education, but on the plantation they were removed from village life and learnt some new ways of living from the European plantation manager. . . . Both our parents spoke Motu and Pidgin fluently. They also knew Hula and they had picked up a bit of English. Such words as: go, come, good, bad, naughty boy, silly girl, good morning, good evening, hello . . . were often used by them though they pronounced them with little ease. We children understood these few words and phrases. We could not express abstract ideas in English, but we knew how to name spoon, pot, pan, plate, knife and fork. My parents took some pride in such knowledge and even gave us European names: Jimmy, John and Susan – names that were quite unknown back home in the village.[8]

The captive and the free are never simply placed at either ends of a carceral spectacle. For example, within the physical confines of a bricks-and-mortar prison, an ongoing narrative of moral and ethical negotiation continues (the topic, needless to say, of enough imaginative literature and film to need no further introduction). This point, to return to Ferro, some critics seem entirely to miss. 'Sensitive only to what had been their misfortune,' he writes, 'they [the convicts] strove to transform New South Wales into the *land of justice* which their motherland failed to be for them.'

The myth of egalitarianism which pervaded a great deal of white Australia in the nineteenth and early twentieth centuries has long been shown to be a sham – and not only because it denies the social disadvantage of the indigenous population. Nevertheless, it is true to say that the colonial carceral produces, as does the general prison environment, a set of new hierarchies often only partially connected to the social structures which dominate the outside world. Thus, in the cults of intrusion ('cargo-cultism') developed in Pacific islands, the connection is between power and new goods, between religio-political prestige and the transformations that these goods promise. Thus, also, there is the intriguing amalgam of Maori and Pakeha in the following sections from two New Zealand works, Keri Hulme's Booker Prize-winning *The Bone People* and a stanza from Hone Tuwhare's *Lament*, a poem of war:

'This place used to have one of the finest stands of kahikatea in the country.'
  'And they cut it down to make room for those?'
  'She did,' she says sourly. 'Pines grow faster. When they grow. The poor old kahikatea takes two or three hundred years to get to its best, and that's not fast enough for the moneyminded.'
  She pulls up hard. 'I hate pines,' she says unnecessarily.
  Joe grins. 'I gathered. They've got their uses though.'
  'O, there's room in the land for them, I grant you, but why do they have to cut down good bush just to plant sickening pinus? Look at that lot, dripping with needle blight dammit . . . this land isn't suitable for immigrants from Monterey or bloody wherever. Bring the kete, eh.'[9]

> In that strident summer of battle
> when cannon grape and ball
> tore down the pointed walls
> and women snarled at men
> and blood boiled in the eyes:
> in the proud winter of defeat
> he stood unweary
> and a god among men.[10]

Power and privilege in a prison are often built on giving certain personal attributes a heightened sense of importance. This is redoubled when incarceration occurs *across* cultures: thus the heightened interest in narratives of the colonial carceral portraying stoicism, physical and mental strength, self-reliance and self-respect. The diary narrations of 'colonized persons' – narrations such as Ngũgĩ a Thiong'o's *Detained: A Writer's Prison Diary*,[11] or Harriet Jacobs's *Incidents in the Life of a Slave Girl*,[12] or Phan Boi Chau's 'Nguc Trung Thu'[13] – are subtly different in this regard from other prison narratives such as Jean Genet's *The Thief's Journal*[14] and Timothy Leary's *Jail Notes*.[15] Both sets of narration are politically charged, but it is the strength of natural justice, based on the personal qualities of the narrator, which ring strongest in the narratives of the colonial carceral. Harriet Jacobs writes:

> The secrets of slavery are concealed like those of the Inquisition. My master was, to my knowledge, the father of eleven slaves. But did the mothers dare to tell who was the father of their children? Did the other slaves dare to allude to it, except in whispers among themselves? No, indeed! They knew too well the terrible consequences.[16]

And bore them stoically. A sense of defeat, such as that hinted at in Hulme's and Tuwhare's writing, is contextualized within the colonial carceral as part and parcel of not simply a *resistance* mentality but of a burgeoning, stronger *new character*, built on the meeting of the pre-colonial culture with imperialism. If there is a more general sense of justice contained in these narratives of the colonial carceral it is in the formation of a 'new', evolved indigenity – a new indigenous culture.

Does this negate the old culture? Hardly: it is the natural consequence of an enforced evolution. And yet, the rhetorical movement from old to new is in so many ways the very crux of the ethical superiority afforded the colonized in their personal narratives of imprisonment. Not so much resistance as *refraction* of the imperial aims and desires of the colonizers; not so much open to evolution as determined to be the natural, indigenous bridge by which it occurs.

While the idea expressed earlier by Ferro – that convict New South Wales was a society constructed as a 'land of justice' – is both a romantic myth and an historiographical misjudgement, his failure to grasp the nature of the Australian white convict carceral is paradoxically helpful here. It is the construction of a new ideal of justice, born out of colonial hybridity, out of the progress of (albeit often brutal) negotiation, out of the 'colonization of freedom' in the wider prison of colonial society, that gives the appearance of having a new spatial form.

This is not as dubious a statement as at first it seems. It is the spatial condition of the prison which has been largely at the core of colonial incarceration, far and above the temporal condition. Whereas generic imprisonment relies on a neat mesh of temporal and spatial rhetoric (a prison sentence, after all, involves both a period of incarceration and confinement to a specific carceral site), the broader context of the colonial carceral is entirely a spatial consideration. It is, of course, most often resistance to giving up rightful ownership of space which brings about the clash between the colonizers and the colonized in the first place.

We could seemingly ignore Ferro's final, offhand observation that 'a large number of their descendants [of convicts sent to Australia] hate England' if it were not that it too reflects on how difficult it is to summarize a sense of colonial nationalism borne on conditions of enforced separation from a 'home culture'. The fact remains that the majority of Australians are still of British descent and that, at the time of writing, the issue of whether to become a republic or not and rejecting the British crown as sovereign has been decided in the imperial power's favour. What helps bolster a discussion of the colonial carceral, however (given that its wider context is as broad as national and regional boundaries themselves and the many colonial histories the world has experienced), is a narrower consideration of the physical attributes of day-to-day colonial imprisonment.

Bricks and chains

To break down a wider discussion of the colonial carceral into a consideration of the day-to-day attributes of the colonial prison is simple enough. Where the problem lies is in moving between these physical sites of enclosure – which often, by the nature of the models brought to bear, resemble the prisons of the imperialists – and the human activities of the prison's interior.

To discuss the 'bricks and chains' of the colonial carceral we must see them first as attributes of the condition discussed above, the result of specific instances of political, economic and cultural imperialism. Only then can the reality of the bricks and chains colonial carceral not be sensationalized but, rather, provide insight into the differences between generic imprisonment and colonial imprisonment.

In 1995, publishing in the *Prison Journal* and basing his discussion on 1992 figures, Marc Mauer noted that in relation to the international use of incarceration both Russia and the USA were the highest users in the world – the USA incarcerating 519 citizens per 100,000 of the population and Russia incarcerating 558 per 100,000. While direct comparisons are difficult, because they would require additional information about the rates of sentencing on crimes of property, crimes against the person and so on, it is notable that colonial South Africa had a level of incarceration of 368 per 100,000, Northern Ireland, 126 per 100,000, while India had a rate of only 23 per 100,000. Population size clearly bore relatively little direct relation to incarceration rates. A racial breakdown of the US inmate population, however, revealed that compared to 306 per 100,000 white persons incarcerated, 1,947 per 100,000 African Americans met the same fate.[17] The US white population is, of course, substantially larger than the African American.

Were crime rates higher amongst African Americans than whites *generically*? Or was this substantial difference in incarceration levels the result of a legal system which favours the white population (not necessarily explicitly but in implicit notions connected to property ownership, codes of moral conduct and so forth)? Simply put, these figures reveal that the use of incarceration is inherently imbued not just with generic cultural *significance*, but with specific cultural *intention*. How we interpret this intention is, in part, relative; though common sense tells us that certain actions are immoral or unjust in any political system.

Cultural intention can best be understood in terms of the relationship of power to force and authority – authority as a social relationship, force as a compulsion used by those having power or holding authority, and power as the ability to elicit compliance and/or obedience to the holder's will, in whatever fashion.

As the power to imprison is invested in the state, the authority to do so is created by laws which purport to serve the interests of persons who abide by these laws. Suffice it that under different political orientations of State, such as in the case of the colonial State, there are different types, terms, interpretations of imprisonment – note, for example, the expression 'House Arrest' which gained a new, distinctive currency in colonial South African history.

This situating of the specific attributes of incarceration gets complicated under the weight of tradition, the living standards of the population, the influence of various penological theories, etc. It is as varied as the common law (an obvious example being the differing sentences handed down for the same crimes in culturally similar countries such as Australia, the USA and Great Britain). What is considered an undue use of force in one country is legitimate under the regime of another. The treatment of drug traffickers in a number of Asian countries is a case in point, often being criticized by Western observers as harsh.

Suffice it to say that the significance of specific 'bricks and chains' attributes of colonial incarceration can best be considered under the general inter-connected headings of *enclosure, physical abuse* and *removal*. But it must always be remembered that our interpretation of such attributes is, in itself, a political act. In the increasingly neo-colonial condition of the intellectualization of that condition we have identified as *post*colonialism, this must not go unsaid.

Enclosure is, by definition, enforced. It is, by definition, culturally and personally specific. To choose almost too bald an example: to enclose a nomad in a cell designed by a sedentary gaoler is a form of what Foucault has called 'rectification',[18] which carries with it the straightforward aim of 'enclosing' cultural spread, discontinuing routes of communication, cutting off avenues of dissent.

Enclosure is, by nature, relative to the size and shape of the enclosures themselves and also, in the case of the colonial carceral specifically, to the expectations of punishment prevalent in the indigenous and settler populations. The following is a response from Native Americans to the Bursum Bill of 1922, which took 60,000 acres of land away from the Pueblos. It is specifically concerned with *enclosure*:

> We, the Pueblo Indians, have always been self-supporting and have not been a burden on the government. We have lived in peace with our fellow Americans even while we have watched the gradual taking of our lands and waters. Today many of our Pueblos have the use of less than an acre per person of irrigated land, whereas in New Mexico ten acres of irrigated land are considered necessary for a man to live on. We have reached a point where we must either live or die.[19]

Contrast this with this extract from Ngũgĩ wa Thiong'o's *Detained: A Writer's Prison Notes* which largely concerns itself with *physical abuse* in Kenya:

> The huge prison gates, like the jaws of a ravenous monster, now slowly swung open to swallow me within its walls, which still dripped with the blood of many Kenyan patriots who have been hanged there for their courageous Mau Mau guerrilla struggle against British imperialism. . . .
>
> Even then my place of detention, as in the case of all other detainees, remained a top secret known only to an initiated few. The KANU government would in fact go to ridiculous lengths to mystify people about our whereabouts . . .
>
> The rituals of mystery and secrecy are exercises in psychological terror aimed at a whole people – part of the culture of fear – and at the individual detainee – part of the strategy of eventually breaking him.[20]

And contrast this with a section from Pramoedya Ananta Toer's diary. It concerns itself with *removal*. Javanese Toer, imprisoned in an Indonesian colonial jail, writes as he is taken by ship to the notorious Buru Island detention centre:

> Our cabin is a cell, a forced enclosure, with a huge door of iron bars, locked, as are the doors to the other two cells that are found below deck.
>
> We no longer own our right to look at the sky, or so it seems. We are the coolies. For many of my mates, this journey is their first time at sea, the first

time they have ever set foot out of their villages. . . . Many of them have come here directly from prisons where, for a year, their food ration was no more than three shoe-wax tins per day. You have never ever witnessed the abnormality of a man's bodily movements or that of a man's mental processes whose body weight is less than fifty per cent of what it should be. . . .

You have never known real hunger. You are the child of a free people and as a free person you should never have to experience hunger just because of other people's incompetence. But I am a child of a colonized people and if, in my life, I have sustained long periods of bitter hunger, that is not extraordinary.[21]

Of course, the rhetorical position adopted here is fatally flawed. It has been adopted to make a point clear, that is, to show that in all cases of colonial carceral, enclosure, physical abuse and removal work in conjunction to overpower cultural integrity, and to suggest conduct norms[22] which are out of keeping with the norms of personal and social interaction prevalent in the colonized society. In this sense, the colonial carceral is distinctive. Whereas generic incarceration uses its modes of coercion, its rhetoric of rehabilitation, its sites of retribution to normalize a member of an established culture, the colonial carceral uses its methods to ensure cultural evolution through pathologization.

The brutality of much of this comes about because the carceral is the site of greatest conflict, the point at which one conduct norm and another have reached an impasse. Of course, the Native American Pueblo is equally physically abused, Ngũgĩ equally removed, Toer equally enclosed. They can only be so because of pathologizing by the dominant culture – the prevailing imperial politics, the economics of colonial imposition – of activities which do not support its evolutionist aims (i.e. such things as indigenous ideals, philosophies, economic and social systems, personal and cultural needs).

In this sense, Foucault's discussion of the carceral in terms of 'a new form of "law": a mixture of legality and nature, prescription and constitution'[23] fails to fully contextualize the relationship of authority, force and power in the colonial context. The notion of legality is doubly edged by a forced cultural evolution. The unnatural state of both personal and public narratives is so heightened as to become the focus of cultural discourse generally. And so the 'prescriptive' far exceeds the 'constitutional', to the point at which authority as a social relationship breaks down, and power and force are the dominant modes of human interaction.

Conclusion

When the broader elements of the colonial carceral – those that are seen in the general make-up of colonial societies – are taken in conjunction with the specific instances of 'bricks and chains' incarceration, considerations of the normative role of the penal system in any society break down, and the penal system loses any sense of legitimacy.

Speaking colloquially, as an Other for gauging the moral actions of the free, the colonial carceral condemns the imperialist. As the location of the dangerous in a world we would otherwise believe to be largely safe (that is, as a site of what we would normally regard as 'civilization') it fails – often destabilizing the safety of the majority. As a place of judgement and legal definition it undermines legality by its failure to recognize the strength of illogic on which it depends (the world made it plain long before the fall of South African apartheid that it considered this neither an equitable system nor legally sound). As something to do with retribution and rehabilitation the colonial carceral favours the former and makes rehabilitation a matter of enforced cultural change, rather than favouring adherence to conduct norms within the imprisoned's own society. As an arena for the modelling of better citizens it connects citizenship to subjugation and promotes subservience as a matter of a new political correctness.

The cultural context of the colonial carceral changes. Its history, the social structures which create it, the personal records it creates, and the public politics it represents, benefit very little from being contained beneath the overarching term 'colonialism'. Yet we see today in the determination of intellectuals to discuss a state of affairs *after* colonialism, a *post*colonialism, a will to recognize the urgent political needs of colonial societies. Within this urgent need, the colonial carceral represents a distinctive mode of engagement between people and cultures, which identifies itself not simply by its theoretical importance but by the actual, real foundation on which it has existed – and still exists.

Notes

1. Marc Ferro, *Colonization: A Global History* (London, Routledge, 1997), p. 147.

2. Stephen Slemon, 'The scramble for Post-Colonialism', in Bill Ashcroft, Gareth Griffiths and Helen Tiffin, *The Post-Colonial Studies Reader* (London, Routledge, 1995), p. 52.

3. Michel Foucault, *Discipline and Punish: The Birth of the Prison* (Harmondsworth, Penguin, 1979), p. 305.

4. Salman Rushdie, *Midnight's Children* (London, Picador, 1982), p. 95.

5. *Ibid.*, p. 97.

6. William Modisane, 'The dignity of begging', in Peggy Rutherfoord (ed.), *Darkness and Light: An Anthology of African Writing* (London, Faith, 1958), p. 51.

7. Nadine Gordimer, 'Read all about it: the way they see us', in Liam Browne and Graeme Harper (eds), *Touchpaper Contemporary Pamphlets*, no. 1 (London, Waterstones/Arts Council of England, 2000), p. 1.

8. John Kadiba, 'Growing up in Mailu', in Ulli Beier (ed.), *Black Writing from New Guinea* (St Lucia, University of Queensland Press, 1973), p. 5.

9. Keri Hulme, *The Bone People* (London, Hodder & Stoughton, 1984), p. 157.

10. Hone Tuwhare, 'Lament', in Vincent O'Sullivan (ed.), *An Anthology of Twentieth Century New Zealand Poetry* (Wellington, Oxford University Press, 1976), p. 216.

11. Ngũgĩ wa Thiong'o, *Detained: A Writer's Prison Diary* (London, Heinemann, 1981).

12. Harriet Jacobs, *Incidents in the Life of a Slave Girl*. Introduction by Valerie Smith (New York, Oxford University Press, 1988). (First published 1861.)

13. Phan Boi Chau, 'Nguc Trung Thu', in Christopher Jenkins, Tran Khanh Tuyet and Huynh Sanh-Thong (trans.), David G. Marr (ed.), *Reflections from Captivity* (Athens, Ohio University Press, 1978).

14. Jean Genet, *The Thief's Journal* (Harmondsworth, Penguin, 1971).

15. Timothy Leary, *Jail Notes* (London, New English Library, 1972).

16. Jacobs, *Incidents in the Life*, p. 55.

17. Marc Mauer, 'The international use of incarceration,' *Prison Journal*, vol. 75, no. 1, March (1995): 113.

18. Foucault, *Discipline and Punish*, p. 305.

19. Quoted in James Wilson, *The Earth Shall Weep: A History of Native America* (London, Picador, 1998), p. 337.

20. Thiong'o, *Detained*, pp. 20–1.

21. Pramoedya Ananta Toer, 'Transportation', in Siobhan Dowd (ed.), *This Prison Where I Live: The PEN Anthology of Imprisoned Writers* (London, Cassell, 1996), pp. 112–13.

22. Thorstein Sellin, 'Culture conflict and crime', in Stuart H. Traub and Craig B. Little (eds), *Theories of Deviance* (New York, Peacock, 1975), p. 51.

23. Foucault, *Discipline and Punish*, p. 304.

CHAPTER TWO

The circulation of bodies: slavery, maritime commerce and English captivity narratives in the early modern period

DANIEL J. VITKUS

The heritage

During the early modern period, the dominant religious ideology of English Protestantism defined itself against Roman Catholic 'idolatry', Islamic 'infidelity', Jewish 'stubbornness' and African 'paganism'. But these demonizations of foreign peoples and their beliefs had to be held in abeyance when English merchants sought profit in a maritime market-place that stretched from Turkey to Trinidad. A violent contradiction arose within English culture: the old forces of ethnocentric, sectarian and nationalistic feeling produced a repulsion for the alien, while at the same time the attractive forces of colonial land, valuable commodities and the general appeal of the exotic drew English culture out to mix with other cultures beyond their shores. The centrifugal force of commerce was irresistible, however, and a dispersal and circulation of bodies was necessary to sustain the growth of overseas trade. This brought more and more English subjects in contact with other cultures during an age of economic and imperial expansion. During the late sixteenth and then the seventeenth centuries, English culture produced representations of exotic, cross-cultural encounters and conversions that sought desperately to define English identity in an increasingly unstable context. For the early modern English, one of the most anxious and conflicted cross-cultural exchanges was the encounter with Islamic culture, in both the Ottoman dominions and in the Barbary States of North Africa.

During the late sixteenth century, Elizabeth I and many of the leading merchants in London led an effort to form a stable, profitable alliance with the Ottoman sultanate. An English ambassador, William Harborne, was sent to Istanbul in 1578 to negotiate for trade privileges in areas under Ottoman rule; the Levant Company was formed in 1580; and between 1579 and 1581 Queen Elizabeth and the Sultan, Murad III, exchanged letters full of praise for each other.[1] At the same time, trade and diplomatic relations were developed with some of the autonomous princes of North Africa (or Barbary, as it was called). An important part of this commercial movement, exchange and expansion involved the labour of the English workers who sailed these vessels, and the labourers who were transported in those ships to the new plantations. The purchase of slaves in West Africa and their transportation to the colonies in North America by English merchants was not a new form of economic activity. It was merely an expansion and adaptation of old forms of doing business to the new context of the English colonies and the developing transatlantic economy.

Historians investigating the development of the transatlantic slave trade have pointed to a sustained connection, from the sixteenth to the eighteenth centuries, between two important historical developments: the rise of capitalism and the expansion of slavery.[2] Eric Williams, M. I. Finley, Eugene Genovese, David Brion Davis, Orlando Patterson and Robin Blackburn, among others, have convincingly demonstrated the foundational role of the triangular trade (between Europe, Africa and the New World) in the economic development and expansion of England and the other colonial powers of Western Europe. By the end of the seventeenth century, the slave trade that carried goods and bodies between England, West Africa and the Caribbean was well established along its traditional routes. Before the eighteenth-century Atlantic slave trade was fully developed, however, the Mediterranean was already an important sphere of activity for the commercial maritime enterprise of the English.[3] And slavery was a central feature of the Mediterranean economy long before it became important in the Atlantic and the New World colonies.[4] David Brion Davis, in *Slavery and Human Progress*, emphasizes the continuity between the institution of slavery in Europe and the Mediterranean and its establishment later in the New World: 'The story [of New World slavery] begins,' he writes, 'with the revival of the ancient Mediterranean slave trade that accompanied the early expansion of western Europe'.[5]

The slave trade was thriving throughout the Mediterranean world during the early modern period, and violent rivalries between competing Christians, as well as Islamic–Christian conflict, helped to supply the trade with bodies. As the quest for profit directed more English ships and English people to distant lands, from India to the Caribbean, those English men and women were increasingly caught up in the multicultural circulation of bodies that included the slave trade but also involved other forms of unfree labour and servitude. In New England, for example, colonial masters bought and sold indentured servants who often worked under conditions of disease and hunger so severe that in 1620 one colonist complained at Plymouth, in the Massachusetts Bay settlement, 'that the people are used with more slavery than if they were under the Turk'.[6]

In general, though, servitude in the English colonies was far less harsh than the conditions endured by African 'chattel' slaves taken to the New

World colonies.[7] And if we compare the condition of an indentured servant in Virginia or Massachusetts in 1620 to the plight of an English slave chained to the oar in a Turkish or Algerian galley, certainly the average servant in the American colonies enjoyed greater freedom and more privileges. Some Englishmen owned by Muslim slavemasters, however, were given a great deal of autonomy. In occasional cases, they were allowed to manage their own shops and to move about freely within the city in order to conduct their business, though they could not leave the area entirely; and, if engaged in trade, slaves had to pay their masters a large portion of their profits. Others worked as household servants and could be given positions of some authority, acting as overseers or property managers. One English slave in Algiers, William Okeley, was lent some money by his owner so that he could set up trade in a small shop where he sold tobacco, wine and other commodities. He was so successful that, before making his escape, he had a trunk with a false bottom made and hid his gold and silver there. This trunk was successfully smuggled out of Algiers and taken to England by a Protestant minister named Devereux Spratt who was being ransomed.[8] Okeley's second master treated him well but Okeley thought that this man was planning to send him to 'a fair Farm in the Countrey ... to manage the Farm for him'.[9] In 1644, Okeley and four other English slaves escaped Algiers in a homemade boat and made their way to Majorca where they were hospitably received.

Trade relations

Between the 1580s, when formal trade relations with the Ottomans were established, and the middle of the seventeenth century, when Okeley made his escape, maritime traffic between Europe and the New World had increased markedly and in the second half of the seventeenth century there were more English vessels operating in both the Mediterranean and the American colonies. This increased activity created a tighter web of economic relations linking the Atlantic and Mediterranean regions. Captivity narratives by authors like Abraham Browne (a captive in Salee in 1655) and Joshua Gee (a captive in Algiers from 1680 to 1687) recount how ships sailing from New England or Newfoundland to Europe were intercepted by 'Turkish' corsairs, often with European-born renegades among their crews, and then sold into slavery in Salee or Algiers.[10]

Many of the same English merchants who invested in colonial enterprise in the New World were also involved in the Mediterranean trade. Several chartered members of the Levant Company were leading investors in the Massachusetts Bay Company and the other North American plantations.[11] Large numbers of Englishmen laboured for the profit of such men in both the American colonies and the Mediterranean trade. Thousands of sailors, servants and labourers who worked for English masters in the colonies, in the British Isles or on the high seas were subject to the dangerous conditions of maritime travel and exchange. Some were taken captive by 'Turkish' pirates (who sailed in the western Atlantic as well as in the Mediterranean) and transported to areas under Muslim rule, where they were enslaved in the galleys, put to work on shore or held for ransom.

Beginning in the late sixteenth century, a series of printed texts started to appear in England describing the fascinating and terrifying experiences of English captives who escaped from bondage, returned to England and lived to tell the tale.[12] These texts always make strong claims for the authority of the eyewitness narrator and for the truth and validity of the narration, but they are inevitably filtered through the distorting lens of an English Protestant ideology. Although they are told from a Eurocentric perspective and prepared for a Christian readership, these narratives nonetheless convey a vivid, though partial, picture of Muslim culture in North Africa, and they communicate a sense of the identity crisis and cultural displacement that accompanied the experience of bondage.

Accounts of slavery, piracy and apostasy in North Africa appear frequently in print throughout the seventeenth century, and form a group of writings that might be said to comprise a distinct narrative genre, similar to but in fact earlier in date than the American captivity narratives that have received much recent attention. (The earliest and most renowned of these, the . . . Narrative of the Captivity and Restauration of Mary Rowlandson, appeared in 1682.[13]) One scholar, G. A. Starr, argues that the 'Barbary escape account' became a distinct literary genre in the seventeenth century and influenced later English writers like Defoe and Swift.[14] This generic category might be extended to include the series of Barbary captivity accounts written by or about American men and women who were taken captive in North Africa during the eighteenth century.[15]

I wish to read the English captivity narratives not in terms of a strictly literary history but in the context of the larger circulation of bodies that was carried out in the commercial system of the time. The circulation, exchange and conversion of human beings as commodities was not only a strictly economic phenomenon but was strongly affected by an ideological matrix from which national, religious and racial categories were constructed, categories that allowed for conflict or affiliation. The English captivity narratives, though they sometimes communicate conventional anti-Islamic messages, are not simply exercises in the demonization of the Other, along the lines of a reductive Saidian 'orientalism'. In fact, they are much more interesting, complex and conflicted. Merely pointing to the construction of English identity and selfhood by means of an Islamic or 'oriental' Other is only a preliminary step in any rigorous analysis of such texts. The binary opposition of Self and Other, Christian and Turk, is sometimes present as a rough framework, but it is not the only ideological formation at work and to see the captivity narratives only in such polarized terms would be reductive. In these texts, there occurs a fragmentation and multiplication of identities that produces a shifting array of cultural positions: Christianity is divided into Protestant, Roman Catholic, and other sects; Islam into Turkish and Moorish. The renegade pirate is a figure whose identity is no longer Christian, but is also not fully Islamic and remains 'redeemable'. Muslims and their customs are sometimes admired and praised by the authors of the captivity narratives – and they were the ones who wanted to go home. Many stayed, and many converted to Islam. They were happy to leave behind the agonies of seafaring life on an English ship or the conditions of lower-class society in a nation with serious socio-economic problems, including frequent outbreaks of famine and plague.

In the early modern period, English contact with Islamic culture was often accompanied by other cross-cultural encounters in the Mediterranean, including relations with Spain and Portugal. Spanish and Portuguese contact and conflict with Islamic culture began earlier, went deeper and were closer to home. Slavery was already a well-established institution in Spain, Portugal and their colonies by the late fifteenth century.[16] The English admired the success of the Portuguese slavers, the Brazilian sugar plantations and the Spanish sugar industries in the Caribbean that employed slave labour. One scholar traces the lineage of English slave-trading back even further, arguing that

> there had been a developmental continuity between the plantations that first appeared in the eastern Mediterranean in the early 12th century and those to be found in the Atlantic Ocean in the 15th [in Madeira] and in tropical America in the 16th, 17th and 18th centuries.[17]

In England, commercial energies and imperial ambitions built up momentum and by the mid-sixteenth century an increased maritime commerce, especially international trade, took the English further afloat in vessels that were designed for longer journeys than the galleys or carracks of old. During the second half of the sixteenth century, English merchants revived maritime trade in the Levant[18] and began to develop the slave trade in West Africa and the Caribbean. John Hawkins's voyage of 1562 marked the commencement of the English slave-trading enterprise.

As the space of maritime enterprise opened up, English merchants, seamen and travellers were exposed to new experiences, new dangers and new sources of profit. The Mediterranean littoral during this period was a region in which many peoples met and exchanged goods – sometimes under conditions of mutual agreement, and sometimes under circumstances of coercion, force or violence. The system of 'free' trade, then as now, was conducted with power, force and fraud as basic strategies, and human bodies were at stake. The galleys of the Mediterranean fleets were propelled by slave labour, and human beings were bought and sold throughout the region, in the Ottoman and Barbary states as well as in the areas under Christian rule. There were large slave markets in Spain, Portugal, France, Italy and Malta, as well as in Tunis, Tripoli, Algiers,

Salee and Istanbul, and there were pirates and privateers in every region of the Mediterranean looking for vulnerable ships.[19] Capture by pirates was a danger well known to those who followed the sea for a living and, by the early seventeenth century, the number of Englishmen and women held in the Barbary ports reached a crisis level. The number of captivity narratives printed at the time indicates the fascination and concern with which people regarded this phenomenon.

Each of the English captivity narrators begin their accounts with a description of their departure from a British port, where they had already entered into the service of a master – the captain or the master of the vessel would have exercised considerable power over them. After setting sail from home, the narrator describes his voyage, his labour and his commercial purposes up to the point of his capture. The loss of freedom could occur in various ways; it usually began with a corsair assault, but sometimes with a storm or shipwreck.

In 1655, Abraham Browne, who had settled in New England but was working for his master, a Plymouth merchant, 'agreed . . . to go' on a voyage of trade from Plymouth (in England) 'to Madeira, next to Barbados and thence to New England'.[20] Like many merchantmen of the time, Browne's ship travelled in a convoy to discourage pirates but, when a storm separated his ship from the others, the vessel was pursued and attacked by 'our most cruel enemies, two Turk's men of war belonging to Sally'.[21] After a fierce resistance, the captain of Browne's ship surrendered and the crew was taken, an event which Browne interprets as 'the just judgments of God and the desert of our sins'.[22]

The process of conversion from 'free' man to commodity was painful and humiliating. Browne describes how, though he was already bleeding from wounds he suffered during the fight, he was stripped naked, bound and then beaten with his own shoe by his captors. Back in Salee, he changed hands when he was sold by the pirates to a slave dealer who kept the newly acquired slaves in a room for a week where potential buyers could come to see the merchandise. Then they were well 'fed up' for the market. Browne describes the experience of being sold as a slave:

> we were led about, two or three at a time, in the midst of a great concourse of people . . . who have the full sight of you; and if that will not satisfy they come and feel your hand and look in your mouth to see whether you are sound and in health or to see by the hardness of your hand whether you have been a worker or no. The manner of buying is by assuring that he [who] gives the greatest price hath you, they bidding one upon another until the highest profferer whose slave you must be whatever he is or wherever he dwells.[23]

Browne's experience is in many ways typical of the captivity narrators, though he was lucky to receive good treatment from his owner in Sallee. Those who became galley slaves faced much harsher conditions, but it was more lucrative for the Sallee pirates and slave dealers to encourage ransom at the highest possible price rather than keep a slave in labour for many years, with the risk of escape or early death that would mean complete loss of the slave owner's investment.

Browne was enslaved for only three months, when he was redeemed by an English merchant, Philip Payne, who was authorized to ransom forty captives. Browne's ransom was £125, and part of that was a bill of exchange for £60 drawn on the account of Browne's master, Nicholas Opie of Plymouth. The relatively quick turnaround time in Browne's case – from captivity to sale to ransom – reflects the profit-driven pace of circulation in the economy of slavery and redemption, and relies upon the role of go-betweens (like Payne) who traded in ransomed bodies.

Redemption and work

Some English captives, especially those with useful skills, were treated well and given considerable responsibility and autonomy but, for those less fortunate, slavery could be similar to the treatment given prisoners of war who were chained to the oars in the galleys of Venice, Spain, Ottoman Turkey and other Mediterranean nations.[24] Piracy, slavery and forced labour were business-as-usual in the Mediterranean and Atlantic maritime world. Slavery could be a form of punishment involving forced labour, or forced labour could be a form of coercion verging on slavery. Traitors, prisoners of war and victims of piracy shared the same conditions of servitude.

The practices of impressment, the spiriting away of children, the selling of children and of young men and women into apprenticeship or indentured servitude: all these were common forms of 'white slavery' that prevailed even before the English commitment to the African-Caribbean slave trade. David W. Galenson reminds us that

> the use of bound white labourers preceded the use of black slaves in every British American colony, and it was only after an initial reliance on indentured servants for the bulk of their labour needs that the planters of the West Indies and the southern mainland colonies turned to slaves.[25]

An important example of white slavery is the forced deportation and enslavement under Cromwell of Irish and Scottish prisoners of war who were sent to Barbados to become indentured servants on the English sugar plantations there. Throughout the seventeenth century, 'incorrigible rogues' who were held in the Bridewell or other houses of correction were sentenced to be shipped to the colonies in North America as indentured servants, and various groups from Ireland, Scotland and England, ranging from military prisoners to Quakers to Irish-Catholic girls, were transported. Indentured servants, including Irish, had been brought to Barbados since 1627, but there were 12,000 prisoners shipped involuntarily between 1648 and 1655 and they laboured under conditions of severe hardship.[26] Many of those transported were not used to agricultural labour, and the cultivation of sugar or tobacco in a much hotter climate than that of the British Isles was difficult work. 'As for the usage of the Servants,' remarked Richard Ligon in *A True and Exact History of the Island of Barbadoes* (1673), 'it is much as the Master is; merciful or cruel'.[27] Ligon also described the working conditions endured by bondservants in Barbados:

> I have seen an Overseer beat a servant with a can about the head, till the blood has followed, for a fault that is not worth the speaking of; and yet he must have patience or worse will follow.... Their salt Provisions are weighed out, and they have nothing but what the Law obliges the Master to give.[28]

In 1649, Royalists attacked Cromwell and others for 'enslaving' British subjects. The same accusation was raised again in Parliament in 1659, in a petition which was printed as *Englands slavery, or Barbados merchandize; represented in a petition to the high court of Parliament, by Marcellus Rivers and Oxenbridge Foyle gentelmen, on behalf of themselves and three-score and ten more free-born Englishmen sold (uncondemned) into slavery.*[29]

Not only in Barbados, but as early as 1619 in Virginia, we find lower-class men and women from England, categorized as 'rogues' or 'vaga-bonds', being forcibly transported to the colonies where they were sent for seven years' service or longer.[30] Whether they were shipped volun-tarily or not, these colonial bondservants could be traded, bought and sold by their masters – even won or lost in a card game. According to James Curtis Ballagh, 'The depressed condition of the [Virginia] colony following the Indian massacre of 1622 made the sale of servants a very common practice among both officers and planters', and in one case 'a planter sold the seven men on his plantation for a hundred and fifty pounds of tobacco'.[31] In the second decade of the seventeenth century, under Governor Thomas Gates, violation of gubernatorial edicts was punishable by 'three years' slavery' to the Virginia colony; persistent neglect of labour on the part of a servant was punishable by galley service of one to three years; and for 'petty offenses', servants worked as slaves in irons for a term of years.[32]

Some of the Barbary captives lived in far more comfortable circum-stances than the bondservants toiling in Virginia and Barbados, or the African slaves who were first introduced in Virginia in 1619.[33] For Chris-tian slaves in North Africa, conditions ranged from miserable to comfort-able. One possible avenue leading to greater freedom and even financial gain was conversion to Islam. Those who 'turned Turk' could achieve a high quality of life; though for some this was considered a 'Satanic temptation'.

Edward Webbe was captured in 1572 and served as a galley slave and then as a gunner in the Turkish army. His narrative, dedicated to Elizabeth I, describes his suffering in the galleys and his (allegedly) forced service as 'chief master gunner in the Turkish wars'. But he claims that the greatest trial was the temptation of conversion:

> the torture and torment of conscience which troubled me and all true Christians to the very soul: for the Turk by all means possible would still persuade me and other my fellow Christians ... to forsake Christ, to deny Him, and to believe in their god Mahomet; which if I would have done, I might have had wonderful preferment of the Turk, and have lived in as great felicity as any lord in that country; but I utterly denied their request, though by them grievously beaten naked for my labour.[34]

A hundred years later, for another English captive, Joseph Pitts, the pressure to convert was too strong. In 1678, at the age of sixteen, he and his fellow crew members were sailing from Newfoundland to Bilbao, Spain, with a cargo of fish, when they were taken by an Algerine pirate ship commanded by a Dutch renegade. After being sold into slavery, he converted to Islam but excused his apostasy by reason of 'the cruelties exercised upon me by the Turks ... which were so many and so great, that I being then but young, too, could no longer endure them, and therefore turned Turk to avoid them'.[35] After making the pilgrimage to Mecca, Pitts was freed by his master and entered military service in the Algerian galleys. He later slipped away at Smyrna and made his way back home to Exeter. His narrative asks forgiveness for his apostasy and he claims 'that though I was forced by that cruelty that was exercised upon me to turn Turk, yet I was really a Christian in my heart'.[36]

Many of the captivity narratives, including those by Webbe and Pitts, give detailed, suspenseful accounts of escape attempts, both successful and unsuccessful. Recapture by Moors or Turks resulted in punishment and increased restrictions. Some captives succeeded in fleeing from Muslim territory, only to be taken and imprisoned by their fellow Christians. Richard Hasleton was able to escape when the galley in which he served as a slave was shipwrecked on the Italian coast but the year was 1587 and, when one of his fellow galley slaves told the authorities that Hasleton was a 'Lutheran', he was sent to Majorca where he was imprisoned and tortured by the Inquisition. When Hasleton escaped from the Inquisition, he made for the Barbary Coast where he attempted to get aboard an English ship; however, he failed to do so and was returned to slavery in the Algerian galleys. In 1592 he was finally ransomed by Richard Staper, one of the merchants who had founded the Elizabethan trade with Turkey.

Pitts reports that 'Another Englishman I knew, who was bred to the trade of a gunsmith, who after he was ransomed, and only waited for his passage, reneged and chose rather to be a Mahometan than to return to his own country'.[37] And there were certainly many others without the good fortune or family connections needed to raise a ransom. This was only one of the risks involved in seafaring capitalism, a risk which perhaps could be offset by another form of business speculation – the 'putting out of five for one' mentioned by Gonzalo in *The Tempest* and described by Jonson's Puntarvolo in *Every Man Out of His Humor*:

> I do intend ... to travel, and ... I am determined to put forth some five thousand pound to be paid me five for one upon the return of myself, my wife, and my dog from the Turk's court in Constantinople. (3.3.245–8)

Jonson ridicules this practice, but the fact that there were established brokers willing to take the risk indicates that the journey was a perilous one, and many travellers did not return. Some captives languished for years in captivity before being ransomed. Cervantes is a case in point: he was a prisoner in Algiers from 1575 until 1580, when he was finally ransomed by Fray Juan Gil, the procurator-general of the Trinitarian redemptionists.

The profits of captivity

The merchants, consuls, factors and priests who mediated between the captors and those paying ransom helped to stimulate the early economy of piracy and captivity. Between the late sixteenth century and the mid-seventeenth century, the circulation of bodies had increased, not only because there were more English vessels sailing in the Mediterranean and Atlantic but because the collection of ransom and the use of slave labour had stimulated and empowered the corsair economies of the Barbary States. The more money they collected as ransom, the more the corsairs of Sallee, Algiers and Tunis were able to reinvest in supplies, ships, guns and fortifications for their harbours to outfit and support further expeditions. And the more successful and numerous their piratical operations became, the more Christians were attracted to join them, turn Turk and partake of the profits. Then, as today, the paying of ransom to redeem captives was not an unproblematic act of charity: it encouraged the taking of more captives. In her study of *Spanish Captives in North Africa in the Early Modern Age*, Ellen Friedman concludes that 'the efforts of the redemptionist fathers helped make corsairing a profitable endeavor'.[38] It was only when the battle fleets of England and France became so over-whelmingly powerful at the end of the seventeenth century that the corsairs were forced to submit to peace treaties restricting their depreda-tions, or face artillery bombardments that were increasingly destructive to their walled cities.

As the circulation of bodies accelerated in the seventeenth century, English merchants and courtiers with the resources to pay ransom were not able to keep up with the number of slaves being held for redemption. Ransoms were high and unaffordable by many families back home, and merchants and the government argued about who should pay ransom or how funds for ransom should be collected and distributed. Only by appealing to the government could some relatives hope to get their loved ones back home. In the 1640s, female petitioners besieged Parliament asking for the government to ransom their husbands.[39] It is not surprising that many slaves turned Turk or died while waiting. Algerian pirates raided the coast of Iceland in 1627 and brought 400 Icelandic hostages – men, women and children – back to Algiers. About one hundred of the captives converted to Islam and only twenty-seven were ransomed and returned home years later, in 1636. Those who did make it back were made to undergo a period of religious reinstruction and were 'reChristianized' in Copenhagen by a Lutheran divinity student before being returned to their communities in Iceland.

In England during the seventeenth century there were enough returned renegades that in 1635 the Church of England promulgated a formal rite of reinstatement, the 'Form of Penance and Reconciliation of a Renegado, or Apostate from the Christian Church to Turcism', presumably a ceremony that Pitts and other apostates underwent upon their return. The 'offender' was made

> to stand, all the time of divine service and sermon in the forenoon, in the porch of the church . . . in a penitent fashion in a white sheet, and with a white wand in his hand, his head uncovered, his countenance dejected, not taking any particular notice of any person that passeth by him; and when the people come in and go out of the church, let him upon his knees humbly crave their prayers and acknowledge his offence in this form, 'Good Christians, remember in your prayers a poor wretched apostate or renegado'.[40]

The next Sunday he is made to stand inside the church next to the minister, before whom the apostate would make a formal statement of remorse and beg forgiveness. After this, the minister removes the renegade's white robe and wand and recognizes him as a 'brother'. He is then permitted to rejoin the Christian community and to take Holy Communion at the next service he attends.

The captives and renegades like Pitts or Okeley who 'escaped' and returned to England are exceptional, not typical – most captives were ransomed, died or turned Turk without printing their stories. The captivity narrators (and those who helped arrange for their texts to be printed) had special motives for bringing these stories to the public eye. Even their claims to have 'escaped' are sometimes dubious, for they were not always physically captive but, rather, *captivated* by Islamic culture. Their accounts may distort the facts to serve ideological or personal agendas (for example, Pitts's desperate need to convince his audience that he was not really a convinced Muslim, though he did formally turn Turk; or Webbe's insistence that he did not willingly supply military technology to the infidel). The very urgency and insistence of the author's rhetoric of truth-telling testifies to the captivity narratives' reception as mere travellers' tales.

In many of the texts, anxious truth claims, based on the authority of plain speech and supported by vehement assertions for the authority and authenticity of firsthand experience, are linked to claims for the religious truth of Christianity, and particularly Protestantism. The religious framework that is present in most of the captivity narratives serves the function of clearing the good name of the former captive or slave by describing the endurance of suffering or the resistance to temptation as Christian, Protestant virtue. Those who escape or refuse to convert are presented as personifications of Anglo-Protestant virtue and fortitude. For the returned captives whose stories were printed, this was also an effort to clear themselves of contamination.

These texts also served a larger ideological function: they attempted to elide the fact of unfree labour and suffering within the larger maritime-colonial economy by emphasizing the cruel mastery or religious 'superstition' of the Muslims in North Africa, and by constructing a role for English merchants as tenacious victims and underdogs, not oppressors. Both Spanish and Ottoman powers are represented as evil forces, though the Inquisition often comes across as the greater of these two evils (especially in the Elizabethan narratives). Turks, Moors, Jews, renegades and Roman Catholics – all of these groups are condemned for their role in persecuting or enslaving English Protestants. At the same time there are sympathetic or even admiring reports of Islamic culture's wealth, sophistication, discipline, etc., and the same groups that were denouncing the 'Turkish' cruelty and 'Mahometan' barbarism were trafficking in profitable commodities with Muslim merchants in North Africa and the Levant.

In England, and in ships or colonial settlements run by Englishmen, there were customary forms of social control exerted over 'human resources' that are hardly distinguishable from some forms of slavery or captivity. An English crew member taken captive by the Barbary pirates and sold into slavery in Tunis or Algiers might, depending on his master and circumstances, live under conditions preferable to those of an indentured servant suffering virtual slavery in places like Barbados or Jamaica during the seventeenth century. Or, if unfortunate, an English slave might be sent to the Sultan's galleys and be worked to death without much hope of ransom. By working seven years or more for their freedom, English 'redemptioners', as they were termed, were essentially ransoming themselves from a form of slavery – buying back their freedom, which had been taken away when they were indentured. While these redemptioners in America toiled and waited for their day of release, there were redemptionist friars in North Africa working to redeem Christian slaves in Tunis and Algiers. These systems of servitude were not only comparable in terms of the power dynamic and conditions of unfree labour that existed in the colonies and in the Barbary States, they were also interconnected through the commercial, maritime system that circulated bodies back and forth, from North America to North Africa to England. Dealers, agents and factors in North Africa functioned in much the same way, and with the same population of labourers, as the merchants transporting or supplying labour to the New World colonies.

The captivity narratives attempt to create a distinction between Mediterranean and New World bond service when, in spite of the historically specific differences, they are branches of the same invasive and aggressive system. The captivity accounts attempt to distract the reader from the fact of unfree labour and suffering within English society and in English colonies, but they can never quite conceal the contradiction – especially in those accounts that highlight the positive allure, the 'temptation' of wealth, pleasure, ease and sex offered to those who 'turn'. An important ideological function of the captivity narratives is to displace the onus of 'master' or 'patron' from the domestic or colonial English masters who controlled and exploited lower-class labourers onto a demonized Islamic Other who could be condemned for 'barbaric' and cruel behaviour, leaving the readers of the narrative with a self-satisfied, ethnocentric sense of their own nation's 'liberty' and cultural superiority.

Notes

1. The original documents pertaining to these exchanges are reprinted in S. A. Skilliter, *William Harborne and the Trade with Turkey, 1578–1582: A Documentary Study of the First Anglo-Ottoman Relations* (London, Oxford University Press for the British Academy, 1979).

2. See Eric Williams, *Capitalism and Slavery* (Chapel Hill, University of North Carolina Press, 1944); M. I. Finley, *Ancient Slavery and Modern Ideology* (New York, Viking Press, 1980); Eugene Genovese, *The Political Economy of Slavery* (New York, Vintage Books, 1968); Eugene Genovese and Elizabeth Fox-Genovese, *The Fruits of Merchant Capital: Slavery and Bourgeois Property in the Rise and Expansion of Capitalism* (Oxford, Oxford University Press, 1983); David Brion Davis, *The Problem of Slavery in Western Culture* (Ithaca, NY, Cornell University Press, 1966) and *Slavery and Human Progress* (Oxford, Oxford University Press, 1984); Orlando Patterson, *Slavery and Social Death* (Cambridge, MA, Harvard University Press, 1982); Robin Blackburn, *The Making of New World Slavery* (London, Verso, 1997).

3. See 'The Renaissance triangle: Britons, Muslims, and American Indians', in Nabil Matar, *Turks, Moors, and Englishmen in the Age of Discovery* (New York, Columbia University Press, 1999).

4. See Chapter 1, 'The Old World background to New World slavery', in Blackburn, *The Making of New World Slavery*, pp. 31–93.

5. Davis, *Slavery and Human Progress*, p. 52.

6. Cited in Matar, *Turks, Moors, and Englishmen*, p. 92.

7. On the system of servitude in Virginia, this study is still useful: James Curtis Ballagh, *White Servitude in the Colony of Virginia: A Study of the System of Indentured Labor in the American Colonies* (1895; reprinted New York, Burt Franklin, 1969).

8. William Okeley, *Eben-Ezer, or A Small Monument of Great Mercy Appearing in the Miraculous Deliverance of William Okeley* (London, 1676), pp. 18–19; 59–60.

9. *Ibid.*, p. 41.

10. 'Abraham Browne's Captivity' is printed in Stephen T. Riley (ed.), *Seafaring in Colonial Massachusetts* (Boston, Colonial Society of Massachusetts, 1980), pp. 31–43. Joshua Gee's manuscript narrative is printed as the *Narrative of Joshua Gee of Boston, Mass., while he was captive in Algeria of the Barbary States, 1680–1687*, ed. Albert C. Bates (Hartford, 1943).

11. Two excellent accounts of English mercantile enterprise during this period, both colonial and commercial, are Robert Brenner, *Merchants and Revolution: Commercial Change, Political Conflict, and London's Overseas Traders, 1550–1653* (Princeton, Princeton University

Press, 1993) and Kenneth R. Andrews, *Trade, Plunder and Settlement: Maritime Enterprise and the Genesis of the British Empire, 1480–1630* (Cambridge, Cambridge University Press, 1984).

12. The titles of some English captivity narratives written in the sixteenth and seventeenth centuries are to be found in the Bibliography.

13. For examples of the American captivity narratives, see the texts in Alden T. Vaughan and Edward W. Clark (eds), *Puritans among the Indians: Accounts of Captivity and Redemption, 1676–1724* (Cambridge, MA, Harvard University Press, 1981).

14. G. A. Starr, 'Escape from Barbary: a seventeenth-century genre', *Huntington Library Quarterly*, vol. 29 (1965). Other treatments of the captivity narratives as a genre include Joe Snader, 'The Oriental captivity narrative and early English fiction', *Eighteenth-Century Fiction*, vol. 9 (1997), and Paul Baepler, 'The Barbary captivity narrative in early America', *Early American Literature*, vol. 30, no. 2 (1995). See also James R. Lewis, 'Savages of the seas: Barbary captivity tales and images of Muslims in the early Republic', *Journal of American Culture*, vol. 13, no. 2 (Summer 1990).

15. See Paul Baepler (ed.), *White Slaves, African Masters: An Anthology of American Barbary Captivity Narratives* (Chicago, University of Chicago Press, 1999).

16. For information on slavery in Portugal, consult A. C. de C. M. Saunders, *A Social History of Black Slaves and Freedmen in Portugal, 1441–1555* (Cambridge, Cambridge University Press, 1982).

17. Sidney M. Greenfield, 'Plantations, sugar cane and slavery', in Michael Craton (ed.), *Roots and Branches: Current Directions in Slave Studies* (Toronto, Pergamon Press, 1979), p. 86.

18. On English trade in the Levant, see T. S. Willan, 'Some aspects of English trade with the Levant in the sixteenth century', *English History Review*, vol. 70 (1955), and Ralph Davis, 'England and the Mediterranean, 1570–1670', in F. J. Fisher (ed.), *Essays in the Economic and Social History of Tudor and Stuart England* (London, Cambridge University Press, 1961), pp. 117–37.

19. On early modern piracy in the Mediterranean and along European coasts, consult Peter Earle, *Corsairs of Malta and Barbary* (London, Sidgwick & Jackson, 1970); G. Fisher, *Barbary Legend: War, Trade, and Piracy in North Africa 1415–1830* (Oxford, Clarendon Press, 1957); David Delison Hebb, *Piracy and the English Government, 1616–1642* (Aldershot, Scolar Press, 1994); Alberto Tenenti, *Piracy and the Decline of Venice, 1580–1615* (London, Longmans, 1967); and John B. Wolf, *The Barbary Coast: Algiers under the Turks, 1500 to 1830* (New York, W. W. Norton, 1979).

20. Browne, 'Abraham Browne's Captivity', in Riley, p. 35.

21. *Ibid.*

22. *Ibid.*, p. 37.

23. *Ibid.*, pp. 40–1.

24. For a description of the conditions of slavery in Algiers, see Ellen G. Friedman, 'Christian captives at "hard labor" in Algiers, 16th-18th centuries', *International Journal of African Historical Studies*, vol. 13, no. 4 (1980).

25. Cited in Davis, *Slavery and Human Progress*, p. 52.

26. Kevin Brady, 'The Irish as slaves in the Caribbean', in Paul Finkelman and Joseph C. Miller (eds), *The Macmillan Encyclopedia of World Slavery* (London, Simon & Schuster and Prentice-Hall International, 1998), p. 369.

27. Richard Ligon, *A True and Exact History of the Island of Barbadoes* (London, 1673), p. 44.

28. *Ibid.*

29. An earlier text is John Harris, *The grand designe: or a discovery of that forme of slavery, extended, and in part brought upon the free people of England; by a powerful party in Parliament: and L. G. Crumwell . . . tending to the utter ruine, and enslaving of the whole nation* (London, 1647). Readers who might like to seek out a comparison between the 1647 and the 1659 texts (one 'Printed in the last yeare of Englands slavery, 1647' and the other 'printed in the eleventh year of Englands liberty, 1659') will find some indication of the change in political rhetoric over this 12-year period.

30. Abbot Emerson Smith, *Colonists in Bondage: White Servitude and Convict Labor in America, 1607–1776* (Gloucester, MA, Peter Smith, 1965), pp. 139–40.

31. Ballagh, *White Servitude*, p. 43.

32. *Ibid.*, p. 23.

33. For a brief introduction to how 'chattel slavery based on race . . . became an established feature in American society' (p. 185), see Steven Deyle, ' "By Farr the Most profitable Trade": slave trading in British colonial North America', in Patrick Manning (ed.), *Slave Trades, 1500–1800: Globalization of Forced Labour* (Aldershot and Brookfield, VT, Variorum, 1996), pp. 185–211.

34. Edward Arber (ed.), *Edward Webbe, Chief Master Gunner, His Travailes* (reprinted London, 1869), p. 29.

35. Joseph Pitts, *A True and Faithful Account of the Religion and Manners of the Mahometans* (London, 1704), p. 129.

36. *Ibid.*, p. 145.

37. *Ibid.*, p. 143.

38. Ellen Friedman, *Spanish Captives in North Africa in the Early Modern Age* (Madison, University of Wisconsin Press, 1983), p. xxv.

39. See Nabil Matar, 'Wives, captive husbands, and Turks: the first women petitioners in Caroline England', *Explorations in Renaissance Culture*, vol. 23 (1997).

40. *The Works of the Most Reverend Father in God, William Laud, D. D., Sometime Lord Archbishop of Canterbury* (Oxford, John Henry Parker, 1853), vol. 5, book 2, pp. 372–3.

CHAPTER THREE

Captivating reading: or captivity fiction as tourist guide to a non-Aboriginal Tasmania

SUSAN K. MARTIN

'Planting natives' in Tasmania

In August 1893, the Launceston meeting of the Tasmanian Amateur Gardener's Association heard a paper presented by Mr Thomas Carr on 'The Wild Flowers of Tasmania'. *The Tasmanian Mail* reported him as

> giving an outline of the characteristics of the different sort of native flora, and before concluding he strongly urged upon the Committee of the City and Suburban Improvement Association the cultivation of native flora at the Catar- act Gorge and Park. He said it would not only be ornamental, but would have an educational influence on the rising generation.[1]

In the nineteenth century, white Tasmanians of reasonable means could sit down on a Sunday and read *The Tasmanian Mail: A Weekly Journal of Politics, Literature, Science, Agriculture, News and Notes for Tasmania*, a publication from the Hobart *Mercury* office. Soon to take up Mr Carr's call to 'plant natives' in Cataract Gorge, though not quite in the way that he meant, was Mrs W. I. Thrower, whose short novel *Younâh!: A Tasmanian Aboriginal Romance of the Cataract Gorge* commenced serialization in the journal on 14 October 1893, before its publication as a separate volume in 1894. Mrs Thrower planted not indigenous plants, but indigenous peoples in the gorge in this fiction, which was one of the few nineteenth-century Australian captivity narratives. My comparison here is not intended to be flippant or disrespectful, but to point out the ways in which the notions behind Mr Carr's paper and Mrs Thrower's novel were extremely similar, and similarly bizarre.

In the 1890s Cataract Gorge was a well established and much visited tourist spot for Launceston and Tasmanian residents, as well as for interstate Australian and overseas visitors. Initially, it was visited for its untouched picturesque beauty: a set of rapids and two deep pools, the first and second basins, embedded in a gorge on the South Esk River at the edge of Launceston. By the 1890s, as is clear from Mr Carr's paper, the picturesqueness had been enhanced by considerable plantings of European species and some clearing as well as by the erection of various built structures, including the 'Crusoe Hut'. The Gorge's accessibility had been facilitated by the erection of a raised walkway along the north side. In early 1893, work commenced on a hydroelectric generating plant upstream from the Gorge.[2]

Clearly, there was almost no sense in which Cataract Gorge remained a pristine site when Mrs Thrower wrote her novel *Younâh!*. The novel, however, produces a pristine moment, in a kind of pre-lapsarian world at the very beginning of white encroachment onto Aboriginal land in Tasmania. It recounts the kidnap of a three-year-old white girl, Keitha St Clair, by a group of local Aborigines, the Pialummas. Keitha is taken in retaliation for depredations by local white settlers. There is some suggestion that Keitha is to be sacrificed to avenge the theft of Pialumma girls, but the chief's son, Eumarrah, becomes the child's protector. She is renamed Younâh, and brought up amongst the Pialummas. Eumarrah believes she may be useful as an intermediary between them and the whites in the future.[3]

When white encroachment again threatens the group, Eumarrah's mother decides that they should kill Younâh. Eumarrah conceals Younâh and her best friend, Natone, but they are discovered by a couple of English squires out exploring in the antipodean wilds. Younâh's whiteness is instantly recognized. She and Natone, who gets little choice in the matter, return with the men to 'civilization'. Younâh is identified by her coral necklace as Keitha, lost heiress of the St Clairs. Younâh is able to rapidly and miraculously acquire language, manners and class in a few months in Australia before she is sent home to her family. In a few years she is engaged to her rescuer, Jack Ormond. Jack and Keitha take their honeymoon trip to Tasmania so that Younâh/Keitha can repay Eumarrah for all his kindness, but the Black Wars have been perpetrated in her absence, and she finds Eumarrah dying of consumption on Flinders Island with the remaining Tasmanian Aborigines. The novel closes with Eumarrah and his people remembered only through the tales Keitha tells her enthralled children.

Younâh! is an obscure but valuable text. Valuable because it is a fiction about Tasmanian Aboriginal people at a time when the white population regarded them as extinct and, more particularly, because the Aborigines depicted are not just anonymous plot elements. A large part of the narrative is taken up with a version, however fanciful, of Tasmanian first peoples' daily life and culture. *Younâh!* is also distinct because it is one of relatively few captivity narratives published in nineteenth-century Australia, and because it is a novel with a local setting, by a local woman, published locally at a time when much Australian long fiction, women's and men's, was still being published in Britain.

Australian captivity fictions

Despite its distinctness, *Younâh!* can be taken as representative, even emblematic, of a number of the effects and uses of similar, better known fictions published in Australia around the same time, and as symptomatic of the production of race relations in the 1890s, the alleged seminal decade in the development of Australian nationalism. That it is part of some wider discourse becomes evident when one looks at the serial immediately preceding *Younâh!* in *The Tasmanian Mail*: Rosa Praed's *Outlaw and Lawmaker*.

This novel also contains a brief captivity scene, in which the desired heroine Elsie is lured from a picnic and exploring party, with the complicity of Aboriginal workers, into a concealed hideaway strongly associated with the local Aborigines. Praed's novel uses the captivity and associated events to negotiate similar anxieties about race, sexuality, nation and the environment. Like Younâh, Elsie is seen as both congruent with the wild environment and threatened by it. In both novels, miscegenation is a present, unspeakable and unspoken threat. Elsie's reputation is in danger of being lost after her rescue from the kidnap, in that she has been away from the surveillance and guarantee of white female chaperonage, though the possibility of interracial sex or rape is displaced because Elsie's immediate threat during the kidnap is the white leader of the Aboriginal workers. As in many of Praed's novels, national identity and loyalties are debated through the main female characters' choice of romantic partners, in this case the rough, true, home-grown variety versus the more sophisticated but potentially corrupt European. The ambivalence of *Outlaw and Lawmaker* is not matched by *Younâh!*, a novel which does not question the Britishness of the colony, its allegiance to Britain or British superiority.

Many of the other existent nineteenth-century Australian *fictional* captivity narratives, or narratives which contain a captivity episode, are more or less contemporary with *Younâh!*. I am excepting here what might be called 'reverse' captivity narratives – fictions which contain the implicit or explicit kidnap of Aboriginal characters by Europeans, though *Younâh!* belongs in this group also. The European-victim narratives – which include Rosa Praed's *Fugitive Anne* (1902) and *Outlaw and Lawmaker* (1893), Ernest Favenc's *The Secret of the Australian Desert* (1895), various short stories and a number of tales inspired by the White Woman of Gippsland – work in similar ways and have some very similar elements.[4]

These fictions all produced representations of indigenous people which worked to a greater or lesser extent to displace actual Aboriginal people; this was not just to the degree in which any representation displaces or replaces that which it ostensibly represents or encapsulates, but through the violent rewriting of the, or an, indigenous people. *Fugitive Anne* and *The Secret of the Australian Desert*, for instance, as well as producing dubious and unauthorized versions of Aboriginality, populate their fantasy Australian interiors with another 'superior' indigenous race.

Furthermore, in Australia, any version of the 'white captured by Aborigines' works to obscure the facts and history of the common and systematic abduction and rape of *Aboriginal* women by white men, and the abduction of Aboriginal children by white men and women. Aboriginal children were removed from their parents and adopted out or, more commonly, placed in institutions from the nineteenth century to the 1970s. These children are now known as the Stolen Generations. Recently, the efforts of the reconciliation process in Australia have been disrupted by the comments of the Minister for Aboriginal Affairs, John Herron, questioning the scope and impact of such removals. Herron's comments can be seen as a continuation of nineteenth-century representations which routinely erased or overlaid such captures. Intimately connected to this obfuscation of atrocities are the moves these fictions made to produce and perform a romantic history of place for the non-Aboriginal population. They might also be seen to partake of, and duplicate, the discourses of the growing industry of tourism, in order to map the country as both unfamiliar, exotic and unexplored *and* as familiar, picturesque, historically inscribed, owned and available.

Younâh! as captivity narrative

In the strictest sense, neither *Younâh!* nor the other novels mentioned are captivity narratives. They are fictional and make no specific claims to the sort of authenticity found in the North American 'Indian captivity narratives' which give rise to the term. Nor do they draw on the sort of broad historical record and cultural tradition around actual captivities of settler or invader peoples by indigenous peoples that the American narratives do. Obviously, there are actual tales and myths in Australia which inform them – Eliza Fraser, and the 'White Woman of Gippsland' stories and the story of William Buckley.[5]

But the term 'captivity narrative' can also register the circulation of particular understandings of captivity or cohabitation with indigenous people that are informed directly or indirectly by the ideologies and forms of North American captivity narratives. The Australian fictions, including *Younâh!*, can be seen in relation to the North American narratives in a number of ways. The Australian fictional narratives, like many of their North American counterparts (such as the 'Panther Captivity' story), are obviously concerned with notions of race – racial identification, nineteenth-century hierarchies of racial development and, especially, intense anxieties about miscegenation and sexual contact between indigenous men and European women. The Australian fictions likewise negotiate anxieties and desires circulating around the environment, ideas of wilderness and possession of the country through the captivity narrative.[6] While there are discernible similarities between the European concerns which such narratives are used to confront, there are extreme and significant differences in the actual environment encountered, the actual indigenous peoples and the historical and geographical details of the different places. Australia was less amenable to fantasies of a fresh welcoming new world because of its less familiar and mostly drier environment, and because settlement took place mainly in the nineteenth century, in a different cultural moment from the celebrations of eastern North America. Though Tasmania was perhaps the most English-like environment in terms of climate, appearance and potential crops, it was also a part of Australia primarily associated with exile, incarceration and cruelty. The original name, Van Diemen's Land, became synonymous with convictism and such famously vicious and isolated penal settlements as Port Arthur. It is important to stress that it is the *uses* to which captive figures and captive stories were put, and not necessarily the stories themselves or their settings, which seem similar.

The unsettling familiarity of woman with wilderness, common to American captivity narratives and described by Annette Kolodny in her discussion of the Panther Captivity, is matched in *Younâh!*, and doubled.[7] Younâh's bush skills and closeness to indigeneity are mapped on her body – 'the natural fairness of her skin had deepened into an almost brunette-like tint, by reason of continued exposure to the open air' (p. 42) – *and* through her proximity to her Aboriginal companion Natone. Despite this, femininity and class are clearly legible after years in the supposed wilderness. Jack, one of her discoverers, comments confidently:

> If she had parents in this wilderness they could be none other than runaway convicts. This girl belongs to a better type of race than is generally found among that class. I am of the opinion that she has been lost, or it may be that she was stolen from her home by some of the tribes . . . (p. 42)

Such figures enact that unsettling association of women with nature, with the physical and earthy, and of white women with indigeneity, even as they are being used to rehearse and dispel that fear. The woman's recuperation is into a 'civilization' that for her consists of both a libidinal economy and a mercantile one. The female prize of the wilderness is both beautiful and (soon to be) well endowed with cash. It is tempting to see the unsettling vision of a feminized wilderness/wilderness-woman converted into the attractive domestic lucrative property.[8]

There is a limit to general comparisons between captivity narratives however. In *The Indian Captivity Narrative 1550–1900*, Kathryn Z. Derounian-Stodola and James A. Levernier read one of the Eliza Fraser narratives unproblematically as an extension of the North American captivity narrative's westward trajectory across the Pacific. In a consistently USA-centric, if somewhat bizarre, geographical slippage they read the narrative as set not in Australia, but New Guinea.[9] Such a slippage should alert us to the distinct cultural, historical and geographic differences between North American captivity narratives, and Australian narratives of captivity.[10]

Derounian-Stodola and Levernier acknowledge what might be called the shifting use-value of North American captivity stories, but they seem to adhere to a notion that such stories' 'archetypal patterns' are more important to their surviving popularity than their 'cultural significances'.[11] In contradiction to such a stance, Chris Healy argues, in *From the Ruins of Colonialism*, that Eliza Fraser does not stand at the centre of a stable narrative but is rather a multiple figure, an 'event under description', a name used and useful in various forms of cultural work, including attempts to stabilize the impossibly unstable categories of race and gender which circulate in captivity narratives.[12] Though the Fraser narratives are a separate case from the later fictions, Healy's argument is relevant because it highlights the geographical and cultural specificity, and the distinct historical and cultural circulations of such tales. While the European colonial context of captivity narratives makes likely some commonality of narrative form and narrative anxiety, this should not be taken to override the specificity of moment, use and circulation, to the extent that Eliza Fraser becomes some vague Pacific extension of a North American form and archetype.[13]

Younâh! and Tasmanian Aboriginal culture

The sources for Thrower's fiction are not clear. Some of her material presumably came from local folklore. Thrower's lifespan would overlap with the lives of the surviving Tasmanian Aboriginal community on Flinders Island (to which they were exiled in the 1830s) and at Oyster Cove.[14] She almost certainly would have read in the Tasmanian *Mercury* in 1876 of the death of Truganini, and of the theft of her body.[15] Truganini was neither the last 'full-blood' Tasmanian Aborigine to die, nor did her death mark the end of the Tasmanian Aborigines as claimed, but the white Tasmanian community largely used her as a marker of Aboriginal pastness, and the wider non-Aboriginal Australian community has continued to do so, despite ample evidence to the contrary.

Many of the features of Thrower's representation seem completely spurious but the novel does have a complicated relation to knowledge about the Aboriginal groups around Launceston. The land occupied by the Pialummas in their seasonal migrations vaguely matches what is known of the movements of the Panninher people of the North Midlands.[16] Certainly Thrower's representation is anachronistic and in the whites' favour – suggesting as it does that peaceful occupation of Cataract Gorge would have been possible up until the late 1820s and the 'Black Line', the military-run expedition intended to round up the remaining population and remove them from the mainland.[17] Thrower's flights of fancy are in fact enabled by the early dispossession and disruption in this area, which resulted in a dearth of information about the pre-invasion boundaries and culture of these people.[18]

While the character Eumarrah coincides in age, place and authority with the historic guerilla fighter Umarrah,[19] other names seem to have been chosen more overtly for some effect of authenticity unconnected to historical accuracy or respect for persons. For instance, Younâh was the name of a child, who died as a young woman sometime between 1847 and 1851. Her father was a white sealer.[20] Considering the importance of names for the Tasmanian Aboriginal people, as noted in Thrower's Chapter 2, her theft of these names is callous. They do, however, work to fracture the narrative, marking the romantic text of the found heiress with the names of dispossessed and prematurely dead female children – and raising the spectre of miscegenation in Younâh's very name. Yet the text works so hard to obviate and obscure any such possibility, with Younâh's sparkling and unmistakable whiteness and middle-classness and with her instant removal from the Aborigines to permanent European female chaperonage as soon as she reaches puberty.

The use of the name Eumarrah seems to have been more self-conscious on Thrower's part. In the novel, the only raid Eumarrah is depicted as being involved in is the one in which Younâh is kidnapped, where the hut is burnt but no blood is shed. Eumarrah dies in Christian resignation. No further mention is made of the other Aborigines, except that many are also dying from consumption.

The novel converts Eumarrah from a freedom fighter to an Uncle Tom figure. His gentleness and the representations of the Pialummas' culture to some extent dispute contemporary understandings of the Tasmanian Aborigines as mindlessly violent and without culture, but the use of *parts* of the history of Umarrah, while excluding the history of his sustained resistance, his imprisonment and the role of George Augustus Robinson, the 'Aboriginal Protector' (who is not named in the novel), erases political history in favour of personal stories.

On a personal level, with Eumarrah dead and the Governor forbidding Aboriginal return to the Tasmanian mainland, Keitha's well-meaning scheme is pointless. This erases the political fact of genocidal policies and the failure or refusal to address the situation of the Flinders Island community. George Augustus Robinson led a number of excursions from 1830 to 1834 to gather the remaining mainland Tasmanian Aboriginal population and relocate them on Flinders Island, off the north-east coast of Tasmania.[21] Robinson and his followers attempted to impose European lifestyles and values on these people, and the resulting conditions at Flinders Island – damp accommodation and clothing, restricted movement, cultural genocide – were fatal for many. In *Younâh!*, the English squirearchy are exonerated from any connection to such policies through ignorance:

When Jack Ormond and his wife reached Hobart Town . . . they learned for the first time that all the survivors of that race, to whom the land had formerly belonged, had been banished from it by the stronger one which had ousted them. (p. 60)

The honeymoon of the English propertied classes in Tasmania, then, takes place across the territory and via the deathbeds of the Tasmanian Aborigines, without irony.[22]

Younâh! as tour guide

Chapter 2 of *Younâh!* begins with a lengthy argument for the connection between land and Aboriginal people, through occupation, tradition, intimate familiarity and sacred association. The placement is interesting. It follows the narrative of the capture of the child Keitha in which the normal Manichean opposition of black and white, savage and civilized operates, and so might carry less power. Yet, because of its length and tone, it works to justify the attack and Younâh's captivity, and to invert many of the assumptions set up in the opening chapter. Younâh is taken captive as revenge for the capture of Pialumma women, but more broadly as revenge for the capture and misuse of their land. This chapter sets up a complicated argument for an Aboriginal understanding and appreciation of place, both of which are radically different from the European; and yet, because it represents Aboriginal life in part in terms of familiar European domestic imagery – in particular the hearth as centre and proof of the home – it renders the uncanny familiar:

> For generation after generation had the ancestors of Warnee owned all the mountains and valleys of Pialumma; there were the vast forests wherein to track down, and catch the timid kangaroo and wallaby,[23] the brightly plumaged birds belonged to them alone, and for whom else did the agile opossum surrender at once its life and the furry covering of its body! . . .
>
> How well they knew each giant of the forest, remembered every streamlet as it dashed impetuously over its brown and rocky bed ere it mingled its clear waters with those of some deeper, calmer stream! Familiar to them, not alone from the associations of a lifetime spent amid these wilds, but by reason of the legends which tradition had preserved to the tribe, were every steep, tree-crowned summit, each ferny moss-carpeted glade.
>
> And no less dear than familiar were all their well-known haunts. . . .
>
> Amid the depths of the sombre forest reposed the relics of many a brave, and reverently moved the tribe as they passed by the spots made hallowed to them by the presence of their dead. For so great an awe possessed the Tasmanians of those days, when death severed their family ties, that the name of a departed one was never again mentioned among them, nor any reference made to him. Nevertheless his memory lingered with the relatives and friends as something too sacred to be touched upon.
>
> Household gods, such as civilisation prizes, they had not, it is true, for the great vault of heaven was their canopy, the soft, springy turf their carpet. They

needed not tables, chairs, nor couches; and yet they possessed one element which they treasured with jealous care, for although the household was to them unknown – the household fire was theirs.

Certain members of the tribe had the care of this. . . . Individual families possessed, when they were in settled quarters, their own household fires. . . .

The dismay and anger which filled the breasts of Warnee and his savages may easily be gauged by the feelings which might be expected to animate those of a peaceful settlement of civilised beings were a horde of barbarians suddenly to descend into their midst, assume to themselves the right of possession and treat as trespassers the original owners.

Such had been the bitter experience of the Pialumma tribe, as one settler after another marked off and occupied selections of the hunting grounds which had belonged to them and their ancestors for countless ages. Week after week they found the area within which they were permitted to remain unmolested growing more circumscribed, until at length, driven by hunger and the impossibility of obtaining in their old haunts the game which had been their chief means of subsistence, they sought and found among the flocks of the settlers upon their own grounds that food without which they could not exist. (pp. 4–5)

It is important to read this against the background of the claimed extinction, at the time of the writing of *Younâh!*, of Tasmanian Aboriginal people which enables a level of sympathy and elegiac rhetoric always liable to be more vexed in the face of an existing indigenous population.[24] Nevertheless, in the wider context of Australian relations with mainland Aboriginal peoples, its tone is interesting. The narrative makes a strong claim for rightful ownership through traditional usage, knowledge and occupation, association and religious significance[25] and against the founding notions of what is now known as *terra nullius* – the idea that the land was not morally occupied because inhabited by 'barbarians'.[26] Some version of the notion of *terra nullius* in nineteenth- and twentieth-century Australia formed the foundation for the European occupation of Australia without treaty with the existing population. This was based on the idea that the land was 'waste' and was not being 'used' in a civilized sense by the inhabitants. This notion was legally overturned by the landmark Mabo decision in 1992 – a ruling by the Australian High Court which established for the first time that Native title was not automatically extinguished by the British colonization of Australia, and instituted the principle of indigenous ownership of traditional lands – and the later Wik ruling (1996). Thrower's is one of a few early texts which throw doubt on the barbarian, non-domestic nature of Aboriginal occupation.

Thrower describes a domestic society, a society with household arrangements not absent because they dwell in the bush but present in that very environment, symbolized by and centred on the fire as household emblem. The domestication of the landscape is not uncommon in nineteenth-century Australian women's fiction, which frequently represents the natural environment in non-threatening terms through a kind of imaginative extension or opening out of the internal domestic sphere into the garden and surrounding bush. This is reiterated, and also inverted here: the bush *is* the household, and fire is not an uncontrollable element but a clear sign of domesticity and, therefore, civilization. It renders the bush a domestic site.

This is, of course, enhanced by the complete reversal of common understandings of the processes of settlement and of a common trope of early fictions and settler accounts, in which the domestic hearth of a 'peaceful settlement of civilized beings' (the whites) is rudely disrupted by a 'horde of barbarians' (the indigenes). In Thrower's version, Warnee's 'tribe' are the peaceful beings, at this moment and throughout this chapter, and the white settlers become 'hordes of barbarians', with no respect for the domestic, peaceful civilization depicted.

Another notable aspect of the passage is the extent to which this fiction makes an argument for the discursive production of landscape and the ways in which narratives of place forge connections and signify ownership; the place is '[f]amiliar to them, not alone from the associations of a lifetime spent amid these wilds, but by reason of the legends which tradition had preserved to the tribe' (p. 3).[27]

This passage is employed to demonstrate Aboriginal connection to the land, but ultimately the story of *Younâh!* replaces the Aboriginal tales described. Thus this story, as one which inserts the white settler into the landscape and traditions of Aboriginal land, becomes also a story of right and habitation; it produces the scene as the space of white experience, white narrative and white history and takes the land justifiably captive. The telling and retelling of the history of Younâh's capture and rescue within the tale contribute to this, but the narrative itself enacts it.

Part of the way it does this is through selling Cataract Gorge to Tasmanians as a tourist site of uniqueness and naturalness. The novel peoples the Gorge with colourful indigenes as at the same moment it erases those occupants and turns the Gorge back into wild but available space – space which had been *both* occupied *and* untouched. It buys into the rhetoric of barbarism used a hundred years earlier to occupy the land in the first place – that it is physically but not morally occupied 'wasteland'; available, first, for the settlement described and, second, for the specular occupation encouraged. Its familiarity is repeatedly pointed out in the story, usually in contexts which highlight the historical separation which enables the romance and (perhaps) denies responsibility for the emptiness produced. For instance, when Eumarrah withdraws for a conference with his father and mother, Warnee and Makooi, they retreat to a private area in the Gorge. The narrator locates it specifically as an unexplored site, at the same time as mourning the 'vandalism' that has befallen it:

As 'Mossy Dell' it still exists for modern explorers, although the hand of the vandal, who rejoices in destruction, has shorn it of its pristine beauty, and neither clematis, woodbine, nor other beauteous climber of the woodlands clothes it as with a veil to conceal its cool, inmost recesses. (p. 12)

Colin and Jack are proto-tourists for nineteenth-century Cataract Gorge. As tourists, they are not responsible for the dispossession disapproved of by the narrative, even while tourism is implicated in this through its interconnectedness with the entire process and economy of settlement and development. Colin and Jack's trip to Australia is a sequel or alternative to the Grand Tour. They are landed gentlemen in search of the new. They:

left England behind them in a spirit of adventurous longing for 'something new under the sun' – something new to them at least, for they had used up all the resources of travel and exploration which Europe could present to them at the period of which I write, when the facilities for moving from one country to another were by no means so numerous or so convenient as they are in these Cook-tourist days. The great invention of steam was as yet in its infancy, and did not extend to foreign countries so that a Continental tour was an event in the lifetime of the few who were fortunate, while a trip to the Antipodes was equivalent to a sentence of exile. For there were no 'ocean greyhounds' in those remote days . . . [so travel was a serious matter to those who went by necessity] . . . But Jack Ormond and his friend were not impelled by such motives as these, as fortune had smiled upon them from the time at which they had commenced life's journey.

They were the eldest sons and heirs of wealthy Englishmen, whose large estates in Sussex adjoined . . . they had spent a considerable time abroad when their education was completed, had gone through a London season together, and emerged thence heart-whole. (pp. 36–7)

They follow Jack's sister to Australia, because,

'You see, old fellow, there is not much European ground that we have left untrodden. We have explored a goodly part of Asia, been to Egypt, and would have been certain to make for America next. We can go there some other time.' (p. 37)

As Dona Brown points out in relation to America:

Tourism offered tourists satisfaction through acquisition (. . . the acquisition of *experiences*), emotional fulfilment through spending money. Throughout the nineteenth century the product that tourism offered most consistently was some form of antidote to industrial capitalism. [But] . . . far from opposing that order, tourism was an integral part of it.[28]

Jack and Keitha's wedding tour is similarly composed of ownership and sentimental inscription:

The settlement, which had consisted but of a few straggling, small houses when Jack had visited Launceston before, had increased to very respectable dimensions, and there was even an hotel at which fair accommodation was to be obtained. [They hire a boat and go] up the Gorge as far as they could be rowed; then they scrambled across rocks and through shrubs and dense undergrowth afterwards, until they reached the spot where they two had first met. (p. 37)

Keitha sends Jack into the cave to retrieve the skeleton of her little pet albino kangaroo, which she proposes to keep as a 'relic of a faithful, although dumb friend' (p. 60).

The touristic acts of visiting romantic spots and collecting souvenirs are the same here. It is just that such forms of tourism as ways of owning and knowing the landscape are more clearly connected to their implications and sources through the grim echo in this passage of the thieving and keeping of Tasmanian Aboriginal remains by 'scientific' whites and collectors in Australia.[29] There might be a further level of cultural appropriation at work also. According to Lyndall Ryan, the Tasmanian Aborigines sometimes kept the bones of their own dead as 'relics'.[30]

For Tasmania, more intensively than for other colonies in the 1890s, tourism was becoming a potentially vital industry. Tasmania, across treacherous Bass Strait south of mainland Australia, was physically isolated from the main markets for its primary goods. Its physical isolation has always been matched by a kind of psychological isolation. Van Diemen's Land was the penal colony for mainland Australia: recalcitrant prisoners were sent to sites like Macquarie Harbour, or Port Arthur which is on an isolated, almost detached, peninsula in the south. From the first white settlements the island was associated with exile and incarceration, and stereotyped views of a corrupt, cruel society were assisted by such successful depictions as Marcus Clarke's convict novel *His Natural Life* (1874). Though white convicts were further up the social scale than Aboriginal Tasmanians, there are similarities in the enaction of social control of them through captivity, exile to still more isolated parts of the colony, indoctrination and surveillance. Port Arthur is the site of an extensive model or ideal prison, operating on and designed according to the Benthamite panoptic disciplinary methods examined by Foucault.[31] In the early part of the nineteenth century it is possible to see anxiety about the unruly bodies of convicts and of Aborigines being acted upon in similar ways. By the end of the century the surveillance had become touristic: Port Arthur was a stop on the tour of Tasmania, and the remains of Tasmanian Aboriginal people were on display in the museum of the Royal Society of Tasmania in Hobart. From 1904 to 1947, Truganini's skeleton was one of the exhibits.[32]

In August 1891 the Van Diemen's Land Bank collapsed, an event which prefaced a major economic depression in the colony, by some accounts more severe than that on the mainland.[33] Most Tasmanians experienced some degree of financial hardship. Thrower's publication might have been partly motivated by financial need – a little pocket money for herself or necessary funds for the family.

In any case, Thrower appears to have had a strong interest in promoting the Cataract Gorge and environs as a specular site, a destination for local tourists but, more importantly, also for those further afield. Thrower Street in Launceston runs parallel to Basin Road, the road leading down to the south side of the Gorge. This land belonged to William Ignatius Thrower, husband of Mrs W. I. Thrower. For whatever economic purpose the land adjoining the Basin might have been used, the other property owned by the Throwers in Launceston would clearly have benefited from any touristic side-effects of Mrs Thrower's romantic fictional exercise: it was Thrower's Court House Hotel.

It is seldom that fiction so clearly displays its use-value – the hotel with 'fair accommodation' may be the Throwers' own. It is surely not just the case that Mrs Thrower's novel is trash fiction, or glorified advertising, but rather that the bare bones and implied use of national fictions are a little more evident in this as a raw product. Captivity narratives, romance fictions and Lemurian novels open up and make the country available in a new way. The trope of the white, lost, stolen captive who disappears in the landscape is used in a project of inserting the figure of the white into the landscape. Younâh is kept captive with the intention of making her into an intercessor for the Aboriginal people but, of course, in her textual use she becomes an intercessor between the white reader/Tasmanian/ Australian and the native landscape. In this configuration it is not just the represented Aborigines who displace the original Tasmanians and their descendants' rights' but the native landscape also.

Conclusions

Thomas Carr's call for the planting of natives in Cataract Gorge seems to have been part of a popular movement to re-authenticate the environment, to restore what had been lost and make it available for the visual pleasure of those inheriting that loss. Mrs Thrower installs in the Gorge a dispossessed and fantasized indigenous population, who are replaced only to be dispossessed again in the space of the novel. The novel inevitably has to reiterate their doom in order to legitimate the colonial adventure it is proposing, yet it has to reinvoke them to remake/make it adventurous. Such a project inevitably disintegrates under the pressure of its own contradictory discourses. Unlike introduced plants, Anglo settlers have entirely refused any idea of sharing or coexistence, much as in the present day the Australian Government led by Prime Minister John Howard seems incapable of comprehending, explaining or tolerating the notion that pastoral leases can co-exist with native title on mainland Australia.[34] Thrower's indigenous plantings are ghosts whose removal forms the romance of her tale and the attraction of her vacated site, but her placement of them reveals a different sort of haunting.

Notes

1. *The Tasmanian Mail*, no. 41, issue 841 (1893), p. 29.

2. John Reynolds, *Launceston: History of an Australian City* (South Melbourne, Macmillan/ Adult Education Board of Tasmania, 1969), p. 129.

3. Mrs W. I. Thrower [Marian Teresa or Mary Theresa], *Younâh! A Tasmanian Aboriginal Romance of the Cataract Gorge* (Hobart, The *Mercury* Office, 1894), p. 13. All page references are to the book. The story was serialized in *The Tasmanian Mail*, 1893–1894.

4. See Robert Dixon's discussion of the way in which these captivity fictions, like other 'Lemurian' romances, are implicated in *fin-de-siècle* anxieties about gender, sexuality and the 'New Woman' in *Writing the Colonial Adventure: Race, Gender and Nation in Anglo-Australian Popular Fiction 1875–1914* (Oakleigh, Melbourne, Cambridge University Press, 1995), pp. 82–99. For a discussion of the White Woman tales, see Julie Carr, 'Unsettling settlement: re-reading the legends of the White Woman of Gippsland', unpublished PhD thesis (La Trobe University, 1998).

5. See Kay Schaffer, *In the Wake of First Contact: The Eliza Fraser Stories* (Cambridge, Cambridge University Press, 1995); Chris Healy, *From the Ruins of Colonialism: History as Social Memory* (Oakleigh, Melbourne, Cambridge University Press, 1997); also on the Fraser story, Julie Carr, 'Unsettling settlement', and Kate Darian-Smith (ed.), *Captive Lives: Australian Captivity Narratives* (Working Papers in Australian Studies 85, 86, 87) (London, Sir Robert Menzies Centre for Australian Studies, 1993).

6. It is possible that *Younâh!* was directly influenced by two 'real' Australian captivity tales. Thrower may have seen a version of the White Woman of Gippsland tale in the March 1893 edition of *Austral Light*, p. 6; and she may, like other Australian children, have encountered the Eliza Fraser story in [Charlotte Barton] A Lady Long Resident in New South Wales, *A Mother's Offering to Her Children* (Sydney Gazette Office, 1841). *Younâh!* also reveals some intertextual echoes of (or coincidences with) North American narratives, especially the Panther Captivity, a well-known eighteenth-century story in which two men find a lost woman who later becomes an heiress.

7. Annette Kolodny, *The Land Before Her: Fantasy and Experience of the American Frontiers, 1630–1860* (Chapel Hill, University of North Carolina Press, 1984).

8. This is in accordance with Annette Kolodny's desire in both *The Land Before Her* and *The Lay of the Land: Metaphor as Experience and History in American Life and Letters* (Chapel Hill, University of North Carolina Press, 1975) to read the female as representative of the land-as-female.

9. Kathryn Z. Derounian-Stodola and James A. Levernier, *The Indian Captivity Narrative, 1550–1900* (New York, Twayne, 1993), p. 32.

10. Various cultural practices of capture in Native American societies have been documented, and the numbers taken in the eighteenth and nineteenth centuries are relatively substantial. Most of the North American narratives, whether they claim or feign truth or fiction, are in the first person. The nineteenth- and very early twentieth-century Australian fictions are not. North American captivity narratives date from the seventeenth to the twentieth centuries, but what might be called the key texts of the genre – narratives like that of Mary Rowlandson, captured in America in the seventeenth century – are mostly considerably earlier than the Australian stories. Mary Rowlandson, *A True History of the Captivity and Restoration of Mrs. Rowlandson* (New York, Garland, 1977, first published 1682).

11. Derounian-Stodola and Levernier, *The Indian Captivity Narrative*, p. 40, quoting VanDerBeets.

12. Healy, *Ruins of Colonialism*, p. 165.

13. Bob Hodge and Vijay Mishra make clear the uses and dangers of such parallel readings of postcolonial societies in *Dark Side of the Dream: Australian Literature and the Postcolonial Mind* (Sydney, Allen & Unwin, 1991), preface.

14. Lyndall Ryan, *The Aboriginal Tasmanians*, 2nd edition (St Leonards, NSW, Allen & Unwin, 1996), pp. 195–204.

15. *Ibid.*, pp. 218–20.

16. *Ibid.*, pp. 29–32; 30, Map 11; 31, Map 12.

17. Sharon Morgan, *Land Settlement in Early Tasmania: Creating an Antipodean England* (Cambridge, Cambridge University Press, 1992), p. 15, is one of a number of sources that demonstrates that this was not the case.

18. Ryan, *Aboriginal Tasmanians*, p. 31. Thrower would have had many sources available to her in the 1890s. Both James Fenton's *The Jubilee History of Tasmania* (Melbourne, Wells & Leavitt, 1888), and his *Bush Life in Tasmania* (London and Aylesbury, Hazell, Watson & Viney, 1891) were available, as was H. Ling Roth's *The Aborigines of Tasmania* published in 1890. She might also have consulted James Bonwick's *The Last of the Tasmanians* (London, Low, 1870). Bonwick was also the author of *The Tasmanian Lily* (London, H. S. King, 1873).

19. Ryan, *Aboriginal Tasmanians*, pp. 67–70.

20. Pillah, the name of Younâh's female protector in the novel, was one of the names of a young girl who died in 1837 at the age of eleven. She was from the Pieman River area (Peternidic), on the north-west coast of Tasmania (Ryan, *Aboriginal Tasmanians*, Appendix 3).

21. *Ibid.*, pp. 124–73; see also pp. 170–1. Robinson's sons led additional expeditions on his orders in late 1836 and early 1837.

22. The character who might be seen to disrupt this happy closure is Natone. From being Younâh's friend and equal, by the time they reach England Natone has become Younâh's servant. But on their return to Tasmania she does not rejoin her people and their implied fate, but returns to England. Natone disappears out of the narrative at this juncture – the unnarratable subaltern perhaps. (See Gayatri Spivak, 'Three women's texts and the discourse of imperialism', *Critical Inquiry*, vol. 12 (1985): 243–61, who gives some suggestion of the surviving community of Tasmanian Aborigines, uncontained, though not unaffected, by such narratives.)

23. Ryan notes that the North Midlands people occupied the area with 'the biggest kangaroo hunting grounds in the country . . . at Campbell Town and Norfolk Plains', *Aboriginal Tasmanians*, p. 32.

24. See Tim Bonyhady, *Images in Opposition: Australian Landscape Painting 1801–1890* (Melbourne, Oxford University Press, 1985), where he argues that elegiac images of Aboriginal people in Australian art only emerge once they no longer represent a realistic threat to the non-Aboriginal colonial project.

25. The language and proofs are echoed in post-Mabo definitions of traditional evidence: 'history, moral obligation, legend and mythology, religion, an organized society, personal assertion of descent, cultural artefacts and an explanation of their significance, customs, territory, the traditions of family ownership, its acquisitions, succession and divestiture': B. A. Keon-Cohen, 'Some problems of proof: the admissibility of traditional evidence', in M. A. Stephenson and Suri Ratnapala (eds), *Mabo: A Judicial Revolution – The Aboriginal Land Rights Decision and Its Impact on Australian Law* (St Lucia, University of Queensland Press, 1993), p. 197. (I am indebted to Simon McCart for this reference.)

26. Harry Gibbs, 'Foreword', in Stephenson and Ratnapala, *Mabo: A Judicial Revolution*.

27. Interestingly, this is the sort of evidence of belonging to and knowing the land used in contemporary Aboriginal fiction, such as Mudrooroo's novel of Tasmanian Aboriginal dispossession, *Dr Wooreddy's Prescription for Enduring the Ending of the World* (Melbourne, Hyland House, 1987), pp. 191–7.

28. Dona Brown, *Inventing New England: Regional Tourism in the Nineteenth Century* (Washington, Smithsonian Institution Press, 1995), p. 12.

29. See, for example, Tom Griffiths, *Hunters and Collectors* (Melbourne, Cambridge University Press, 1996).

30. Ryan, *Aboriginal Tasmanians*, p. 184.

31. Michel Foucault, *Discipline and Punish: The Birth of the Prison* (London, Penguin, 1991), p. 220.

32. Ryan, *Aboriginal Tasmanians*, p. 220.

33. Reynolds, *Launceston*, pp. 133, 135. Note that Tasmania was originally known as Van Diemen's Land.

34. For discussions of this see Stephenson and Ratnapala, *Mabo*, and Ken Gelder and Jane Jacobs, *Uncanny Australia: Sacredness and Identity in a Postcolonial Nation* (Melbourne, Melbourne University Press, 1998).

CHAPTER FOUR

Colonizing the mind:
'Leo Africanus' in the Renaissance and today

JOHN C. HAWLEY

> Noises from afar were calling me, and it was written that I
> should not remain deaf to their temptations.
>
> Amin Maalouf, *Leo Africanus*

No place like home

In many ways, someone like Meena Alexander would seem to be one of the powerful individuals in society, one of the freest. Professor of English and Women's Studies at the Graduate Center and Hunter College, City University of New York, and Lecturer in Poetry in the Writing Program at Columbia University, she surely has assimilated well to her adopted homeland. Yet she herself suggests that the facts are otherwise. The inscription that opens her book *The Shock of Arrival: Reflections on Post-colonial Experience* sets the tone.[1] Here, quoting from Banabhatta's *Kadam-bari*, she has the king ask a suka bird, 'How were you caught in this cage?', making for some readers, no doubt, an ironic allusion to Maya Angelou's *I Know Why the Caged Bird Sings*. With a cage as golden as Professor Alexander's, some might ask, why *not* sing?

And yet, as the present volume on colonial and postcolonial incarceration makes repeatedly clear, there are types and degrees of captivity, and that of the *mind* is the most painful and the most elusive to dissect.[2] Its description, despite its resistance to easy categorization, has become an obsession for a growing number of intellectuals in the West, and for migrants from the Middle East, South Asia and elsewhere. 'Over the fault lines of my life,' writes Alexander, 'I have unfurled a resolute picture, a flag that fluttered into a sheet and grew and grew. A simple shining topography.'[3] This flag, this map, this tapestry of memories from her childhood in India, is one that she wraps around her raw ego against the winds of Western indifference. But, as in some Greek myth, the cloth has offered a deceptive comfort; it has clung to her skin and burned it. 'That shining picture [of her youth] has tormented me,' she writes.

> Faced with it, my real life has dwindled and diminished. And my words have recoiled back into a vacant space in the mind, a place of waste, dingy detritus or a life uncared for, no images to offer it hospitality. I ask myself, am I a creature with no home, no nation? And if so, what new genus could I possibly be?[4]

The 'real' life is, apparently, the world of New York, the one that somehow 'Others' her and forces a self-reflexive biologism. Her body transports her through the crowds to the subway and on to her classroom on the east side of Manhattan. Her mind and soul, however, are only partially there among the students and the lively mayhem of the city. And the existential question persists: how was I caught in *this* cage?

What Alexander describes as a shock, V. S. Naipaul earlier described as an enigma. Beyond the semantic difference, their experience at the heart of their books seems remarkably similar. Naipaul, for example, upon arrival in England is 'like a man entering the world of a novel, a book; entering *the real world*' (emphasis added).[5] Again, the reality of this new world is projected from within, viewed through a tissue of memories and, apparently, literary encounters. He notes that England is a disappointment, that he had arrived somehow too late to find the country he had created in his fantasy world. And Naipaul has the sensitivity to realize that this disorientation, prepared for by years of anticipation and, in his case, reading, did not rely on arrival in a colonizing country like England. As he notes of an older generation that had moved from India to Trinidad, for example,

> The older people in our Asian-Indian community in Trinidad – especially the poor ones, who could never manage English or get used to the strange races – looked back to an India that became more and more golden in their memory. They were living in Trinidad and were going to die there; but for them it was the wrong place. Something of that feeling was passed down to me. I didn't look back to India, couldn't do so; my ambition caused me to look ahead and outwards, to England; but it led to a similar feeling of wrongness. In Trinidad, feeling myself far away, I had held myself back, as it were, for life at the centre of things. . . . As a child in Trinidad I had put this world at a far distance, in London perhaps. In London now I was able to put this perfect world at another time, an earlier time. The mental or emotional processes were the same.[6]

Thus, it is not the attempt to retrieve the past that ties Naipaul to Alexander and those with similar 'captive' histories, but the existential displacement of identity tied to a place. The assertion of agency in no longer seeking out but creating a home, seems to characterize the migrant intellectual of the twenty-first century.

But one need not be a writer at an Ivy League institution like Columbia to suffer under this dislocation. In Sam Selvon's classic, *The Lonely Londoners* (1956), labourers from the Caribbean islands regularly drink together to shore up some sense of who they (once?) were, but meet with very limited and fleeting success. 'Under the kiff-kiff laughter,' Selvon's narrator relates,

> behind the ballad and the episode, the what-happening, the summer-is-hearts, he could see a great aimlessness, a great restless, swaying movement that leaving you standing in the same spot. As if a forlorn shadow of doom fall on all the spades in the country. As if he could see the black faces bobbing up and down in the millions of white, strained faces, everybody hustling along the Strand, the spades jostling in the crowd, bewildered, hopeless. As if, on the surface, things don't look so bad, but when you go down a little, you bounce up a kind of misery and pathos and a frightening – what? He don't know the right word, but he have the right feeling in his heart.[7]

This narrator with this 'right' feeling is the 'subaltern' without a voice – in some sense just as happy that words will not easily give shape to the sense of place-less-ness that tugs at his heart and the hearts of his casual friends. But even those who have not yet grasped their dislocation, who have, one might say, blurred their memories in favour of an uncertain assimilation with the forces of deracination, also find a place in recent fiction, as in Caryl Phillips's multiply ironic novel *A State of Independence* (1995).[8] As Phillips (born in St Kitts, raised in Britain, now spending half the year in Manhattan and half in London) himself no doubt has learned and as he relentlessly teaches his protagonist, one can never return home again.

The world of memories, the tapestry that both warms and torments Meena Alexander, simply does not exist any more except in the *minds* of those who have dropped it somewhere along the way. 'I am what others see me as,' writes Alexander, 'but I am also my longings, my desire, my speech.'[9] This strange enslavement to potential is therefore more than nostalgia; it is something with a keener edge because it threatens to dislodge the individual even from the flimsy home that has been newly constructed. Throughout the centuries, these and the other adjustments that immigration demands have been endured and sometimes chronicled by a great many people. But in recent decades, with the emergence of postcolonial awareness among the highly educated, its impact on the individual psyche has become the most pressing theme in world literature. Globalization has loosened the cultural moorings upon which identities are constructed. 'What the immigrant must work with is what she must invent in order to live'[10] – retrieval and invention, two sources of tension and of creation.

There are, of course, peculiar differences in any example of such dislocation of subjectivity, but the postcolonial 'moment' at the close of the twentieth century and opening of the twenty-first brings with it a far more focused, persistent and multi-faceted examination than at any other time in history. Offering a somewhat unlikely approach to this contemporary crisis, this chapter attempts something of an etiology of the 'disease' that seems so similar to melancholy by rehearsing the case of perhaps the most famous migrant intellectual of the fifteenth century: Leo Africanus. What he endured, how he portrayed his adventures and how they have, in turn, been portrayed by others, offer some suggestive angles of vision on the more recent adventurers who have crossed borders or found themselves adrift across cultures, attempting to negotiate a self-presentation that plays well in both the old and the newer settings.

The 'real' Othello

Born al-Hassan ibn Muhammad al-Wezaz al-Fasi in Granada in 1488, Leo Africanus, as he later came to be known, moved with his family to Fez in what is now Morocco a few years after Ferdinand and Isabella conquered southern Spain in 1492, caught up in that 'other' significant Spanish event of that year. In Fez he received an excellent education. He subsequently travelled a great deal, often in diplomatic service, and became a wealthy merchant; in these capacities he moved throughout a great part of northern Africa, visiting Cairo, Timbuktu, Mali and Bornu, as well as Istanbul. He was captured by Italian pirates in 1518 just off the coast of Tunisia, and was given as a slave to the current Pope, Leo X (Giovanni de Medici). The Pope was delighted to have such an educated contact with the Islamic world, especially the threatening Ottoman Empire; he quickly gave the slave his freedom and, in a sense, adopted him. He had him baptized – in a stunningly patriarchal move, christening the convert with his own name (Giovanni Leo Africanus) and serving as his godfather. The Pope asked him to teach Arabic and African history, which he did to several prominent clerics, including the future Cardinal Egidio Antonini. Though it is not certain, historians generally believe Leo Africanus lived in Italy approximately eight years, eventually returning to Tunisia and, reportedly, to Islam, and that he died around 1552. Before leaving, however, he gave the Pope his *Geographical Historie* of Africa. Written in 1526 from travel notes he had kept with him at the time of his capture, the book was published in Italian in 1550, in Latin in 1556, later in French, and in English in 1600 by John Pory. Shakespeare's *Othello*, written between 1602 and 1604 and first produced in 1604, reflected the great popularity of Africanus's work, which replaced Pliny's *Natural History* and the later *Book of John Mandeville* as definitive of Africa (especially Sudan) in the European mind for the next two hundred years.

Immigration, whether forced or chosen, sets in motion (and in most cases is the result of) influences that move in two directions. Al-Hassan ibn Muhammad, in the guise of Leo Africanus, mysterious 'son' of the Pope and purveyor of the exoticism of the Orient, surely shaped Europe as significantly as it, by literally enslaving him, shaped the chameleon traveller he had long since become. In turn, his writings took on a life of their own and ramified in other cultural artefacts. The possible influence of the *Geographical Historie* on the composition of *Othello* and on the shaping of Shakespeare's flawed protagonist has been commented upon at great length.[11] Carole Levin argues that the play was built not only upon Leo's book but upon several sources, including the story as recounted by Giambattista Cinzio Giraldi (1504–73); she further argues that blacks had appeared on the Elizabethan stage (principally as villains) before *Othello*.[12] But, however it happened, Levin points out that 'Shakespeare's Othello is a far more textured and complex character than any previous depiction of an African on the English stage,' and that 'some of the nobility of Othello echoes the story of Leo Africanus's life as it appeared in his *Historie*, and was newly and readily available to Shakespeare'.[13] Both Leo and Othello were enslaved and set free; both had to demonstrate their trustworthiness before they could be listened to by European society. And, of more immediate significance for this chapter, both felt themselves alienated and both had to deal with this fact in their subsequent self-representation.

Leo had to prove his trustworthiness as a truthful raconteur and, as we shall see, as a worthy historian as well. But beyond the self-justification, perhaps as part of it, is the educated voice of outrage. Rosalind R. Johnson is among those who recognize a parallel between *Othello* and the *Geographical Historie* in their common 'critique of the Christian European as a devious, hypocritical demoralizer of the innocent, trusting African'.[14] In fact, Johnson considers this to be the most important parallel between the two characters, sees 'an intense struggle between the European-Christian and the African infidel throughout both works',[15] and discusses their criticisms of Christian society in convincing detail (principally focusing on Leo in her 1985 article, and on Othello in its 1986 sequel).[16] Furthermore, since Leo is clearly attempting to offer a less fanciful (and thereby more balanced) version of his homeland than those accounts familiar to Europeans, he had a difficult balancing act indeed. Pliny's ancient, fanciful and scary version, for example, would be published in 1556, offering up monsters and cannibals and confirming the European's worst suspicions – and all this from a venerable source. A Moor of Venice, let alone this unlikely godson of the Italian Pope, might find such a compelling narrative as Pliny's to be fearsome competition in the market for the minds and hearts of those who clearly felt a fascination with Africa and points beyond the pale, but who might not easily accept Leo Africanus's race as a likely source for veracity. Making matters worse, Levin reports that 'a common sixteenth century proverb stated that three Moors were equal to one Portuguese, and three Portuguese equal to one Englishman'.[17] The consequences of such xenophobia were various: Elizabeth, for example, decreed in 1601 that all 'Blackamoors' who had 'crept' into the realm (there were not that many) had to leave her kingdom.[18] In addressing

Italians in the early edition of the book, Leo faced prejudices similar to those that would later greet other such 'Blackamoors'. Furthermore, Leo as narrator would be encumbered not only by his race but also by his religion. His conversion, though its authenticity could be vouched for by none other than the Vicar of Christ on Earth himself, might nonetheless meet with a certain cynicism among many, as did the conversions of many Jews under Ferdinand and Isabella.

It is this implied high-wire act in creating a public self that draws the attention of several observers with a postcolonial interest. Ania Loomba (1989) and Peter Stallybrass (1986) discuss the importance of race in the construction of Othello's Otherness, and Jonathan Burton (1998) convincingly advances this argument by adding the important element of religious difference (see also Stephen Greenblatt).[19] Burton imbricates the historical placement of Leo Africanus in the presentation of Africa to a European audience, and then underscores the parallel in *Othello*. Burton notes, regarding Shakespeare's positioning of the protagonist, that

> even before he appears on stage, Othello's irrevocably non-Christian origins are foregrounded in the terms of Christianity's narrative of Islamic error. Yet, when Othello first appears before the audience, his impeccable behavior reveals him to be, in some ways, more like the idealized New World savage (tractable but noble) who gratefully embraces Christianity. Indeed, he has become a Christian and defends his adopted world 'against the general enemy Ottoman'. (I.iii.49)[20]

And this is much the same way that Leo's various editors present him to their European readers as, for example, John Pory to the English. Introducing Leo, Pory remarks of him that

> albeit by birth a More, and by religion for many yeeres a Mahumetan: yet if you consider his Parentage, Witte, Education, Learning, Emploiments, Trauels, and his conuersion to Christianitie; you shall finde him not altogether vnfit to vndertake such an enterprize; nor unwoorthy to be regarded.[21]

And not only Leo's editors but Leo himself seem intent on anticipating the suspicions of his readers that a supposed convert from Islam would not be capable of disguising sympathies for his former compatriots. While it is true that he points out the injustices and hypocrisies he has observed among his 'fellow' Christians, Leo seems, in fact, to bend over backwards in confirming many of the impressions expressed by Europeans regarding the brutality of Africans. Why is that? Has the writer simply accepted his cage, and learned to trim his sails?

This is near to the conclusion of commentators like Emily Bartels (1990), Kim Hall and Jack D'Amico.[22] They emphasize that Leo makes great efforts to make his text acceptable to Europeans, thereby deconstructing his purported desire to restore a correct reading of his African heritage. The result, in their minds, is a Leo who is something of a toady, assimilated in the most neocolonial manner. Even a more subtle commentary like Jonathan Burton's suggests that Leo, like Othello, may be 'prone to a brand of self-doubt founded in what [Frantz] Fanon terms "affiliation neuroses"' [sic].[23] In the case of Othello, these self-doubts and unsure footing in the new society result in his 'purple speech, his position at the vanguard of Christendom's forces against the Turks (and verbal positioning as part of the Christian "we" in his question, "Are we turn'd Turks?") and his marriage to Desdemona'.[24] In the case of Leo, the need to confirm a place in Roman (Catholic) society expresses itself in a portrayal of the worst faults of many of the Africans he describes, alongside a vigorous defence of the glories of Timbuktu civilization, etc. He will even offer apparently contradictory accounts of the same people, praising them as sincerely religious and then condemning them as covetous and deceitful. He makes no attempt to reconcile the conflict; the discrepancy is easily noticed by anyone reading the text. Even without the self-doubts, Burton reasonably stresses that 'an alien author like Africanus would have found himself in a position requiring a degree of ideological conformity toward his audience'.[25] If this is true for most authors, it is doubly so for those who are immigrants. In any event, the result is an odd mix, perhaps a determined attempt on Leo's part to appear objective, above the fray, malleable in the face of new facts and, therefore, as a trustworthy historian without the vested interests that one would surely understand and possibly forgive. As Burton concludes, 'what distinguishes Africanus from Othello is his ability successfully to employ hybridity as a strategy to maintain the resulting compound'.[26]

Self-revelation vs wily evasion

This strategic use of 'hybridity' nicely describes the condition of those who are the subjects of this chapter. A Meena Alexander, a V. S. Naipaul, are in many ways reaping the benefits of maintaining a certain chameleon-like presentation of self. But it comes at the price of exposing the discomfort at the heart of their sense of self. The apparent need to express this crisis for all the world (all the English-speaking metropolitan world) to read results from the type of captivity of the mind that colonial education has produced. The number of writers from former British and French colonies who have centred on this theme is truly overwhelming but Naipaul is, again, emblematic of the problem. 'It wasn't only that I was unformed at the age of eighteen or had no idea what I was going to write about,' he records,

> It was that the idea given me by my education – and by the more 'cultural,' the nicest, part of the education – was that the writer was a person possessed of sensibility; that the writer was someone who recorded or displayed an inward development. So, in an unlikely way, the ideas of the aesthetic movement of

the end of the nineteenth century and the ideas of Bloomsbury, ideas bred essentially out of empire, wealth and imperial security, had been transmitted to me in Trinidad. To be that kind of writer (as I interpreted it) I had to be false; I had to pretend to be other than I was, other than what a man of my background could be. Concealing this colonial-Hindu self below the writing personality, I did both my material and myself much damage.[27]

Such concealment of self, destructive though it may in some senses be, characterizes the trickster narratives of Native American and African American tale-tellers, and surely goes a long way to suggesting the rationale behind the 'conflicts' in Leo Africanus's testimony. (See, also, the 'mimicry' classically described by Homi Bhabha.)[28] Concealing his Muslim self below the writing personality allowed him to fit the shape of a European writer; furthermore, as a (freed) slave to the most powerful ruler in Rome he had every reason for care in self-expression, perhaps in gratitude as well and even, on some level, in admiration for the conquering culture – though that status was coming under increasing attack from the encroaching Ottoman empire.

As Burton nicely underscores, Leo Africanus makes no bones about his decision to adjust to whatever situation he falls into. He had, after all, faced many similar threats before finally ending as a slave in Rome. Thus, in his description of Africa he offers a tale about the origin of amphibians that could easily have been written by Pliny or by Aesop. In his account, the animal is really a bird, but can live with the fishes just as easily. When the king of birds demands tribute, the bird 'determined forthwith to change her element, and to delude the king'. She moves in with the fish. But when the king of fishes eventually decides to demand tribute, 'Amphibia' returns to the air. And the process continues ad infinitum. Then a straightfaced Leo draws the moral of his tale:

all men do most affect that place, where they find least damage and inconvenience. For mine own part, when I hear the Africans evil spoken of, I will affirm my self to be one of Granada: and when I perceive the nation of Granada to be discommended, then I will profess my self to be an African.[29]

With no apparent sense that he has just confessed to duplicity, this proto-postcolonial writer offers a pragmatic example of what others might call hybridity, the ability (or curse) of multiculturalism, often imposed upon its recipients in what must appear to be an enslavement.

Colonization of the public persona

But self-creation must, in time, be rounded by a sleep. Leo Africanus does not have the last word in declaring his identity and, as even with someone like Shakespeare, we invent him anew for our own purposes. In the case of Leo, perhaps the most bizarre reincarnation, almost literally, is the use to which he was put by W. B. Yeats. In what must be considered one of the most highly strung cases of orientalization, Yeats projects a version of Leo Africanus as his own muse. Thus, he records that Leo appears to him and explains that

> he was no secondary personality, with a symbolic biography as I thought possible but the person he claimed to be. He was drawn to me because in life he had been all undoubting impulse, all that his name and Africa might suggest symbolically for his biography was both symbolical and actual. I was doubting, conscientious and timid. His contrary and by association with me would be made not one but two perfected natures. He asked me to write him a letter addressed to him as if to Africa giving all my doubts about spiritual things and then to write a reply as from him to me. He would control me in that reply so that it would be really from him.[30]

Coming as it does from arguably the greatest lyric poet of the twentieth century, this passage and its aftermath, a truly fascinating reminder of how bizarre Yeats really was, also demonstrate the mutual captivity – of Yeats by what he has imagined Leo Africanus to be (his own hidden animus, perhaps, 'all undoubting impulse'), of Leo by a latter-day colonial (Leo *should* be more 'doubting, conscientious and timid'). This unlikely marriage would, in Yeats's mind, result in 'two perfected natures'. But something goes haywire a bit later and Leo becomes a 'frustrator', a spirit who cannot be trusted, and finally, after seven years of involvement, possibly not the genuine Leo Africanus after all but only someone who knew him in real life (another take on 'real' life). As quirky as this incident obviously is, Yeats's imagined relationship with a vaguely imagined figure, who apparently represented the creative energies that the poet hoped to use, offers a stark example of several relevant ideas: the power of projection in self-creation; the invention of Others by the society that captures or captivates them; the ongoing refiguring of 'fixed' subjects who have been possessed by a culture.

The most recent manifestation of this partially remembered Renaissance figure is *Leo Africanus* (1986), by the Lebanese novelist Amin Maalouf. Maalouf, a resident of Paris, does a generally believable job of imagining and reconstructing al-Hassan ibn Muhammad's life, presenting the story in the first person.[31] What will immediately strike Western readers, intent on getting to the events in Rome, is the great percentage of the novel (75 per cent) devoted to the Islamic life prior to the enslavement. This is clearly a function not only of the expectations of the audience but of the agenda that the Christian Arab writer has set for himself, which would seem to be at least partially revisionary of the orientalized Renaissance view. Maalouf intends to contextualize the convert and provide a solid sense of the many captivities that shaped Leo before his final capture by pirates and the various exiles imposed upon him. The role of Ferdinand and Isabella and the duplicity of the Christians in extending their control throughout southern Spain and beyond, the corruption of Islamic princes who converted to Christianity to retain their lands, the emergence of pre-Islamic practices among wayward believers, the defensive embrace of fundamentalism: 'And then came the drying up of the spirit and of the pen. To defend themselves against the ideas and customs of the Franks, men turned Tradition into a citadel in which they shut themselves up'[32] – the list of examples could extend throughout much of the book. Moreover, they all seem to serve a purpose much like that of Leo Africanus's double critique of European and African societies: they authenticate Maalouf, though he is not a Muslim, as a fair-minded spokesman, for concerns common throughout the Arab world but also as a Janus-faced advocate who recognizes a good Christian when he describes one. Though living in Paris, he wishes to remain Lebanese. He tells the story of Boabdil who departs into exile expressing

> 'the Moor's last sigh', because, it was said, the fallen sultan had shed tears there, of shame and remorse. 'You weep like a woman for the kingdom which you did not defend like a man,' his mother Fatima would have said.[33]

And what sort of tears might a Lebanese, living in comfort in self-imposed exile in Paris, shed for his troubled land? More to the point, what sort of tears might a Lebanese, even in Beirut, shed for his imagined version of a country, fratricidal to this day, 'imprisoned' by Syria?

'A lost homeland,' writes Maalouf as *his* Leo goes into exile in Fez, 'is like the corpse of a near relative; bury it with respect and believe in eternal life.'[34] Some would interpret that eternal life much as V. S. Naipaul seems to do: as the unfolding of the next day, the future of one's life rather than a sentimentalized version of one's past or of one's country. Later, he struggles lest he give in to 'the shameful nostalgia of the exiled'.[35] Thus, when Maalouf's protagonist is later exiled from Fez by the Islamic prince, he writes that 'my departure from Fez was flamboyant. I decided to go into exile with my head high, dressed in brocade, not at night but right in the middle of the day.'[36] Still later, fleeing from Egypt, this Leo writes: 'I had no other ambition than to survive, with my family, no other ambition than to go away, in order one day to relate on a piece of glazed paper the fall of Cairo, of her empire, of her last hero.'[37] When he later arrives at the palace of the Pope, the desire to write finally bears fruit; the desire simply to survive becomes more complex. Faced with threats from the kings of France and of Spain, besieged increasingly by the forces of the Protestant Reformation, the Pope is seen by Leo as a worthy leader. He tells a young and enthusiastic Lutheran that 'whatever my feelings might be, I cannot betray my protector', and later writes that 'it was impossible for me to follow my own rational inclinations on this subject'.[38]

If this might be described, as some of the critics to whom we have referred have described the historical Leo Africanus, as capitulation to one's captor, as a symptom of a colonized mind, Maalouf does his best to get inside Leo's head and suggest how loyalties more personal than national or ethnic might intervene. Here is how the novelist describes the day of Leo's baptism:

> The Pope was triumphant beneath his tiara: 'On this day of Epiphany, when we celebrate the baptism of Christ at the hands of John the Baptist, and when we also celebrate, according to Tradition, the arrival of the three Magi from Arabia to adore Our Lord, what greater happiness could there be for us than to welcome, into the bosom of Our Holy Church, a new Magian King, come from the furthest corners of Barbary to make his offering in the House of Peter!' . . . None of the people assembled in this place was unaware that this 'Magian King' had been captured on a summer night by a pirate on a beach in Jerba, and brought to Rome as a slave. Everything which was said about me and everything which was happening to me was so insane, so immoderate, so grotesque! Wasn't I the victim of some bad dream, some mirage? Wasn't I really in a mosque in Fez, Cairo, or Timbuktu, as on every Friday, my mind affected by a long sleepless night? Suddenly, in the heart of my doubts, the voice of the Pope rose again, addressing me: 'And you, Our well-beloved son John-Leo, whom Providence has singled out among all men.' . . . By God, I have loved him since that moment. . . . I had no feelings of resentment or bitterness about my captivity any more. A few weeks of heavy chains, a few months of soft servitude, and lo and behold I had become a traveller again, a migrant creature.[39]

Some could read this as a typical conversion experience, a Patty Hearst-style identification with one's captors. Some would see it as an emotional attempt to disguise from oneself the powerlessness of one's situation. Some would be reminded of Meena Alexander's (and Maya Angelou's) image of a gilded cage, especially when Maalouf's Leo finds 'refuge in the calm of [his] former prison' just a few paragraphs further in the narrative. This Lebanese Leo writes:

> I no longer knew what to think. Good and Bad, truth and untruth, beauty and rottenness were so muddled up in my mind! But perhaps that was it, the Rome of Leo X, the Rome of Leo the African. . . . Had the time passed when I could be genuinely proud of my own without needing to brag about them?[40]

The inadequacy of cells

If the Renaissance had its reasons for fascination with Leo Africanus, shaping him into the Moor of Venice, and if W. B. Yeats could later exoticize him and listen to his own creative urges through this unlikely projection, it is perhaps clear that a twentieth-century writer like Maalouf has his reasons for choosing him as the subject for his first important novel. In recent interviews (with François Bénichou and Gunther Verheyen) he has expressed his own sense of exile, of a sort of imprisonment in full view in the world, and of his own complex and ambiguous relationship with Lebanon.[41] For him, it elicits a curious sentiment, like visiting a sick relative in the hospital.[42] Its troubled history has convinced him that the most important influences in one's life are beyond one's control – a sentiment earlier expressed by his Leo ('Of all this I had chosen nothing; life had chosen for me, as well as my temperament').[43] He has also concluded that national divisions arise from the sort of intolerance that he has vowed to work against: thus, in *Leo Africanus* his protagonist concludes that 'faith quickly becomes cruel if it is not subdued by certain doubts'.[44] He describes himself as a minority, very consciously so, and very alert, therefore, to the minor voices of society. These, he notes, will determine the shape of democracy in the future and must be given a place at the table. When asked if he would have written his books if he had stayed in his own country, he becomes somewhat fatalistic. The war would have denied him that possibility. In writing, he has found what he calls a safe haven. So much so, that little by little he has thrown off everything else and chosen the life of a hermit (almost as if he has voluntarily chosen a simple cell), and, as he puts it, 'ma patrie, c'est l'écriture' (writing has become his country).[45]

In his other interview (with Verheyen) he makes clear what aspects of a character like Leo Africanus appeal to his imagination, and they principally centre on what some have criticized as Leo's wily adaptability. It is as if Leo, if not a carbon copy of the person Maalouf imagines himself to be, at least symbolizes much the same thing that a country like Lebanon has the potential to symbolize for its citizens: 'des communautés nombreuses et différentes' (diverse and numerous communities).[46] How such communities will be able to live together is, in his view, the most important question for the future of the world. Rather than a future that exacerbates narrow affiliations, exclusivity and hatreds, a country like Lebanon can serve as a workshop for cooperation and toleration of potentially conflicting hermeneutical frameworks. The alternative is seen in the rearguard action of fundamentalists of all stripes, who threaten to set the planet afire and devour several generations with bloody conflict. At the heart of his work, Maalouf says, is his ongoing preoccupation with the peaceful exchange between different cultures.[47] This is seen most clearly, he notes, on the first page of *Leo Africanus*. 'I come from no country,' begins the narrator,

> from no city, no tribe. I am the son of the road, my country is the caravan, my life the most unexpected of voyages. . . . From my mouth you will hear Arabic, Turkish, Castilian, Berber, Hebrew, Latin and vulgar Italian, because all tongues and all prayers belong to me. But I belong to none of them.[48]

And such a beginning marks an appropriate place to conclude our consideration of this protean and fascinating figure from the Renaissance. His meaning cannot be held captive by any age.

Regarding the fundamentalists of today, seeking to maintain purity, consistency and some certainty in the face of what appears to be *excessive* freedom, Maalouf declares that despite all their affirmations, today's Muslims do not resemble the Muslims of yesterday; despite their denials, they have been and continue to be influenced in their thinking and in their daily lives by all sorts of ideas, inventions and modes of production in the Christian world and elsewhere.[49] The lesson of a Leo Africanus may be the inescapability of freedom in a world where migrancy has become perhaps *the* major source for creative writing. Meena Alexander, perhaps with thoughts of someone like Leo Africanus in her head, muses that

> if I were a man, I might have turned myself into something large and heroic, a creature of quest and adventure, a visionary with power in his grasp. Instead, as a woman, the best I can be is something small and stubborn, delicate perhaps at the best of times, but irrefutably persistent. After all, when has my life gone according to plan? It seems a poor thing to say, but the best I have learnt has to do with unlearning the fixed positionings I was taught, trusting my own nose, diving into the waves, tale telling.[50]

That sounds like freedom, to me.

Notes

1. Meena Alexander, *The Shock of Arrival: Reflections on Postcolonial Experience* (Boston, South End Press, 1996).

2. See, for example, Ngūgī wa Thiong'o, *Decolonising the Mind: The Politics of Language in African Literature* (London, James Currey, 1986).

3. Alexander, *Shock of Arrival*, p. 116.

4. *Ibid.*

5. V. S. Naipaul, *The Enigma of Arrival* (London, Penguin, 1987), p. 119.

6. *Ibid.*, pp. 120–1.

7. Sam Selvon, *The Lonely Londoners* (New York, Longman, 1997), p. 142.

8. Caryl Phillips, *A State of Independence* (New York, Vintage, 1995).

9. Alexander, *Shock of Arrival*, p. 1.

10. *Ibid.*

11. See, for example, Lois Whitney, 'Did Shakespeare know Leo Africanus?', *PMLA*, vol. 37 (1922), and Eldred Jones, *The Elizabethans and Africa* (Charlottesville, University of Virginia Press for the Folger Shakespeare Library, 1968).

12. Carole Levin, 'Backgrounds and echoes of *Othello*: from Leo Africanus to Ignatius Sancho', *Lamar Journal of the Humanities*, vol. 22, no. 2 (1996): 45–68.

13. *Ibid.*, p. 51.

14. Rosalind R. Johnson, 'African presence in Shakespearean drama: parallels between *Othello* and the historical Leo Africanus', *Journal of African Civilizations*, vol. 7, no. 2 (1985): 277.

15. *Ibid.*

16. *Ibid.*, pp. 276–87; Rosalind R. Johnson, 'Parallels between Othello and the historical Leo Africanus', *Bim*, vol. 18, no. 70 (1986): 9–34.

17. Levin, 'Backgrounds and echoes of *Othello*', p. 54.

18. *Ibid.*, p. 59.

19. Ania Loomba, *Gender, Race, Renaissance Drama* (New York, St. Martin's Press, 1989); Peter Stallybrass, 'Patriarchal territories: the body enclosed', in M. W. Ferguson, M. Quilligan and N. Vickers (eds), *Rewriting the Renaissance: The Discourse of Sexual Difference in Early Modern Europe* (Chicago, University of Chicago Press, 1986); Jonathan Burton,

'"A most wily bird": Leo Africanus, Othello and the trafficking in difference', in Ania Loomba and Martin Orkin, *Post-colonial Shakespeare*, pp. 43–63. See also Stephen Greenblatt, *Marvelous Possessions: The Wonder of the New World* (Chicago, University of Chicago Press, 1991), pp. 25–61.

20. Burton, '"A most wily bird"', p. 56.

21. Luther Jones (ed.), *A Geographical Histories of Africa Written in Arabic and Italian by John Leo, a Moor Born in Granada Brought up in Barbarie*, trans. and collected by John Pory (Pittsburgh, Jones's Research and Publishing Company, 1994), p. 2.

22. Emily Bartels, 'Making more of the Moor: Aaron, Othello, and Renaissance refashionings of race', *Shakespeare Quarterly*, vol. 41, no. 4 (1990): 433–54; Kim F. Hall, *Things of Darkness: Economies of Race and Gender in Early Modern England* (New York, Cornell University Press, 1995); Jack D'Amico, *The Moor in English Renaissance Drama* (Tampa, University of South Florida Press, 1991).

23. Burton, '"A most wily bird"', p. 57.

24. *Ibid.*

25. *Ibid.*, p. 49.

26. *Ibid.*, p. 46.

27. Naipaul, *Enigma of Arrival*, p. 134.

28. Homi Bhabha, *The Location of Culture* (London, Routledge, 1994), p. 86.

29. Cited in Burton, '"A most wily bird"', pp. 52–3.

30. Steve L. Adams and George Mills Harper (eds), 'The manuscript of "Leo Africanus"', *Yeats Annual*, vol. 1 (1982), p. 13.

31. Amin Maalouf, *Leo Africanus*, trans. Peter Sluglett (Lanham, MD, New Amsterdam Books, 1992).

32. *Ibid.*, p. 38.

33. *Ibid.*, p. 57.

34. *Ibid.*, p. 71.

35. *Ibid.*, p. 281.

36. *Ibid.*, p. 209.

37. *Ibid.*, p. 273.

38. *Ibid.*, pp. 295, 296.

39. *Ibid.*, pp. 296–8.

40. *Ibid.*, pp. 301, 317.

41. François Bénichou, 'Amin Maalouf: "Ma patrie, c'est l'écriture"', *Magazine littéraire*, vol. 359 (1997): 114–15; Gunther Verheyen, '"Faire vivre les gens ensemble". Un entretien avec Amin Maalouf', *Französisch heute*, vol. 1 (1996): 36–8.

42. Bénichou, 'Amin Maalouf', pp. 114–15.

43. Maalouf, *Leo Africanus*, p. 246.

44. *Ibid.*, p. 308.

45. Bénichou, 'Amin Maalouf', p. 115.

46. Verheyen, 'Un entretien avec Amin Maalouf', p. 37.

47. *Ibid.*, p. 38.

48. Maalouf, *Leo Africanus*, p. 1.

49. Verheyen, 'Un entretien avec Amin Maalouf', p. 38.

50. Alexander, *Shock of Arrival*, p. 117.

CHAPTER FIVE

Trading places: slave traders as slaves

KERRY SINANAN

A genteel employment

In 1746 John Newton, a dissatisfied naval recruit, was exchanged into the service of a resident slave dealer, a Mr Clow, on the Guinea Coast. In the words of his contemporary biographer Richard Cecil, Clow's 'example impressed Mr Newton with hopes of the same success and he obtained his discharge upon condition of entry into the trader's service to whose generosity he trusted without the precondition of terms.'[1]

Newton's experience over the next two years was to show him that he could not rely on anyone's generosity in the privatizing world of the slave trade and that he, like so many others, could be reduced to the status of chattel, to be exchanged at the behest of his owners. His illusion of free choice undertaken in his self-commodification was shattered when Clow left Newton at the service of Clow's black mistress, who put him to work on their lime tree plantation with the other slaves. Newton continued in this condition for over a year until he was able to negotiate his way out of this undesirable situation. By 1750 Newton would return to the island of the Benanoes to trade with Clow for slaves to fill the ship he was captaining.

In 1788 James Irving, captaining his first slave-trading voyage, was shipwrecked on the coast of Morocco. The crew was captured by a nomadic Arab tribe and sold several times until, in April 1790, the Emperor Mawlay al-Yazid, into whose custody they came, reached terms with the British Government under which he would release the incarcerated Englishmen.

While in captivity, the men laboured for their various masters and were almost sold off as slaves to work for private traders. The complex negotiations between Morocco and Britain were bound up with issues of trade and tariffs in the wider economic sphere. In June 1791 Irving, having returned to England, succeeded in reaching the west coast of Africa to fill his ship, bound for Trinidad, with slaves. As Suzanne Schwarz, who has edited Irving's letters and journal writes:

> The use of the term 'slavery' to describe Irving's condition in Morocco as well as the economic and social status of the 3,000 or so Africans that he helped to

transport to the colonies of the West Indies and America is misleading if it implies homogeneity of experience.[2]

While Schwarz goes on to highlight the crucial differences between Irving's slave condition and that of those whom he enslaved, her point that the term 'slavery' may be used to incorporate a range of experiences is crucial. Not all black slaves who crossed the mid-Atlantic passage had the same experiences; indeed, in his autobiography, Olaudah Equiano details how he became a slave owner after buying his own freedom from white masters.[3]

Newton and Irving left behind many representations of their enslavement, and the different moments when they wrote mark their different positions within the slave trade. Newton's versions are all retrospective: in 1764 he published his spiritual autobiography, *An Authentic Narrative*, as an example of how he had been called and saved by God through his turbulent career.[4] He was later to rise to prominence in the Anglican Church and became a founder of the evangelical movement in the late 1780s. His vision of divine intervention in his life was perfectly expressed in the words to the hymn, 'Amazing Grace' which he penned after surviving a sea storm on his return from Africa to England. Also, in various letters to his wife written throughout his career he describes his period of enslavement and, finally, he alludes to it in his abolitionist tract, 'Thoughts upon the African slave trade' (1788). Newton's captain's journals also survive in their entirety. Many letters written by Irving during the time of his enslavement also survive and these are corroborated by letters from James Matra and John Hutchison, respectively Consul General and Vice-Consul to Morocco, and who played vital roles in securing the release of Irving and his crew. A year after his release, Irving compiled a journal of his experience written, he states, for his brother-in-law, George Dalston Tunstall. Many of the details in this journal are supported by other evidence, yet the journal is also interesting for the ways in which it rewrites Irving's enslavement.[5]

Most of the accounts left by Newton and Irving, then, are retrospective and attempt to rationalize this perceived rupture in a natural order. The actual capture of these men exposes the purely discursive status of their identities as civilized, white, Christian natural masters and colonizers. Despite their redefinitions and rewritings of their enslavement, both men's texts highlight the fact that their capture and release were the result of economic forces, as was their participation in the slave trade itself.

The slave trade at this time can easily be seen as the institutional paradigm of colonial power. Commentators from Adam Smith to contemporary historians, such as Eric Williams, have discussed the slave trade as the epitome of an eighteenth-century mercantilist trading practice which flourished under a European colonial agenda. The creation in England of the Royal African Company in 1672 was the establishment of a monopoly, which was strenuously opposed by private colonialists until abolition in

1808 when the interests of the colonial planters became synonymous with those of the state.[6] The enslavement of these slave traders enacts an upheaval of colonial power. Moreover, the slave traders' representations of their enslavement show that the trade's mercantilist thrust was destabilized by the process of exchange inevitably acting as a two-way transaction, in which the privatizing, unrestricted nature of trade gave rise to a fluidity not accounted for by monopolistic trade structures. In the slave traders' representations, the perspective of the representing subject is presented as a monopolistic one; the inevitable cultural exchange, which makes their representations possible, is masked behind the ironic ideal of an objective representing perspective – that of the colonial subject.

In *The Order of Things* (1970), Michel Foucault explicitly links the structure of exchange to that of mercantilism in what he terms the Classical episteme: 'Throughout the mercantilist experience, the domain of wealth was constituted in the same mode as that of representations.'[7] Both exchange in mercantilism and the representations of colonial discourse at this time regard themselves as one-way processes in which the perspective of the exchanging/representing individual is prioritized. In the slave traders' representations of their own enslavement, the representation/production of Self and Other becomes problematized by the economic force of reality, which undercuts the slavers' attempts to contain practice within the terms of dualistic principles such as civility and religion. The economy of the slave traders' language is disturbed as their discursive limits actually produce identities not accounted for by the logic of colonialism: their own identities as slaves most powerfully exemplify this production. The productivity of the mercantilist slave trade was an inevitable result of a system which protected the individual trader. Robin Blackburn has shown that, in the eighteenth century, the mercantilist system, especially in the slave trade, actually worked to foster *private* interests. He asserts that 'primitive accumulation'

> [W]as orchestrated by an inverted mercantilism – that is to say, not by financiers and merchants serving *raison d'état* but by the state serving capitalist purposes. The whole point was that the state created a free zone of imperial 'free trade' for its merchants and manufacturers, offered them protection, and gained favourable terms for their entry to other markets.[8]

Newton's and Irving's writings show that, in the slave trade, it was private economic interest on both sides of the exchanging couple, and not the dictates of state policy, that determined the trade's organization at a grass-roots level. This destabilization of monopoly is perfectly expressed by the fact that both men actually trade places with those they would enslave and come to embody a value as a commodity themselves.

As Sara Suleri has noted: 'In historical terms, colonialism precludes the concept of "exchange" by granting the idea of power a greater literalism than it deserves'.[9] Newton's and Irving's quick transformation into slaves not only undermines their power as colonizers but it also articulates the intersection of economics with the category of the Self, so pertinent to the formulation of identity in the eighteenth century. Their writings show that the logic of colonialism, mercantilism and representation, with their attendant hierarchies, are under constant pressure from the realities of an exchanging practice.

A slave to sin

> During the time I was engaged in the slave trade, I never had the least scruple as to its lawfulness. I was upon the whole satisfied with it as the appointment Providence had worked out for me; yet it was, in many respects, far from eligible. It is, indeed, accounted a genteel employment and is usually very profitable, though to me it did not prove so, the Lord seeing that a large increase of wealth would not be good for me. However, I considered myself a sort of a gaoler or turnkey and I was sometimes shocked with an employment that was perpetually conversant with chains, bolts and shackles. In this view I had often petitioned in my prayers that the Lord (in his own time) would be pleased to fix me in a more humane calling, and (if it might be) place me where I might have more frequent converse with his people and ordinances and be freed from those long separations from home which were very often hard to bear. My prayers were now answered.[10]

It was a sudden illness that prevented Newton from undertaking a fourth voyage as captain of a slave ship in 1754, at the age of twenty-nine. The above passage shows that, by 1764, Newton had begun to question the eligibility of his profession as a slave captain. His language reveals much, not only about his own ambiguity with regard to the slave trade; it also expresses the interconnection of many issues, economics, morality and religion which, for him at least, are all inseparable from the trade itself.

Newton's career at sea, begun at the age of ten, had been turbulent. In a letter to his wife written on his first journey as a slave trader and dated 22 March 1751, Newton describes himself as having been as 'changeable as the Weather'[11] in his early seafaring years. In 1743, after visiting his future wife, Mary Catlett, whilst on leave from his duty in the Mediterranean trade, Newton was impressed by the Navy on the Kentish coast. Although his father used his influence to promote him to midshipman, this did not prevent Newton from attempting desertion after returning to England in 1744. This rebelliousness resulted in severe punishment, flogging and demotion. Newton was, once more, on the lowest rung of the ship's hierarchy and a virtual slave to the Navy. In his *Narrative*, he describes how, at this time, he was heavily influenced by Deism and became 'one of the loudest in the Free-thinking strain'.[12] He describes this phase of religious dissent as one of the factors behind his own personal fall, and so a precursor to his time on the African coast. As David Hindmarsh writes in his biography of Newton:

Recurring Dialectical imagery in Newton's narrative reiterated the central theme or pattern of conversion [and] . . . he often wrote of his experience in terms of bondage and freedom. In his moral decline he was 'fast bound in chains', and only illness could 'break the fatal chain'; he was 'delivered' from the dominion of sin and gradually set at 'liberty' from complaisance in worldly diversions.[13]

Newton's enslavement is drawn as part of his spiritual distance from God and actually becomes a metaphor for his unsaved condition. However, when Newton describes how he came to be in a slave trader's possession, he makes it clear that it was a personal choice which allowed him to escape from the enforced subjection of the Navy.[14] Despite the fact that Newton's decision to remain on the west coast was motivated by pragmatism, he describes his actual arrival on the coast in very different terms: 'The day before the vessel sailed I landed upon the island of the Benanoes, with little more than the clothes upon my back as if I had been shipwrecked.'[15] Newton translates his self-commodification into a familiar scene of nautical adventure, in which the European hero becomes subjected to the vicissitudes of fortune until a Crusoe-like personal reformation takes place. This narrative also fits in with the religious purpose of the autobiography, which was to demonstrate God's direction of Newton's predetermined path.

Once on the windward coast and in Clow's service, Newton finds himself an outcast and at the very bottom of the social hierarchy. Again, this degradation is placed within the context of his becoming removed from God, laying the way for future self-realization. He writes:

> The few I had to converse with were too much like myself and I was soon brought into such abject circumstances that I was too low to have any influence. I was rather shunned and despised than intimidated; there being few, even of the negroes themselves, during the first year of my residence amongst them, but thought themselves too good to speak to me.[16]

Not for the last time does Newton find the conventional colonial order reversed. Newton himself attributes his enslavement to a woman he refers to as P. I., Clow's black mistress.[17] Newton states that it was due to this woman's influence that his position shifted from being an employee to being a slave. When Clow went on a slave-buying trip, Newton took ill and found himself mistreated by P. I.:

> [H]e left me in her hands. At first I was taken some care of; but as I did not recover very soon, she grew weary and entirely neglected me . . . She lived in plenty herself but hardly allowed me to sustain life . . . she lived much in the *European manner* . . . I had sometimes been relieved by strangers; nay even by the slaves in chains who secretly brought me victuals.[18]

P. I.'s authority as a slave owner and mistress of a White trader is accompanied by her assuming the figure of the European 'domestic subject' who, as Newton tells us, uses imported furniture, eats European food and dresses in European style. Her adoption of a 'white' lifestyle, defined by a collection of appropriate objects, dislocates European civility from its link to colour and resituates it in the realm of commodities. P. I.'s self-styling, defined by a plethora of appropriate objects, is commensurate with the plethora of discursive definitions Newton needs to represent himself as the 'natural' civilized subject. In this instance, the realms of representation and trade serve the same function in defining identity – P. I. can approximate to the European manner because of the objects gleaned from trade and has her position because of the slave trade. Newton, at this point, must rely on discursive definitions only being literally stripped of external signifiers. P. I.'s authority over Newton is a clear inversion of their roles within the scheme of an order defined by colour and gender difference. This exchanging of roles highlights the radical contingency of the central principles such as freedom, providential ordering and the racially defined position of the individual which Newton articulates in his writings. Moreover, in this passage, Newton represents the black slaves as generous and self-sacrificing, qualities which were central to Christianity. When he finally recovered, P. I. convinced Clow he should send Newton to work with the Black slaves on their lime tree plantation, providing him with the same food and living quarters as the slaves. Whilst Newton attempts to rationalize his enslavement within the narrative of personal redemption, this is immediately undercut by the fact that it also signifies the collapse of a divine and colonial ordering of the world: Europeans can become commodities for Africans to exploit economically.

As Bernard Martin and Martin Spurrell point out, Newton's experience of slavery was recounted by William Wordsworth in *The Prelude* (1805). Newton's own account of his isolation whilst enslaved clearly appealed to the Romantic poet's interest in the individual's reflective capacities:

> One thing, though strange, is most true. Though destitute of food and clothing, depressed to a degree beyond common wretchedness, I could sometimes collect my mind to mathematical studies. I had bought Barrow's *Euclid* at Portsmouth; it was the only volume I brought on shore; it was always with me and I used to take it to remote corners of the island by the seaside and draw diagrams with a long stick upon the sand. Thus I often beguiled my sorrows and almost forgot my feeling.[19]

This passage is the source for Book six of *The Prelude*:

> And I have read of one by shipwreck thrown
> With fellow-sufferers whom the waves had spared
> Upon a region uninhabited
> An island of the deep, who, having brought
> To land a single volume and no more,
> A treatise of geometry was used,

Although of food and clothing destitute
And beyond all common wretchedness depressed,
To part from company and take this book
(Then first a self-taught pupil in those truths)
To spots remote and corners of the isle
By the seaside, and draw his diagrams
With a long stick upon the sand, and thus
Did oft beguile his sorrow and almost
Forget his feeling . . .

(lines 160–74)[20]

Taking his cue from Newton, Wordsworth has him shipwrecked on a deserted island. In this passage, Wordsworth draws on Newton's autobiography in order to compare his own experience of studying geometry in his youth with Newton's perusal of the *Euclid* whilst held in captivity. For Wordsworth, examining:

. . . the alliance of those simple, pure
Proportions and relations with the frame
And laws of nature . . .

(lines 144–6)

leads to a deep personal sense of inner calm prompted by the idea of a fixed, eternal order which ultimately regulates the universe. Here, the Romantic moves from classic introspection to the idea of external order and is momentarily comforted by the idea of an objective reality being naturally connected to the senses of the individual. Moreover, Wordsworth's appropriation of Newton's writing exemplifies the link between the type of subjectivity expressed in the spiritual biography and Romantic subjectivity: it is the empirical individual who, observing the universal from a perusal of the particular, provides the necessary connection.

Newton's captain's journals provide another context within which to represent his captors Clow and P. I. since he is obliged to trade with them when he arrives on the coast to gather slaves. His material circumstances have changed and now Newton is a slave captain who must work with the very people who had previously exploited him. A letter to his wife conveys the tension of his first meeting with P. I., with whom he now has an equal trading relationship:

I have had a visit from my quondam mistress P. I. I treated her with the greatest complaisance and kindness; if she has any shame in her I believe I made her sorry for her former ill-treatment of me. . . . I have had several such occasions of taking the noblest form of revenge upon persons who once despised me and used me ill. Indeed I have no reason to be angry with them. They were, what they little intended, instrumental to my good.[21]

It is clear that Newton chooses to translate his former enslavement into his personal narrative of conversion in which he 'once was bound, but now am free'. His belief in divine intervention allows him to erase the power of his former captors and to see them as similarly under the direction of an all-powerful God. It is evident, however, that Newton has not entirely forgiven his quondam mistress. His cynicism undermines his insistence that he accepts his former imprisonment as part of God's plan and for which he is therefore thankful. Newton's ability to behave well towards his 'quondam mistress' and master is clearly the result of his need to gather slaves.

Indeed, it seems to be commerce alone and not religious belief which encourages Newton to forge any type of relationship with P. I. and Clow at all. On his second journey he writes:

> Sent likewise a letter to Mr Clow to beg it as a great favour (*necessity dictating*) that he would sell me a few slaves to forward me off the coast. Our slow purchase and the pressing season reduces me to court those whose behaviour I have reason to resent and despise.[22] (emphasis added)

Newton's attempt to maintain an objective discourse slips into a tone of personal anxiety and, once more, this anxiety is caused by economic pressures. Newton needs Clow, and the *appearance* of civility takes the place of any sincerely felt bond between the traders. This extract certainly contradicts Newton's attempts to frame his slavery within the context of predestination – a context which would allow him objectively and rationally to accept the vicissitudes of fortune. Despite claiming the year before to have no reason to still be angry with P. I. and Clow, he still is. Nevertheless, as he states himself, he is able to *behave* with a civility born of the necessity of trade.

Newton had spent one year in Clow's possession before persuading him that it was unacceptable for a white man to be treated in the same manner as the black slaves. He persuaded his master to let him go and live with another slave trader, as his aspirations for succeeding in this trade himself had not been dimmed by his own experience. Newton was sent to Kittam and quickly rose to the station of manager at a slave factory there.

> Here I began to be wretch enough to think myself happy. There is such a significant phrase frequently used in those parts that such a *white man is grown black*. It does not intend an alteration of complexion, but disposition ... they have become dupes to all the pretended charms, necromances, amulets and divinations of the blinded negroes.[23] (emphasis added)

Ignorance and blackness are linked, literally *incorporated* into the powerful binarism of the discourse of civility and enlightenment. In Newton's autobiography, the image of a benighted Africa becomes a powerful metaphor for his own distance from God, for his own ignorance before being saved. In this passage, this ignorance which allows Newton to be 'happy', shifts into actual blindness thereby completing the totality of blackness which is Africa – he once 'was blind but now I see'.

However, Newton's account of his time on the Guinea Coast shifts according to the context provided by his representations. This is what he writes in his abolitionist 'Thoughts' (1788):

> My headstrong passions and follies plunged me, in early life, into a succession of difficulties and hardships, which at length, reduced me to seek a refuge among the natives of Africa. There, for about the space of eighteen months, I was in effect a slave myself; and was depressed to the lowest degree of human wretchedness. Possibly I should not have been so completely miserable had I lived among natives only, but it was my lot to reside with white men.[24]

The abolitionist context within which he writes results in a reversal of the correlation between colour and morality which Newton had formulated in his autobiography. Thus we see the ways in which his various texts influence Newton's accounts and even opinions. In the journals, the morality signified by colour is contested by the impact of trade; in his *Narrative*, colour becomes a metaphor for ungodliness and barbarity from which Newton has been saved; and, in his 'Thoughts', the conventional equation between morality and colour is overturned as abolitionism attempts to portray the slave trade itself as barbaric.

Slaves to infidels

James Irving first entered the slave trade as a ship's surgeon in the early 1780s. Although not much is known about his education before this, it is clear that he had considerable capabilities at a young age and, by the time he was twenty-nine, Irving had achieved his first captaincy, of the *Anna*, bound for the Guinea Coast from Liverpool. Having arrived in Tobago, Irving writes:

> We have ... not yet disposed of our very disagreeable cargo, but expect it in the 7th instant when our sale opens. ... Often, very often have I perused my dear girl's letter and each time with redoubled pleasure. ... I'm nearly wearied of this unnatural and accursed trade and think (if no change of station takes place) when convenience suits of adopting some other mode of life, although I'm fully sensible and aware of the difficultys attending any new undertaking, yet I will at least look around me. ... I think I'll desist as our black cattle are intolerably noisy and I'm almost melted in the midst of five or six hundred of them.[25]

While Irving's distaste for the slave trade is quite evident, the reasons why he regards it as 'unnatural' are not so clear. He speaks of the slaves as mere chattels to be traded, yet they are a troublesome cargo and he is not comfortable with his proximity to them. While the slaves themselves are largely absent from Newton's writings, referred to in the main as lists of numbers in his captain's journals, this invasion of the slaves into Irving's letter reflects not only the horrific conditions on a ship packed with in excess of five hundred slaves but also the pressure which their existence actually exerts on Irving as he writes. The limits of his civil discourse cannot contain their matter. In a letter in which he conveys his feelings for his wife and family and muses on his future employment prospects, the incongruity between domestic civility and the necessary brutality involved in being a slave trader is brought into sharp relief. What is also clear is that Irving regards his employment as one of the few options open to him at this time and the nexus between civility and economic necessity, here, is a fraught coincidence.

By May 1789, Irving had received the promotion necessary to his continuation in the slave trade and was given the captaincy of the *Anna* by the company Baker and Dawson, for whom he had worked as a ship's surgeon. The ship was considerably smaller than those Irving would have previously served on, weighing only 50 tons 'burthen' and only able to carry about eighty slaves. As Schwarz points out, this preference by the company for a smaller ship was probably an attempt to comply with newly introduced legislation to monitor the slave trade, the Dolben Act.[26] Writing to his wife upon his departure from Liverpool, Irving sounds confident about his journey:

> Providence if you confide in him is able and willing to support you in every situation in life. Think on these little matters and the reflection will afford balm to your mind. Go to church now and then or as often as you please. . . . As the wind is so exceeding favourable the vessel runs out very fast so that I really cannot find time to say what I have within, but do rest satisfied my sweet girl the next I shall write shall be a very long one.[27]

Irving would soon have to put his faith in Providence to the test. The next surviving letter, written by him on 24 June 1789, is very long and is addressed to John Hutchison the Vice-Consul at Mogodore, Morocco:

> Sir,
>
> The subscriber a most distrest and suffering object takes the liberty to inform you that he had the most grievous misfortune to lose his vessell on the Arab Coast opposite the west end of Forte Ventura on 26th May ultimo. He and his crew, eleven in number inclusive, have been since that time in the hands of Arabs and Moors in a condition miserable beyond conception. . . . For the sake of Almighty God neglect us not. We are Englishmen, and we hope good and loyal ones. . . . Suffer us not any longer like some poor Frenchmen about ten or twelve miles from hence to be the slaves of Negroes . . . If we are allowed to stay here to toil and be maltreated under a vertical sun we shall soon be lost forever to ourselves, our wives and familys, our country and all we hold dear. . . . The people who at present claim me are pretty civil. Sheak Braham is my master, and he boards me with a Jew merchant named Aaron Debauny. . . . Pardon the freedom I've treated you with, and the shameful scrawl done with a reed. I am this moment told that 500 dollars per man is the sum to be expected.[28]

Irving's distress and frustration are clear as he finds himself a slave to those he would enslave. His capture seems to overturn every system of order – divine, racial and civil – within which his current status is an unnatural aberration. Yet, as his letter shows, it is the economic order which dictates his identity as a slave and which allows him to write this letter in the first place, since his direct appeal lends weight to his owner's negotiations. He invokes Almighty God, the spirit of humanity in England, his crew's identity as Englishmen, and his horror at the idea of their becoming 'slaves to Negroes'; these references to providential, national and racial discourses assert Irving's and his crew's innate destiny to be masters, not slaves. Yet, such phrases contrast with the sense of cultural disorientation and the fragility of the domestic self which can 'soon be lost'. As Anthony Pagden writes: 'The spaces that separated the European from those "others" he was eventually to encounter were spaces of dissolution, menacing areas where civility could so easily dissolve into barbarism.'[29]

The 'space' of Irving's letter shows that dissolution to be a very real fear: the barbarity he is wary of is also the barbarity of the self which, due to a spatial and temporal distance from the domus,[30] is not too far below the surface of his Englishness. Even his letter, the signifier of his civility, is scrawled with a reed. In this letter, Irving provides Hutchison with a full list of his crew of eleven men which included his cousin, also James Irving, and three 'Portuguese blacks'. It was not unusual for there to be blacks on slaving voyages but their presence in this particular adventure further complicates Irving's reference to racial and national orders. They are, crucially, named as Portuguese but for now Irving includes them as part of his crew although whether he considers them to be 'Englishmen' is less certain.

Irving's description of the crew's capture in this letter is echoed in his journal, which was written a year after his captivity.[31] It was a strong 'easterly current'[32] which brought the *Anna* onto the Barbary Coast on the wrong side of the Canaries. As Schwarz notes, Newton's captain's journal of 21 September 1750 records a similar 'strong current setting to the eastward' which also brought his ship, *The Duke of Argyle* dangerously close to the Barbary Coast.[33] Irving, like Newton, did not discern 'the least shadow of land'[34] once he had realized the ship was off course but, by the early hours of 4 May 1789, the ship had run aground on a reef, was damaged and filled with water. Irving records the crew's response after having spent the night on the heavily leaning ship:

> we resolved to travel by land to the eastward in hopes of reaching Santa Crux or falling in with some hospitable inhabitants ... We set out about eight or nine in the morning, and in about an hour perceived the print of a human foot in the sand. Before this discovery, we had believed the country uninhabited.[35]

Allusions to *Robinson Crusoe* pervade Irving's journal. Schwarz writes 'At first, this almost fictional quality led me to doubt the authenticity of this copy journal'.[36] However, as Newton's accounts show, this intertex-tuality can also be seen as a common mode of representation which, in fact, bolsters the validity of the account since references to other stories, narratives and discourses provide a legitimate and familiar context around the 'new' story. What it also shows is the degree to which other discourses actually influence Irving's perception of reality. He does not seem to have noticed the contradiction in these few sentences in which he at once hopes to meet some 'hospitable inhabitants' *and* is of the opinion that the area is 'uninhabited'. The fact that the journal is written retrospectively allows Irving to hint ominously at the savage, perhaps even cannibalistic, nature of the natives whom, like Crusoe, he has not yet encountered.

Irving's journal is also full of proto-imperial surveys of the Moroccan landscape. His first accounts of the landscape combine the impression of a deserted wilderness with that of an agricultural rural scene. He sees the footprints of cattle and writes that, as they climbed higher:

> we had an extensive view of the country, which appeared a brown trackless sand with some herbs sprouting here and there. About ten o'clock in the forenoon, perceived live animals at a great distance and soon after observed a flock of sheep, and almost at the same instant observed three people running from us over a small eminence that lay before us.[37]

Although this would seem to be a fairly familiar scene, and one which could promise help from the local inhabitants, in retrospect Irving inserts a tone which anticipates their capture:

> We were all now big with anxiety, hopes, fears, resolutions and cowardice, a strange medley of ideas ... In this condition of mind three copper colored naked savages appeared before us, running at full speed and shouting hide-ously. They were followed by a tribe, some armed with long knives, others with muskets; you cannot conceive a scene more shocking ... We were seized by the throats and our bundles instantly disappeared, as well as our neck handkerchiefs. They then cut and tore the clothes from our backs and so eager were they for the plunder that the weakest who in all probability would get a small share of it, attempted to stab us.... During this scene of rapine, had frequent opportunity of seeing my unfortunate shipmates served in the same manner and fresh parties of Arabs coming from tents that lay at a greater distance, occasioned a repetition of the scene several times, till we were stripped almost naked.[38]

In this passage, the barbarity, violence and greed of the Arabs is unequivo-cally asserted. Irving portrays his crew's capture as a haphazard attack by a disorganized pack of bandits. However, the crew are immediately dealt with efficiently as they are separated and guarded, and their captors are well aware of their economic value. It is clear that being stripped is a significant form of debasement for Irving; losing his clothes perhaps reduces him to an instantly inferior position and means that he cannot easily be recognized as an Englishman. Within a few hours, their captors

had divided the crew and had gone in search of the ship. Irving, like
Newton, was left 'under the charge of women'.[39]

In captivity under the nomadic Arabs, Irving and the members of his
crew remaining in the same group met up when they could and fed on
scraps and shellfish. Some of the crew had already been taken away to be
sold as slaves. The very idea of being captured by nomads resonated with
the cultural meanings granted to a central domus as the heart of a civil
society, and to its absence as the signifier of barbarity:

> In all European cultures ... migration and nomadism were looked upon as
> either the 'barbaric' phase in the evolution of cultures, or as an integral part of
> the process whereby once civil peoples, who had been driven from their lands,
> became progressively decivilized. Such migrations had always been perceiveed
> as a menace by the inhabitants of the 'civilized' West.[40]

The desert, like the sea, is a liminal space for Irving, where the laws
governing civility are absent and where the territory of North Africa
comes to have a different meaning from that given to it by the European
perspective of the slave economy.

The nomads took the crew towards Goulimine, Agadir. Throughout his
relation of this journey, Irving provides his reader with detailed descriptions of the land and vegetation. Mary Louise Pratt points out that travel
writing in the eighteenth century reflected the shift from the colonizer's
charting of coastlines to an imperial stocktaking of the natural resources
within the interior of the potential colonies.[41] Indeed, Irving employs this
'imperial gaze' as a means of recuperating power and of asserting his true
status as a natural superior. The account of the next day undermines this
assumption, however, as Irving and the crew are made to cut their hair
and beards. He writes: 'That action, as it too much resembled the practice
followed by slave traders gave us much trouble.'[42] As a slave ship's
surgeon, Irving would have had to perform this very task on the slaves
just before they were sold, yet his language here indicates a distancing of
himself from his occupation. It is clear that Irving was a slave to be sold
and he relates how he was made to walk along with a 'Negro slave, who
had been also purchased by my master'.[43]

Irving's new master was Sheik Brahim, who took him from Goulimene
to a village he refers to as Tellin. In an entry for 24 June, Irving writes:

> In an extensive valley below I could perceive a town, where my new master
> (by name Sheik Brahim) informed me, the French people who had been
> shipwrecked some months before us, were in slavery. Their employment was
> chiefly in cultivating ground and gathering in the crop. He also told me I was
> not going to Mogodore, but to a place called Tellin where he resided, where I
> must write to the consul, who would purchase me and all the others. In the
> meantime he promised to use me well.[44]

From this point on, Irving's journal and letters from the corresponding
dates exhibit the tensions between his consciousness of his status as an

economic commodity and his objections to this condition, which are expressed as assertions of his natural superiority over a 'savage race'.[45] In his second letter to John Hutchison, dated 25 June 1789, Irving writes to give the names of several men who would act as vouchers for the sum of his release and that of his cousin. He is highly pragmatic in his attempts to secure his release. His pragmatism means that he is willing to exclude the 'Portuguese blacks' from his attempts if this means he will be more successful. In making this distinction, Irving is once more asserting the white or Englishman's innate right to freedom despite the fact that, at this moment, he is as much a slave as the black members of his crew. His recourse to racial and religious definitions of identity results in an ironic assertion of power from a position of powerlessness.

In the journal, Irving frequently attempts to rewrite his slavery by describing it within terms which assert a paradoxical claim to colonial authority. In Tellin, he writes:

> About this time I was informed by the Jew that I had been bought from Bilade at Gulimene by Sheik Brahim, my present master, for a hundred and thirty five ducats and that the least price he would accept was two hundred. Had I been master of the Indies, I would most cheerfully have parted with them for liberty, a privilege so dear to Englishmen. . . . I wrought as a servant to the Jew, who was a kind of merchant. This service, though unavoidable, I cordially detested, as I discovered that Jews in this country are little better than slaves to the Mahometans, their property, yea, their lives are at their disposal.[46]

Clearly, Irving is loath to find himself at the very bottom of the Moroccan social hierarchy. His Jewish keeper, Aaron Debauny, is, like Irving himself, 'a kind of merchant' and his emphasis on the lowly status of the Jews in Morocco ultimately highlights the extremity of his own condition. Within this context, then, his reiteration of the natural right of Englishmen to freedom is shown to be no more than a discursive construction, one that his own experience does not uphold.

Not withstanding Irving's textual reconstructions of his situation, the real state of the balance of power is reflected in the letters from Hutchison, the Vice-Consul at Mogodore. In a letter dated 28 August 1789, Hutchison writes:

> I must beg leave to caution you not to make use of the *term* infidels, either in your *letters or discourse* when speaking of the Moors. They look upon the term as the most opprobrious in their language, and as they have the power in their hands, it may operate to your prejudice.[47] (emphasis added)

Within the delicate negotiations to achieve the crew's release, Irving's language has a currency; yet its effect, in contrast to his intention of asserting his superiority as Christian, actually reinforces his subjection. Here, the Vice-Consul urges Irving to relinquish the specifically textual and discursive strategies through which he constructs his own identity and that of his captors. Since Irving is the Moors' property, he must respect their language and engage in a textual economy which reflects his actual economic status as a slave within their system. This imperative reinforces the fact that Irving's slave status is not one which he can circumvent through discursive ruses. It also registers the Moors' resentment of Irving's (mis)representation, and shows them to be as conscious of their religious identity as he is.

By the end of January 1790, Irving and the crew, although now the property of the Emperor of Morocco, were allowed to go to Mogodore and were placed in the charge of Hutchison. Their release, however, was not secured until the summer and, throughout the intervening months, they remained slaves in status and were not able to move freely whilst the complex political situation determining their release fluctuated. A letter of 25 March 1790 from Irving to his wife explains the final stages in the process:

> [T]he Emperor has wrote to the Governor of Gibraltar for the loan of a frigate to go to Alexandria with one of his sones who is going a pilgrimage to Mecca which if the Governor will grant, and there is no doubt but he will, the Emperor will deliver all of us up to him and likewise allow the trade of fresh provisions (duty free) from Tangier to Gilbraltar which has been stopt for some time past.[48]

Clearly, the Emperor was not the only party with interests to protect or with gains to be made in the transactions involving the crew. This final stage shows that Irving and his crew were not only slaves within the Moroccan system, but that the means through which they achieved their 'freedom' were absolutely determined by economic concerns and that they themselves became exchangeable commodities for both trading partners. Despite its rhetoric, the British government's actions subverted the idea of English liberty and reduced it to something to be traded for.

On 9 August 1790, Irving wrote to his wife from Mogodore to inform her at last of his definite release. At the end of his letter he includes a list of his new clothes:

> 1 coat, waistcoat and breeches
> 1 pair black sattin breech
> 1 shirt
> 2 neck cloths
> 2 pocket handkerchiefs
> 1 pair of black silk stockings
> 2 Guinea cloths
> 2 pieces of nonkeen
> 8 sillk handkerchiefs.[49]

This list, essentially a textual representation of the objects which outwardly define Irving's freedom for himself as well as for others, reads like a trader's account of his stock. After having been 'stripped naked' by the Arabs at the beginning of his ordeal, Irving can now re-dress himself in the uniform of the civilized Englishman. This passage explicitly represents freedom in terms of objects, and the list is an important way for Irving to reinforce his possession of these objects. Irving finally arrived back in Liverpool in November 1791. He spent just one month with his wife and son before embarking on another slaving venture.[50]

In trading places with African slaves, Newton and Irving filled positions not traditionally accounted for in the slave/slaver binary relationship. Their experiences typify the literal productivity of the slave trade in terms of identity, as well as of economics, their own slavehood being the product of the fluid exchanging practices which were the reality of the slave trade. Mercantilist trade inevitably gave way to the production of unregulated types of trade not allowed for by the limits of dominant economic logic. Similarly, the discursive limits within which Newton and Irving attempted to represent their experiences of slavery are shown to be productive of other identities which cannot be contained within civil, religious, national or racial ideals – most obviously, their own status as slaves. The institution of the slave trade figured the fluidity of the border between civilization and exploitation which a burgeoning eighteenth-century European commercial culture put under increasing pressure. These men's experiences of slavery highlighted to them the level to which civil ideals were denigrated in the slave trade. However, what is most astounding is that their enslavement did not at all prevent them from continuing in their profession as slavers as soon as they were free to do so. This testifies to the power of context: despite having had their view of the world literally turned upside down by being enslaved, both Newton and Irving were able to maintain their identity as natural slavers or masters, defined by the very terms which had failed to prevent them being enslaved.

Irving met an untimely death. Newton, however, rose to prominence in the Anglican Church and become a founder member of the Abolitionist Society in 1787, along with William Wilberforce, Thomas Clarkson and Granville Sharp. Newton's abolitionism marked not so much a renunciation of past beliefs but, rather, the effects of a new Europe-wide revision which had to take account of emerging economic and political situations, some of which were the result of colonial slavery, as well as of new identities which embodied the exchange and contamination between cultures and peoples. The recurrence of the trope of exchange in his abolitionist tract, 'Thoughts upon the African Slave Trade', highlights that slavery was an institution in which contamination was inevitable and that the reciprocity that gave rise to fluid identities and practices could not be compartmentalized. As he writes:

> For the sake of method, I could wish to consider the African trade first, with regard to the effect it has upon our own people; and secondly, as it concerns the blacks, or, as they are more contemptuously styled, the negro slaves, whom

we purchase upon the coast. *But these topics are so interwoven, that it will not be easy to keep them exactly separate.*[51] (emphasis added)

Notes

1. Richard Cecil, *Memoirs of Him* (1808), p. 39. Cecil states that this was a collaboration, saying that Newton

> promised to afford whatever materials might be necessary beyond those which his printed 'Narrative' contained. He promised also to read over and revise whatever was added from my own observation; and soon he brought me an account in writing containing everything memorable which he recollected before the commencement of his 'Narrative'. (p. vi)

As this shows, Newton was continually revising his life within different contexts. In the preface, Cecil states his reason for undertaking this rewrite of Newton's original *Narrative*: 'I considered how striking a display such a life affords of the nature of true religion – of the power of divine grace – of the mysterious but all-wise course of "Divine Providence"' (p. vi).

2. Suzanne Schwarz (ed.), *Slave Captain: The Career of James Irving in the Liverpool Slave Trade* (Wrexham, Bridge Books, 1995), p. 68.

3. Olaudah Equiano, *The Interesting Narrative and Other Writings* (1789), ed. Vincent Carretta (London, Penguin, 1995).

4. This autobiography was reprinted several times. The primary source used here for all quotes from Newton's autobiography is *The Life of John Newton, Written by Himself with a Continuation by the Reverend Richard Cecil* (Edinburgh, Johnstone and Hunter, 1855), p. 6.

5. Suzanne Schwarz has edited Irving's letters and other relevant surviving documents in *Slave Captain*. She writes:

> This discussion of James Irving's life and career is based largely on a collection of documents that has recently come to light in the Lancashire Record Office. This archive, held at reference DDX 1126, includes a copy of a journal written by James Irving which vividly reconstructs his shipwreck and period in captivity. The main part of the collection comprises Irving's correspondence spanning a period of five years. . . . The [journal] contained in the Lancashire Record Office is a copy written in a hardbacked, lined exercise book which probably dates from the early to mid-twentieth century. . . . Not only are the details in the journal supported by many of the eighteenth-century letters in the collection in the Lancashire Record Office, but many other sources confirm as well as expand upon the account in the journal.

In addition to these, William Lempriere's published writings, *A tour from Gibraltar to Tangier, Salee, Mogodore, Santa Cruz, Tarudant, and thence over Mount Atlas to Morocco*, 3rd edition (London, 1804), detail his meeting with Irving in Morocco.

6. As Eric Williams writes in *Capitalism and Slavery* (London, Andre Deutsch, 1964), p. 31:

> The case against monopoly was succinctly stated by the free traders . . . to the Board of Trade in 1711. The monopoly meant that the purchase of British manufactures for sale on the coast of Africa, control of ships employed in the slave trade, sale of Negroes to the plantations, importation of plantation produce . . . on which the livelihood, direct and indirect, of many thousands depended would be under the control of a single company.

7. Michel Foucault, *The Order of Things* (London, Routledge, 1994), p. 176. For Foucault, representation in the classical era is based on itself:

> If the sign is the pure and simple connection between what signifies and what is signified (a connection that may be arbitrary or not, voluntary or imposed, individual or collective) then the relation can be established only within the general element of representation: the signifying element and the signified element are linked only in so far as they are (or have been or can be) represented, and in so far as the one actually represents the other. (p. 67)

Just as representation is able to represent with itself as the basis of representation, so wealth (in mercantilism) receives its value from its exchangeability, or representative function. 'Wealth is wealth because we estimate it, just as our ideas are what they are because we represent them' (p. 176).

8. Robin Blackburn, *The Making of New World Slavery from the Baroque to the Modern 1492–1800* (London, Verso, 1997), p. 515.

9. Sara Suleri, *The Rhetoric of English India* (Chicago, Chicago University Press, 1992), p. 3.

10. John Newton, *The Journal of a Slave Trader*, ed. Bernard Martin and Martin Spurrell (London, Epworth Press, 1962), pp. 95–6.

11. Newton, *Letters to a Wife* (Philadelphia, William Young, 1793).

12. In Josiah Bull, *John Newton, an Autobiography and Narrative* (1849), pp. 51–2.

13. David Hindmarsh, *John Newton and the Evangelical Tradition between the Conversions of Wesley and Wilberforce* (Oxford, Clarendon Press, 1996), p. 43.

14. See Newton, *Journal*, p. x.

15. Newton, *The Life*, p. 27.

16. *Ibid.*, p. 28.

17. *Ibid.*, p. 30.

18. *Ibid.*, p. 32.

19. *Ibid.*, p. 34.

20. William Wordsworth, *The Prelude* (London, Penguin Classics, 1986).

21. Newton, *Letters*, 21 November 1750.

22. Newton, *Journal*, p. 42.

23. Newton, *The Life*, p. 38.

24. Newton, *Journal*, p. 98.

25. Irving in *Slave Captain*, Letter 4, pp. 112–13.

26. 'An act to regulate, for a limited time, the shipping and carrying of slaves in British vessels from the coast of Africa', clause 1, Elizabeth Donnan (ed.), *Documents Illustrative of the History of the Slave Trade to America, vol. 2* (Carnegie Institution, Washington, DC, 1931), p. 583. This act, introduced by Sir William Dolben in 1788, aimed at general control of the slave trade in order to lower mortality rates of both slaves and crews. Ships were only allowed to carry 'five slaves for every three tons of "burthen"', Schwarz, *Slave Captain*, p. 73.

27. Irving in Schwarz, *Slave Captain*, p. 118.

28. *Ibid.*, p. 120.

29. Anthony Pagden, *European Encounters with the New World: From Renaissance to Romanticism* (New Haven, Yale University Press, 1993), p. 3.

30. *Ibid.* As Pagden writes:

> Europeans have for long been preoccupied with the difficulties involved in encountering other worlds and their often fiercely 'other' inhabitants. Since antiquity European culture has been founded on the concept of the *oikos*, the *domus*, the household.

Pagden's introduction argues that this concept of a static point, which defined the centre of the domestic civilization, was fundamental to European representations of the New World as travellers and discoverers attempted to portray these spaces in terms of 'cultural commensurability'.

31. Schwarz (ed.) writes in *Slave Captain*, p. 10:

> I suspect that Irving's original journal still survives in private ownership. He may have written more than one as a way of informing family and friends of his experiences. . . . His uncle, living in London, may have been the recipient of one volume, whereas the copy in the Lancashire Record Office suggests that the original from which it was transcribed was 'wrote by Mr Irving for his much loved brother-in-law, George Dalston Tunstall'.

32. Irving in Schwarz, *Slave Captain*, p. 34.

33. Newton, *Journal*, p. 8. In this entry, Newton is much surprised to find himself 'not less than 50 leagues to the eastward of my reckoning' despite 'fair winds and weather and frequent observations'.

34. Irving in Schwarz, *Slave Captain*, p. 83.

35. *Ibid.*

36. Schwarz, *Slave Captain*, p. 103.

37. Irving in Schwarz, *Slave Captain*, p. 84.

38. *Ibid.*, p. 85.

39. *Ibid.*

40. Pagden, *European Encounters*, p. 2.

41. Although something of an accidental tourist, Irving nevertheless produces an account of Morocco and its inhabitants which can also be read as a travelogue. If we regard travel writing in the late-eighteenth-century colonial sphere as a broad, fluid continuum, ranging from travelogues of explorers to the written accounts of those who travelled for various purposes, then both Irving's and Newton's multiple accounts of Africa are travelogues in the sense that they provided accounts of journeys within colonial power structures and they consciously contributed to colonial representations of Africa and the colonies. As Mary Louise Pratt writes in *Imperial Eyes: Travel Writing and Transculturation* (London, Routledge, 1992), p. 7, the term 'contact zone', in which travel writing was produced,

> is an attempt to invoke the spatial and temporal copresence of subjects previously separated by geographies and historical disjunctures, and whose trajectories now intersect. . . . A 'contact' perspective emphasizes how subjects are constituted in and by their relations to each other. It treats the relations among colonizers and colonized, or travelers and 'travelees', not in terms of separateness or apartheid, but in terms of copresence, interaction, interlocking understandings and practices, often within radically asymmetrical relations of power.

42. Irving in Schwarz, *Slave Captain*, p. 92.

43. *Ibid.*, p. 93.

44. *Ibid.*, p. 94. In a letter, dated 21 July, from James Matra, Consul-General to the Secretary of State, Matra describes the difficulties they face in trying to negotiate for the crew's release. He also writes, 'At this time there are eight French seamen in the hands of the Arabs, who will not sell them to the Emperor, and he has refused to let anybody else buy them', p. 122.

45. *Ibid.*, p. 94.

46. *Ibid.*, p. 96.

47. *Ibid.*, p. 129.

48. *Ibid.*, p. 138.

49. Schwarz, *Slave Captain*, p. 142.

50. See *ibid.*, p. 66.

51. Newton, *Journal*, p. 100.

CHAPTER SIX

Urban captivity narratives: the literature of the yellow fever epidemics of the 1790s

CYNTHIA L. RAGLAND

Yellow fever in America

> The attack . . . was very sudden; few had any particular sensations of approaching disease; many went to bed in the evening to all appearance in the enjoyment of perfect health, and at break of day they were often at death's door. This unmerciful enemy most commonly made his first deadly attack on the body with a severe chill.[1]

The words of Reverend Jutus Helmuth, Lutheran minister in Philadelphia during 1793, echoed the sentiments of many Philadelphians who thought, like Helmuth, that few cities 'have been plunged by his just judgment into a deeper abyss of distress, than our now weeping Philadelphia'.[2] The minister and many early chroniclers of yellow fever epidemics frequently depicted the onset of these calamitous events in the redolent language used to portray Indian attacks in the seventeenth and eighteenth centuries. When Dr Samuel Brown of Boston recounted the epidemics of the 1790s in his 1800 published chronicle, he likewise relied upon captivity language to describe yellow fever: 'But the work of death is not always performed by legions and battalions. . . . This is a foe, against which neither ramparts nor intrenchments afford any security'.[3]

The preponderance of captivity language and the thematic and structural similarities of the Indian captivity narrative to the epidemic prose of the late eighteenth century in America is striking. A study of these urban captivity narratives helps us understand how Americans first grappled with the problems of national identity in the early decades after independence by relying on familiar genres from their colonial history.[4]

The narrative of yellow fever forms a complicated story of tragic dimensions, national anxieties and national hopes. It is a story that began in the nation's capital and one that continued to touch directly the lives of the citizens of the major seaboard cities. People living beyond the reaches of the epidemics participated through their reading of those events or by their contact with epidemic survivors. Eventually, most of those in the nation experienced yellow fever either directly in their own cities or vicariously by reading and hearing accounts from others.

This American tale, however, proved difficult to narrate. When Moses Bartram wrote to his brother Isaac on 3 October 1793, he ended his anecdotes about the condition of the city, lamenting that 'I could add a great number more but am tired of this Dismal tale.'[5] Yet this 'dismal tale' kept repeating itself through the 1790s, spurring an outpouring of material, all of which was highly narrative-driven. Thus, the story not only found its emotional outlet in novels and poetry but also in many non-fiction genres popular during the eighteenth century.[6]

Hundreds of accounts of the epidemics attempted to narrate the events of Philadelphia, New York and other cities. Tales of the epidemics embraced the histories and the aftermaths of the devastation as well as the events themselves. Letters, diaries, autobiographies, medical records, city reports, sermons, jeremiads, histories, medical treatises, political tracts, court documents and newspaper items all framed the published or unpublished material into narratives. People tried these different literary genres to explain the inexplicable and, eventually, the genre of the Indian captivity narrative provided many narratives with organization, thematic unity and the moral and religious symbolism needed to elaborate the yellow fever debate.

Indian captivity rhetoric

Much like the Indian captivity narratives, at the centre of the difficulties of recording the incomprehensible story of yellow fever was the impossibility of separating the personal from public destiny. Survival of Indian captivity marked more than personal endurance; it signalled community survival in a hostile new world. The new nation attempted to survive during the spate of epidemics soon after the inauguration of a new political system. The need to elude national destruction had a profound personal effect on the lives of the new citizens, influencing public perceptions as well, and made it difficult for writers to isolate personal considerations. John de Peyster, writing to Philadelphia's painter Charles Willson Peale from New York on 2 October 1793, appropriates the dual public-personal anxiety of captivity rhetoric:

> it affords me great consolation to find your family still in the Land of the Living – but how long this may be the case God only knows – Death's Shafts fly thick around you, and no one knows who they will light on, – I am well convinced that no man can paint the present distresses of your City . . . so many Dreadfull and Contradictory Reports prevail here that we know not which to believe.[7]

De Peyster, like the rest of the nation, felt the helplessness of watching his country's capital and his close friends besieged by disease. And for the many Philadelphians who later struggled to explain the 1793 epidemic – anonymous citizens who hyperbolically decreed it 'a crisis of inconceivable consternation' brought about by a 'potent malady [which] hath laughed to scorn our wisdom' – language seemingly failed in providing expression for the inexpressible, just as it failed to explain the new nation.[8] This failure of language, however, did not prevent writers from trying to find the particular rhetorical designs which would illuminate their and their nation's sufferings. What they found, however, was the rhetoric of captivity, which thus became embedded in tales of the epidemics precisely because this rhetoric, while it seemed to focus on the personal narrative, actually privileged the public chronicle.

The rhetoric of yellow fever identified an enemy, albeit misunderstood and oversimplified, and construed that enemy from the perspective of the helpless captive. Further characterizing the transformed captivity genre, this rhetoric helped narrators depict the onset of captivity, the survival and eventual escape, and provided the subsequent narrations with the theme of public redemption. Most important, however, was the depiction of the captive as victim and the extension of that victimization to America in general. Searching for the significance of captivity and the intentions of the captors, chroniclers defined captivity and redemption in terms of early national identity crises. The motivations for framing these urban captivity experiences in words and the resulting popularity of these texts are as complex as those of the Indian captivity narratives.

Although colonists had experienced the continued effects of Indian captivity since the first European attempts at North American settlement, making Indian raids endemic on the frontier, the great urban epidemics of Europe had spared most Euro-Americans in the seventeenth and eighteenth centuries. However, shortly after national independence, during the late summer and autumn of 1793, almost a tenth of Philadelphia's population died. By the beginning of Thomas Jefferson's administration in 1801, yellow fever, the 'plague' of Philadelphia, killed thousands of eastern seaboard residents. Epidemics continued to appear annually during the 1790s, relentlessly snatching victims in a seemingly random pattern, leaving stunned survivors to make sense of mass burials, horrible deaths, government and commercial paralysis, and social disintegration. Unable to explain the transmission of the fever and unable to find a cure against its ravages, numerous theories arose to explain why the nation suffered such punishment.[9]

Yellow fever and the jeremiad

Doctors disagreed about where the epidemics came from: were they local or were they imported? At first a medical controversy, the political implications of the yellow fever debate infused the new citizens with deeply felt anxieties about the nature and the future of their country. The lack of knowledge about the origins of the epidemics suggested both internal and external national security concerns. Thus emerged an explicit expression of American exceptionalism, implicitly finding its expression in the theory of importationism. Yellow fever, the unseen enemy arriving from outside the country, captured not only individuals but an entire nation. Elements of the jeremiad, a popular American genre describing declension and redemption, appeared, as they had in Indian captivity accounts, but ironically the jeremiad suggested localism as an informing theory. The spiritual declension supposedly responsible for Indian wars in the seventeenth century was transformed into urban declension at the end of the eighteenth century. In this way, the same narrative often contained two distinct theories about the origins of the epidemics. Although this appears illogical, these theories paradoxically enabled the rhetoric of yellow fever to help Americans explore national self-definition.

Clarifying national identity meant understanding the national psyche, and from a psychological perspective, both Indian attacks and epidemics shared similarities. Ironically, the 'attackers' could be seen as analogous: the lack of colonial understanding of the Indians as distinct tribes led to seeing the Indians in general terms as the 'Other' or, in seventeenth-century terms, 'heathens' or 'savages'. Although the origination of yellow fever defied detection, the colonists lacked the desire to comprehend both the origination and motivations of the Indians.

Furthermore, the suddenness of onset and the lack of preparedness by both groups of sufferers served to wrench those inflicted out of their regular worlds. For example, by the time an epidemic seemed inevitable it was already too late for many of the inhabitants, who would have been infected but who were not yet showing symptoms. While Puritan settlers, according to Colin Calloway, 'didn't try to understand Indian captors or their reasons for taking captives',[10] the urban population vainly attempted to trace the disease's origins which, however, eluded scientists for a hundred years after Philadelphia's 1793 epidemic. However, like Puritans who saw Indian attacks both as 'a form of divine punishment visited upon erring communities', with the Indians as an extension of Satan, and as part of 'the intrigues of French Catholics in Canada',[11] yellow fever chroniclers believed in divine or secular punishment (domestic origin) or blamed the French for importing the disease into American cities (importationism).

In fact, many Philadelphians stressed the city's rather than individuals' sins and warned that God meant the city to suffer, claiming that 'The wrath of the Almighty seems inflamed against this City – his wrath impregnated with death! – His fiery indignation scatters terror around!' Philadelphian Thomas Dunn made sure his congregation understood that 'Indeed in these awful visitations of an angry God, he spares not his own people. . . . In no other light perhaps should we view our late calamity than the judgments of God.'[12]

During the epidemic years, sermons printed in Boston, a city mostly unaffected by yellow fever, tend to exhibit the more formalized aspects of the jeremiad, a genre highly developed in New England since the seventeenth century.[13] However, the focus of such yellow fever jeremiads frequently pointed to regional tensions (therefore, secular anxieties) between the mid-Atlantic and New England regions, in addition to highlighting what some thought of as Boston's bitterness at being eclipsed by Philadelphia after the Revolutionary War. Clearly, the redemption of a particular Boston congregation remained in the background when the Reverend John Lathrop reminded them that 'a small number were protected among the savages in an inhospitable wilderness', but now the 'Capitol of the United States . . . is now a city, almost left solitary'.[14]

Jeremiads from New York, on the other hand, focused more subtly on the rivalry between the two major port cities of the mid-Atlantic region. Before New York felt the effects of yellow fever, John Mitchell Mason questioned his New York congregation in late September 1793, 'Have *we* escaped because we are better than they? No . . . A sovereign God has made them an example of his righteous vengeance.' Mitchell concluded, of course, that New Yorkers had an opportunity to repent, 'that our condition . . . though sad, is not hopeless . . . [that] there is no citizen present, who will not find . . . that he has abundant reason to say, not as a *man*, but as an *American, God be merciful to ME*'. Although Mason's message clearly intended to spark national spiritual re-examination, he reminded New Yorkers of their privileged position with God, especially during a time when Philadelphia was struck by his 'righteous vengeance'.[15]

The jeremiad, by its nature, suggests localism as an informing theory for the origin of yellow fever. Punishment, whether framed in religious or secular language, was deserved because America had strayed from the path of righteousness or republican values. The jeremiad warned its audience against ignoring the meaning of the punishment; if they were to do so, further punishment would certainly follow.

Anonymous, religious jeremiads, unconnected with sermons, abounded as well, accusing 'Her inhabitants [of Philadelphia] indulg[ing] themselves in all the gratifications of luxury and dissipation. . . . The citizens too generally had forgotten the Fountain from whom all their blessings flowed.'[16] According to this writer, Philadelphians experienced their traumas because they concentrated their energies unwisely on the accumulation of possessions. Likewise, Hannah Swarton, captured by the Indians at Casco Bay in 1690, had denounced her own community's behaviour as being responsible for her punishment:

> so we turned our backs upon God's ordinances to get this world's goods. But now God hath stripped me of these things also so that I must justify the Lord in all that has befallen me and acknowledged that He hath punished me. . . . I was now bereaved of husband, children, friends, neighbors, house, estate, bread, clothes, or lodgings suitable.[17]

Swarton pinpoints the origins of her sorrows as rooted in the decision to leave her former community's values behind. She paid a high price for that decision: she was a captive for five and a half years and her husband and one of her children died. Two other children were never redeemed. Similar religious concerns distressed many Philadelphians, particularly Quakers, who claimed the origin of yellow fever germinated in the community's loss of spiritual vision. For these critics, creating wealth and prosperity had eclipsed religious piety.

Secular jeremiads likewise condemned Philadelphia for social sins. The publisher, Mathew Carey, in stating that 'something was waiting to humble the pride of a city, which was running on in full career, to the goal of prodigality and dissipation',[18] blamed the epidemic on civic extravagances and a severe housing shortage. In a similar fashion, as if writing a secular jeremiad, Dr Rush warned the citizens of Philadelphia in 1799 to heed his directives:

> Should this attempt be unsuccessful in producing the effect intended by it, as my former ones have been, I shall hereafter mourn in secret over the continuance of an error which has been so fatal to the citizens of Philadelphia.[19]

Rush, a doctor who stood as a secular god in a world filled with fever, invoked the same sense of dread as did the contemporary harbingers of religious punishment.

Importationism and American exceptionalism

Many Philadelphia doctors and inhabitants like Dr Adam Kuhn and Richard Folwell, however, strongly believed that the French imported yellow fever from their rebellious islands in the Caribbean. Although Dr Charles Caldwell persisted in countering these claims throughout the 1790s by reminding the Academy of Medicine of Philadelphia that cries of importation always accompanied these epidemics, 'Hence the evils of pestilence have been generally charged to the account of commerce', many disbelieved him. He maintained that the ignorance of these views stemmed from the 'powerful principle of self-interest' because admitting domestic origin would 'prove injurious to its population and prosperity'.[20] Thus, Caldwell questioned the underlying idea of American exceptionalism embedded in importation theory as well as identifying the source of what he saw as a denial of urban accountability. Instead of understanding that the punishment of yellow fever originated from the sins of civic irresponsibility, the community, according to Caldwell, would be doomed to continue its suffering if it tried to place the blame elsewhere.

Separating domestic origin from importationism (and, by extension, American exceptionalism) in urban captivity narratives is not uncomplicated, as the following example illustrates and, because of this, the solutions (or redemption) present equal complexities. The papers of

Dr Benjamin Barton, a Philadelphia physician and an avid naturalist, include a number of unpublished genres: correspondence with the London scientific community, detailed descriptions of American specimens, medical notes and records and a manuscript clearly intended as an early draft of a full narrative of the 1793 epidemic. Barton never published his manuscript, although it is not clear why he did not finish the project. In a March 1794 letter to Thomas Pennant of London, whom he had never met but had communicated with frequently, Barton discussed the 1793 epidemic, claiming that he intended to publish a long account. His tone in the letter remained unemotional and he did not refer to his own role during the epidemic as a doctor, nor did he tell Pennant that he had survived a case of yellow fever himself.[21]

Barton's response to the epidemic differs little from captivity survivors or victims of trauma. The emotional numbness evinced by his narrative is one method of surviving trauma. Mary Rowlandson, for example, could not include the name of her daughter, wounded by the Indians in a 1676 attack, even though she carried the six-year-old for days until the child died. Rowlandson's captivity narrative, the first published in British North America, chronicles her initial capture in 1676, her separation from her remaining children and her redemption eleven weeks later. This desensitization constitutes what trauma scholars refer to as dissociation and is another form of denying the experience of captivity. Viewed in this light, Barton's refusal to include his very recent personal epidemic experience explicitly illustrates his own trauma.[22]

What Barton did write, however, bears exploration. In this and subsequent letters, he quickly directed the subject away from yellow fever, taking the opportunity to exalt America's political system as compared to that of Britain's. He championed America's recovery from yellow fever, claiming that the fever was imported, and he extolled America's natural superiority over other countries.

Barton's overt references to American exceptionalism are not uncommon in epidemic materials. What emerges as uncommon is that Barton held ambiguous views as to the origin of the fever, never specifically taking sides in the controversy between domestic or imported origination. In fact, near the end of the epidemic, Barton wrote in his notes: 'I am not going to describe the yellow fever, nor enter into an inquiry concerning its origin.' Yet Barton did attempt to draft a narrative, one whose language surprisingly emerges as imprecise compared to his scientific and naturalist prose, and he did tell Pennant of his desire to bring the project to completion.[23]

Despite his intention of not inquiring into the epidemic's origin, Barton provides confident expression of American exceptionalism in his letters to Pennant, which links him by *cultural assumptions* to the importationists, even if he did not fully advocate their views. Therefore, Barton's intentions, noted in several genres of his unpublished work, contradict the public persona he projected for the benefit of a European audience. The eighteenth-century epidemic chronicler found himself caught between the simultaneous desires of decrying the threat posed to the nation from the outside and boasting of the nation's capacity to overcome those threats. He fits what trauma expert Judith Herman calls a pattern for trauma chroniclers:

> It is difficult for an observer . . . to retain all the pieces, and fit them together. It is even more difficult to find a language that conveys fully and persuasively what one has seen. . . . To speak publicly about one's knowledge of atrocities is to invite the stigma that attaches to victims.[24]

Therefore, the survivor also becomes the victim, one who perceives 'victimization as punishment'.[25]

According to Herman's characterization, in order to cope with trauma Barton, like many survivors, exhibits the duality embedded in such narratives: 'The survivor is called upon to articulate the values and beliefs . . . that the trauma destroyed'.[26] Just as Benjamin Tompson's words during King Philip's war struck a note of despair over the 'Slaughter, Captivating, Deaths and wounds', they also captured 'New-Englands Glory'.[27] The nation's potential, although assaulted by yellow fever or Indians, persisted to override the jeopardy of nation building in order to champion national glory.

By the end of the 1790s, when epidemics had struck repeatedly at all the major middle-seaboard cities, the sins of the individual or the particular city dimmed when compared to the lack of fulfilling national promise. Never do we feel 'more completely helpless, and more entirely in the hands of God, than when he sends forth pestilence, as a messenger of his to chastise a guilty society', said Samuel Miller in 1799 to his New York congregation. America, he claimed, had forgotten God's 'national blessings; for civil and religious liberty; for governments of our own choice and laws of our formation'.[28] Therefore, the sins of the individual, the community and the nation defined the religious, secular and political backsliding responsible for God's wrath and undermined the stability of the country's new political system. Both the individual and the nation respond to the annihilation of 'the sense of connection between individual and community, creating a crisis of faith',[29] a common reaction prompted by the perils threatened in the jeremiad.

Captivity and narrative

The emphasis on origination, whether domestic or imported, whether described in a secular or religious jeremiad, framed the yellow fever captivity experience slightly differently from that of the Indian captivity. There was rarely a yellow fever captive who related the experience of epidemic captivity solely in individual terms, showing how 'denial, repression and dissociation operate on a social as well as individual level'.[30] Although captives of the Indians were taken frequently in groups, those groups never approached the size of the city population; yellow fever captivity extended always to a whole city, and this difference is crucial. By the time several people had died of yellow fever, many more were already infected and, hence, already captive prior to the onset of symptoms. By its very nature, an epidemic cannot exist without a great number of victims. Therefore, the period of captivity must be refigured in ways that allow for urban differences.

Calloway reminds us that the 'Puritan chroniclers and early New England historians depicted the triumph of English settlers over what they saw as savage wilderness', using the 'theme of bondage and redemption', where the captive 'was abducted from home, dragged through the wilderness, taken into Indian society, but eventually liberated and returned home'. This pattern of 'Separation', 'Transformation' and 'Return', what anthropologist Victor Turner describes as an experience marked by separation, marginality (liminality) and reaggregation, at first seems to defy the yellow fever captivity structure.[31] Victims were not abducted from the city: they fled. And there was little wilderness to be found in eighteenth-century cities.

Yet the underlying formation of the urban captivity experience captured precisely those stages which inform Puritan captivity narratives. Citizens of Philadelphia, New York and Baltimore were wrenched from their daily lives, abducted from their families by disease and death. As a modern fictional account notes, Philadelphia faced 'the long hot dry summer of '93, when the dead and dying wrested control of the city from the living'.[32]

Those who fled the cities were imprisoned in more diverse ways than those who remained; frequently shunned by people believing that yellow fever was contagious, many refugees were turned back to the cities or, if allowed to stay, were avoided by others and unable to have contact with their families or businesses in the cities. Their burden of captivity was an enforced isolation away from their lives, causing a sense of helplessness, constant worry and the overwhelming guilt of surviving while others were dying.[33] The desperation of subsisting on few or no resources continued to plague those who supposedly escaped, while their property and resources in the cities were lost or diminished. For example, the Philadelphia businessman Levi Hollingsworth received scores of letters from friends and business acquaintances in September and October of 1793, asking him for financial assistance so they could survive what I call their 'reverse captivity'.[34]

Those who remained behind did so because their choices were limited. The fever had attacked them or their families already, or they felt a duty to help others or to manage businesses. Many people, however, had no resources to leave the city, and for all who stayed survival was a continual problem. Money had little currency in a city where nurses could not be obtained, where food and firewood ceased to be brought daily into the city and aid of any kind was unpredictable. Like captives of the Indians, the captives of yellow fever never felt that the danger had abated until redemption from the enemy provided them with alleviation from fear.

The pestilence also turned the cities into the wilderness, where civic order ceased to function. Not unlike captivity communities of the seventeenth century, the metamorphosis of the city mimicked the transformation of those who found themselves in psychological and physical disarray, who moved through different sets of perceptions, gaining new insight about their society.[35] What they saw in the new republican wilderness of the city did not measure up to republican rhetoric: their leaders frequently abandoned them and anarchy quickly overwhelmed many attempts to stem the chaos. Widows and orphaned children clamoured for relief that was not available, class and race concerns overtly intruded and an entire nation's cultural values were called into question.[36]

As Alden Vaughan and Edward Clark have noted, 'during the liminal phase the [Puritan] captive witnessed the bulk of what he recorded in his narrative', and the urban captive did likewise.[37] Redemption came with the frosts, ending several months of epidemic captivity, and the accounts of what transpired appeared immediately. One is struck by the number of reports which promote the rhetorical structure of captivity narratives (i.e. attack, captivity and redemption) by beginning their titles with the words, 'The Rise, Progress and Termination' of yellow fever. Although the brevity of this chapter does not allow for a full explanation of the publishing aspects of the urban captivity narrative, the issue of redemption must be addressed.[38]

De Peyster's letter to Peale, noted earlier, highlights an important consideration in studying the rhetoric and publication of this period – that of audience. The intended audience for both private and public discourse dictated a variety of rhetorical strategies. Where the audience lived was a crucial point: were they outside the reach of the epidemic or at the epicentre? Did this audience live in a major city or in a particular region? These basic questions shed light on how the events of yellow fever were explained and *why* particular narrative strategies and genres were used to interpret those events.

Interestingly, whether the audience was a private or a public one had less effect than the locality. Private discourse suffered from the lack of the personal: there was little which was not public in tone. Even private grief became a footnote in a city's public narrative of suffering. In fact, the rhetoric of manuscripts tends to be surprisingly reserved in both content and tone, often more unemotional than that of the printed texts. The writers seem to sense a public audience always hovering just beyond their words. Assessment of this dulling of the personal sensibility in private discourse and the expansion of overly personalized rhetoric at the public level defies a complete explanation. Undoubtedly, the trauma of the epidemic restrained the personal voice; however, this same restraint appeared in manuscripts written long after any particular epidemic.

Herman maintains that trauma survivors' 'first attempts to develop a narrative language may be partially dissociated', that their initial accounts 'may be repetitious, stereotyped, and emotionless'. She sees such accounts functioning like 'pre-narrative', because any one of these given narratives 'does not develop or progress in time, and it does not reveal the story teller's feelings or interpretation of events'.[39] Herman's theories could also explain the emotional restraints present in material written long after the epidemics. She notes that 'reconstructing the trauma story also included a systematic review of the meaning of the event', but that continued emotional suppression can indicate that 'the chronic trauma of captivity cannot be integrated into the person's ongoing life story'.[40]

Herman's theories, developed in part from modern narratives of political incarceration and the subsequent torture of the captive, illuminate causes for a restrained personal voice in urban captivity narratives. Nevertheless, while most Indian captives were captured only once in their lifetimes, epidemic survivors re-entered captivity numerous times between 1793 and 1820, guaranteeing that yellow fever epidemics became the 'life story', rather than merely an event to incorporate into that story. In addition, without knowing where yellow fever came from or why, and not knowing how to cure it, the impossibility of wresting meaning from the event prevailed.

Yellow fever narratives, in which the public voice shifts to the personal voice in printed materials, may offer some additional useful insights. Such passages frequently appeared in the texts when the writers tried to explain the situation in their city beyond the most general of descriptions. Difficulty in explaining the horrors of the epidemics made it all the harder to maintain the disinterested voice of the public commentator, and the uncertainty of surviving any particular epidemic was compounded by the stark certainty of future epidemics at regular intervals. Language simply failed these writers because, as Cathy Caruth explains in her work on trauma narrative, the act of writing is 'the very attempt to claim one's own survival'. However, claiming one's own survival means little if the individual will be thrust back into yet another epidemic and yet another attempt to survive.[41] Additionally, Caruth's premises, like Herman's, focus entirely upon the individual. Whereas urban captives prefigured their survival in individual terms, their desire for their city (nation) to survive was more paramount. Therefore, these writers published narratives which fluctuate between their individual desires to survive and their public voices of dispassionate chroniclers of a city and nation in calamity.

Audiences of yellow fever

Unpublished manuscripts also supply a wealth of material for scholars studying intended audiences and their responses in non-fiction prose. Not only are these audiences frequently difficult to identify but also, more important, in some cases the writer seems to have tried to obfuscate his intended audience. In other cases, the writer seems to have been genuinely perplexed as to which audience he was targeting. Albeit the writer might have been struggling to maintain his own identity in the midst of continued assault, but personal identity rarely emerges as a concern in these writings, with the exception of doctors who are desirous of creating identities as those who can cure the disease. The writer equally seems to be trying to retrieve or even discover a larger national identity, one in which he can transform his personal sense of punishment into national retribution.

However, when the intended audience appears detectable, it is linked tightly to the issue of authorial purpose. For example, Mary Rowlandson's seventeenth-century narrative reflected many of these considerations. As Lorrayne Carroll notes, the captive Rowlandson 'earns the experiential authority to speak to the public – to publish – the particulars and the consequences of her captivity'.[42] Yellow fever survivors also earned a certain respect for their captivity. Mathew Carey (although not always in Philadelphia during the epidemics), Benjamin Rush and Charles Caldwell all brought to their narratives the authenticity of experience. In fact, many reviews of yellow fever narratives found in the *Medical Repository*, the country's first national medical journal, first established the experiential credentials of the author before reviewing the work. Likewise, the veracity of accounts offered for review was challenged if the author lacked authentic urban captivity experience. The captivity component continued to be privileged even in the communities of scientific discourse.[43]

However, much like secular ministers, Carey, Rush and Caldwell tried to use their positions as survivors and chroniclers of the epidemics to solidify their particular social views. Unlike solely individual accounts of the epidemics, the secular historians produced within their narratives a collection of accounts which direct the reader to templates of specific social policy. Rowlandson's narrative, under Increase Mather's translation, 'establishes the female captivity narrative as a genre with standard images: privation in the woods, loss of kin, spiritual conversion', and reinforces that the 'representations of power, powerlessness, and social authority exist in a dynamic relationship to one another'. Therefore, Rowlandson's account, directed most likely by ministerial intercession, reflected 'several cultural preoccupations', such as the 'shrinking spheres of Puritan influ-ence' and the 'control of historiography'.[44] Moreover, Increase Mather's interpretation of Rowlandson's captivity, as Lorrayne Carroll notes, trans-forms 'the personal experience . . . into a providential sign for all to read'. However, 'Mather uses the Swarton narrative to address contemporary social and political concerns'.[45] Tara Fitzpatrick also explores the Puritan 'clergy's attempts to impose a socially and doctrinally unified and ortho-dox interpretation of the captives' experiences'.[46] Yellow fever chroniclers, on the other hand, did not have a unified audience to address, but that did not stop them from trying to create one.

Identifying the intended audience of these published accounts is frequently as difficult as ascertaining particular audiences for post-Puritan Indian captivity narratives. Occasionally, an author even obscured his intentions by pretending to address a wholly different audience. Mathew Carey's first account of the 1793 epidemic shows that, because of his profession, he was acutely aware of national publishing opportunities. In April of 1794, he justified the success of his first account by noting:

> When I began to write, I had not the smallest view to profit. For it is a fact well-known to printers, that pamphlets rarely defray themselves. My intention was to prevent such an utter deficiency of records on the subject of our late scourge, as has been often regretted, respecting the former instances of this kind. But the profit was speedily altered, through the avidity, with which the pamphlet was bought up by the public.[47]

Although this seems like a straightforward explanation, Carey's response was not due to criticism over making a profit. Critics charged that Carey fled at the height of the epidemic and that his first narrative not only glossed over this fact but also condemned the behaviour of the black population of the city who, in fact, had stayed and helped the city to survive. Therefore, Carey's multiple accounts of one epidemic discern aspects of his personal justification shaping those narratives, purportedly written as factual regional history.

Like Mathew Carey's, Benjamin Rush's audience at first seems to encompass the general public. Yet, upon closer examination, it becomes apparent that Rush's intended audience comprised the national medical community with whom Rush attempted to establish himself as the country's yellow fever expert. Later, his audience narrowed even more when he sought to defend his local reputation against what he felt were scurrilous attacks against his methods of treatment. Also carefully compiling his accounts to appeal to a specific audience near the end of the 1790s, Noah Webster based his compilation mostly on accounts already in existence, shaping those sources to support his political and cultural ideas of American exceptionalism.[48]

Historical narratives

The attempts and subsequent failures to define a unified audience due to the writers' inability to delineate the ideas of a unified nation were only part of the anxiety plaguing yellow fever narrators. Rhetorical uneasiness highlights the sense of frustration by those fighting the epidemics in not being able to discover the knowledge which could have helped them combat the yellow fever. This inability to find consensus, a crucial rhetorical strategy in the newly constituted republic, continued to vex the chroniclers.[49] Their 'evidence' and 'testimonies' read as second- or third-hand information. Historically, much of their information remained anecdotal, impossible to confirm and layered with the uncertain biases of several narrators, some of whom were unnamed. Consequently, these narratives floundered expressly at the point where they strove for clarity and, more important, muddled the third level of the captivity narrative: redemption. History precedes redemption, which serves as an interpretation of that history. The conduct of Indian captives and their communities guided the possible resolutions for deliverance. Without historical consensus and lacking at times in historical veracity, these narratives thwarted the comprehension of national identity.

This lack of knowledge, particularly of the origins of yellow fever, especially hampered the historical narratives, at least in terms of seventeenth-century historiography where, according to Stephen Arch, a writer like John Winthrop attempted 'to balance, or reconcile, a series of dichotomies: public and private, society and self, order and disorder'.[50] In addition, compared to the American histories written at the end of the eighteenth century, many of which recounted the Revolutionary War, yellow fever histories are antihistorical rather than historical in form, despite their titles which frequently begin with 'A History of Yellow Fever', clearly indicating that 'traumatic memories ... are not encoded like the ordinary memories of adults in a verbal, linear narrative'.[51] Without a tightly knit society which, for example, shared the religious and cultural foundations of Puritanism – leading to a unified conception of redemption – these narratives provided little or no documentation, did not attempt to evaluate evidence, made no effort to search for corroborating information, ignored public records and made few pretences of impartiality. Yet, these writers noted that they were participating in the documentation of social history out of a sense of duty to record events factually.

Dr Joseph Mackrill claimed in his 1796 *History of the Yellow Fever* that 'I am well aware, that a weak credulity on facts has injured every science, but none so materially as Medicine.' However, an anonymous reviewer found much to complain about, remarking that Mackrill 'resided in the West Indies' during Philadelphia's 1793 epidemic and, therefore, lacked the firsthand knowledge he claimed. Furthermore, the reviewer pointed out that 'notwithstanding [Mackrill] assures us that his work is "the fruit of his experience", that he must have derived what knowledge he may have acquired of this disease, through other channels than his own observation'. The importance of those channels struck the reviewer as insignificant, for he found that 'Dr Mackrill has not suggested one new or useful fact.'[52] The reviewer's complaint was not without foundation and it applies to many manuscripts which claimed historical veracity but ignored or distorted facts in order to promote a particular theory of the origin of yellow fever, something seen with the introduction of fictionalized Indian captivity narratives that began appearing in the 1790s. Dr Charles Caldwell, a lifelong local-origin supporter, berated those accounts decades later when writing his autobiography because of what he saw as the flawed historiography presented by the medical community: 'All their matter is derivative – the product of neither their own observation nor their own thought – the mere fruit, or rather excretion of their memory, which has imbibed it from books, or from some form of oral communication.'[53]

Apparently unaware of his own prejudices, Caldwell forgot his own oration to the Philadelphia Medical Society in 1807, when he exhorted physicians not only to write about the epidemics but also to wrest public health decisions from elected officials and public opinion:

> It is an enterprise worthy of ambition – worthy of your exertions – enterprise not confined in its effects to your own country, nor limited in its duration to present times; but enfolding in its wide embrace nations the most distant and extending to ages the most remote. It is an enterprise which will, in future times, be regarded as the first effectual blow aimed at that false idol [of superstition].[54]

Caldwell's plan for redemption of the world is evocative of the promotion of American exceptionalism, as well as the desire to participate consensually or historically in a new democracy. Such redemption reflected cultural attitudes which, in turn, drove the narrative structures of yellow fever chronicles. The end result of the expressive American exceptionalism clearly anticipated the redemption of the nation at large.

Redemption

Most Puritan narratives were clear on this point: redemption came through God's mercy and that redemption was both physical and spiritual. But for the urban captives of epidemics in the late eighteenth century, what constituted redemption? What were the sins? Redemption could be depicted in Herman's three stages of trauma recovery: 'safety', 'remembrance and mourning' and 'reconnection with ordinary life'.[55] But the citizens of Philadelphia, New York, and other cities found only temporary liberation in the annual changes in temperature, which were related to the ebb and flow of the epidemic. 'Remembrance' was marred by the anti-historical and 'reconnection' only functioned until the next humid summer. Redemption likewise became as much of an annual concern; the epidemics returned to the eastern seaboard like clockwork almost every August until the early 1820s. Some narratives claimed redemption came in the form of improved public health measures. Waterworks and hospitals were erected, quarantines and redesigned wharves improved public safety, citizens more willingly paid for street-cleaning and supported public institutions for the poor and orphaned.

But just as tied to the domestic or imported origination controversies of yellow fever was the question about where the sins of the captive – the whole nation – originated. Were they domestic or imported? If they were imported, would the measures taken to protect America from invasion put the country in more jeopardy, as witnessed by the blows to trade caused by quarantines or the blows to liberty generated by enacting Alien and Sedition Laws? If the sins arose domestically, would the physical efforts to clean up the cities be enough if the spiritual soul of republican experiment could not be redeemed because it had already been sold for profit? At least, Levi Hollingsworth might have thought the latter when he read the barely literate letter sent to him by Jeremiah Brown of New Brittain [sic] in the midst of Philadelphia's 1793 epidemic:

> Lately I am very Sorry to here of the Sickness In your City . . . I am afraid there is too much Truth in the Reports and think it must be a very alarming Time in the City not knowing whose turn may be next . . . Please to write me a Particular acct. of the Sickness & whether it Increased & also Respecting the flour Market.[56]

For Brown, the 'flour Market', or the economy, anteceded the epidemics, retaining privilege over calamity.

Conclusion

For almost thirty years, at the end of the eighteenth and the beginning of the nineteenth centuries, the new republic in North America struggled not only to understand itself as a separate nation but also to survive its infancy despite overwhelming obstacles. The political health of the country suffered dreadfully as frightening epidemics swept repeatedly through the country's major cities. In order to protect the nation's political survival, its inhabitants had to comprehend the mysterious yellow fever epidemics. Shrouded in mystery, these epidemics defied easy explanation, so writers searched for rhetorical strategies to express their trauma. Indian captivity narratives had championed survival during the colonial period and, therefore, this genre, if subsumed into the epidemic narratives, could help shape the survival of the new nation. Indian captivity narrative gave to a massive body of epidemic materials the organizational structures and rhetorical strategies needed to express the psychology of the new nation. Jeremiads verbalized the citizen's anxiety about the possibility of political failure and the exhortations of American exceptionalism kept the population firmly pointed towards a better future. Capture, captivity and redemption – the major themes of the Indian captivity narrative – mirrored, albeit imperfectly, the experiences of the urban captives of yellow fever. Using the familiar genre to explain the foreign ordeal of urban epidemics, the writers of yellow fever narratives have left us with a better understanding of their aspirations and their apprehensions during the dawn of their nationhood.

They should leave us as well with a firmer desire to explore the experience of captivity beyond the individual captive and the concrete occurrence of captivity. While the discourse of the individual captive enhances our scholarship, it also constrains our understanding of the simultaneous captivity experience of large numbers of people. Just as we see the difficulty of separating the individual's destiny from the city's or nation's destiny during yellow fever epidemics, we should furthermore pause when we leap to explain the effects of captivity on Native Americans when they were placed on reservations, or the deeper effects of the incarceration of so many young black men in the United States today. Additionally, we cannot afford to ignore the combined effects of repeated captivity on a group's psyche because survival becomes endemic, not epidemic.

Notes

1. Jutus Henry Christian Helmuth, *A Short Account of the Yellow Fever in Philadelphia for the Reflecting Christian* (Philadelphia, Jones, Hoff & Derrick, 1974), p. 6.

2. *Ibid.*, p. 1.

3. Samuel Brown, *A Treatise on the Nature, Origin and Progress of the Yellow Fever* (Boston, Manning and Loring, 1800), p. vi.

4. For background on the Indian captivity narrative, see especially the following works: Alden T. Vaughan and Edward W. Clark (eds), *Puritans among the Indians: Accounts of Captivity and Redemption, 1676–1724* (Cambridge, MA, Harvard University Press, 1981); Colin Calloway, *North Country Captives: Narratives of Indian Captivity from Vermont and New Hampshire* (Hanover, University Press of New England, 1992); Wilcomb E. Washburn, 'Introduction', in Alden T. Vaughan (ed.), *Narratives of North American Indian Captivity: A Selective Bibliography* (New York, Garland, 1983), pp. xi–liii; Richard VanDerBeets, *The Indian Captivity Narrative: An American Genre* (Lantham, MD, University Press of America, 1984); James Levernier, 'The captivity narrative as regional, military, and ethnic history', *Research Studies*, vol. 45 (1977): 30–7; and Kathryn Z. Derounian-Stodola and James A. Levernier, *The Indian Captivity Narrative, 1550–1900* (New York, Twayne, 1993).

5. Moses Bartram, Letter to Isaac Bartram, 3 October 1793, Miscellaneous Manuscript Collection, American Philosophical Society, Philadelphia, Pennsylvania.

6. The fictional accounts of yellow fever epidemics can be found especially in the novels of Charles Brockden Brown and in the poetry and satire of Philip Freneau. See, especially, Charles Brockden Brown, *Ormond; or, the Secret Witness* (New York, Hafner, 1937); Charles Brockden Brown, *Arthur Mervyn; or, Memoirs of the Year 1793* (New York, Holt, 1962); Philip Freneau, *The Poems of Philip Freneau: Poet of the American Revolution*, Fred Lewis Pattee (ed.), 3 vols (New York, Russell, 1963); Philip Freneau, *The Prose of Philip Freneau*, Philip Marshall (ed.) (New Brunswick, Scarecrow, 1955); and Philip Freneau, *Letters on Various and Interesting Subjects* (New York, Scholars' Facsimiles, 1943).

7. John de Peyster, Letter to Charles Willson Peale, 2 October 1793, Peale-Sellers Papers, American Philosophical Society, Philadelphia, Pennsylvania.

8. Anonymous, *An Account of the Rise, Progress, and Termination of the Malignant Fever, Lately Prevalent in Philadelphia. Briefly Stated from Authentic Documents* (Philadelphia, Benjamin Johnson, 1793), pp. 13, 17.

9. For background on the yellow fever epidemics, see especially Theodore E. Woodward, 'Yellow fever: from colonial Philadelphia and Baltimore to the mid-twentieth century', Zigerist Supplement to the *Bulletin of the History of Medicine* (1980); Richard H. Shryock, *The Yellow Fever Epidemics, 1793–1805* (New York, New York University Press, 1952); John Duffy, *Epidemics in Colonial America* (Baton Rouge, Louisiana State University Press, 1953); J. M. Powell, *Bring out Your Dead: The Great Plague of Yellow Fever in Philadelphia in 1793* (Philadelphia, University of Pennsylvania Press, 1949); and John Blake, 'Yellow fever in eighteenth century America', *Bulletin for the New York Academy of Medicine*, 2nd series, vol. 44 (1968): 673–86.

10. Calloway, *North Country Captives*, p. viii.

11. *Ibid.*, pp. vii, viii; VanDerBeets, *Indian Captivity*, p. 14; Vaughan and Clark, *Puritans*, pp. 4, 5.

12. Anonymous, *An Earnest Call Occasioned by the Alarming Pestilential Contagion, Addressed to the Inhabitants of Philadelphia* (Philadelphia, Jones, Hoff & Derrick, 1793), p. 7; Thomas Dunn, *Equality of Rich and Poor* (Philadelphia, Dobson, 1793), p. 12.

13. For background on the development and uses of the jeremiad in America, see especially Sacvan Bercovitch, *The American Jeremiad* (Madison, University of Wisconsin Press, 1978).

14. John Lathrop, *A Sermon Preached at the Church in Brattle-Street, Boston, Thursday, September 27, 1798* (Boston, T. & J. Swords, 1798), pp. 19, 22.

15. John Mitchell Mason, *A Sermon, Preached September 20th, 1793; A Day Set Apart, in the City of New-York, for the Public Fasting, Humiliation and Prayer, on Account of a Malignant and Mortal Fever Prevailing in the City of Philadelphia* (New York, Loudons, 1793), p. 15.

16. Anonymous, *An Account*, p. 4.

17. Vaughan and Clark, *Puritans*, p. 151.

18. Mathew Carey, *A Short Account of the Malignant Fever Lately Prevalent in Philadelphia* (Philadelphia, Mathew Carey, 1793), pp. 12, 13–15.

19. Benjamin Rush, *A Second Address to the Citizens of Philadelphia* (Philadelphia, printed by Budd and Bartram for Thomas Dobson, 1799), p. 40.

20. Richard Folwell, *Short History of the Yellow Fever That Lately Broke out in the City of Philadelphia in July 1797* (Philadelphia, Richard Folwell, 1799); Charles Caldwell, *A Semi-Annual Oration, on the Origin of Pestilential Diseases, Delivered before the Academy of Medicine of Philadelphia, on the 17th Day of December, 1798* (Philadelphia, Samuel Bradford, 1799), pp. 16, 20.

21. Benjamin Barton, Letters to Thomas Pennant, 26 March and 11 April 1794, Benjamin Barton Papers (1790–1794), American Philosophical Society, Philadelphia, Pennsylvania.

22. Ronnie Janoff-Bulman, *Shattered Assumptions: Towards a Psychology of Trauma* (New York, Free Press, 1992), pp. 101–2.

23. Barton, MSS, Benjamin Barton Papers, November 1793–February 1794, Medical Box, American Philosophical Society, Philadelphia, Pennsylvania.

24. Judith L. Herman, *Trauma and Recovery* (New York, HarperCollins, 1992), p. 2.

25. Janoff-Bulman, *Shattered Assumptions*, p. 134.

26. Herman, *Trauma*, p. 178.

27. Peter White (ed.), *Benjamin Tompson, Colonial Bard: A Critical Edition* (University Park, Pennsylvania State University Press, 1980), p. 93.

28. Samuel Miller, *A Sermon, Delivered February 5, 1799; Recommended by the Clergy of the City of New York . . . on Account of the Removal of a Malignant and Mortal Disease . . .* (New York, George Forman, 1799), pp. 9, 7.

29. Herman, *Trauma*, p. 55.

30. *Ibid.*, p. 2.

31. Calloway, *North Country Captives*, pp. viii, vii; VanDerBeets, *The Indian Captivity*, p. x; Vaughan and Clark, *Puritans*, p. 11.

32. John Edgar Wideman, 'Fever', in *Fever: Twelve Stories* (New York, Holt, 1989), p. 128.

33. Janoff-Bulman, *Shattered Assumptions*, p. 130.

34. See the Hollingsworth Family Collection at the Historical Society of Pennsylvania, Philadelphia, Pennsylvania. Levi Hollingsworth received 77 letters in September 1793, and 87 letters in October 1793.

35. Vaughan and Clark, *Puritans*, pp. 11, 10.

36. *Ibid.*, p. 12.

37. *Ibid.*

38. Accounts of the epidemics frequently sold well, especially if they included an appendix listing the dead. Mathew Carey's firm presents a good example of the economics of epidemic publishing for a company which had a distribution network in place.

He published four editions of his account of the 1793 epidemic before the end of 1794, when it was printed in French, German and Dutch. Eleven editions eventually reached press, and Carey acted as publisher for numerous epidemic narratives throughout the 1790s and early 1800s. By 1817, Carey's firm was the largest in America. See Earl L. Bradsher, *Mathew Carey: Editor, Author and Publisher; A Study in America's Literary Development* (New York, AMS, 1966), pp. 10, 14.

39. Herman, *Trauma*, pp. 177, 173.

40. *Ibid.*, pp. 178, 89.

41. Cathy Caruth, 'Traumatic departures: survival and history in Freud', in Charles B. Strozier and Michael Flynn (eds), *Trauma and Self* (Lantham, MD, Rowan and Littlefield, 1996), p. 34.

42. Lorrayne Carroll, '"My Outward Man": the curious case of Hannah Swarton', *Early American Literature*, vol. 31, no. 1 (1996): 45. See also Mary Rowlandson, *A True History of the Captivity and Restoration of Mrs. Rowlandson* (New York, Garland, 1977; first published 1682).

43. See review articles in the *Medical Repository* (New York), vol. 1, no. 1 – vol. 3 (1797), no. 4 (1800).

44. Carroll, 'Hannah Swarton', pp. 58, 45, 46, 47.

45. *Ibid.*, pp. 47, 59.

46. Tara Fitzpatrick, 'The figure of captivity: the cultural work of the Puritan captivity narrative', *American Literary History*, vol. 3 (1991): 2.

47. Carey, *Address of M. Carey to the Public* (Philadelphia, Mathew Carey, 1794), p. 4.

48. Benjamin Rush, *An Account of the Bilious Remitting Fever in Philadelphia . . .* (Philadelphia, Dobson, 1794); Noah Webster, *A Collection of Papers on the Subject of Bilious Fevers . . .* (New York, Hopkins, Webb and Co., 1796).

49. Robert Ferguson, '"We hold these truths": strategies of control in the literature of the Founders', in Sacvan Bercovitch (ed.), *Reconstructing American History* (Cambridge, MA, Harvard University Press, 1986), p. 2.

50. Stephen Carl Arch, *Authorizing the Past: The Rhetoric of History in Seventeenth-century New England* (Dekalb, Northern Illinois University Press, 1994), p. 24.

51. Herman, *Trauma*, p. 37.

52. Joseph Mackrill, *The History of the Yellow Fever . . .* (Baltimore, John Haynes, 1796); Anonymous, *Observations on Doctor Mackrill's History of the Yellow Fever* (Baltimore, John Haynes, 1796), pp. 2, 8, 12.

53. Charles Caldwell, *Autobiography of Charles Caldwell, M.D.*, preface, notes and appendix by Harriot W. Warner (Philadelphia, Lippincott, Grambo, 1855), p. 187.

54. Charles Caldwell, *An Anniversary Oration on the Subject of Quarantines, Delivered to the Philadelphia Medical Society, on the 21st of January, 1807* (Philadelphia, Fry and Kammerer, 1807), p. 5.

55. Herman, *Trauma*, p. 89.

56. Jeremiah Brown, Letter to Levi Hollingsworth, Philadelphia, September 9, 1793, Hollingsworth Family Collection, Historical Society of Pennsylvania, Philadelphia, Pennsylvania.

CHAPTER SEVEN

Transglobal translations:
the Eliza Fraser and Rachel Plummer
captivity narratives

KAY SCHAFFER AND D'ARCY RANDALL

Amazing synchronicities: three women's tales from the 1830s

The names of Eliza Fraser, Rachel Plummer and Cynthia Ann Parker resonate through the histories of Australia and North America and, specifically, Texas.[1] In May 1836, all three women were reputedly 'captured' by indigenous tribes – Eliza Fraser by the Badtjala people, Australian Aborigines of the Northeast coast; Rachel Plummer and Cynthia Ann Parker by the Comanches at Fort Parker, Texas – and all were eventually returned to white society. Fraser's and Plummer's tales of 'barbarous captivity' at the distant borders of civilization in the 1830s fed the popular imagination and fuelled formations of national and self-identity in their respective nations. In twentieth-century Australia, the Eliza Fraser saga became a national legend, re-emerging in the works of Patrick White, Sidney Nolan, Tim Burstall and David Williamson.[2] Similarly, Rachel Plummer and Cynthia Ann Parker haunt Texas legend and literature. Both novel and film versions of *The Searchers* (1954, 1956) and *Dances with Wolves* (1988, 1991) recall stories associated with both women, and the Parker legend continues to figure in regional histories, essays and novels.[3]

For women to attain such cultural status in nations dominated by myths of diggers and mates, cowboys and Indian warriors is unusual. Moreover, the clusters of stories around Eliza Fraser, Rachel Plummer and Cynthia Ann Parker display not only a startling synchronicity of life and timing but also of art and cultural production. At almost the same moment, on opposite ends of the globe, these women's lives suddenly changed; later, their experiences fed legends that met and merged. Eliza Fraser and Rachel Plummer returned with accounts of their experiences, accounts that were quickly transformed into the captivity narrative genre. Remarkably, narratives drawn from both the Texas and the Australian events were published in New York in 1837–8 as *American Indian* captivity narratives, with the Badtjala Aboriginal people transformed into teepee-housed, toga-clad and moccasined Indians and squaws with papooses. In addition, the popular publications of the tales share the same illustrations, narrative formula, rhetorical devices, tropes and imagery. Indeed, the Eliza Fraser narrative, published in New York in 1837, appears to have had a direct and striking influence on a version of the Plummer tale, published in New York the following year.

The textual translation of both the women's ordeals from event to tale and the transglobal 'conversation' between the Eliza Fraser and the Rachel Plummer captivity narratives are striking for how they enlarge the frame of reference for both the stories and for studies of the genre itself. Most scholarship on captivity narratives emerges from within the disciplines of American history, literature or cultural studies. That scholarship, whether attempting to recover historical data or to study the work of narrative, seldom acknowledges a number of aspects which our research has made evident. In particular, we would like to call attention to two areas neglected in both historical and literary studies: namely, the significance of regional variations of captivities within the expanding American nation and the transglobal influences in the transmission of the tales as they served various forms of colonial conquest.

Regional variations and transglobal effects

A New England focus, a critical attention to the coherence of captivities and their role in nation building are marked features of Richard Slotkin's highly influential study, *Regeneration through Violence*. Slotkin argues that the captivity narrative 'constitutes the first coherent myth-literature developed in America for American audiences'.[4] This claim set the parameters for a number of studies to come. Slotkin stresses its enormous popularity from the publication of Mary Rowlandson's narrative in 1682 until the late eighteenth century.[5] Although captivity narratives were published well into the nineteenth century, and variations continue today, Slotkin and other scholars tend to focus on the early, foundational examples from colonial America. Partly because their captivities occurred in Texas in 1836, a century after the genre passed its prime, the stories of Rachel Plummer and Cynthia Ann Parker were, until recently, treated as regional tales and located in the even more geographically specific fields of Texas and southwestern history, literature, myth and legend.[6] Over the past decade, research into captivity narratives has flourished,[7] and nineteenth-century narratives, including Rachel Plummer's, have been mentioned or discussed in several recent critical studies. Unfortunately, however, the complex publication history of the Plummer narratives and the importance of their regional inflections are seldom acknowledged.[8]

Meanwhile, the Eliza Fraser legend is known within a separate framework of Australian or British postcolonial studies. Kay Schaffer's *In the Wake of First Contact: The Eliza Fraser Stories* (1995/6), analyses the cultural effects of the Fraser legend. Drawing from a number of cultural, postcolonial and feminist theories, she presents the Eliza Fraser legend as a 'foundational fiction' for the British Empire and, later, the nation of Australia. Schaffer's discussion covers representations of Eliza Fraser in a range of media spanning 150 years: official reports, journalism, literature, drama, art and film, and includes indigenous Australian anticolonial responses to the legend. Her research comes primarily from Australia and other former British colonies. Nevertheless, *In the Wake*'s second chapter notes the Fraser story's curious, early transformation into an American captivity narrative. Schaffer suggests that despite the considerable differences between America and the Empire, 'the Eliza Fraser story functioned to extend patterns of Western colonial dominance in both contexts'.[9] As Schaffer traces the reach of the Fraser story from Australia to England and thence to America, she expands the traditional American perspective beyond the narrow, northeastern American focus by viewing the Fraser material in terms of an Anglo-American exchange. Since the publication of *In the Wake of First Contact*, several North American texts have taken up this theme. James Hartman (1999), for instance, locates sources for the early New England narratives in English providence tales, and other scholars trace English and Canadian influences on and borrowings from the 'American' genre.[10] Our research on the confluences between the Fraser and Plummer tales not only contributes to the extended, trans-Atlantic line of inquiry but also stretches it by presenting a Texas story's little-known Australian connection.

Women's agency

Our understanding of the complex publication histories of the Fraser and Plummer tales also challenges another recent tendency in captivity narrative criticism regarding assumptions about woman's agency. From Nancy Armstrong's ground-breaking feminist historical perspective onward, a number of critical studies have argued that the American captivity genre gives evidence of women's agency through their writing/authorship and by demonstrating their active participation in the public sphere.[11] We are wary of this trend. Arguments for women's agency in captivity narratives too often assume what may be a highly dubious and contested form of historic agency. Typically, they rely on the existence of a 'real' woman behind the 'authoritative' or 'authentic' first-person account, who relates her experiences and exerts considerable authorial control over her published story.[12] Our research into the various versions of the Fraser and Plummer narratives reveals marked differences between early and later accounts of their ordeals, raising questions about how the publication of popular captivity narratives occurred. Furthermore, our inspection into the originating events and the contexts of the narratives' publication opens up further gaps and contradictions between what might be known historically about these women's experiences and the events that are disclosed in the narratives and ascribed to the women. It is clear that, in the case of both the Fraser and Plummer stories, the captivity narratives went through a series of transformations. Some were tailored to address specific local demands, like reports to the police and local authorities, others were fashioned for local newspaper consumption, and still others for broader, popular readership markets in Texas, Australia and, soon thereafter, a transglobal readership. Clearly the later, more popular and lurid tales show little regard for historic accuracy or evidence of what the real women might have experienced, thought or felt.[13]

Because the voluminous captivity narrative scholarship and criticism over the past decade has resulted in an abundance of strategies for approaching these texts, we first offer an overview of how our work builds from or relates to the foundation works in the field. Then, to demonstrate the expanded frame of reference for both stories, we detail the specific publication histories of the early Eliza Fraser accounts and the Rachel Plummer narratives of 1838 and 1844. Finally, we consider the conversational exchange between these published New York tales as they were transformed into sensational captivity narratives and marketed to a transglobal, white, colonial readership.

Captivity narratives

Our research joins a spate of recent, and abundant, captivity narrative scholarship which challenges, expands and complicates earlier paradigms posed by Richard Slotkin and others (like Roy Harvey Pearce, Leslie Fiedler and Richard VanDerBeets), whose scholarship presaged his land-mark text. The history of the genre developed by these earlier critics, however, remains pertinent to our current discussion. Pearce, for example, reads captivity narrative as belonging to a family of 'genres' whose 'significances' varied over time.[14] According to Pearce, the captivity nar-rative began with early 'simple, direct religious documents' that described the captive experience with convincing 'immediacy'. Later, the genre modified into an instrument of anti-Indian propaganda, featuring violent 'savages'. Later still, as 'Indian wars' in the northeast receded into memory, captivity narratives became increasingly stylized, melodramatic and sensational. Under the influence of the nineteenth-century 'novel of sensibility', the violent 'savages' were sometimes poignantly ennobled as the last survivors of a dying race, but the brutal violent types held on in the vast scurrilous wash of sensational texts that flooded the American (and English) markets in the 1830s.

Meanwhile, as warfare between whites and Native Americans continued on the western and southwestern frontiers, new captivities took place, resulting in the appearance of new captivity narratives. But Pearce argues that even historically verified events (like the Fort Parker raid) were distorted into obviously fake accounts. Commenting on forty narratives published between 1813 and 1873, he remarks that although they may have originated in 'real enough experiences, [they] have been worked up into something terrible and strange. Their language is most often that of the hack writer gone wild.'[15] Richard VanDerBeets also addresses the melo-dramatic flourishes of these derivative tales and concludes that, because of them, few readers would have believed the historical accuracy of the stories.[16] Pearce notes, with some astonishment, that the pulp thriller narratives, like those of Rachel Plummer and Eliza Fraser which we discuss here, were eventually included in serious ethnographic anthologies.[17]

In the last twenty or so years, several critics have taken Pearce to task on a number of fronts. June Namias, for example, critiques Pearce for underestimating the importance of the 'sentimental' appeal displayed in the nineteenth-century narratives.[18] The 'frail flower' heroine that Namias recognizes in these late texts was a common trope in the nineteenth century, contributing to 'highly saleable' captivity narratives.[19] Gary Eber-sole insists on a recognition of the difference between nineteenth- and twentieth-century reading practices, pointing out that Pearce's aesthetic preference for the early colonial narratives unfairly positions the later nineteenth-century versions as 'corrupt'.[20] Others, like Lucy Maddox, Susan Scheckel and Rebecca Blevins Faery, address the narratives as fictions, connecting them with early nineteenth-century anxieties over the new American national identity. These anxieties were addressed – and cultivated – by literature, which defined the mythical, white American by constructing and valorizing exaggerated distinctions of class, gender and race.[21] Our own, early twenty-first century, postcolonial reading views the late Fraser and Plummer narratives as cultural artefacts that helped to produce, rather than reflect, asymmetrical hierarchies of gender, race and class. The amendments and changes to these texts to suit various markets also interpolate readers in specific ways, constructing subjectivities and shaping national and regional affiliations. Clearly, then, there are other approaches to these texts than writing them off as a debased genre.

The identity of the white American (or colonial) hero emerges out of discourses and texts which construct categories of sameness with reference to difference or Otherness. In the captivity narrative, for example, a number of binary oppositions structure the tales. They set white against dark-skinned peoples, civilization against wilderness, Christian against savage, Catholic against Protestant and masculine against feminine. The white man is positioned against his various physical and symbolic Others. Robert Berkhofer's study, *The White Man's Indian*, was one of the first to provide a structuralist account of these Self–Other relations. Although it does not trouble to deconstruct the asymmetrical nature of the hierarchies, it nonetheless demonstrates how the captivity narrative as a genre stereo-types Indians into 'good' or 'bad' types in a way that is remarkably consistent with the stereotypes that attend the Plummer and Fraser tales. The bad Indian engages in cruelty to captives, brutal warfare, superstition and passion. The good Indian exists in primitive harmony with nature. Honest and loyal to the white man, he furthers white destiny.[22] The bad Indian becomes the negative image of the white man through which white civilization formulates a stable identity, here in the conquest of good over evil. Berkhofer's approach sets up rigid and static binary oppositions between the national self and its others. His analysis is complicated by postcolonial, deconstructive and feminist critiques of the race and gender asymmetries which attend these stereotypes and by how these differences are mediated through the figure of the white woman. His delineation of 'bad' Indian traits, however, can be traced through the Fraser and Plummer narratives published in New York. Not only are these attributes heralded by the textual tropes of racial difference but also by the graphic illustrations which accompanied the narratives.

Numerous critics read the white woman captive figuratively as a symbol for the land, the 'territory' under dispute. Annette Kolodny shows how, before the advent of the captivity narrative genre, the European male imaginary had constructed the New World wilderness as an unspoiled female body. Captain John Smith wrote of 'her treasures hauing yet neuer beene opened, nor her originalls wasted, consumed, nor abused'.[23] Kolodny explains, 'The American husbandman was cast as both son and lover in a primal paradise where the maternal and the erotic were harmoniously intermingled.'[24] Real English and European women had no part in creating this 'metaphorical landscape'; hence, they were 'captive, as it were, in the garden of someone else's imagination'.[25] If these women were – literally – taken captive by Indians and returned to white communities to tell the tale, their attempts to relate their experiences were challenged by, and confused with, the compelling, symbolic significance of their captive body. In a deconstructive manner much like Schaffer's, Rebecca Blevins Faery writes that the woman in captivity narratives was 'a mediating space between emergent races and cultures in conflict, a terrain for which and on which the ideological struggle between the two cultures took place'.[26] Faery concerns herself primarily with the Mary Rowlandson narrative, but her statement applies particularly well to the later New York variations of the Eliza Fraser and Rachel Plummer narratives, in which the symbolic role of the woman captive overrides other considerations.

As Hartman demonstrates, captivity narratives arose within the context of cultural exchange between the colonies and England right from the start. Mary Rowlandson's narrative borrows the trope of the seventeenth-century English providence tale and adapts it to a frontier context. The Rowlandson narrative was then reprinted in England, where it found a different market, a different negotiation of 'English' and 'colonial' identities in the trans-Atlantic exchange.[27] The migrations of the Eliza Fraser tale in the 1830s trace a similar but ultimately far more complex conversation. As the Fraser account shifted from the Australian to the English markets, certain features of her shipwreck ordeal in the antipodes were elaborated in keeping with the public taste for melodrama and sentimentality. The popularized Fraser story was then well positioned to make its way to New York and throughout the English colonial world.

Eliza Fraser

On 22 May 1836, the merchant ship *Stirling Castle* was returning to Liverpool from Van Dieman's Land (Tasmania) when it was wrecked approximately 800 kilometres off the coast of what is now Queensland.[28] The survivors of the wreck included crew members, the Scottish Captain James Fraser and his wife Eliza, who may have been pregnant at the time. (The couple had three other children, who had remained behind in Scotland.) They crowded into two lifeboats and spent the following six weeks battling rough weather and stormy, shark-infested seas. Although all members of the party were debilitated by exhaustion, hunger, thirst and illness, Captain Fraser refused to pull ashore because he feared the company would be attacked by cannibals. It is said that Eliza Fraser gave birth during the ordeal but the infant died, drowning in the waist-high water of the lifeboat. Finally, after one team mutinied and sailed south and the remaining crew threatened to 'draw lots', the Captain agreed to land on the coast of what is now known as Fraser Island.

> A party of Aborigines came across the exhausted party on the beach and took them to the southern part of the island, where they were distributed among several family groups. Eliza Fraser was taken in by the Badtjala people, who separated her from her husband and put her to work with the other native women. She was given a sick child to care for and was assigned demanding and unfamiliar tasks, like being prodded by firesticks to climb trees in order to gather honey from honey ant's nests. When, after three weeks, she saw Captain Fraser again, he was emaciated and weak. He was subsequently speared in the back of the shoulder by the natives, presumably for his intransigence to native demands, and died of the wound. Other crew members suffered privations; one was possibly tortured and another reputedly burned at the stake.[29] Finally, in August of that year, Eliza Fraser and the second mate, John Baxter, were rescued by John Graham, a convict from the Moreton Bay penal colony who, hoping for a pardon, had volunteered to lead a search party. Graham bartered with the Aborigines, with whom he had lived previously for seven years, arguing that Eliza Fraser was the trumped up ghost of his dead (native) wife. He delivered Fraser and Baxter to the Lieutenant in command, and they sailed back to the Moreton Bay settlement on a ship crewed by convicts. Historians speculate, on the basis of other evidence surrounding the event, that Eliza Fraser may have been raped by another absconding convict during the time of her rescue. For innumerable reasons, she is reported to have returned to 'civilization' mentally and physically debilitated.[30]

Our version of Eliza Fraser's ordeal has been pieced together from many conflicting and contradictory accounts. Among these accounts,

Aboriginal perspectives are conspicuous by their absence, although Schaffer speculates it is likely that the Badtjala people considered themselves the hosts of Eliza Fraser, not her captors, and that their behaviours, which were reinterpreted as 'torture' by the white survivors, may have been in keeping with indigenous practices designed to educate and heal the survivors and inculcate them into the group. During this period, when other shipwreck victims or escaped convicts, including some members of the *Stirling Castle* crew, encountered indigenous Fraser Islanders they later reported to the English authorities that they were treated with 'uniform kindness'.[31] As for Eliza Fraser's own story, Schaffer reports that she offered at least three versions, 'each one becoming more and more exaggerated, more and more sensational, as it reached a wider, less discriminating, and more eager public'.[32]

Rachel Plummer

Three days before the shipwreck of the *Stirling Castle*, on 19 May 1836, a group of Caddo, Comanche and Kiowa warriors raided Parker's Fort, Texas, taking with them several captives, including Rachel Plummer and nine-year-old Cynthia Ann Parker.[33] The fort itself had been established shortly after the founding of the Republic of Texas, an event that emboldened Anglo-American settlers like the extended Parker family to move onto the contested frontier of east and central Texas. Apparently, on that warm May morning, the Parkers felt secure enough to leave open the gates of the Fort. The warriors destroyed houses, crops and livestock. Several settlers managed to escape, including Rachel Plummer's father, the Rev. James W. Parker, and her husband, L. T. M. Plummer. Those unable to flee were killed and scalped, or taken prisoner. In addition to Rachel Plummer and Cynthia Ann Parker, the other captives included Rachel Plummer's son James Pratt, Cynthia Ann Parker's brother, John Parker and Elizabeth Kellogg.

American captivity narratives (and many accounts of the Parker's Fort raid) never offer a reason for the attack, thereby inviting the reader to assume it was unprovoked. However, the raid on Parker's Fort could well have been prompted by the behaviour of a band of Texas Rangers, which included James W. Parker and was led by his brother Silas. Margaret Hacker, in her historical biography of Cynthia Ann Parker, speculates that 'Silas and his Rangers attacked any Indian they met, so it is likely they provoked hostility among peaceful bands in the area.'[34] Unlike the Badtjala people whom Eliza Fraser encountered, the Comanches had in the 1830s a long-established custom of taking captives: they ransomed most captives for economic reasons but they adopted others, usually children, to sustain their numbers.[35]

Within six years all captives would be returned to white society, with the exception of Cynthia Ann Parker who was adopted by the Comanches.

From the white point of view, Cynthia Ann Parker's famous 'captivity' lasted twenty-four years. Rachel Plummer's captivity lasted a terrifying thirteen months. She was finally sold to traders in June 1837 then returned to her husband and family eight months later, in February 1838. She died exactly a year after her return. *Rachael Plummer's Narrative of Twenty-One Months Servitude as a Prisoner Among the Commanchee Indians* (1838) was the first captivity narrative to be published in Texas. In his introduction to a reprinted edition, William S. Reese relates the interesting bibliographical history of the text.[36] For years *Rachael Plummer's Narrative* was a lost text, one of the publications long sought by bibliographers of Western Americana. Until a copy of the first 1838 edition was found by a Houston book dealer in 1975, Plummer's story was known only through the later, embellished, enlarged edition and its multiple derivatives.

Sensational transformations: Eliza Fraser and Rachel Plummer meet in New York

For the American audience, the story of the *Stirling Castle* shipwreck was transformed into a North American literary and cultural context. Eliza appears at the mercy not of Australian Aborigines but North American 'Indians' wielding 'tomahawks', and 'squaws' tending 'papooses'. The *Narrative of the Capture, Sufferings, and Miraculous Escape of Mrs. Eliza Fraser*, published in New York by Charles Webb and Sons in 1837, translates the story into an American captivity narrative.[37] This American version of the story, however, goes further than swapping ethnic vocabularies. *Narrative of the Capture . . .* follows the formula of the captivity narrative, tracing a tale of capture, suffering and deliverance, but the melodramatic language and style identify it with a later era of narratives which Pearce identifies as 'pulp thrillers'.

The narrative opens with the shipwreck and the survivors' first night on the island. Eliza awakes to find 'a band of frightful looking savages, approaching us, apparently with the ferocity of wild beasts; all armed with knives or dirks, and long spears' (p. 7). She is separated from her husband, beaten mercilessly by the squaws and children of the tribe and forced to live in a 'hovel' filled with 'vermin'.

One of the most significant textual features of an English account, which was carried over into the American captivity narrative version, is the death scene of Captain Fraser. After Eliza had been separated from her husband for three weeks, enslaved and beaten by jealous 'squaws', she is at last allowed a conversation with her husband, who is by now 'a sad and melancholy spectacle' of a man:

> The final separation was now about to take place! his strength having in the course of the night so far failed as to render him unable longer to obey the commands of his savage task masters, who, to revenge themselves had most

inhumanly stabbed him with their knives – a spear was thrust into his body in my presence, which caused me in a fit of despair to explain (as I seized and pulled the spear out of his body) 'Jesus of Nazareth, I can endure this no longer!' – he retained his senses until a few moments before he expired. The last words he uttered were, 'Eliza, I am gone!' (p. 15)

Although the (historical) Captain Fraser perished during his ordeal on the island, he died not by murder but of spear wounds, compounded by his already weakened condition. According to Eliza Fraser's testimony at the Mayoral Inquiry into her case, it was never the intention of the natives to kill him. Yet the 'murder' of Captain Fraser has achieved the status of fact in countless authoritative accounts of the story.[38] This passage also contains the narrative's only instance of dialogue, which highlights the status of Captain Fraser, Eliza's male protector. Eliza, the hapless heroine, in a panic over losing her earthly lord and master, turns to her spiritual one. She cries out: 'Jesus of Nazareth, I can endure this no longer!' The Captain responds with his dying breath, 'Eliza, I am gone!' These two exhortations draw dramatic attention to the symbolic significance of the demise of Captain Fraser and the vulnerability of his widow, while also adding 'authenticity' to the account in the mind of the reader.

The 'murder of Captain Fraser' presages a moral crisis in the text, one represented by the heroine's sexual vulnerability. Eliza is asked to submit sexually to one of the 'most ugly and frightful looking Indians that my eyes ever beheld': 'I must (he represented to me) either voluntarily become his "mate", or become so by compulsion!' (p. 17). After a 'good Indian' intervenes and is killed in the process, Eliza is finally rescued 'not from the devouring jaws of a ravenous lion, but from the hands of a savage ruffian, far more to be dreaded!' (p. 18).

An appendix to the story adds the detail that Mrs Fraser's 'modesty' has caused her to neglect another detail: that she had given birth in the lifeboat, 'up to her waist in water' to a child who drowned 'after a few gasps'. The narrative ends with an appeal to the power of 'Divine Providence', a typical trope of the captivity narrative genre.

Two woodcut illustrations introduce the New York version of the tale. The first foregrounds the death of Captain Fraser under the shade of a North American oak, accompanied in the background by three groups of Indians carrying bows and arrows and dressed in moccasins, feathered head-dresses and loincloths. The 'savages' enact the traits of Berkhofer's 'bad Indians': they are unfeeling, murderous, cruel and lustful. One group observes the scene with stoic indifference; another pair threatens each other with knives and tomahawk; the third group burns a struggling white captive at the stake (Figure 7.1). The second illustration portrays the hapless Mrs. Fraser in the hands of a rapacious Indian. It carries the caption: 'An Indian Chief in the act of forcibly conveying Mrs. Fraser to his hut or wigwam' (Figure 7.2).

Figure 7.1 The frontispiece of *Narrative of the Capture, Sufferings, and Miraculous Escape of Mrs. Eliza Fraser.* Illustration by courtesy of the Everett D. Graff Collection, Newberry Library, Chicago

Figure 7.2 'An Indian Chief in the act of forcibly conveying Mrs. Fraser to his hut or wigwam', the title page of *Narrative of the Capture, Sufferings, and Miraculous Escape of Mrs. Eliza Fraser.*
Illustration by courtesy of the Everett D. Graff Collection, Newberry Library, Chicago

The efforts of the New York publisher to fit an Australian first-contact story into an American captivity narrative illustrates the imposing force of the genre, and of the appetite for these stories within American popular culture. In her book, Kay Schaffer studies the Eliza Fraser narrative in relation to the North American formula, making some important distinctions:

The shipwreck of the *Stirling Castle* and the fate of its crew is not a captivity in the classic American sense – no one was captured nor coerced to live against their will. The white party fell upon the island after floundering at sea for nearly [six] weeks. Upon arrival they were met by the island's native inhabitants who faced the dilemma of how to deal with the ghostly strangers. The members of the party were separated and passed from one group of natives to another as they made their way south on the island and then across to the mainland. There is no evidence of 'capture' or coercion until the point of rescue which occurred just before a corroboree in which Mrs. Fraser was dressed for display before a gathering of clans. At that time, but only at that time, she had been placed under guard, necessitating careful negotiation for her release. The event itself occurred in a liminal environment without plot or structure, where meanings were indeterminate. The captivity narrative genre gives the tale a structure and purpose, placing it in a field of previously determined meanings. It translates the diffuse nature of a woman's experience into a coherent colonial myth, justifying the white settler's presence in a new land.[39]

This last function of the sensational captivity narrative also gave purpose and coherence to Rachel Plummer's experiences.

In 1838, the year after the *Narrative of ... Eliza Fraser* was published, another ephemeral New York publisher, Perry and Cooke, produced a sensationalized, melodramatic version of Rachel Plummer's story in the form of a captivity narrative which would overshadow the Texas original. In fact, Perry and Cooke published at least two sensationalized captivity narratives drawing from this story. The first, *History of the Captivity and Providential Release Therefrom of Mrs. Caroline Harris*, contains within it the main elements of the second, separately published text, *The Narrative of the Captivity of Mrs.* [not Rachel but] *Clarissa Plummer*.[40] These publications borrowed Plummer's name and details of her and others' captivities – like the motif of the lost children – but wove them into different, racier stories.[41] The hallmarks of these new narratives are sex and savagery, much like the Eliza Fraser narrative published the previous year. In fact, the confluence of all three texts is striking. If the American captivity narrative genre directed the production of the Eliza Fraser story, the (compromised) Australian story appears to have influenced the popular Texas tale.

Both texts, however, introduce a familiar, significant deviation from Rachel Plummer's first published account. Although Rachel Plummer's husband had escaped from the raid at Parker's Fort, in these narratives both husbands are killed trying to rescue their wives. Again, for the pulp-thriller writers, killing off the husbands frees the way for each story's lurid climax. The Caroline Harris text explains how she was 'not only compelled to cohabit, but to yield to the beastly will of a Savage brute!': 'If I ever felt a willingness, nay, an anxious desire, to be called hence to the world of spirits, it was at that moment!'[42] In Clarissa Plummer's narrative, her husband's death leads to a lengthy discussion of her 'mock marriage' to the 'savage ruffian to whose will I had been obliged to yield without a murmur' (p. 13). Finally, a fur trader frees both women from the 'yoke of bondage'. For Clarissa Plummer and Caroline Harris, as well as for Eliza Fraser, the death of the husband sets up the crisis in the narrative which brings about the heroine's 'fate worse than death', a fate that then provides the context for her rescue. In the symbolic realm of the captivity narrative, her rescue carries a mythic dimension for the white man.

The illustrations that accompany the Caroline Harris narrative (Figure 7.3) emphasize the story's lascivious dimension. They will look familiar.

Figure 7.3 The frontispiece of *History of the Captivity and Providential Release Therefrom of Mrs. Caroline Harris.* Illustration by courtesy of the Everett D. Graff Collection, Newberry Library, Chicago

Caroline's husband lies dying, speared by 'savages', while in an adjoining illustration, the chief pulls Caroline into his hut. The frontispiece description of the tale tells readers:

> It was the misfortune of Mrs. *Harris*, and her unfortunate female companion (soon after the deaths of their husbands), to be separated by, and compelled to become the companions of, and to cohabit with, two disgusting Indian Chiefs, and from whom they received the most cruel and beastly treatment.

They are, indeed, the very Indians that appeared the previous year in the Eliza Fraser narrative. To the New York publishers, Eliza Fraser and Rachel Plummer were interchangeable figures, as were the Comanches and indigenous Australians.

The sexual interface of the frontier

What accounts for this market for sex and savagery, that drew from such distant corners of the Anglo-American colonial world? Popular 1830s entertainment like the 1838 Eliza Fraser, Clarissa Plummer and Caroline Harris narratives ply their white, nineteenth-century audiences with fears and fantasies of cross-racial sexual relations. The stylistic excesses of these pulp thrillers would have distracted from their more serious appeal to white readers, who typically feared (or assumed) women captured by Indians to have been sexually violated. These fantasies turn the woman's body into an object, a spectacle; they also define the indigenous body, not only as savage but also as lecherous, for the purposes of glorifying Empire and nation. The thinly disguised rape rhetoric keeps in circulation a sexualized threat to American or European manhood inherent in the idea of a white woman and an 'Indian' man engaging in *any* sort of sexual relationship, consensual or not. The tragic 'rescue' of the fully assimilated Comanche Cynthia Ann Parker in 1860 demonstrates the degree to which this myth was internalized by nineteenth-century Americans.[43]

This heightened nineteenth-century Anglo-American interest in the sexual interface of the frontier encounter would seem to mask a number of anxieties and ambivalences for white Englishmen and Americans about racial identities. During the 1830s the English were freeing slaves at home while still contributing to ethnic genocide in distant colonies like Australia. In the northeastern USA, white Americans were becoming increasingly attached to the idea of the 'noble savage' but at the same time, on the frontiers, the attacks on 'savage brutes' would continue for decades. Such ambivalences touched close to home in the 1830s when, after many years of debate, the Jacksonian administration's Indian Removal policies were implemented and Native American tribes remaining in the eastern states were forced westward, even though many of these tribes had been assimilated into white society and shared familial ties with whites. Perhaps in an effort to justify these policies, and to remind urban Americans that 'Indian wars' continued on the southwestern frontiers, the pulp thrillers displaced the central issues of brutality and violence by white settlers towards indigenous peoples – the brutality and violence that made colonization possible.

Conclusion

The stories behind the Fraser and Plummer tales offer a case study in how two vastly different events were transformed into accounts that first addressed specific local markets but were soon tailored to suit a trans-national colonial readership. These tales have been taken up differently by historians and literary and cultural critics since the time of their publication. For historians, when read in isolation outside the network of their textual families, some versions of the Fraser and Plummer narratives have been assumed to relate true events from women's lives on the frontiers. However, a close inspection of their publication histories, like the one we have undertaken here, raises questions about the authenticity of many of these accounts and narratives and the purposes of their publication. For the literary and cultural critic, the tales clearly have moral, ideological and cultural intentions and effects. The construction and transmission of the stories produced and maintained conditions necessary for the advance of nation and empire. The 'conversation' between the Fraser and the Plummer/Harris stories in New York shows how, despite considerable geographic and historical differences between England and America, the two countries shared common cultural desires that manifest themselves through popular culture in the trans-Atlantic assertion of white, male national identities. The Americans may have been labouring to distinguish themselves from the English parent culture of the past, but the trans-Atlantic exchange of popular colonial tales tells another story.

Although the genre functioned differently when placed within the various contexts of colony, nation and empire, its popularity, malleable adaptations, and the ideologies of racial superiority which it maintained, sustained varied colonial, imperial and national enterprises. Its transformations over time, and the receptivity of new audiences to its popular and ethnographic appeal, demonstrate the impossibility of dividing colonial discourse from the evolution of Western relations of power and dominance or frontier histories from an analysis of their representations. The frameworks for understanding the importance of the genre may have altered over time, but the beliefs and imaginings it produced in America, Britain and Australia helped to constitute hierarchies of power and their regulation through constructions of race, class and gender which, although widely contested, continue to have their effects today.

Notes

1. This chapter extends the discussion of the histories, myths and legends concerning Eliza Fraser which were analysed in depth in Kay Schaffer, *In the Wake of First Contact: The Eliza Fraser Stories* (Melbourne, Cambridge University Press, 1995/6). Here we compare Eliza Fraser's story with extant tales from Texas during the same period.

2. Patrick White, *A Fringe of Leaves* (Harmondsworth, Penguin, 1976); Sidney Nolan, 'Mrs Fraser' (painting series, 1947–77); Tim Burstall (director) and David Williamson (screenplay), *A Faithful Narrative of the Capture, Sufferings, and Miraculous Escape of Eliza Fraser* (Sydney, Hexagon Films, 1976), cited in Schaffer, *In the Wake*, p. 1.

3. Some examples include James T. DeShields, *Cynthia Ann Parker: The Story of Her Capture* (New York, Garland, 1976, originally published in St Louis, printed for the author, 1886); T. R. Fehrenbach, *Lone Star* (New York, Wings, 1968), pp. 449–51, 543–51; Margaret Schmidt Hacker, *Cynthia Ann Parker: The Life and the Legend* (Southwestern Studies, no. 9) (El Paso, TX, Texas Western Press, 1990); Steve Harrigan, 'Comanche midnight', in *Comanche Midnight* (Austin, University of Texas Press, 1995); Lucia St Clair Robson, *Ride the Wind: The Story of Cynthia Ann Parker and the Last Days of the Comanche* (New York, Ballantine, 1982).

4. Richard Slotkin, *Regeneration through Violence: Mythology of the American Frontier, 1600–1860* (Middletown, CT, Wesleyan University Press, 1973), pp. 94–5.

5. Slotkin writes that captivity narratives would 'completely dominate the list of frontier narratives published in America between 1680 and 1716', *Regeneration through Violence*, p. 95.

6. Fehrenbach, *Lone Star*, Hacker, *Cynthia Ann Parker*, and Harrigan, 'Comanche midnight', give twentieth-century accounts, although the Plummer and Parker stories are best known from DeShields, *Cynthia Ann Parker*.

7. Scholarship published over the last decade includes Michelle Burnham, *Captivity and Sentiment: Cultural Exchange in American Literature, 1682–1861* (Hanover, University Press of New England, 1997); Sarah Carter, *Capturing Women: The Manipulation of Cultural Imagery in Canada's Prairie West* (Montreal, McGill–Queen's University Press, 1997); Christopher Castiglia, *Bound and Determined: Captivity, Culture-Crossing and White Womanhood from Mary Rowlandson to Patty Hearst* (Chicago, University of Chicago Press, 1996); Kathryn Z. Derounian-Stodola and James A. Levernier, *The Indian Captivity Narrative, 1550–1900* (New York, Twayne, 1993); Gary Ebersole, *Captured by Texts: Puritan to Postmodern Images of Indian Captivity* (Charlottesville, University Press of Virginia, 1995); Rebecca Blevins Faery, *Cartographies of Desire: Captivity, Race and Sex in the Shaping of an American Nation* (Norman, University of Oklahoma Press, 1999); James D. Hartman, *Providence Tales and the Birth of American Literature* (Baltimore, Johns Hopkins University Press, 1999); Lucy Maddox, *Removals: Nineteenth-Century American Literature and the Politics of Indian Affairs* (New York, Oxford University Press, 1991); June Namias, *White Captives: Gender and Ethnicity on the American Frontier* (Chapel Hill, University of North Carolina Press, 1993); Kay Schaffer, *In the Wake of First Contact: The Eliza Fraser Stories*; Susan Scheckel, *The Insistence of the Indian: Race and Nationalism in Nineteenth-Century American Culture* (Princeton, Princeton University Press, 1998); Pauline Turner Strong, *Captive Slaves, Captivating Others: The Politics and Poetics of Colonial American Captivity Narratives* (Boulder, CO: Westview Press, 1999); Richard VanDerBeets (ed.), *Held Captive by Indians: Selected Narratives, 1642–1836*, 2nd edition (Knoxville, University of Tennessee Press, 1994).

8. Faery is an important exception to this general trend. Towards the end of her *Cartographies of Desire* she brings in an informed discussion of the Parker and Plummer stories. See pp. 189, 196–7.

9. See Schaffer, *In the Wake of First Contact*, p. 59. In her discussion of American captivity narratives, Schaffer notes the illustrative and stylistic overlap between the Fraser and the Caroline Harris narrative discussed below. She does not, however, develop the comparison between the Fraser and the extensive Parker/Plummer stories. See especially pp. 29–65.

10. See Sarah Carter, *Capturing Women*, which studies popular representations of race and gender in Canadian captivity narratives. See also Richard Joseph Snader's dissertation, 'Caught between worlds: British captivity narratives in fact and fiction', PhD thesis (University of Maryland, 1998), which also expands the framework of captivity narrative scholarship from the American-centred model and reads the captivity narrative in a more transglobal, Anglophone tradition.

11. See the debates about the significance of the captivity narrative in expressing women's agency in Nancy Armstrong, *Desire and Domestic Fiction: A Political History of the Novel* (New York, Oxford University Press, 1987); Jane Tompkins, *Sensational Designs: The Cultural Work of American Fiction 1790–1860* (New York, Oxford University Press, 1985); Pat Gill, 'The conduct of ideology: musings on the origin of the bourgeois self', *Genre: Forms of Discourse and Culture*, vol. 25, no. 4 (1993): 461–78; Christopher Castiglia, *Bound and Determined*; Michelle Burnham, *Captivity and Sentiment*.

12. This is particularly apparent in the first chapter of Castiglia's study, although his frequent parenthetical reference to male editors bely the instability of this assumption of authorial authenticity or agency. See pp. 39ff.

13. The word 'agency' carries different meanings in different disciplinary contexts. Schaffer's *In the Wake*, for example, distinguishes between historical agency and textual agency, in which the narrator's authority is produced by the text itself. We will be addressing this issue more extensively in forthcoming publications.

14. Roy Harvey Pearce, 'The significance of the captivity narrative', *American Literature*, vol. 19 (1948): 1–2.

15. *Ibid.*, p. 16.

16. See Richard VanDerBeets, 'A surfeit of style: the Indian Captivity Narrative as penny dreadful', *Research Studies*, vol. 39, no. 4 (1971): 303.

17. Pearce, 'Significance', p. 17.

18. Namias, *White Captives*, p. 36.

19. *Ibid.*, p. 37. Namias organizes the heroines of the American captivity narrative into three general types: Survivor, Amazon, and the Frail Flower of the nineteenth-century narratives.

20. Ebersole, *Captured by Texts*, p. 100. Ebersole argues that for nineteenth-century readers, this literature 'functioned didactically, conveying a moral message to readers and helping them to evaluate their lives' (p. 109).

21. June Namias's *White Captives* attends to the gender and racial constructions of the narratives. Lucy Maddox, *Removals*, Susan Scheckel, *The Insistence of the Indian*, and Rebecca Blevins Faery, *Cartographies of Desire*, contextualize some of the nineteenth-century narratives with the increasing debates over Indian removal in the 1820s, and the controversial enactment of removal policies during the 1830s. Such scholarship overlaps, to some degree, with the increasingly serious attention given to nineteenth-century 'popular fiction' by literary critics. See, for example, David S. Reynolds, *Beneath the American Renaissance: The Subversive Imagination in the Age of Emerson and Melville* (New York, Knopf, 1988).

22. Robert Berkhofer, *The White Man's Indian: Images of the American Indian from Columbus to the Present* (New York, Knopf, 1978), pp. 28–30. For an extended discussion of the permutations of these stereotypes over several white settler cultures see Terry Goldie, *Fear and Temptation: The Image of the Indigene in Canadian, Australian and New Zealand Literature* (Kingston, ON, McGill–Queen's University Press, 1989).

23. John Smith, 'A Description of New England; or, The Observations, Discoueries of Captain John Smith (Admirall of that Country) in the North of America, in the year of our Lord 1614' (London, 1616), in Peter Force (compiler), *Tracts and Other Papers, Relating Principally to the Origin, Settlement, And Progress of the Colonies in North America, From the Discovery Of the Country To The Year 1776*, 3 vols (Washington, DC, 1836–38), p. 9, quoted in Annette Kolodny, *The Land Before Her: Fantasy and Experience of the American Frontiers, 1630–1830* (Chapel Hill, University of North Carolina Press, 1984), p. 3, n. 5. See also Kay Schaffer, *Women and the Bush: Forces of Desire in the Australian Cultural Imaginary* (Cambridge University Press, 1988/9) for a deconstructive feminist analysis of these dimensions in regard to Australian nationalism.

24. Kolodny, *The Land Before Her*, p. 4.

25. *Ibid.*, p. 6.

26. Faery, *Cartographies*, p. 41. Mary Rowlandson was captured in 1676, with her 6-year-old daughter who died, and was held for eleven weeks. Her narrative was published in 1682.

27. Benedict Anderson points out that Rowlandson's text describes herself and the community she came from as 'English', but the English did not necessarily see her that way; he speculates that, for English readers at the time, the Rowlandson narrative served another

purpose: 'The photographic negative of the colonial, the non-English Englishwoman, was coming into view', 'Exodus', *Critical Inquiry*, vol. 20, no. 2 (Winter 1984): 315.

28. See Note 1. This section closely follows Schaffer's *In the Wake*, Chapters 1 and 2.

29. These assertions have been subsequently refuted by anthropologists and attributed to the conflict between Western and indigenous understandings of native behaviours and practices.

30. This version of the Eliza Fraser story follows the historical account of Neil Buchanan and Barry Dwyer, *The Rescue of Eliza Fraser* (Noosa, Queensland, Noosa Graphica, 1986).

31. See J. G. Steele (ed.), *Explorers of the Moreton Bay District, 1780–1830* (St Lucia, University of Queensland Press, 1972), pp. 84–5; and J. G. Steele (ed.), *Brisbane Town in Convict Days, 1824–1842* (St Lucia, University of Queensland Press, 1975), p. 12. (Quoted in Schaffer, *In the Wake*, p. 10.)

32. Schaffer, *In the Wake*, p. 45.

33. The historical dimensions of the Plummer/Parker story follow the fuller historical account in Hacker, *Cynthia Ann Parker*.

34. *Ibid.*, pp. 6–7.

35. James W. Brooks explains that, by the early 1800s, the trade of women and children had long been an intrinsic part of the complex social and cultural networks of the borderlands region now known as Texas, New Mexico and Mexico. Brooks argues that 'thousands of Indian and hundreds of Spanish women and children "crossed cultures" through the workings of a captive-exchange system that knit diverse communities into vital, and violent, webs of interdependence'. See James Brooks, ' "This evil extends especially . . . to the feminine sex": negotiating captivity in the New Mexico Borderlands', *Feminist Studies*, vol. 22, no. 2 (Summer 1996): 279–310.

36. See William S. Reese's introduction to the reprinted, first edition of *Rachael Plummer's Narrative of Twenty-one Months Servitude as a Prisoner among Commanchee Indians*. Reproduced from the only known copy. Preface by Archibald Hanna (Austin, Jenkins Publishing Press, 1977/Houston, Telegraph Power Press, 1838).

37. *Narrative of the Capture, Sufferings, and Miraculous Escape of Mrs. Eliza Fraser* (New York, Charles Webb and Sons, 1837). There is also an alternative version published by Dean and Munday in the same year. In 1838, John Curtis published a full-length account of the shipwreck, Mrs Fraser's captivity, and her subsequent fate upon her return to England. John Curtis, *Shipwreck of the Stirling Castle* (London, George Vertue, Ivy Lane, 1838). For more, see Schaffer, *In the Wake*, Chapters 2–5.

38. See the entry for Eliza Fraser in William H. Wilde, Joy Hooton and Barry Andrews, *The Oxford Companion to Australian Literature* (Melbourne and Oxford, Oxford University Press, 1985), p. 281.

39. Schaffer, *In the Wake*, p. 52.

40. Caroline Harris, *History of the Captivity and Providential Release Therefrom of Mrs. Caroline Harris, Wife of the Late Mr. Richard Harris, of Franklin County . . . New-York, who, with Mrs. Clarissa Plummer, Wife of Mr. James Plummer Were, in the Spring of 1835 (with their Unfortunate Husbands) Taken Prisoner by the Camanche Tribe of Indians, while Emigrating from said Franklin County (N.Y.) to Texas . . .* (New York, Perry and Cooke, 1838).

41. Reese cites *Rachael Plummer's Narrative* (1838) as a source for the *Clarissa Plummer* and *Caroline Harris* texts, stating that 'the New York publishers lifted not only the basic story but many details and phrases as well from the Texas original'; see 'Introduction', *Rachael Plummer's Narrative*, n.p. Pearce notes another source for *Clarissa Plummer* in *A Narrative of the Captivity of Mrs. Horn*; see 'The significance of the captivity narrative', p. 16.

42. *Caroline Harris*, pp. 13, 11.

43. After living twenty-four years as a Comanche, Cynthia Ann Parker was 'rescued' by Texas Rangers at the Pease River Massacre, in which a combined force of US troops and Texas Rangers attacked and killed most members of a Comanche party composed largely of women and children. Cynthia Ann Parker and her infant daughter Topsannah were taken to the home of her Parker relatives, but Cynthia Ann mourned the loss of her Comanche family and tried many times to escape. As Hacker comments, 'After she returned to the whites, she became another captive' (p. 40). Topsannah's death in 1863 caused Cynthia Ann Parker even greater suffering, and she died in 1870.

CHAPTER EIGHT

Body and belonging(s): property in the captivity of Mungo Park

EMILY A. HADDAD

Park's mission and incarceration

In 1795, the young Scottish physician Mungo Park (1771–1806) was commissioned to 'ascertain the course, and, if possible, the rise and termination' of the Niger River.[1] The English gentlemen who engaged him called themselves the African Association; they were dedicated to expanding opportunities for British trade in Africa through the advancement of geographical knowledge.[2] Although Park's expedition did help prepare the way for future imperialist and colonialist exploitation of western Africa, his efforts had no immediate commercial results. Park did not find the rise or termination of the Niger, but he did confirm the reports of his predecessor, Daniel Houghton, that the river flowed eastward, not westward as European wisdom had it.

Park was the only one of the Association's first four employees to return alive and report some measure of success.[3] Throughout his journey, he worried about the various threats to his life – from climate and disease, to warfare and famine. His inability to protect or control his property intensified his anxiety, particularly in the period following his capture on 7 March 1796 by 'Moors', Muslims from central or northern West Africa.[4] Soon after he arrived at the residence of Ali, the Moors' leader, all of his belongings were taken from him and he was strip-searched. Other humiliations and privations followed in Park's more than three months of incarceration, at the end of which a small portion of his possessions was returned to him.

Park's narrative of his captivity occupies about a fifth of his very popular *Travels in the Interior Districts of Africa* (1799).[5] I analyse this narrative to show how Africans' violations of Park's ownership of his belongings and his body during his incarceration involved him in an unwitting reversal of the usual power relations between Europeans and Africans, and in a similar inversion of traditional relations between the sexes. Park responds to the redefinition of racial and national values by producing an alternate system of cultural organization based on his understanding of property rights; however, there is no corresponding revision of gender boundaries.

In this respect, *Travels* does not entirely fulfil what Christopher Castiglia has identified as a 'primary function' of the captivity narrative: 'to maintain the established interlocking hierarchies of race and gender'.[6] Moreover, unlike the Anglo-American female captives Castiglia discusses, Park does not reliably 'subvert and disrupt' these hierarchies.[7] *Travels* instead occupies an intermediate position, opening the possibility for a reconsideration of essentialist, race-based categories in a colonial context while also reasserting conventional, domestic gender roles. Castiglia's central argument is that 'the captives' experience of captivity and crossing cultures occasioned their revision of identities . . ., which in turn became a way for white women to survive captivity not only by Indians but by patriarchal prescription at home as well'.[8] Park's reluctance to reformulate gender roles can then be easily explained in terms of his privileged position as a man in the patriarchal domestic hierarchy. Castiglia depicts the revision of racial divisions as proceeding from the reconstruction of gender categories; obviously this linkage is not operative in Park's narrative, which presents gender and race as less fully interlocking than Castiglia proposes. Where, according to Castiglia, captivity narratives engage critically with, but ultimately reinforce, white male supremacy, Park's narrative projects an economically driven vision of social value, one that privileges a notion of private property rights essential to capitalism. Insofar as *Travels* 'condemn[s] . . . the political and socio-economic practices' of the region, the account conforms to the model of the 'Oriental captivity narrative' outlined by Joe Snader.[9] However, this narrative lacks the emphasis on 'individualistic autonomy' and 'resourcefulness' that, in Snader's view, form the basis for the genre's 'expansionist ideology'.[10] More importantly, Park's incorporation of the region's non-Moorish population into a relatively unracialized framework of shared economic practice has little in common with the 'aggressively antagonistic and totalizing epistemological stance' identified by Snader as characteristic of eighteenth-century records of captivity in North Africa.[11]

Trade and commerce

Park gave the impression that he had accepted the African Association's capitalist goals as his own. At the beginning of his book he announced his 'passionate desire to examine into the productions of a country so little known', and expressed his hope that he 'should succeed . . . in opening to [my countrymen's] ambition and industry new sources of wealth, and new channels of commerce'.[12] Near the end of *Travels*, Park offered a summary of his research:

> I have now, I trust, . . . explained with sufficient minuteness, the nature and extent of the commercial connection which at present prevails, and has long subsisted, between the Negro natives of those parts of Africa which I visited,

and the nations of Europe; and it appears that slaves, gold, and ivory, together with the few articles enumerated in the beginning of my work, . . . constitute the whole catalogue of exportable commodities. . . . It cannot, however, admit of a doubt, that all the rich and valuable productions, both of the East and West Indies, might easily be naturalized, and brought to the utmost perfection, in the tropical parts of this immense continent. Nothing is wanting to this end, but example, to enlighten the minds of the natives; and instruction, to enable them to direct their industry to proper objects. It is not possible for me to behold the wonderful fertility of the soil, the vast herds of cattle, proper both for labour and food, and a variety of other circumstances favourable to colonization and agriculture; and reflect, withal, on the means which presented themselves of a vast inland navigation, without lamenting that a country, so abundantly gifted and favoured by nature, should remain in its present savage and neglected state.[13]

Park did not explicitly locate himself in this utopian export economy, managed by European mercantile imperialists for their own benefit, nor does his behaviour during this trip suggest that he perceived himself as one of these potential imperialists.[14] Park's primary mission was not trade but exploration: to 'render the geography of Africa more familiar to my countrymen'.[15] Once in Africa, he used the merchandise he had with him only to exchange for necessities, especially food and lodging; he never traded for profit.

Mary Louise Pratt proposes that Park's refusal to trade actually concealed a compulsion to exchange – not towards profit, of course, but rather towards 'reciprocity, or . . . equivalence between parties'.[16] 'Reciprocity,' she argues,

> is the dynamic that above all organizes Park's . . . narrative. . . . [W]hat sets up drama and tension is almost invariably the desire to achieve reciprocity, to establish equilibrium through exchange. . . . Negotiating his way across Africa, Park is the picture of the entrepreneur. Yet the decidedly non-reciprocal momentum of European capitalism can scarcely be discerned in his lone and long-suffering figure, no matter how long you (the reader or the Africans) stare at him.[17]

According to Pratt, then, Park's mode of acting the trader disengaged him (at least metaphorically) from the larger capitalist project represented by the African Association. Once again, it seems clear that while Park represented this project (both materially as an employee and rhetorically as a writer), he did not necessarily align himself with it.

Pratt is no doubt right that Park's intricate relationship with European capitalism would hardly have been detectable by Africans who encountered him. However, his apparent lack of interest in commerce was both obvious and unintelligible to the locals. In general, members of the various communities inhabiting the region willingly interacted with one another only to wage war or to trade.[18] They knew Europeans almost exclusively as traders, if they knew them at all. Park, who travelled with little baggage and no more than half a dozen African companions, was clearly neither a warrior nor a trader. Some of the communities he passed through seem to have accepted his inability to fit either category.[19] More commonly, though, his hosts expressed surprise, puzzlement or hostility. To consider him a military threat was no doubt preposterous, so most of the people he encountered looked for some commercial rationale for his journey. Almami of Bondou, for instance, listened to Park's tale without response, then 'asked if I wished to purchase any slaves, or gold. being [sic] answered in the negative, he seemed rather surprised'.[20] When Park repeated his story later, the ruler

> seemed, however, but half satisfied. The notion of travelling for curiosity, was quite new to him. He thought it impossible, he said, that any man in his senses would undertake so dangerous a journey, merely to look at the country, and its inhabitants: however, when I offered to shew him the contents of my portmanteau, and every thing belonging to me, he was convinced; and it was evident that his suspicion had arisen from a belief, that every white man must of necessity be a trader.[21]

Park's narrative here constructs his identity in terms of his possessions and of his relationship with them, while simultaneously making clear that this construction was comprehensible to his African host. So long as this explanatory strategy worked, Park was able to travel relatively unobstructed. His incarceration was due largely to his inability to find an intelligible subject position from which to make his explanations; in its absence, the Moors assumed 'that I had come as a *spy* into the country', and maltreated him accordingly.[22] It would not have been logistically feasible for Park to carry goods for trade, yet his failure to engage in the type of trading partnerships typical of the region obviously did not promote good diplomatic relations, nor did the non-commercial reciprocity outlined in Pratt's analysis adequately compensate for it.

(Dis)possession

Park's location of his subject position in terms of his possessions establishes property as a fundamental component of his conceptualization of culture. Reading the narrative of his incarceration in terms of Enlightenment theories of property, we see the extent to which both his experience of African cultures and his relationship with his own culture are constituted by the role he ascribes to property rights in each. Park's journey entails a progressive dispossession, both of tangible belongings and of the ability to exercise what he presents as rights and qualities, intangible entities which tend to become functionally analogous to property.

By the start of his captivity, Park had been cheated once, robbed four times and forced to part with belongings as 'presents' eleven times; he had lost well over three-quarters of his baggage.[23] He survived his incarceration virtually without possessions, and was robbed again immediately after his escape. He realized early that 'every body could rob me with impunity' but at the same time resisted the notion that 'my property was lawful plunder'.[24] The essential aspects of Park's view of the right to property are consistent with those of his time; after all, *Travels* was published only a decade after the French Revolutionary Assembly's 'Declaration of the Rights of Man and of the Citizen' had announced that 'liberty, property, security and resistance to oppression' were the 'natural and imprescriptible rights of man' and, in particular, that 'property is an inviolable and sacred right'.[25] Similarly, Adam Smith (1723–90), one of the economic theorists most influential in Park's milieu, concluded in his 1759 book *The Theory of Moral Sentiments*, that the 'most sacred laws of justice ... are the laws which guard the life and person of our neighbour; the next are those which guard his property and possessions'.[26]

Although Smith, his contemporary Edmund Burke (1729–97) and his predecessor John Locke (1632–1704) all stressed the role of labour in the right to property,[27] Park was not interested in this feature of the (proto-)Enlightenment theory of property, and gave virtually no attention to the basis for the right to acquire or possess property. Rather, he implied that the fact of a person's possession of an item justified his possession, so long as he had acquired the item without taking it illegitimately from someone else. His assumptions here are consistent with Locke's definition of property as that 'whereof we may not be deprived without our consent', provided that 'there is no legitimate objection' to our use of the materials from which the property derives.[28]

Park's assumptions about property are clearest in his comments on the Moors' violations of the right to property, but they can also be detected in his representation of his own incarceration experience. Park objected often to his captors' failure to satisfy his most basic needs, especially food, water and clothing, while he was dependent upon their charity. Obviously, he perceived as a violation of his right to his property the Moors' confiscation, 'with their usual rudeness', of '[m]y clothes, instruments, and every thing that belonged to me'.[29] Left thus destitute, Park rhetorically appropriated for himself the hut which Ali provided for him at Ali's camp in Benowm (in today's Mali), calling it 'my ... habitation' or 'my hut' even though he would have had no right to dispose of this hut and he could be readily deprived of it without his consent.[30] Park never mentioned any sign of former inhabitants, implying that his occupation of the hut did not dispossess anyone else. Even this rather tenuous ownership status entailed an obligation to charity, however. Park was willing to share the hut if it were needed – as when a salt trader arrived in camp and required shelter.[31]

Thus Park's *Travels* implies two fundamental conditions on the legitimate possession of property. First, the possessor must have acquired the property without knowingly depriving someone else of it. Second, to the extent that his means allow, the possessor must offer the use of his property to the needy. The first of these conditions relies firmly though implicitly upon the Lockean view, already cited, that property is what cannot be taken without its possessor's consent. Accordingly, if the item in question is taken without the consent of the original possessor, it is not legitimately the property of its new possessor. Similarly, a basis for the second of Park's fundamental conditions can be found in Locke's view that a person has first of all 'a right to the means of preservation'; if he has enough for his own preservation, he must allow others access (at a subsistence level) to his surplus.[32] According to Locke, 'Charity gives every Man a Title to so much out of another's Plenty, as will keep him from extream want, where he has no means to subsist otherwise.'[33] As a captive who lacked any way to transform his labour into the water or food that would 'keep him from extream want', Park would qualify for charity even under Locke's strict criteria; he falls into the category of 'those who, through poverty or misfortune, suffer from temporary disability'.[34] So too, the visiting salt trader, however able-bodied, apparently had no way to convert labour into shelter and therefore was owed Park's charity.

Moors, Negroes and the right to property

In effect, Park's status as a prisoner, which left those around him the obligation to offer charity, laid the groundwork for his alliance with Africans who shared his economic disempowerment. Park began the chapter in which he narrated his capture by explaining the political relationship between Moors and other African ethnic groups, collectively referred to as 'Negroes' in keeping with the practice of his European milieu. The Negroes, he said,

> prefer a precarious protection under the Moors, which they purchase by a tribute, rather than continue exposed to their predatory hostilities. The tribute they pay is considerable; and they manifest towards their Moorish superiors the most unlimited obedience and submission, and are treated by them with the utmost indignity and contempt.[35]

This introduction implies for the first time the unstated alliance between Park and these Negroes that persisted throughout his captivity. The alliance was based on shared oppression; the exaggerated emphasis on 'tribute' as a tactic of oppression here suggests that the three parties' understanding of the right to property stood at the centre of their relationship. Park observed repeatedly that, despite universal shortages of food and water, he was able to obtain these necessities more easily from Negroes than from Moors, who typically tormented those in need.[36] Moreover, he shared with Negroes the experience of being plundered by Moors. Thus both in their exercise of charity towards the indigent Park and in their indignation at the Moors' practices of extortion and confiscation, the Negroes seemed to share his view of the rights and obligations of ownership.[37]

Throughout *Travels*, but especially in the captivity narrative, Park maintained a binary division between the Moors on the one side and on the other all others, including himself and the non-Moorish inhabitants of the region. 'I was fully convinced,' he said, 'that whatever difference there is between the Negro and European in the conformation of the nose and the colour of the skin, there is none in the genuine sympathies and characteristic feelings of our common nature.'[38] In contrast, the Moors were 'the rudest savages on earth', whose 'rudeness, ferocity, and fanaticism ... distinguish [them] from the rest of mankind'.[39] Park discussed racial and other differences between the Moors and the Negroes in some detail, but it was the Moors' handling of others' property that truly set them apart, defining their 'rudeness' and their 'ferocity'.[40] The Moors met neither of Park's fundamental conditions for the possession of property. Repeatedly and without compunction, they violated both the first, by acquiring property by depriving others of it, and the second, by refusing to make their property available to the needy. Park did admit that 'the most prominent defect in [the Negroes'] character, is that insurmountable propensity, which the reader must have observed to prevail in all classes of them, to steal from me the few effects I was possessed of'.[41] However, he then explained that 'theft is a crime in their own estimation';[42] such an assertion would be impossible had not Park accepted their understanding of property ownership as being similar to his own, despite their failure to implement that understanding. His apologia continued:

> it were well to consider whether the lower order of people in any part of Europe, would have acted, under similar circumstances, with greater honesty towards a stranger, than the Negroes acted towards me. . . . Notwithstanding I was so great a sufferer by [their pilfering disposition], I do not consider that their natural sense of justice was perverted or extinguished: it was overpowered only, for the moment, by the strength of a temptation which it required not common virtue to resist.[43]

If Negroes' cultural identity is constituted by their philosophy of property, Europeans' identity is also integrally linked with their possession of property. Returning at the very end of his travels to Pisania, the village on the Gambia River (in today's Senegal) where he had begun, Park was careful to note that he 'lost no time in resuming the English dress'.[44] At the same time, he described his Negro benefactor Karfa Taura's awed reaction to European furnishings: 'Every thing he saw seemed wonderful.'[45] Material objects – 'property' – came to define the essence of Europeanness, against which Karfa would 'exclaim with an involuntary sigh, *fato fing inta feng*, "black men are nothing" '.[46]

On the one hand, Park's depiction of his final days in Africa reveals the very real limitations of his affiliation with Negroes, who are presented in the final analysis as stereotypically backward and primitive, albeit at least aware of their supposed deficiencies. On the other hand, it shows how fully he identified his Europeanness in terms of property – in this case, furniture and clothing – and simultaneously, how entirely Karfa Taura is portrayed as having concurred. If indeed 'black men are nothing', that is because they did not have the property which characterized Europeans. Re-examining this phenomenon in terms of Pratt's argument that 'Park's everyday struggles, then, consist mainly of attempts to achieve reciprocity between himself and others, or to endure its absence',[47] we can see that his characteristic inability to achieve reciprocity with the Moors can best be read as a consequence or manifestation of the divergence between his understanding of property and theirs. Both the Moors and Park, for instance, privileged certain types of property, yet the hierarchies they developed were the inverse of one another. The failure of reciprocity occurred because neither the property itself nor the parties' relationships with it offered common ground on which to make an exchange.

Human property

The notion of persons as property arose inevitably in a context where slavery was presented as integral to the customs and economic system of the region. Park estimated that in many locales 'persons of *free condition* ... constitute ... not more than one-fourth part of the inhabitants at large'.[48] He concluded his chapter on 'Observations concerning the State and Sources of Slavery in Africa' by arguing that, because slavery was endemic to Africa, the effect of 'a discontinuance of [European] commerce [in slaves] would neither be so extensive or beneficial, as many wise and worthy persons fondly expect'.[49] Park himself did occasionally participate marginally in the slavery-based economic system, but he did not purchase any slaves on this trip nor did he explicitly condone slavery.

On the other hand, Park's recounting of his own experience was structured to an important extent by his perception of the situation of slaves. During his captivity, he was subject to many of the circumstances of slavery, including poor living conditions, deprivation, and (obviously) lack of liberty. The rhetoric of his narrative often juxtaposes or equates captivity and slavery, repeatedly using the word 'captive' to refer to a slave, for instance.[50] As Maria Grosz-Ngaté points out, Park's narrative strongly emphasises his 'powerlessness'.[51] I would add that, on several occasions, Park appropriated slavery as a figure for his own impotence or as a standard of comparison. For example, he was not forced to work as a slave would be and, in fact, exerted every effort 'to make myself as useless and insignificant as possible, as the only means of recovering my liberty'.[52] Implicit here is a fear of actual enslavement were he to prove useful. Later, at a particularly trying stage of his incarceration, he found himself yearning for 'solitude and reflection' and 'env[ying] the situation of a slave, who, amidst all his calamities, could still possess the enjoyment of his own thoughts; a happiness to which I had for some time been a stranger'.[53]

The status of Park's body as a possession must also be addressed here. Locke contended that 'every Man has a Property in his own Person. This no Body has any Right to but himself.'[54] Park seems to have perceived his body as his own property, indirectly accepting Locke's understanding both of a human being's own person as his property and of the exclusivity of his right to it. Park presented his notion of the body as property through an extended, three-part analogy between human life and non-human forms of property; the concept which unifies the three parts is that of (un)lawful possession. First, Park stated the Moors' view that his material possessions were 'lawful plunder'. Later, he announced their presumption that he himself was their 'lawful prisoner'. Finally, Park declared that they would 'consider it nearly as lawful to murder a European, as it would be to kill a dog'.[55] In general, he presented theft as a crime of the same type as murder, albeit of lesser degree.[56] Any person or group – and the Moors were Park's prime example here – that failed to respect his right to his property was unlikely, in Park's estimation, to respect his right to continued life or liberty. Captivity, the denial of liberty, entails the taking possession of another's body. But since Park was not enslaved, one cannot argue that the Moors actually took possession of his body-as-property. Nor did they permanently deprive Park of the use of his body by murdering him. In short, they violated Park's right to his body-as-property not by actually taking it from him, but by preventing him from fully exercising his own right to it.

Property on display: whiteness

This mode of violation was especially prominent on the many occasions when Park became a local spectacle. During the first such episode, the local ruler

> observed, that his women were very desirous to see me, and requested that I would favour them with a visit. . . . I had no sooner entered the court appropriated to the ladies, than the whole seraglio surrounded me. . . . They rallied me with a good deal of gaiety on different subjects; particularly upon the whiteness of my skin, and the prominency of my nose.[57]

Park responded by 'pa[ying] them many compliments on African beauty'.[58] Weeks later, in a less cordial encounter elsewhere, Park reported: 'I was so completely surrounded by the gazing multitude, that I did not attempt to dismount.'[59] In another town, Park spent hours 'surrounded by so great a crowd, as made it necessary for me to satisfy their curiosity, by sitting still'.[60]

The scene repeated itself yet again at Ali's camp: 'I soon found myself surrounded by such a crowd, that I could scarcely move; one pulled my clothes, another took off my hat, a third stopped me to examine my waistcoat buttons.'[61] Once in Ali's tent,

> [t]he surrounding attendants, and especially the ladies, were abundantly more inquisitive: they asked a thousand questions; inspected every part of my apparel, searched my pockets, and obliged me to unbutton my waistcoat and display the whiteness of my skin; they even counted my toes and fingers, as if they doubted whether I was in truth a human being.[62]

Park was then conducted to his hut, but

> I was no sooner seated in this my new habitation, than the Moors assembled in crowds to behold me; but I found it rather a troublesome levee, for I was obliged to take off one of my stockings, and show them my foot, and even to take off my jacket and waistcoat, to show them how my clothes were put on and off; they were much delighted with the curious contrivance of buttons. All this was to be repeated to every succeeding visitor; for such as had already seen these wonders, insisted on their friends seeing the same; and in this manner I was employed, dressing and undressing, buttoning and unbuttoning, from noon to night.[63]

Assuming that those gazing upon a human spectacle have more power than the person who is the object of their gaze, Park as spectacle was disempowered vis-à-vis the African onlookers.[64] Because he never had the resources to exercise substantial power as an individual, that disempowerment is more important in a global than a local sense. Although the 'scramble for Africa' was many decades away, Africa had already begun to feel the British colonial influence implicit (and later explicit) in the mission of the African Association.[65] *Travels* makes clear that British and other European merchants were well established in coastal areas. Their demand for gold, ivory and (especially) slaves had clearly affected the indigenous economies and social structures.[66] It is difficult to believe Park's assertion that the European slave trade had relatively insignificant consequences in western Africa; the mechanisms necessary to remove 26,000 Africans a year from West Africa onto British slaving ships could scarcely have existed without substantial social and economic impact on the region.[67] Overall, despite their tiny numbers and their limited access to direct political power, Europeans exerted substantial economic power in Africa.[68] Clearly, then, it would be a mistake to interpret Park's apparent powerlessness as indicative of European impotence in West Africa. At least in the important arena of European, and particularly British, economic influence in the region, Europe evidently dominated African/European power relations – relations which Park's transformation into a spectacle inverts.

Using an approach related to Pratt's argument that this phenomenon represents a 'reciprocal seeing' or 'mutual appropriation',[69] Denise

Brahimi depicts the situation as a kind of visual exchange. Brahimi proposes that

> if it is true that the explorer discovers in the interior of Africa a virgin country, entirely unknown to him and to his readers, it is equally true that the Africans discover in him for the first time a white man fully accessible to exploration.[70]

Although Brahimi's language here is suggestive, she does not examine this reciprocity politically or economically, as Pratt's analysis shows us the necessity of doing. Moreover, neither Pratt nor Brahimi observe that the inversion of global-scale power relations was then (re-)enacted on a more intimate level through the spectacle, in that the spectacle entailed Park's metaphorical assumption of the role of a slave. Park-as-spectacle endured not only the gaze but also both the bodily restraint (as when the crowds of onlookers prevented him from moving) and the physical inspection (tugging on clothes, counting fingers) experienced in a much more extreme form by enslaved Africans offered for sale.

So if Park's disqualification from the role of 'white man' began with his refusal to trade, his disenfranchisement from whiteness was in one respect completed when he became a spectacle, physically as well as psychically and politically disempowered by the crowds of gazing and prodding Africans. For extended portions of *Travels*, then, Park's whiteness functioned almost solely as a marker of difference – difference which did not necessarily imply the economic and political power otherwise characteristic of whiteness in the colonial era.[71] Still, it would be a mistake to overstate the political purity of Park's complexion. Park's account suggests that his whiteness (his visible difference), more than his foreignness or his Christianity, made him an object of sustained interest. While uncomfortable, being an object of interest may have enabled Park's achievements and even his survival. One suspects that any young man whose story was the same as his but who looked like a 'Negro' or a 'Moor' would simply have been dismissed as some sort of oddity. The fact that on at least one of the occasions when Park was mistaken for a Moor he 'became the subject of much merriment' suggests that his hypothetical Moorish- or Negro-looking counterpart would have fared much worse than Park did.[72] So it seems that even though Park's transformation into a spectacle mirrored the experience of an enslaved African more closely than that of an economically and politically empowered European, Park's whiteness retains at least some of its protective value. After his release from captivity, as he grew increasingly decrepit and, under the influence of fever, less white and more yellow, Park met more often with contempt than with real interest. His clothes were few and ragged, and he had no more buttons to undo or presents to give. It seems, then, that Park's whiteness was most efficacious in combination with other elements which marked his Otherness; in a sense, his whiteness functioned as a property among other properties.

Analysing whiteness and property in the context of American law and culture, Cheryl I. Harris argues, in part, that 'rights in property are contingent on, intertwined with, and conflated with race'. Whiteness, she says, 'shares the critical characteristics of property.... In particular, whiteness and property share a common premise – a conceptual nucleus – of a right to exclude.' Through slavery, '[r]ace and property were ... conflated by establishing a form of property contingent on race – only Blacks were subjugated as slaves and treated as property'.[73] Harris's complete argument is intricate and, because of its context, not entirely applicable to Park's situation; for instance, I have already shown how Park's implied definition of the right to property is not strictly race-bound. However, her analysis of whiteness as property offers a necessary explanation for certain aspects of the operation of whiteness in *Travels*. Although Park's whiteness cannot be confiscated, it can be degraded to the point where he is deprived of the use of it, in the same way that, as I argue above, he is deprived during his captivity of the use of his body-as-property.[74] The exclusivity of Park's property in whiteness justifies the great demand for it (and, perhaps, his own devotion to maintaining the appearance of it, as evidenced by his unwillingness to adopt non-European attire). No matter how light-skinned, no Moor had whiteness, which was Park's monopoly. When Park was displayed as a spectacle, his whiteness was exhibited along with his other belongings. That whiteness, like the belongings, had material value;[75] he was able, when deprived of all else, to use it to purchase Karfa Taura's protection – only Park's difference convinced Karfa, a careful businessman, that this destitute traveller could actually command the resources to pay the promised fee of 'the value of one prime slave'.[76] Park explained:

> some of the Slatees, who had seen the Europeans upon the Coast, observing the colour of my skin (which was now become very yellow with sickness), my long beard, ragged clothes, and extreme poverty, were unwilling to admit that I was a white man, and told Karfa, that they suspected I was some Arab in disguise.[77]

Karfa successfully documents Park's status as 'a white man' by asking him to read from the Anglican *Book of Common Prayer*. In accordance with Harris's analysis, his whiteness is an absolute that does not depend for its existence upon the shade of his skin colour. Park relies upon his whiteness as property when, in effect, he uses it to secure his promise to pay Karfa. As Harris says of ante-bellum America, 'White identity and whiteness were sources of privilege and protection; their absence meant being the object of property.'[78] Thus the idea of whiteness as property is essential to explain the residual efficacy of Park's whiteness even when, as in this instance, whiteness must operate without its supporting network of other more tangible, and therefore alienable, properties.

Property on display: masculinity

This potential for residual efficacy is shared by another of Park's basic 'properties': his masculinity. It is clear from the examples I have already cited that African women (Moorish and Negro) tended to pursue their curiosity about Park even more assertively than men did, and that in general they appear to have held relatively empowered positions vis-à-vis both Park and the men of their own communities, despite Park's assertion that 'African husbands are possessed of great authority over their wives'.[79] The elevated status of women becomes most obvious in the case of Ali's wife, Fatima, who prompted Park's capture and then delayed but finally arranged for his release. Whereas the life of a Scottish woman of the same class and age (almost 25) as Park would typically have been controlled to a great extent by men – father, husband, brothers – Park's life had been virtually free of female domination. He must have been ill prepared to find his existence circumscribed to a significant extent by the wills of various women, Fatima foremost among them. To a degree, then, Park experienced in Africa the sort of disenfranchisement which his own society designated for women.

I showed earlier how Park-as-spectacle inverted African/European power relations; at least from Park's perspective, there seems to be here a parallel inversion of gender-based power relations. As Pratt argues, he 'becomes the object of the female gaze, whose aggressive voyeurism feminizes him in the process'.[80] Throughout his experience in Africa, his body was subject to scrutiny in a way that tended to deprive his masculinity of its associations with power, rather as his existence as a spectacle also stripped his whiteness of much of its potency. When the African women inspected him, they were also evaluating him. The evaluation of female bodies on the middle- and upper-middle-class British marriage market was – despite the layers of clothing typically covering those bodies – an unquestioned convention for which there was no precise male counterpart. Feminine modesty was an equally conventional value; male modesty was not. Yet, in Benowm, Park found both his modesty and his physical desirability very much at issue, even though he never suggested any possibility of a sexual relationship with any of the inhabitants. On 28 March 1796, for example, Ali wished to take Park 'to shew me to some of his women'.

> But here a new difficulty occurred: the Moors, accustomed to a loose and easy dress, could not reconcile themselves to the appearance of my *nankeen breeches*, which they said were not only inelegant, but, on account of their tightness, very indecent; and as this was a visit to ladies, Ali ordered my boy to bring out the loose cloak which I had always worn since my arrival at Benowm, and told me to wrap it close round me. We visited the tents of four different ladies. . . . They were very inquisitive, and examined my hair and skin with great

attention; but affected to consider me as a sort of inferior being to themselves, and would knit their brows, and seem to shudder, when they looked at the whiteness of my skin. In the course of the evening's excursion, my dress and appearance afforded infinite mirth to the company [of Ali's men], who galloped round me as if they were baiting a wild animal . . . seemingly to display their superior prowess over a miserable captive.[81]

At the opening of this passage, Park appeared desirable enough that he had to cover himself more modestly; in this respect his situation again approximated that of a typical Scottish woman rather than a man. As the encounter continued, however, both his sexual appeal and his masculinity diminished to the point of irrelevance.

Park's masculinity offered him very little power even when it was not blatantly threatened. We can judge this from his description of another episode, occurring a few days earlier, in which he received an embarrassing visit from some women:

The curiosity of the Moorish ladies had been very troublesome to me ever since my arrival at Benowm; and on the evening of the 25th . . . a party of them came into my hut, and gave me plainly to understand that the object of their visit was to ascertain, by actual inspection, whether the rite of circumcision extended to the Nazarenes, (Christians,) as well as to the followers of Mahomet. The reader will easily judge of my surprise at this unexpected declaration; and in order to avoid the proposed scrutiny, I thought it best to treat the business jocularly. I observed to them, that it was not customary in my country to give ocular demonstration in such cases, before so many beautiful women; but that if all of them would retire, except the young lady to whom I pointed, (selecting the youngest and handsomest), I would satisfy her curiosity. The ladies enjoyed the jest; and went away laughing heartily; the young damsel herself to whom I had given the preference, (though she did not avail herself of the privilege of inspection), seemed no way displeased at the compliment; for she soon afterwards sent me some meal and milk for my supper.[82]

Park behaved here like a young woman simultaneously protecting her virtue and encouraging the most attractive of her suitors. Were it not for his maleness, the episode would have been pointless, yet only by adopting flirtatious tactics coded in European society as feminine rather than masculine was he able to regain some control over the situation. That his feminine-coded tactics worked makes sense, given that women in the captivity narrative are typically masculinized by the extent of their empowerment (although, interestingly, not in any other significant way). Park's success in both this encounter and the preceding one is evidenced by the food rewards he received in each case.[83] This compensation for his sexualized display of his body suggests that his masculinity retained some value – as his whiteness did in comparable circumstances. However, in every instance, this value was both limited and atypical (according to European norms).

Christopher Castiglia's analysis of Anglo-American women's captivity narratives suggests that some sort of gender realignment is not unusual in the genre. However, the implications of a man adopting behaviour coded as feminine are not the same as those outlined by Castiglia, who argues that white women could achieve a kind of 'freedom' in their captivities by affiliating as women with their American Indian 'sisters' rather than remaining fully within the restricted feminine roles assigned to them within Anglo-American culture.[84] For Park, in contrast, gender realignment represented disempowerment, not social liberation. Michelle Burnham, another scholar who analyses gender in American captivity narratives, points out that for captives of the American Indians, 'the event of captivity is followed by an almost incessant mobility',[85] a circumstance that must have been particularly challenging for Anglo-American women, who saw themselves chiefly as domestic, stationary settlers and colonists. Park, of course, required constant movement and progress to fulfil his mission as an explorer, whereas his incarceration entailed, for the most part, a stationary existence in which he had to devote endless effort to obtaining food. With the procurement of food replacing exploration as his daily concern, a certain shift in his relationship to conventional gender roles was unavoidable.

If we are to accept Pratt's contention that Park's *Travels* 'embodies ideals not of domesticity, but of commerce and private enterprise',[86] we need to understand the extent to which his narrative attempts to recuperate the apparently feminine as essentially masculine. Park used his rhetoric to assimilate the African women he met to various European female roles. Fatima became 'Queen Fatima' and granted him favours 'with much grace and civility'[87] – England's Queen Charlotte could hardly have done better. The women who intruded to determine the state of his foreskin became flirtation partners whom he described in terms easily appropriate to a typical Scottish social encounter.[88] Generalizing about African women, he declared, 'I do not recollect a single instance of hard-heartedness towards me in the women. In all my wanderings and wretchedness, I found them uniformly kind and compassionate.'[89] The narrative as a whole certainly does not support this generalization. Like his claim, noted above, that 'African husbands are possessed of great authority over their wives', the inconsistency exposes Park's great effort to subsume African women's behaviour under an eighteenth-century British ideal of femininity: soft-hearted, sympathetic and submissive to men. One suspects that this refeminization of African women may have been part of an attempt to assert his own masculinity on a rhetorical basis and to repair metaphorically the disruption of gender categories entailed in his interactions with African women. His own remasculinization signals a rejection of domesticity and, in turn, a resumption of a capitalist/imperialist agency whereby he could negotiate for territory (Africa explored) rather than for food or shelter – an agency restricted more severely during his incarceration than at any other point in his journey.

Conclusion

Although Pratt acknowledges that Park, unlike many of his European peers, 'affirms plausible worlds of African agency and experience [and] raises genuine possibilities of critical self-questioning', she concludes that he 'acts out the values that underwrote the greatest non-reciprocal non-exchange of all time: the Civilizing Mission'.[90] Here and elsewhere, Pratt's argument, like Snader's on the Oriental captivity narrative, relies upon the binary models of race, nationality and gender often asserted by critics of colonial literature. As my own analysis of *Travels* shows, Pratt is right to affirm Park's complicity in the imperialist enterprise, an enterprise founded largely upon binarism. However, despite the racist and chauvinist assumptions evident throughout the narrative, Park's version of imperialist ideology seems less securely grounded upon traditional binary models than Pratt suggests. Park's narrative proposes views on property as a dominant constituent of identity, creating an affiliation between Negroes and Europeans based on a theory of property, rather than on conventional racial or national criteria of the sort entailed in Snader's argument that negative portrayals of indigenous cultures in captivity narratives imply 'a positive characterization of the British'.[91] Although the pre-existing division between Negroes and Moors is maintained in Park's *Travels*, it is justified primarily by the difference between the two groups' theories of property. All three groups' theories of property converge with other characteristics (racial, ethnic, religious, national) to establish the boundaries of group identity, but the conception of property rights has a particular importance not addressed by other scholarly readers of *Travels* nor, indeed, by critics of colonial literature in general.

To a degree, then, Park's *Travels* conforms to the paradigm of the captivity narrative described by Castiglia. '[C]aptivity narratives,' Castiglia contends, 'refuse to be static texts endorsing essential, unchanging identities and hence fixed social hierarchies of race and gender'.[92] However, this particular narrative is typically less willing to reconsider hierarchies of gender than of race. When Park's masculinity was challenged by the empowered behaviour of African women, he strove – mainly rhetorically – to restore the status quo of female subordination. Reading in terms of the now conventional equation between man and colonizer, woman and colonized, one can see Park's apparent retrenchment as an effort to maintain for himself some hypothetical role as an agent of colonization or, at least, of imperialism. On the other hand, as Wendy S. Mercer argues in another context, this equation is unreliable.[93] No such set of simplistic pairings could encompass the world Park depicted, where a white European begged food from Africans owned by other Africans, where a man could protect his masculinity only by behaving like a woman, where whiteness was not self-evident but instead subject to verification, where women exercised power over men. Techniques of human categorization that seem so secure in the usual binary models emerge from Park's narrative as ineffective or insignificant. Filling the void, assumptions about economic systems, patterns and values replace them as determinative factors in cultural relations under colonial conditions.

Notes

1. Mungo Park, *Travels in the Interior Districts of Africa* (New York, Arno Press, 1971), p. 3.

2. This organization (formally, the Association for Promoting the Discovery of the Interior Parts of Africa) was founded in 1788. A leading member was Joseph Banks, Park's patron in London; see John Gascoigne, *Science in the Service of Empire: Joseph Banks, the British State and the Uses of Science in the Age of Revolution* (Cambridge, Cambridge University Press, 1998), pp. 179–82.

3. Houghton died attempting the same route to the Niger that Park followed. Another explorer, John Ledyard, died in Cairo, while Simon Lucas returned to Europe having made little progress.

4. Kenneth Lupton explains in *Mungo Park: The African Traveler* (Oxford, Oxford University Press, 1979) that

> the word 'Moor' at that time seems to have embraced both desert-fringe tribes and Moroccans. They all professed Islam and spoke Arabic, and were of mainly Arab and Berber descent, sometimes mingled with black African blood, but the tribes had little in common with the comfortable merchants and scholars of Fez. (p. 64)

For a relevant discussion of the Moors' culture, see Richard L. Roberts, *Warriors, Merchants, and Slaves: The State and the Economy in the Middle Niger Valley, 1700–1914* (Stanford, Stanford University Press, 1987), pp. 46–8.

5. Park was an inexperienced writer and benefited, as he himself acknowledged in the preface to *Travels*, from the assistance of African Association secretary and (perhaps significantly) anti-abolitionist Bryan Edwards. The extent of Edwards's influence on the 1799 text is not clear; see Maria Grosz-Ngaté, 'Power and knowledge: the representation of the Mande world in the works of Park, Caillié, Monteil, and Delafosse', *Cahiers d'études africaines*, vol. 28, no. 3–4 (1988): 490, and Peter Brent, *Black Nile; Mungo Park and the Search for the Niger* (London, Gordon Cremonesi, 1977), pp. 109–11.

For information on the initial reception and publication history of *Travels*, see Brent, *Black Nile*, p. 112; Mary Louise Pratt, *Imperial Eyes: Travel Writing and Transculturation* (London, Routledge, 1992), p. 74; and Samuel J. Rogal, 'Mungo Park: physician-traveler to Africa', *Exploration: Journal of the MLA Special Session on the Literature of Exploration and Travel*, vol. 7 (1979): 29–30. More than thirty years after its publication, *Travels* was praised for 'the merit of being written in a pleasing and animated style [which] has rendered it one of the most popular books in the English language' (Hugh Murray *et al.*, *Narrative of Discovery and Adventure in Africa, from the Earliest Ages to the Present Time* (Edinburgh, Oliver and Boyd, 1832), p. 140).

6. Catharine R. Stimpson, Foreword to Christopher Castiglia, *Bound and Determined: Captivity, Culture-crossing, and White Womanhood from Mary Rowlandson to Patty Hearst* (Chicago, University of Chicago Press, 1996), p. ix. Castiglia's context is the New World, but he claims this function for captivity narratives as a genre.

7. *Ibid.*, p. x.

8. Castiglia, *Bound*, p. 9.

9. Joe Snader, 'The Oriental Captivity Narrative and early English fiction', *Eighteenth-Century Fiction*, vol. 9, no. 3 (1997): 278.

10. *Ibid.*, pp. 268, 280.

11. *Ibid.*, p. 275.

12. Park, *Travels*, p. 2. Park's biography suggests that, for the ears of the African Association, he may have exaggerated his devotion to commerce; more plausible motivating factors for this trip (in addition to Park's unemployment at the time) were his interests in botany and geography, along with his evident desire for adventure.

13. *Ibid.*, pp. 311–12. Denise Brahimi suggests that Park limits his material on commerce to two chapters, but this is clearly not the case; see 'Mungo Park en Afrique, ou l'explorateur exploré', *Dix-huitième siècle*, no. 22 (1990): 151.

14. This is not at all true of Park's fatal second trip to the Niger region in 1805. My analysis of Park throughout this chapter applies only to his first trip as represented in the 1799 *Travels*.

Pratt is right to remind us that the African Association was not interested in settlement and did not, at least initially, have an explicitly colonial agenda (*Imperial Eyes*, p. 70). However, one must also keep in mind that their commercial objectives were inextricable from British imperialism. See also n. 65 below.

15. Park, *Travels*, p. 2.

16. Pratt, *Imperial Eyes*, p. 97.

17. *Ibid.*, pp. 80–1.

18. For a comprehensive analysis of the relationship between warfare and the trading economy, see Roberts, *Warriors*. Determining the nature of the existing economic systems of the area is complicated by the fact that for Western historians, including Roberts, Park's account is a principal source; see, for example, *Warriors*, pp. 45, 50–1.

19. See, for example, the reactions of Demba Sego Jalla, King of Kasson, and Daisy Koorabarri, King of Kaarta (Park, *Travels*, pp. 86, 95). Detailed analysis of these leaders' reactions is made difficult by Park's failure to relate exactly what he told them, but it is clear that he did not claim for himself either a military or a commercial role, nor does it seem that he alluded to the commercial objectives of his sponsors. (I have maintained Park's spelling of African names and terms throughout.)

20. Park, *Travels*, p. 53.

21. *Ibid.*, p. 54. See Pratt's complementary reading of this incident in *Imperial Eyes*, p. 84.

22. Park, *Travels*, p. 125; emphasis his. It is unclear whom Demba Sego, Ali and the others thought he might have been spying for. Park noted that Ali used spies liberally himself (*ibid.*, p. 156); possibly he meant to imply that Ali assumed that another local ruler had employed Park for the same purpose. Park never raised the possibility that Ali, or anyone else, might have suspected him of spying on behalf of Europeans to the detriment of Africans; see Lupton, *Mungo Park*, p. 83. And he never admitted either that the activity in which he claimed to be engaged – 'to look at the country, and its inhabitants' (*Travels*, p. 54) – is very difficult to distinguish from espionage, or that he had in fact committed himself to a kind of mercantile espionage at the direction of the African Association.

23. *Ibid.*, p. 81.

24. *Ibid.*, p. 115.

25. James Harvey Robinson (ed.), *Translations and Reprints from The Original Sources in European History: The French Revolution* (n.p., n.d.), pp. 6, 8.

26. Robert L. Heilbroner (ed.), *The Essential Adam Smith* (New York, Norton, 1986), p. 94.

27. See Gopal Sreenivasan, *The Limits of Lockean Rights in Property* (Oxford, Oxford University Press, 1995), p. 5; Adam Smith, *An Inquiry into the Nature and Causes of the Wealth of Nations*, ed. Edwin Cannan (New York, Modern Library, 1937), pp. 121–2; and Francis Canavan, *The Political Economy of Edmund Burke: The Role of Property in His Thought* (New York, Fordham University Press, 1995), pp. 48, 70.

28. Cited in Alan Ryan, *Property and Political Theory* (Oxford, Basil Blackwell, 1984), p. 29; Sreenivasan, *Limits*, p. 5, see also pp. 33, 97.

29. Park, *Travels*, pp. 127, 128.

30. *Ibid.*, pp. 123, 132, 133, 135.

31. *Ibid.*, p. 140. It might be argued that Park's use of 'my' to refer to the hut simply implied a relationship (as in 'my neighbourhood') without suggesting ownership of the hut as property. However, Park's welcoming of the salt trader into the hut suggested that he did perceive some level of control consistent with ownership. Of the eleven elements which, according to Sreenivasan, comprise full individual ownership, Park can be seen to have participated, albeit with substantial limitations, in four: 'the right to possess', 'the right to use', 'the right to manage' and 'the right to security' (*Limits*, pp. 9–10).

32. *Ibid.*, pp. 24, 104. Smith presents charity as a moral obligation but does not legislate it as a duty; see Heilbroner, *Essential*, pp. 92–3, 136.

33. Cited in Sreenivasan, *Limits*, p. 45.

34. *Ibid.*, p. 103.

35. Park, *Travels*, p. 111. As J. Forbes Monro explains, 'The powerful state surrounded by weaker peripheral polities can probably be said to have been typical of pre-colonial Africa' (*Africa and the International Economy, 1800–1960* (London, J. M. Dent, 1976), p. 30).

36. See especially Park, *Travels*, pp. 142–6.

37. See, for example, Park's final exchange with Almami of Bondou (*ibid.*, p. 56). This point is also supported by Park's documentation of a reliable credit system operating among various regions and Negro ethnic groups; see Lupton, *Mungo Park*, pp. 59, 64. Such a credit system depends upon an acceptance of both the right to and the inviolability of property.

38. Park, *Travels*, p. 82.

39. *Ibid.*, p. 125.

40. Brent argues that Park's objections to the Moors were based in religious difference (*Mungo Park*, p. 93). The fact that Park evidently accepted the Negroes as fellow humans despite their paganism casts Brent's interpretation into serious doubt, even if we disregard the importance of property. Assuredly, Park's unhappy experiences in captivity reinforced whatever *idées reçues* he may have had about Islam, but there is no evidence that he was particularly suspicious of Muslims until events taught him to be. For instance, before being taken captive he applied to Ali for passage through his kingdom and seemed willing to accept in good faith Ali's offer of a guide to conduct him safely, until he realized that the offer was a ruse (Park, *Travels*, pp. 113–14).

41. Park, *Travels*, p. 261. It would be easy to assume that Park's accusation here is yet another manifestation of the stereotypical colonialist linkage between dark complexions and criminality. On the other hand, his consistent differentiation of the behaviour and attitude of Negroes from those of Moors (also represented as non-white in *Travels*) suggests that such an assumption would be simplistic.

42. *Ibid.*, p. 262.

43. *Ibid.*

44. *Ibid.*, p. 358.

45. *Ibid.*, p. 357.

46. *Ibid.*, pp. 358, 359.

47. Pratt, *Imperial Eyes*, p. 81.

48. Park, *Travels*, p. 23; emphasis his.

49. *Ibid.*, p. 298. Some have argued that Park's reticence in criticizing slavery and the slave trade originated in his awareness that some members of the African Association, and especially the organization's secretary, Bryan Edwards, opposed abolition. This argument dates from the first publication of *Travels* and is revived in a biographical account appended to the 1815 publication of Park's journal; for fuller discussion, see Lupton, *Mungo Park*, pp. 116–20. The charge is vigorously denied in an 1815 review (*Quarterly Review*, vol. 13 (April 1815): 121–5); indeed, there is no evidence in *Travels* to support it, and very little evidence elsewhere. Moreover, *Travels* includes plenty of evidence that the European slave trade did have a significant impact on the economic and social structures of western Africa; it would not be hard to oppose Park's assertion here using evidence from his own narrative.

50. See, for example, Park, *Travels*, p. 153.

51. Grosz-Ngaté, 'Power', p. 488.

52. Park, *Travels*, p. 127.

53. *Ibid.*, pp. 138, 130.

54. Cited in Sreenivasan, *Limits*, p. 32.

55. Park, *Travels*, pp. 115, 147, 160.

56. A confirming example occurs early in his account of his captivity, when he described how 'a Moor entered the hut, probably with a view to steal something, or perhaps to murder me' (*ibid.*, p. 124).

57. *Ibid.*, pp. 54–5.

58. *Ibid.*, p. 56.

59. *Ibid.*, p. 93.

60. *Ibid.*, p. 117.

61. *Ibid.*, pp. 121–2.

62. *Ibid.*, p. 122.

63. *Ibid.*, p. 124.

64. The following argument relies in a general sense upon Michel Foucault's analysis of visual surveillance in the prison context; see Foucault, *Discipline and Punish: The Birth of the Prison*, trans. Alan Sheridan (New York, Vintage, 1995).

65. After Park's successful return to England, the Association assumed a more pronounced imperialist, even colonialist, orientation. Presenting Park's achievements, for instance, Banks mixed capitalism and militarism according to the classic imperialist recipe: Park, he said, had

> opened a Gate into the Interior of Africa, into which it is easy for every Nation to enter and to extend its commerce and Discovery . . . A Detachment of 500 chosen Troops would soon make that Road easy, and would build Embarkations. (cited in Lupton, *Mungo Park*, p. 111; see also p. 133)

66. Historians disagree about the extent and nature of these effects; see Roberts, *Warriors*, pp. 17–19, 60.

67. For further discussion, see Brent, *Black Nile*, pp. 15–16. Some historians estimate a higher number; for details, see Philip D. Curtin, *The Atlantic Slave Trade: A Census* (Madison, University of Wisconsin Press, 1969). The often remarkable wealth and social prominence of the 'slatees', or African slave traders, including Park's benefactor Karfa Taura, offer a concrete example of the European slave trade's regional impact. As Bill Freund argues, 'a major consequence of the slave trade was the creation of a class that depended for its existence on Euro-African commerce' (Freund, *The Making of Contemporary Africa: The Development of African Society Since 1800* (Bloomington, Indiana University Press, 1984), p. 54). Monro cites the 'overseas demand for slave labour' as 'the greatest single external influence on socio-economic conditions in Subsaharan Africa' (*Africa*, p. 33).

68. *Travels* provides a telling example of European merchants' rapport with indigenous power structures: the three British residents of Pisania, Park said,

> enjoyed perfect security under the king's protection; and being highly esteemed and respected by the natives at large, wanted no accommodation or comfort which the country could supply; and the greatest part of the trade in slaves, ivory, and gold, was in their hands. (p. 7)

For general discussion of such relationships, see E. W. Bovill, *The Golden Trade of the Moors*, 2nd edition (London, Oxford University Press, 1968), p. 210.

69. Pratt, *Imperial Eyes*, pp. 82, 80.

70. Brahimi, 'Mungo Park', p. 154 (my translation).

71. Bovill argues that merchants in North and West Africa resisted European advance into the interior of the continent because they feared the consequences of European traders' encroachment on the markets they dominated (*Golden Trade*, pp. 207–10, and *The Niger Explored* (London, Oxford University Press, 1968), p. 15). Bovill's argument is plausible, but Park's narrative offers little evidence for it. Neither Moors nor Negroes expressed any such anxiety, although some did object to Park on religious grounds or, as already mentioned, because of his alleged spying. Indeed, until he discussed Karfa Taura's reactions to Pisania, Park offered no indication that the Africans he met were aware of global European influence. It is possible to interpret certain slatees' reluctance to help him ('all of them seemed extremely unwilling that I should prosecute my journey' (Park, *Travels*, p. 8)) as an indication that they perceived Park or those he represented as possible competition, but Park himself suggested no explanation for the slatees' conduct. There is absolutely nothing to suggest that Ali's capture of Park was motivated by concern about European political or economic power.

72. Park, *Travels*, p. 193.

73. Cheryl I. Harris, 'Whiteness as property', *Harvard Law Review*, vol. 106, no. 8 (1993): 1714, 1716.

74. See *ibid.*, p. 1734.

75. See *ibid.*, p. 1724.

76. Park, *Travels*, p. 254. For a discussion of the way using slaves as currency 'highlights the degree to which slavery "propertized" human life', see Harris, 'Whiteness', p. 1720.

77. Park, *Travels*, p. 253.

78. Harris, 'Whiteness', p. 1721.

79. Park, *Travels*, p. 268.

80. Pratt, *Imperial Eyes*, p. 82.

81. Park, *Travels*, pp. 133–4 (emphasis his).

82. *Ibid.*, p. 132.

83. See *ibid.*, p. 133. The ladies of Bondou also rewarded Park under very similar circumstances; he received 'a jar of honey and some fish' for displaying himself to them (p. 56).

84. Castiglia, *Bound*, p. 19. Snader observes a related phenomenon in fictional British accounts. 'The Oriental captivity plot can render Western men abject, ineffectual, or mild'; at the same time, 'the Western female subject's . . . sexual virtue' is preserved (Snader, 'Oriental Captivity Narrative', pp. 292, 289). Seen in this light, Park appears doubly (un)gendered: abject and ineffectual, but with virtue intact.

85. Michelle Burnham, 'Between England and America: captivity, sympathy, and the sentimental novel', in Deidre Lynch and William B. Warner (eds), *Cultural Institutions of the Novel* (Durham, NC, Duke University Press, 1996), p. 58.

86. Pratt, *Imperial Eyes*, p. 78.

87. Park, *Travels*, p. 161.

88. Another example may be found in one of the most famous episodes of *Travels*: a Negro woman invited Park into her home and, with the other women of her household, fed him, put him to bed and then sang him a lullaby which, not coincidentally, lamented his lack of a mother to perform these functions for him. Inevitably, these women were cast in the role of mother or nurse.

89. *Ibid.*, p. 263.

90. Pratt, *Imperial Eyes*, pp. 84, 85.

91. Snader, 'Oriental Captivity Narrative', p. 278.

92. Castiglia, *Bound*, p. 4.

93. See Wendy S. Mercer, 'Gender and genre in nineteenth-century travel writing: Leonie d'Aunet and Xavier Marmier', in Steve Clark (ed.), *Travel Writing and Empire: Postcolonial Theory in Transit* (London, Zed, 1999), pp. 147–8.

CHAPTER NINE

Empires of light and dark:
Japanese prisons and narratives
of survival

JAMES WHITLARK

A new Orientalism

Building on the work of A. L. Tibawi, S. H. Alatas, A. Abdel-Malek, H. Djait, Abdullah Laoui, Talal Asad, K. M. Panikkar, Ramila Thapar, Marshal Hodgson and others, Edward Said's *Orientalism* portrayed its subject as a one-way process: Europe's projecting its fantasies on Asia and the Middle East.[1] This Orientalism arose from a political inequality that hindered Asians from representing themselves to the West. Orientalism, however, underwent a marked change during the Japanese victories following Pearl Harbor. This might have ended Orientalist fantasies. Studying the Japanese closely in order to survive, the prisoners could have acquired a realistic view of their guards, beginning an era of global understanding. Conversely, the Japanese might have projected their own fantasies on their prisoners, thereby producing what one might call an 'Occidentalism' (i.e. a projection of indigenous Eastern preconceptions on the West). Indeed, to a small extent, both these things occurred. However, the dominant discourse relating conqueror and conquered was Western in origin, and thus a variant of Orientalism, though in a new form.

What did the new version replace?

The old Orientalism consisted of a series of binary oppositions: white/ non-white, moral/amoral, masculine/effeminate, and so on. The Occident applied the preferred term to itself and the less preferred one to the Eastern Other. Frantz Fanon was one of the first to remark on the 'Manichean' dimension such colonialism assumed when the Other was conceived as a devil to be exterminated.[2] Homi Bhabha has well explored subtler negotiations that allowed some colonizers to avoid the constant holy war that would be required if the colonized were perceived as totally demonic.[3] Since prisoner-of-war camps are by definition products of war, the Japanese ones gravitated toward binary extremes (as with Fanon) but with psychological modifications as subtle as any described by Bhabha, yet in novel configurations. The key difference between this World War II Orientalism and the previous kind was that, even in writing their versions of what had happened, the Western prisoners could not quite echo the old-Orientalist assumption that Asians naturally and inevitably occupied an inferior status.

Competing racisms

The Japanese had indigenous views of Westerns as hairy monsters, but these did not well suit the modernization of the Meiji period (1867–1912). Therefore, along with borrowing the techniques of modern war, the Japanese adapted European Orientalism (particularly its racism) to their own purposes, but with the Occident as the despised Other. During the Meiji period and thereafter, Japan had been increasingly angry at Occidental, particularly American, racism. For instance, to protest the Exclusion Act of 1924 (which, on racial grounds, kept Far Easterners from immigrating to the United States), the Japanese government called the Act's inauguration 'Humiliation Day' and organized protests. In one of these, a Japanese committed *sepuku* near the American Embassy in Tokyo.[4] Following World War I, a Japanese delegation tried unsuccessfully to include a statement of 'world racial equality' in the Covenant of the League of Nations. Japan's early victories in World War II inclined the victors to think that if the West insisted on racial inequality, then the Japanese would be the superiors.

Because it was on the minds of both Japanese guards and Occidental prisoners, race was a major theme in many Pacific POW narratives, as well as in the official documents to which they often allude. For instance, even in promising humane treatment of prisoners, Japan's Minister of Foreign Affairs on 2 March 1942 used the phrase 'racial customs'.[5] This phrase derives from the idea (then widespread) that people's traditions were largely genetic. Consequently, the conqueror could do little to educate the conquered, whose supposed imperfections were ineradicable (except by extermination).

Since this racism was a relatively recent importation, one might suppose that it was a less prominent influence on Japanese behaviour than indigenous ideologies, e.g. Bushido. Actually, however, the Meiji period was one of great intellectual ferment, wherein all traditional values were being redefined to coincide with national modernization. Although Bushido was much discussed, it was a medieval system that needed to be translated into twentieth-century terms. Consequently, there was no universally accepted meaning to it. The best-known book on Bushido, for instance, was by a Quaker, who tried to make it sound like a combination of Christianity, European chivalry and pacifism.[6] Not only was Bushido highly ambiguous in the Meiji context, but it had one rule that kept it from directing relations between custodians and prisoners: it forbade surrender. Consequently, the existence of prisoners was unthinkable. The Japanese did not prepare for large numbers of inmates, either materially or psychologically. This meant that, in some regions, the Japanese merely contained prisoners and otherwise left them largely alone. A few narratives express this situation, notably James Clavel's fictionalization of his time in Changi, *King Rat*.[7] More often however, both in life and story, guards and guarded had close contact. And since indigenous Japanese values offered no guidelines for that interrelationship, the most accessible guide was racist Orientalism, with the prisoners seeing the guards through its filter while the guards applied their own adaptation of it in persecuting the prisoners.

Typical of memoirs written during the war, Gwen Dew recalls a captor thus:

> At one point Colonel Tada went into a long dissertation about Greek and Roman civilization, how it changed from time to time with the inference, of course, that now Japan was going to take charge of the history of the world, and our era of white influence has ceased.[8]

In his preface, Dew makes this even more explicit:

> The lives of millions of men, women, and children have been piled on the pyre of Japan's ambitions to dominate the white men of the world, all yellow men who are not Japanese, and all brown and black men who come under her blood-dripping juggernaut.[9]

The word 'juggernaut', an allusion to Indian religion, implies that the Japanese cruelty is part of some pan-Asian character flaw. Nonetheless, Dew denies that he is in any way prejudiced: 'I love the Orient, as do all who have ever felt her lure, as a man does a mysterious, fascinating, and wise woman.' The East as a female to be subjected to the masculine West is one of the principal metaphors of Orientalism. Faced with Dew's obvious bias, one might presume his charges are purely American propaganda. Based on Japanese sources, nevertheless, the historian Yuki Tanaka concludes:

> By having Korean and Formosans guard white prisoners under Japanese command, the Japanese military hoped that the old 'pecking order' would be reversed – that non-Japanese Asians would come to see whites as inferior, subjugated people and the Japanese as the 'natural' leaders of Asia.[10]

Thus in a manner that might equally be called lamentable and ironic, one form or another of Orientalism was directing the way both sides perceived the camps. Whereas the Nazi concentration camps did not persuade many that the Germans as a people were inherently pernicious, as late as 1973 Clifford Kinvig 'warns that a race that could make a Thailand Railway necessary, and then build it, is a race quite different from any Western race'.[11]

This racism was difficult to escape. Even on those rare occasions when some rapport existed between conqueror and conquered, the suspicion of prejudice tended to set limits to real reciprocity. For instance, Colonel Suga was a fan of the author Agnes Newton Keith and consequently allowed her special privileges in the camp. Indeed, he demanded that she write an account of her experiences and provided her both leisure and opportunities to do so. He risked much to show leniency towards her husband. Nevertheless, he repeatedly accused her of racism despite her denials, and ultimately she had to conclude: 'we were enemies'.[12] Carl S. Nordin's memoir *We Were Next to Nothing* includes a guard whom the prisoners nickname 'Simon LeGree' because he 'had gone to school in the United States and had taken a dislike to Americans there because he had experienced racism'.[13] That nickname implies that the prisoners also thought of themselves as victims of prejudice.

The Bridge over the River Kwai

Pierre Boulle's *The Bridge over the River Kwai* is one of the best-known explorations of the competing racisms of prisoners and jailers. Japan is represented by Colonel Saito, 'roaring drunk, drunk on European alcohol' – a stereotype of the non-Westerner who cannot hold Occidental liquor. Concerning him, a British officer thinks:

> To be quite honest he had to admit that in Saito's speech there were certain basic principles to which the whole world subscribed, East and West alike. In the course of it he was able to recognize and identify the various influences behind the words which spluttered on the lips of this Jap: racial pride, a mystic belief in authority, the dread of not being taken seriously, a strange sort of inferiority complex which gave him a jaundiced, suspicious outlook on life, as though he was in perpetual fear of being laughed at. Saito had lived abroad. He must have seen how the British sometimes made fun of certain aspects of the Japanese character, and how comic the affectations of a humorless nation were in the eyes of one to whom humor was second nature.[14]

This attribution of being humorless is not necessarily by Boulle, for he later mentions instances of Japanese laughter. Similarly, he makes clear that Saito is also scorned by the Japanese. Nonetheless, he makes the core of the book a confrontation with Occidentals who are more courageous and efficient than their Japanese counterparts. This situation flatters an Occidental audience, particularly in the movie version, which does less to disclaim the implication that Saito is a typical Japanese commander. Boulle is obviously also making fun of the British by way of Colonel Nicholson. The latter is so seduced by Orientalism that he betrays his country by building the best possible bridge for the Japanese in order to prove the superiority of his engineers over theirs. He even makes the structure as inconspicuous as possible so that it will be more difficult for the British to bomb! He fears that unless he proves his efficiency thus, 'we'll fall to the level of these brutes'.[15] Now captured and caged himself, Nicholson must reassert his superiority at any cost in order to retain his humanity. Like Joseph Conrad before him, Boulle was a foreign observer of the British. After escaping from a Japanese camp, Boulle served in Britain's Special Force in Calcutta. He begins his book by quoting Conrad, 'it is by folly alone that the world moves'.[16] As so often with Conrad (another sojourner among the British), the implication is that this folly is clearest in colonies where the colonizers catch some kind of crazed, uncivilized behaviour from the colonized. To create this effect, Boulle departs significantly from history, since there is no evidence that any British officer actually strove to assist the Japanese.[17]

Stereotypes

The novel *The Bridge over the River Kwai* is only one of countless narratives where the Occidentals gain psychological advantage over their captors (though at a certain cost). In Norman Carter's ostensibly non-fiction *G-String Jesters*, for instance, there is again a brave British officer constantly protesting violations of human rights.[18] The other officers maintain their equilibrium by secretly deriding the guards, for example, by nicknaming one 'King Kong', as if he were subhuman. Jailers force some prisoners to wear women's sarongs. Later, prisoners in their theatricals don women's clothes. If these events are psychologically connected, one might speculate that the actual prisoners are, in a small way, doing what the fictional character Nicholson does in a larger way: identifying partly with their jailers' point of view, but as part of a defence against it. Nicholson tries to prove his superiority by helping the Japanese cause. Officers cross-dressing for theatricals are accepting the female roles sometimes imposed by the enemy, but in a context that allows the British to feel they have the last laugh. If one recalls that feminizing the Orient was a standard device of Orientalism, this issue of gender fits into a long history of colonial discourse.

Another equally prevalent image in Orientalism is of Occidental light versus Eastern obscurity. This may occur explicitly or be reduced to mere setting, as in the following:

> Through the silvery leaves of the two palm trees near the water's edge a soft wind sighs. High swamp grass hides the horizon in a mysterious haze. A white ricebird, awakened by the full, tropical moon, utters its eerie cry.[19]

These opening sentences from Cornel Lumiere's imprisonment memoir *Kura!* present this trope in unusually condensed and florid manner. The key word is 'mysterious', an effect supported by the cloaking 'haze' and 'eerie' (i.e. unrecognizable) sounds. However graphically POW stories narrate events, they typically allude to other happenings that remain unspeakably beyond the text. Indeed, as in Lumiere's purple passage, there is usually an almost teasing combination of sensuous detail with an indication of something hidden.

Appropriately, Lumiere lights his impressionistic 'haze' with the dim moon. Its connotations are best seen by turning to an extremely well-developed presentation of this lunar image in another narrative of POW torture, Laurens van der Post's *A Bar of Shadow*:

> The attraction, both the keen, conscious and the deep, submerged attraction that all the Japanese feel for the moon seemed to come to a point in Hara. If ever there was a moon-swung, moon-haunted, moon-drawn soul it was he. As the moon waxed we saw it draw a far tide of mythological frenzy to the full in Hara's blood. . . . In fact, the morning after he had cut off the head of one of us, I remember seeing him talking to Lawrence and being struck by the fact that he had an expression of purified, of youthful and almost springlike innocence on his face, as if the sacrifice of the life of an innocent British aircraftman the night before had . . . appeased for the time the hungry, batlike gods of his race.[20]

By implication, the West is solar, the East lunar, the former conscious, the latter unconscious. This difference is one of 'race', treated in terms reminiscent of Nazi propaganda where the Jews were seen as Eastern and parasitic, as here the Japanese serve vampiric 'hungry, batlike gods'. Nevertheless, accompanying van der Post's harangue against Saito is Lawrence's seeing Saito as virtually an embodiment of his own unconscious, so that later in the story he wishes to be reconciled with him.

Continuing tropes from old Orientalism, the tendency is for these POW narratives to associate the Japanese with dim lights or with darkness, but there are some notable exceptions. For instance, in *The Way of a Boy: A Memoir of Java*, Ernest Hillen writes:

> The Japanese used the sun to hurt us. Day in day out they let it burn down for long hours on workers, weakening and dulling them. A prisoner who broke a rule might be dragged to a shadeless spot to stand at attention, or sit there hunched up in a little bamboo cage, for a day, or two days, eyes burning, lips cracking, with no food or water and kicks and slaps if she blacked out. . . . [lectured in the sun] that we had no home and fatherland any more – 'and so you have no religion any more' – and that we must be obedient, polite, humble, and self-disciplined; on and on.[21]

Preceding these remarks, Hillen alludes to the Japanese flag with its conspicuous sun, reminding the reader that the Japanese also claim to represent the light. In turning this claim against them Hillen is, nonetheless, conceding the association of the Japanese with the sun. An earlier Orientalism tended to give this association unthinkingly to the Occident, for example, in Sir Edwin Arnold's contrasting titles *The Light of Asia* (about Buddhism) and *The Light of the World* (about Christianity as the Occidental and thus greater illumination). Being written after the camps ceased to exist, narratives about them can, with relative safety, reassert almost the old Orientalism, but not quite.

Consider how these narratives transform the basic pattern of the Orientalist tale. Its beginning was typically the introduction of an Occidental into the East through travels or, more rarely, through being born there (e.g. *Kim*). In either case, the Occidental is markedly superior to the natives. The POW narratives begin this way also, but with premonitions of a reversal. For instance, in Dieuwke Bonga's *Eight Prison Camps*, one cannot read the following without a sense of how Bonga will soon be the reluctant, colonized labourer:

> The Dutch government had from the beginning of the twentieth century worked towards the development and education of the vast population [of Java]. At first it went slowly. This multitude did not seem to understand the purpose of this decision. A laborer did not work hard.[22]

Bonga does not seem conscious of the irony the POW context gives to these words. Whether consciously or not, in order to frame prison experience, Pacific POW narrators were commonly drawn to allude to the structure of the society that the Japanese interrupted; and that structure took on an ominous quality when followed by the horrifying structure of the camps. Thus, Ernest Hillen's *The Way of a Boy* begins with such plantation characters as the administrator Mr Witte:

> Some [Javanese] women felt his eyes and glanced up and then his eyes would lock on theirs until they looked away.... Chief administrators were kings on their plantations, I heard my father say once. I think he liked Mr Witte, liked his discipline.[23]

The word 'discipline' recalls an earlier scene where Hillen's father is disciplining a dog. As in Michel Foucault's *Discipline and Punish*, the extension of discipline that made possible the modern state had its paradigmatic form in the prison.[24] To the extent that the Japanese had learned to modernize, they had also acquired this paradigm. Admittedly, that modernization was in many respects superficial, and their camps kept running out of barbed wire, but there is little question from whence the idea for that wire had come. Similarly, their admonitions to their prisoners to exhibit 'self-discipline' sound as if they derived from the Occidental texts quoted by Foucault.

In Pacific POW narratives, another analogue of the Oriental tale is the figure of the good Japanese (usually a Christian) who is less cruel than the others. He serves a comparable purpose to the Oriental tale's good native, for example, Gunga Din, willing to die for the colonists. Indeed, some POW narratives include native troops who suffer torture and death rather than betray their British masters to the Japanese. These 'good' figures seem to demonstrate both the narrator's lack of prejudice and how bad in contrast are the other Asians.

Nevertheless, oriental tales and POW ones are almost mirror reversals of each other. For the crowded masses of Asia, one finds the overcrowded prisoners. Instead of spanning fragrant gardens and beautiful vistas, a large part of the POW stories take place in gloomy, fetid latrines. Above all, the Westerners cannot freely impose their fantasies on the Asians but must also resist the reverse process, being subjected to a style of racism the Japanese learned from the West.

The survivor as artist: Ronald Searle

Those least able to resist are the young, who have not yet fully formed their identities. To assess the continuing influence of the camps, consider the works of Ronald Searle and James Graham Ballard, both youthful when they were confined by the Japanese. Ballard writes of Searle:

> I remember coming across his prison-camp drawings within a few months of leaving my own camp, and thinking how exactly he had caught the squalor of camp life. Superficially, Searle's touch lightened when he launched his post-war career . . . [but] one still senses somewhere in the background the perimeter wall of Changi.[25]

Unlike Ballard (who spent his twelfth to fifteenth years imprisoned near Shanghai), Searle was ten years older when he endured a comparable span in Changi, Singapore, and consequently was not as vulnerable as the child. Nonetheless, the experience was intense: 'Searle endured repeated beatings, starvation and malaria, and the deaths of his friends, all the while sketching on pages torn from books, and bartering . . . "orgiastic" drawings with the Japanese guards in return for precious supplies of paper.'[26]

Searle's visual narrative of his confinement is all the more powerful because it consists of sketchy lines on discoloured paper, the austerity of medium conveying the destitution of camp life. In one picture, three troll-like guards squat before a shadowy form in imitation of the centurions dicing below the cross of Christ.[27] Another shows an emaciated inmate crucified on barbed wire. The scrawl outlining him itself resembles jagged filaments, more a pained entanglement than a human being. He has become what confines him (perhaps Searle's recognition of the degree to which he was internalizing the prison). There are also drawings with grim humour, such as 'Christmas Dinner 1944', a page of kittens.[28]

Works that predate his incarceration include art-school nudes and renderings of army life, but Searle shows no predisposition for the depiction of suffering. This came with Changi and never entirely left him. After returning to England, he continued making grotesque sketches, much in his prison style. In the late 1940s, he portrayed war-devastated Yugoslavia and Poland. In the 1950s, he made a pictorial journey for the United Nations High Command on Refugees, painting the privation of those immured in camps. Later, for UNICEF's Year of the Child, he drew little boys playing with skeletons and a black-and-white, starving baby confined in the womb of the world, surrounded by the full-colour toys which that infant would never have.

Presumably, Changi deepened his morbidity. Before imprisonment, he had already launched a series about a girls' school, St Trinian's. After the camp, however, these cartoons assumed a Charles Adams-like grisliness. In a 1951 drawing, students wrestle so viciously that one plunges a knife into the other's back. The teacher comments, 'Some little girl didn't hear me say "unarmed combat".' The sad insight behind the humour is how confinement increases antagonism between inmates. That Searle should transfer the violence of a prison to a girls' school is not surprising, for incarceration inclines towards seeing the rest of existence as a continuation of it. Thus, Searle draws a 'Workaholic', behind the prisonlike bars of a desk, his leg manacled to the telephones and a winged clock as his celestial warden.[29] In a 1963 cartoon, an angel walks the barbed wire of the Berlin Wall, recalling the Changi crucifixion.[30] A 1968 drawing of 'Papa Doc, Haiti' has chained prisoners tortured by the police.[31]

The aspects of Searle's post-Changi art that most link him to Ballard are the depression and self-destruction that came from at least partly seeing themselves as they had been seen by their guards. Indeed, Searle did an entire book entitled, *The Situation Is Hopeless*. Its cover page consists of a dead seagull lying upside down but with a rainbow in the background as if the bird died seeking an unreachable goal. The cartoons are of animals destroyed by their own trust and naiveté, such as a 'Baby seal under the impression that clubs are centres of social activity'.[32] His book *Hello – Where Did All the People Go?* replaces the population with snails, who carry their own prisons.[33] Indeed, his other volumes also abound in dark comedy, such as 'Self-Portrait as a Non-stop Self-Mutilator', where Vincent van Gogh gradually hacks his head to pieces or 'We Will All Go Together When We Go', with a nuclear explosion which a skeleton accompanies on the piano.[34] Individually, these cartoons inspire laughter, but collectively they evidence a tragic, indeed excessive awareness of suffering.

With the immediate appeal of visual art, they can serve as an introduction to J. G. Ballard's prolific opus, which develops far more fully the implications of similar themes. Among the perils of prison, the most insidious is to adopt the guards' attitudes. Nordin's title *We Were Next to Nothing* well captures some prisoners' willingness to internalize the guard's low opinion of them. Such despair was not quite as much a temptation for the adult Searle as for the twelve-year-old Ballard.

The survivor as artist: James Graham Ballard

Because of the academy-award nominated movie made from the first of them, Ballard's best-known works are the autobiographical novels *Empire of the Sun* (1984) and *The Kindness of Women* (1991).[35] Both treat an internment, where his persona (Jamie) 'Far from wanting to escape from the camp ... had been trying to burrow ever more deeply into its heart.'[36] While witnessing Japanese soldiers torturing a Chinese youth to death with wire, Jamie lingers, leaves reluctantly and later wishes he had stayed – a perverse, indeed, suicidal wish. At least as devastating as any sexual encounter can be in prison is the seductiveness of this kind of total surrender to the hostile powers. As with Kurt Vonnegut's *Slaughterhouse Five*, many years intervened between imprisonment and Ballard's being able to describe directly what he had endured. Nonetheless, before his two realistic novels about the imprisonment, science fiction inspired by the camp experience allowed indirect expression in practically everything he wrote. Ballard's first four books, *The Wind from Nowhere*, *The Drowned World*, *The Drought*, and *The Crystal World* are about apocalyptic destruction, which forces the characters into various kinds of self-imposed enclosure and withdrawal. In *The Wind from Nowhere*, for instance, escaping the tornadoes requires a remnant of humanity to lock themselves in fortresses. Except for that first novel, which Ballard wrote in a hurried, formulaic way for the American market, what is unusual in the other novels is the protagonists' willing submission to destruction. *The Drowned World* ends with its main character refusing to return to society. Instead, he is 'following the lagoons southward through the increasing rain and heat, attacked by alligators and giant bats, [becoming] a second Adam searching for the forgotten paradises of the reborn Sun'.[37] This is his quest for 'the drowned world of my uterine childhood', a return to the confinement of the womb.[38] When an editor requested a happier ending, Ballard replied that this suicide *was* 'happy'.[39] In *The Drought*, the withdrawal is to a miserable group enclosed by a vast desert. *The Crystal World* is the most masochistic, a description of the pleasure its characters take in being encased in fatal crystals.

Through their futuristic ambiance, these stories somewhat distance the reader from the protagonists' surrender to confinement. The next three novels (*Crash*, *Concrete Island* and *High Rise*) are more disquieting because the imprisoning withdrawals are set in the present. The first of these is about the pleasure of being injured in automobile accidents. The link between the writing of *Crash* (1973) and Ballard's prison experience is directly referred to in *The Kindness of Women*. In *Crash*, David, a childhood friend of Jamie, continues to be traumatized by the camp. Decades later, his way of working through/reliving the pain is a highly eroticized obsession with car collisions, causing him to crash deliberately. Having a similar background, Jamie finds this obsession with being trapped and wounded in a wrecked car contagious, the closest bourgeois life comes to the helplessness of prison. Consequently, Jamie holds an art exhibition of crashed cars (as Ballard did, preparatory to his writing the novel). Somewhere between fiction and autobiography, *The Kindness of Women* may not present a literally accurate account of *Crash*'s origin, but it at least shows that Ballard connected *Crash* to prison-formed traumas. His next novel, *Concrete Island* (1974), again uses automotive imagery for the persona's surrender. After an accident that leaves the protagonist injured at a motorway intersection, he decides to spend the rest of his life self-confined there with others who have chosen to do the same. *High Rise* (1977) is an even more elaborate depiction of people organizing their own prison. Comparable to the press of inmates in the camp, a high rise block forms what Ballard terms 'Critical Mass', a density that crushes civilization. Upper-middle-class residents of a high rise stop leaving the building and find themselves enmeshed in tribal feuds between the floors. Regressing toward savagery, they eat each other's pets (cf Searle's Christmas dinner of kittens). Eventually, they begin murdering one another. Like prisoners of war, who avoid carrying their conflicts to camp authorities, the characters never summon the police. At the end of the novel, they expect similar psychological implosions in all the high rises of the world.

His other novels have been equally macabre. *The Unlimited Dream Company* (1979) concerns a deranged and dead aircraft cleaner who, in his afterlife, finds himself trapped in Shepperton, England (where Ballard was writing the narrative). *Hello America* (1981) is about isolated, mostly demented groups in what is left of the United States. In *Running Wild* (1988), stringently supervised children massacre their parents. When Ballard was in the camp, bourgeois families such as his found themselves reduced to the same cramped quarters. Whereas the poor vent the tensions of overcrowding through emotional outbursts, upper-class decorum denied access to this. He imagines that contemporary life is building equally dangerous conditions, as the rich wall themselves and their offspring behind electronic security, which is also used on the children. In their seemingly comfortable prison, the children, nonetheless, suffer from a kind of sensory deprivation. Consequently, they seek release into sensuous brutality. That, in a sense, they escape makes this work different from most of Ballard's other fictions, but the escape is pathological and violent, as if the guard-figures that haunt his imagination could not simply be forgotten.

In *Rushing to Paradise* (1994) the teenage protagonist, Neil Dempsey, joins the criminally insane Dr Barbara, apparently to halt nuclear testing on an island, but actually – like the protagonist of *The Kindness of Women*, who flies bombers for Nato – because of 'childish infatuation with nuclear death'.[40] (What finally brought Searle's and Ballard's release from prison was the bombing of Hiroshima and Nagasaki, so nuclear holocausts are tied complexly to the horrors of their incarceration.) Neil finds Dr Barbara more seductive the more homicidal she becomes. When rescued from her attempts to kill him, he still wishes to rejoin her and 'be embraced again by [her] cruel and generous heart'.[41]

To assess how obsessively often Ballard has recast his psychological surrender to imprisonment, one must at least glance at his vast production of short stories, most of them set in prison, asylum, clinic or some other structure similar to these. Consider, for instance, *The Best Short Stories of J. G. Ballard*, a representative selection. It begins with 'The Concentration City', its very title comparing megalopolis to a concentration camp, because the people are packed so densely together. Then come a series of stories reminiscent of the clock dominating Searle's 'Workaholic'. With a prison inmate as its protagonist, 'Chronopolis' has massive population bringing ever more stringent temporal control until it becomes unendurably constraining. In 'Manhole 69', a clinic's inmates are surgically altered to deprive them of sleep, so they can function constantly. Again with a clinical setting, 'The Voices of Time' also mentions surgical suppression of sleep. That the metaphor of time as prison should occur to both Searle and Ballard is not surprising. In a prison, time-keepers are armed and thus difficult to ignore. Ballard's additional fascination with both insomnia and excessive slumber suggests the sleep disturbances of depression, a common reaction to camp life and the post-traumatic stress syndrome it inspires. The volume ends with a series of stories from the volume *The Atrocity Exhibition*. They concern the (real or imaginary) assassinations of John F. Kennedy, Jacqueline Kennedy and Ronald Reagan, as well as other crimes considered from the points of view of asylum inmates. Madhouse and prison merge as depositories for social deviants.

His more recent collection of stories, *War Fever* (1984, reissued 1990), begins with Beirut as a concentration camp with orphans brought there and conditioned to kill each other as an experiment in violence. Most stories in the volume echo this theme of precarious enclosure. Crushed by the wreck of his life, the protagonist of 'The Enormous Space' sequesters himself at home and devours his neighbours' pets, then anyone who visits him. 'Dream Cargoes' is one of Ballard's many tales about islands, this one quarantined by the rest of the world though a couple choose to stay there despite its contamination. Four stories in the volume are experimental. In 'Answers to a Questionnaire', the reader sees only the answers not the questions, but can infer from the former a tale about an ex-convict who believes he has killed the Son of God. 'The Object of the Attack' constitutes forensic diaries about a psychotic prisoner. 'Notes Towards a Mental Breakdown' consists of a sentence of which each word is annotated by an asylum inmate. Finally, 'The Index' purports to be a book's index, but by its contents the (non-existent) book apparently concerns another life of insanity and imprisonment. These four experimental stories show that Ballard can more easily break free from the conventions of traditional narrative than from his obsessive themes.

Perhaps the most psychologically revealing of his short stories is 'The Dead Time' from *Myths of the Near Future* (1982). It reimagines the conclusion of his camp experience in nightmarish terms. The protagonist is transporting a truck loaded with corpses. Arriving at his parents' camp, he stands naked while a little girl sucks his blood. Only when she does this can he call forth the prisoners, bringing them to life as if resurrected from a grave. So evocative a piece might be analysed in many ways, but one of the more obvious implications is that the corpses represent his freight of traumatic memories. His world seems to have died and only by giving up part of himself (the life blood) can it be reborn. As a fantasy about the East, this story is by definition Orientalist, but it is certainly not the old, lush Orientalism of the nineteenth century. It derives from overpowering terrors endured in the East (which, in a sense, all his works may be said to do).

The obvious question is what these may have to do with the often remarked postmodernity of his writings. Gayatri Spivak's *In Other Words: Essays in Cultural Politics* theorizes, 'There is an affinity between the imperialist subject and the subject of humanism.'[42] In other words, the postmodern critique of humanism is related to the effects of colonialism, because both are predicated on centralized knowledge of people in order to control them.

Is such centralization an indigenous Japanese norm? When, for instance, the Americans occupied Tokyo they imposed street signs on the previously unmarked streets; when the occupation ended, one of the first things the Japanese did was to return the streets to anonymity. They were not just showing their repugnance towards American, centralized control but towards any streamlined centralization. This did not lead to anomie. Each police station continued to keep track of locals, but the system was deliberately subtle and complex, striating and decentring the communication network – a vestige of feudalism amidst seeming modernity.

Do Ballard's satires of centralization derive from this Japanese sensibility? Although his attitude toward anything prison-like probably dates from his being interned by the Japanese, the experience did not make him study Oriental philosophy deeply. Indeed, his few references to that subject are hardly very knowledgeable. For instance, in *Hello America*, he confuses Zen with tantrism, two different branches of Buddhism. Similarly, Jamie's desire to surrender to the Japanese did not inspire him to embrace Japanese culture. Ironically, Ballard's postmodern dissatisfaction with centralization does not seem to derive from his captors being Japanese but from the Westernization they underwent to fight a modern war. Through their imitation of colonialism, they made many Westerners trade places with Asian colonials.

Conclusion

Since that war, economic changes, for example, the increases in Japanese and Arab wealth, have (in less dramatic ways) had similar effects.

In a world where no group of nations can practice unrestrained hegemony, postmodernism and postcolonialism are essentially the same phenomenon, a search for some alternative to the old Western/Orientalist/colonialist view of the globe. Admittedly, in a few cases Occidentals have quite explicitly turned eastward as part of that search, for example, Gary Snyder's Buddhism or Ursula Le Guin's Taoism. Such a turning, however, is not common enough for it to be seen as the source of postmodern decentring. Also admittedly, there are such similarities between Far Eastern philosophies and deconstructive postmodernism, as Robert Magliola notes in his *Derrida on the Mend*.[43] Nonetheless, their having much in common comes largely from coincidence.

Various Occidental developments, including the technological, have increased fear that over-centralization may reduce society to a prison. Unlike postmodernism, traditional Asia was not reacting against this problem. From the eighteenth century until World War II, Asian countries did not suffer from as much streamlined centralization as did their Western contemporaries, but the lack placed the Asians at a disadvantage politically, militarily and economically. The bridge over the River Kwai has become a symbol of an Asian attempt at an equally streamlined communication system. Book and movie give the impression that Japan could only attain that through Western help and that the system could fairly easily be severed by Westerners. In this respect, Boulle's novel is representative of all the Japanese imprisonment narratives, for each implies that you too may be colonized/incarcerated by Asians, but you can break free. This is the newer Orientalism. There were stirrings of it in 'yellow peril' fiction prior to World War II, but before those prison camps the Occident did not have to take the idea very seriously. This new Orientalism remains relatively popular, as in the Japan-bashing of Kurt Vonnegut's *Hocus Pocus* (1990) and Michael Crichton's *Rising Sun* (1992). Both use the prison as metaphor, the first with an American prison run for profit by the Japanese, and the latter with a Japanese corporation that covertly exercises overwhelming control on American soil. Such works, however, are merely a subgenre of a larger body of literature about society as prison – the body to which Ballard and Searle usually contribute, even though their own lives tie them to the subgenre. Like them, literature of course should move beyond the new Orientalism of this subgenre to a non-racist view of humanity as a whole: a non-Orientalism. Nonetheless, despite its paranoia, the new Orientalism has one thing to recommend it at least over the old: it takes the East seriously.

Certainly, this new Orientalism should not be dismissed as merely a fad of the last decade. For instance, a follower of Said, Ziauddin Sardar, dates this change in Orientalism from 1991, when S. Ishihara published *The Japan That Can Say No*.[44] Pearl Harbor, however, constituted an earlier saying No to the West. Both rejections of the Occident were based on what Japan had learned from it, a learning tinged with the old Orientalism. That old version consisted of psychological walls that the West built against the East; unfortunately, these walls materialized as the literal and metaphorical prisons of the new.

Notes

1. Edward Said, *Orientalism* (New York, Pantheon, 1978); for Said's debts to these predecessors, see Ziauddin Sardar, *Orientalism* (Philadelphia, Open University Press, 1999), pp. 65–76.
2. Frantz Fanon, *The Wretched of the Earth*, trans. Constance Farrington (New York, Grove Press, 1963), p. 33.
3. For example, Homi K. Bhabha, *The Location of Culture* (London, Routledge, 1994), p. 22; see also Homi Bhabha, *Nation and Narration* (London, Routledge, 1990).
4. E. Bartlett Kerr, *Surrender and Survival: The Experience of American POWs in the Pacific 1941–1945* (New York, William Morrow & Co., 1985), p. 25.
5. *Ibid.*, p. 43.
6. Inazo Nitobe, *Bushido: The Soul of Japan* (New York, G. P. Putnam, 1905; reprinted Tokyo, Charles E. Tuttle, 1969).
7. James Clavel, *King Rat* (New York, Dell, 1958).
8. Gwen Dew, *Prisoner of the Japs* (New York, Alfred A. Knopf, 1943), p. 155.
9. *Ibid.*, p. v.
10. Yuki Tanaka, *Hidden Horrors: Japanese War Crimes in World War II* (Boulder, CO, Westview Press, 1996), p. 38.
11. Clifford Kinvig, *Death Railway*. Ballantine's Illustrated History of the Violent Century, no. 3 (New York, Ballantine, 1973), p. 7.
12. Agnes Newton Keith, *Three Came Home*, introduction by Carl Mydans (New York, Time, 1965), p. 170.
13. Carl S. Nordin, *We Were Next to Nothing: An American POW's Account of Japanese Prison Camps and Deliverance in World War II* (London, McFarland, 1997), p. 77.
14. Pierre Boulle, *The Bridge over the River Kwai*, trans. Xan Fielding (New York, Time, 1954), p. 23.
15. *Ibid.*, p. 55.
16. *Ibid.*, p. vii.
17. Ernest Gordon, *Through the Valley of the Kwai* (New York, Harper, 1962).
18. Norman Carter, *G-String Jesters* (Sydney, Currawong, 1966).
19. Cornel Lumiere, *Kura!* (Brisbane, Jacaranda Press, 1966), p. 1.
20. Laurens van der Post, *A Bar of Shadow* (Hyde Park, NY, Hyde Park Free Library, 1956), p. 21.
21. Ernest Hillen, *The Way of a Boy: A Memoir of Java* (New York, Penguin, 1993), p. 65.
22. Dieuwke Wendelaar Bonga, *Eight Prison Camps: A Dutch Family in Japanese Java*, Monographs in International Studies, Southeast Asia Series, No. 98 (Athens, OH, Ohio University for International Studies, 1996), p. 8.
23. Hillen, *The Way*, p. 13.
24. Michel Foucault, *Discipline and Punish: The Birth of the Prison*, trans. Alan Sheridan (New York, Vintage, 1995).
25. J. G. Ballard, 'Desperate Humours', in *A User's Guide to the Millennium: Essays and Reviews* (New York, Picador, 1996), p. 104.
26. *Ibid.*, p. 105.
27. Ronald Searle, *Ronald Searle in Perspective* (New York, Atlantic Monthly, 1983), p. 14.
28. *Ibid.*, p. 20.
29. *Ibid.*, p. 109.
30. *Ibid.*, p. 82.
31. *Ibid.*, p. 81.

32. Ronald Searle, *The Situation Is Hopeless* (New York, Viking, 1980), unnumbered.

33. Ronald Searle, *Hello – Where Did All the People Go?* (New York, Stephen Crane Press, 1968).

34. Searle, *Perspective*, pp. 161, 208.

35. I discuss the following works by J. G. Ballard: *The Atrocity Exhibition* (London, Cape, 1970, revised, with annotations by Ballard, San Francisco, Re/Search, 1990); *The Best Short Stories of J. G. Ballard* (New York, Holt, Rinehart & Winston, 1978); *The Burning World* (New York, Berkley, 1964); *Concrete Island* (London, Cape, 1974); *Crash* (London, Cape, 1973); *The Crystal World* (New York, Farrar, Straus & Giroux, 1966); 'Desperate Humours', in *A User's Guide to the Millennium* (New York, Picador, 1996); *The Drowned World* (New York, Berkley, 1962); *Empire of the Sun* (London, Gollancz, 1987); *Hello America* (London, Cape, 1981); *High Rise* (London, Cape, 1975); *The Kindness of Women* (New York, Farrar, Straus, Giroux, 1991); *Rushing to Paradise* (New York, Picador, 1994); *War Fever* (1984, reissued Collins, 1990); *Myths of the Near Future* (London, Cape, 1982).

36. Ballard, *Kindness of Women*, p. 17.

37. Ballard, *Drowned World*, p. 162.

38. *Ibid.*, p. 24.

39. James Goddard and David Pringle (eds), *J. G. Ballard: The First Twenty Years* (Hayes, Barn's Head Books, 1976), p. 24.

40. Ballard, *Rushing to Paradise*, p. 224.

41. *Ibid.*, p. 238.

42. Gayatri Spivak, *In Other Words: Essays in Cultural Politics* (New York, Methuen, 1988), p. 202.

43. Robert Magliola, *Derrida on the Mend* (West Lafayette, IN, Purdue University Press, 1984).

44. Ziauddin Sardar, pp. 111–13; S. Ishihara, *The Japan That Can Say No* (New York, Simon & Schuster, 1991).

CHAPTER TEN

Torture and the decolonization of French Algeria: nationalism, 'race' and violence during colonial incarceration

JAMES D. LE SUEUR

The logic of torture

During the decolonization of Algeria (1954–62), torture was the logical outcome of hegemonic France's politico-military system in its final hours. Torture was probably inevitable in Algeria because the French authorities, led by the military and the police, possessed all the structural characteristics of a totalitarian (and, many argued, fascist) regime. French military authorities, in an effort to keep Algeria French, were intent on maintaining European control over the Muslim majority at all costs; and, as a result, during the final stages of colonialism, these authorities – many of whom had been tortured themselves by the Nazis only a decade before – liberally and systematically employed torture against incarcerated Algerian and European revolutionaries with impunity. Moreover, these blatant abuses of the colonial system in Algeria eventually corrupted all levels of the French bureaucracy and administration, especially the French judicial and penal systems. In short, during the French-Algerian War torture became an indispensable and incontrovertible aspect of a continued French colonial presence in Algeria, and it remained a well-known feature of the colonial incarceration throughout the eight-year war of national liberation.

While the use of torture by the French military and police was by no means accidental, its existence remained a contradictory factor in French politics. Many French observers, and especially public intellectuals, reacted with incredulity as they read of the state's blatant and extensive use of torture. Some practitioners of and witnesses to torture broke the code of silence to testify against it; others, especially the high command in Algeria, defended their 'methods' as the most expeditious means of responding to a violent nationalist insurrection and to Algerian 'terrorism'. Thus the torturing of suspects remained abhorrent for many, but legitimated by the men who controlled the police and military apparatus. This paradox was redoubled by the fact that the torturers were immediately amnestied by President Charles de Gaulle's government following the Evian Accords, which offered a lasting peace on 18 March, 1962.

In 1954, when the war began, torture was generally considered a bygone product of the old regime. Even one of the most esteemed historians of the French penal system, Michel Foucault, seems to have believed that traditional forms of torture had faded from French prisons in the modern era. However, despite his usually acute insights into the spirit of modernity, Foucault was surprisingly unaware of (and surprisingly silent about) the recurrence of torture during decolonization. Indeed, Foucault was mistaken when he claimed in *Discipline and Punish* that 'There are no longer any of those long processes in which death was both retarded by calculated interruptions and multiplied by a series of successive attacks.' And his claim that '[t]he reduction of these "thousand deaths" to strict capital punishment defines a whole new morality concerning the act of punishing' should not go unchallenged.[1] Furthermore, Foucault's claims about torture should not prevent historians from reconsidering the history of torture during the decolonization of Algeria and its relationship to the colonial penal and legal system. That torture was not officially sanctioned by the laws of France during the war also does not allow one to conclude that it was not officiated over by the military and police serving the French Fourth and Fifth Republics. In fact, the racial (by which I mean ethnic and religious) power relations expressed during decolonization in the use of torture in the colonial interrogation cells warrant renewed investigation.

Torture was a very real manifestation of French authority in the mid- to late-1950s and early 1960s. It was, moreover, no secret either in colonial Algeria or in metropolitan France. As early as 1955, just months into the conflict, word had already travelled to France that torture was being practised against Algerian Muslims. When suspects were arrested for allegedly aiding revolutionaries, they knew what to expect during interrogation, and the French authorities willingly used torture not only to get victims to speak (and therefore betray) but also to preserve the colonial status quo and to combat anticolonial nationalism. This dual role of the torturer – as protector of colonialism and grand inquisitor of anticolonialism – left no doubt in the minds of those who conducted campaigns to end colonialism in Algeria that France had became, by 1955, a *régime concentrationnaire*.[2] Equally importantly, colonial incarceration destroyed the possibility of Franco-Muslim reconciliation as well as the moral fibre of the French Republic. Ironically, the French in metropolitan France understood that little could be done to prevent torture from spreading like 'gangrene', as it was then called, to the democratic institutions in metropolitan France.[3]

In this sense, the French-Algerian War is truly one of the most salient illustrations of the eventual recolonization of a metropolitan government by its own out-of-control colonial politico-military establishment. As the eminent French historian, Pierre Vidal-Naquet, noted in *Torture: Cancer of Democracy, France and Algeria 1954–1962* (1963), the French government implicitly condoned the use of torture within the Algerian colonial penal system, and this ended by Algerianizing metropolitan France with the same disease. It took very little time before the use of torture against Algerians in France was witnessed. And from torture, it was but a small step to the massacre of more than 300 Algerians in France on 17 October 1961, by the Parisian police.[4]

Whence modern colonial torture?

Torture, of course, was not unknown to humanity when it was introduced into colonial Algeria during French decolonization. Its first legal codification came with the *Theodosian Code* during the Roman Empire.[5] From that time forward, borrowing heavily from Roman law, western Europe employed torture (usually in cases of treason) as one of the principal ways by which to extract confessions from criminals. Torture was authorized by Pope Innocent IV in 1252 in ecclesiastical courts, as long as the clergy did not engage in the act of torture themselves. Hence, according to the historian Edward Peters, from the mid-thirteenth to the end of the eighteenth century, torture remained a central feature of criminal procedure for the Church and of most of the states of Europe.[6] But, by the mid-eighteenth century, torture had come under increasing criticism from Enlightenment thinkers and eventually became a focus of French *philosophes*'s criticisms of the old regime. Following the lead of several other European states (Denmark, Poland, Saxony, etc.), France began the process of abolishing torture in 1780 and the National Assembly rid France of it in 1789. The subsequent Napoleonic regime then took its anti-torture campaign with it as the French empire grew. Ostensibly, torture became a vestige of the past and the worst reminder of the inhumane authority of old regime sovereignty.

However, over the years, torture never truly disappeared. Despite the 1949 Geneva Conventions, torture once again became a matter of serious public concern during the era of post-World War II decolonization. In the colonial context, revelations of the French army's use of torture against Indo-Chinese prisoners of war were widespread by 1949, and remained a problem until the French defeat at Dien Bien Phu on 7 May 1954. Badly defeated, French forces left Hanoi on 9 October 1954, less than four weeks before the war began in Algeria and about three months after the peace agreement was reached in Geneva. The French military vowed never to lose a colonial war again and, when the revolution started in Algeria on 1 November 1954, the military was bitter about the political decision to end the war in Indochina and was poised for revenge. But the Algerian case was different from that in Indochina. Unlike Indochina, there was an enormous European population (approximately one million) in Algeria, and Algeria was considered not an overseas territory but France itself. Algeria was, in this sense, a unique part of the French Empire. The combination of a large European population, a frustrated and humiliated French military, and an enormously underprivileged and exploited Muslim population intent on achieving independence proved to be lethal not only for Algeria but also for the French political and legal institutions. As early as January 1955, the ethnologist Germaine Tillion, arriving in Algeria, confirmed reports of the French police's use of torture against Algerians.[7] And de Gaulle, no advocate of torture, inherited the problem when the army's *coup d'état* in Algiers brought him to power on 13 May 1958, but the unofficial institutionalization of torture in Algeria came in several stages prior to de Gaulle's arrival.

When the war broke out in November 1954, France made no distinction between Algeria's three *départements* (counties) and any of the other *départements* of metropolitan France. Algeria was France and was the only overseas possession (including Indochina) not administrated as a colony. The only true distinction concerned the Muslim population, which numbered about eight million. Muslims were subject to a barrage of discriminatory laws and denied the normal protections and rights (such as voting) of the European citizens (*pieds noirs* or *colons*, and Jews) living in colonial Algeria. The *colon* population was, by and large, intent on preserving these distinctions and would pressure the political, military and police apparatus to do so.

At the same time, the metropolitan government in France gradually allowed its authority in Algeria to be sapped by the French military. For example, giving in to the extraordinary pressures in colonial Algeria, the French Parliament (backed by the French Communist Party) voted in the so-called Special Powers Act on 12 March 1956, which endowed the French military with police authority and virtually unrestricted power to bring an end to the rebellion in Algeria. A few weeks later, on 3 April 1955, Parliament authorized a law that allowed the state to declare a state of emergency in more than one department at a time. According to Vidal-Naquet, this law paved the way for the subsequent violations of freedom throughout Algeria, such as searches, press censorship, the handling of terrorist cases to the French military tribunals, and permission to sequester suspects in detention camps.[8] Vidal-Naquet also pointed out in *Torture: Cancer of Democracy, France and Algeria 1954–1962* (1963) that these special laws did not give rise to torture in themselves; rather, they were made to fulfil the demands of torturers in Algeria.[9]

In other words, the colonial system in Algeria would continue to colonize the French metropolitan legal and political system until it met the requirements of those attempting to maintain unmitigated sovereignty in French Algeria. Since there existed no alternative to the use of torture to maintain European hegemony in Algeria, the National Assembly simply relinquished its authority over the Algerian question to the torturers. Highly placed French officials in Algeria such as Governor General

Jacques Soustelle, whose tenure in Algiers lasted for one year (from February 1955 to January 1956) and resident minister Robert Lacoste, who remained in power from February 1956 to May 1958, turned a blind eye to reports that confirmed the use of torture.[10] As President, de Gaulle pledged to end torture in Algeria and to bring an end to the conflict there; yet, despite his pronouncements, torture continued and, by the summer of 1959, the now infamous book, *La Gangrène* (*The Gangrene*), which was censored by de Gaulle's government, confirmed that not only had torture not stopped, it was conducted with impunity in metropolitan France. Torture, in fact, remained a constant problem and a frequent source of scandal for the French government until the signing of the Evian agreements. But how, and in what ways, did the decolonization of Algeria accelerate the renaissance of torture by the French authorities?

'Race', nationalism and gender

As torture became more openly discussed during the decolonization, its racial and sexual dimensions became important features of the violence. Specific types of torture were aimed at *types* of individuals: men, women, Muslims/Arabs/Kabyles and Europeans. Victims were often attacked sexually, and their sexuality was put into question. For example, some Muslim men's testicles were literally burned away by electric shock. Mouloud Feraoun (the acclaimed Algerian Kabyle writer) even recounts in his *Journal, 1955–1962: Reflections on the French-Algerian War* how the military devised a special tool just for Muslim men that would be introduced into a man's anus: '[it] increases in size when they push on a spring. Then they pull it out brutally, and you felt your entrails tear.'[11] Feraoun and other writers also record how Muslim men were told to strip naked by the French military and pressed down so that broken bottles were forced into their anuses. Similarly, women generally became the targets of special forms of torture, including rape and violence targeting their genitalia. In some cases, Muslim men were tied up and forced to watch their wives and daughters raped in front of them.[12] Moreover, Feraoun frequently comments in his *Journal* on the zeal with which the French tortured the Muslims. He notes on 31 March 1956:

> There are endless ways of torture. In every police station and in the military camps, the policeman and the officer take all sorts of initiatives and think up all sorts of ways to improve techniques that cannot be listed here because there are too many to mention. Those who have endured these treatments will never forget them because they are forever inscribed in their flesh.[13]

Torturers also felt little compunction against inflicting deadly and inhuman violence against 'Europeans'. In this sense, issues of ethnicity, gender and nationalism (described here as 'race') converge in torture sessions in revolutionary Algeria, rendering the French-Algerian War one of the most gruesome and revealing sites for studying extreme experiences of colonial incarceration. There were literally thousands of cases of torture during this eight-year struggle for national liberation, and it would be impossible to analyse each case separately. The few that I have selected here, I believe, are the most illustrative.

I begin with the case of Henri Alleg. At first glance, it might seem odd to begin with the case of a French man. But this case is indeed one of the most revealing of the war, not only for what it says but also for what it does not. A French intellectual living in Algeria, a communist and the editor of the leading communist daily *Alger républicain*, Henri Alleg was forced into clandestine activity in November 1956. He was arrested seven months later, on 10 June 1957, by General Massu's elite 10th Paratrooper Division on the grounds that he had evaded prosecution in 1956 as editor of a banned publication. He was subsequently held for one month at El Biar, a suburb of Algiers, and tortured several times before he was transferred to a detention camp at Lodi in Algeria. While incarcerated at Lodi, he wrote about his torture in notes that were smuggled out of Algeria and into France.

Alleg's text, which was published as *La Question* (*The Question*) in 1958, became an immediate bestseller in France, and had the distinction of being the first book banned in France since the eighteenth century.[14] It was not, however, the first book about torture. In fact, Pierre-Henri Simon's influential *Contre la torture* had appeared just months before, in June 1957. Simon's account was that of a European intellectual condemning the use of torture by France in Algeria. He also tried to maintain a theoretical distinction between the colonial war and the issue of torture. Alleg's work, on the other hand, was a victim's personal testimony. *The Question*'s title itself had deep symbolism because torture was referred to during the old regime simply as 'the question'. News of *The Question* spread quickly throughout France and around the globe. The case gained even more notoriety after Jean-Paul Sartre penned his now famous article about the book for *Les Temps modernes*, which was subsequently printed as the introduction to the book. Other major intellectuals joined Sartre's protests, including three Nobel Laureates – André Malraux, Roger Martin du Gard and François Mauriac – who, along with Sartre, sent a joint letter to the President of the Republic demanding immediate resolution of the matter. France's most recent Laureate, Albert Camus, was conspicuously absent from these protests.[15]

Vividly bringing his experiences to the reader, Alleg chronicles his painful captivity at El Biar: the beatings, the water torture during which he nearly drowned, his nudity, the insults, the electrodes attached to his genitals and the feeling of having the electricity rip through his body. He also records the violence done to others. He wrote of the many Muslims also undergoing similar, if not worse treatment, and he specifically recounted the presence of both French and Muslim women at El Biar, some of whom had been raped, and all of whom were beaten and forced to endure water torture and electric shock. In addition, he noted that he was one of the last people to see his friend and fellow Frenchman, Maurice Audin, alive after Audin was tortured by the same military authorities. (Audin was then murdered by the Parachutists, and his 'disappearance' provoked another national scandal.) In short, *The Question* was intended to be a highly personalized record of one of France's darkest moments and proof that even the French were not immune from the torture committed in France's name.

When Sartre wrote his essay on Alleg, he expressed his unease with the subject. How could France, which had only just survived the atrocities of the Nazi occupation, so quickly become a torturing nation? And while Sartre also admitted his certain pride that Alleg, as a Frenchman, could bring the readers into his world,[16] he also confessed his sense of sadistic voyeurism: 'We fascinate ourselves with the whirlpool of inhumanity; but it only needs a man, hard and stubborn, obstinately doing his duty to his fellow man, to save us from vertigo.'[17] Alleg would allow readers a glimpse into his world and thereby to view with greater clarity the reality of what modern France had become. It was hatred, sparked by the racist composition of the colonial world according to Sartre, that gave free reign to the torturers. Torture was simply the concrete manifestation of this racial hatred against the Algerians. Furthermore, '[t]orture' became a 'systematized form of hatred that create[d] its own instruments'.[18]

Indeed, one of the most remarkable features in Sartre's essay is the use of Alleg's case to increase discussion of the use of torture against Algerian Muslims. Torture, Sartre noted, was going to be France's way of keeping the Muslims in their place and represented the final effort by the European *colons* to affirm their racial superiority over Algerian Muslims. According to Sartre, torture could be employed by the Europeans in Algeria because the Algerian 'natives' were not even considered men. Torture was logical in this case, Sartre noted, because it 'was simply the expression of racial hatred'.[19] Since torture was borne of the colonial condition of racism in Algeria, racism was, he concluded, at the very core of the conflict. The decision to torture a Frenchman such as Alleg, as Alleg himself wrote, resulted from his decision to side with the 'rats' (as his torturers called the Muslims).

There is no doubt that part of the reason that the French edition of *The Question* sold so quickly, despite its suppression, and the reason it provoked a national scandal was because, as Vidal-Naquet noted, the victim was a member of their own race.[20] Indeed, there had been numerous stories of Algerian Muslim men who had been tortured by the French, and many of these provoked national outcries; yet, it was notably Alleg's torture at El Biar that captured the French nation's attention.

Alleg's revelations, though among the most famous, were not the last. Answers for the disappearance of another French man, Maurice Audin, would continue to be sought by Laurent Schwartz and Pierre Vidal-Naquet, who formed the Maurice Audin Committee and published in

1958 a small but influential book on the case, called *L'Affaire Audin*. At the
same time, Georges Arnaud and Jacques Vergès, two lawyers and French
citizens defending the FLN (Front de Libération Nationale) in Algeria,
took up the case of Djamila Bouhired, a militant Algerian nationalist
woman who was caught carrying compromising correspondence between
two of the leaders of the FLN in Algiers (Yacef Saadi and Ali la Pointe).

Djamila Bouhired underwent extreme tortures, even while she was on
the operating table having a bullet removed. From 17 to 19 April 1957,
she endured torture by electrocution, when paratroopers attached electrodes to her genitalia. Published as *Pour Djamila Bouhired* by Les Editions
de Minuit (also the publisher of *L'Affaire Audin* and *La Question*), Arnaud
and Vergès's text caused another national scandal.

The scandals concerning torture did not stop, nor did the French public
stop reading about them. On 16 June 1959, *La Gangrène* (*The Gangrene*) was
made available in bookstores in Paris, but its story was now different. No
longer were the tortures only taking place outside of metropolitan France:
now proof existed that torture had spread to Paris. Jerome Lindon,
director of Les Editions de Minute, published the book as a collection of
texts written by five Algerians arrested between November and December
1958 and tortured in France between 2 December and 12 December 1958.
All of them were tortured by the French secret police known as the DST
(Direction de Surveillance Territoire) under the supervision of Roger
Wybot.

Within hours of the publication of *The Gangrene*, de Gaulle's government seized the book and declared it a danger to the 'internal security of
the state'.[21] It immediately received national and international attention
and provoked panic among many French citizens; it demonstrated that
torture had become a part of everyday life inside metropolitan France and
was thus not merely something afflicted on nationalists on the other side
of the Mediterranean. However, as important as the publication of *The
Gangrene* was, it was the story of Djamila Boupacha, recounted by Gisèle
Halimi and Simone de Beauvoir in *Djamila Boupacha*, which really became
the *cause célebre* and the finale of anti-torture cases.

Boupacha's case was not dissimilar to so many other cases before her.
She was arrested in Algiers along with her father and her brother-in-law
on suspicion that she was a member of the FLN. She was detained without
recourse to proper legal counsel for nearly two months, before Halimi
could take up her case in April 1960. Boupacha chose Halimi, a leading
defendant of Algerians during the war, as her lawyer in March 1960 while
incarcerated in the infamous Barbarossa Jail in Algiers. Boupacha's situation was not only shocking because of the standard application of torture
that victims had come to expect in colonial Algeria (electric shock, beating,
water treatment, etc.) – she, like so many Algerian Muslims, underwent
these forms of torture during her preliminary interrogations[22] – but what
made Boupacha's torture so scandalous were the revelations of how she
was tortured as a Muslim woman.

Like Djamila Bouhired and so many other women (European and Muslims), Boupacha's torturers forced her to strip and she was beaten. On 17 February, after days of beatings and abuse, she was brought into another police torture chamber at the centre at Hussein-Dey, a section of Algiers. Surrounded by men, including men known as *'bleus'* (in this case the *bleus* were mostly former members of the FLN whose allegiance had turned during torture), Boupacha was once again stripped naked by her tormentors. Lashed down and gagged in a dentist's chair, her captors insulted her with obscene jokes about her body while they drank bottled beer. After spitting beer over her until her body was completely soaked, they attached wires from an amplification box (a *gégène*) to her nipples with tape, to her anus and to her vagina. Her torturers watched sadistically as she convulsed. Periodically, one of the inspectors dabbed the tip of his lit cigarette on her chest and shoulders.

During the next couple of days she was tortured by various methods, and three to four days later she was taken for another session where a paratrooper dressed in full uniform joined the *bleus*, the inspectors and other army men. She was again severely beaten and kicked, until the captain and the other men dragged her into another room where she was once again stripped and then hung, feet and arms bound, over a bathtub full of water as if on a skewer. Submerged to the point of drowning, she began to confess to a whole host of crimes she obviously could not have committed. This was the usual form of torture for women, and many other similar revelations confirmed this. Her story differs somewhat from others in that her forced 'confession' succeeded only in producing greater brutality. Feeling that she was mocking them, her torturers tossed her to the ground, fastened a strap around her waist, spread her legs and inserted a toothbrush into her vagina. After the toothbrush, they plunged an empty beer bottle into her. A virgin, Boupacha began to bleed and fainted. Following her rape with the bottle she was examined once by a doctor, who noted only that she had unusual menstruation, and she was then moved from Hussein-Dey back to El Biar on 24 February.

Many women were raped by the French during incarceration. However, what consumed Boupacha was not only the shame of being violated by the beer bottle but the incessant questioning of whether or not this would constitute a loss of virginity. Virginity for a Muslim, as Boupacha noted, was a critical factor of being able to marry and maintain respectability. But Boupacha also had another problem. After being interrogated for thirty-three days, isolated, afraid and violated, she finally agreed to sign a confession under the threat that, if she did not, she would face new rounds of the most severe forms of torture. When she was finally arraigned on 15 March 1960, the French policemen accompanying her to court warned that if she mentioned her ordeal to the judge she would once again find herself in the torture chamber. She disobeyed. Distinguishing between the police, who had not harmed her, and the military men, who had, she told the judge that she had been tortured by the French military at Hussein-Dey. Not mentioning the rape, out of shame, she simply requested to be examined by a medical doctor.

After Gisèle Halimi took up Djamila Boupacha's case, she decided her chief legal tactic would be to call for an inquiry into the methods of gaining the confession (the torture and the rape). Halimi, fully aware of the importance of virginity in the Maghrib (she herself was from Tunisia), decided a full inquiry was necessary in order to highlight the fact that Boupacha had confessed these crimes only under torture, which was illegal. Chief among the crimes to which she had confessed was the planting of a bomb in the University of Algiers's dining hall on 27 February 1959. Eventually, with Halimi's aid, Boupacha withdrew her confession and filed a civil suit against the French authorities under articles 341, 342 and 344 of the Penal Code. Understanding that urgency was required and that she would have to bring French public opinion into this case to keep Boupacha from the death penalty, Halimi swiftly founded the Djamila Boupacha Committee in Paris. Germaine Tillion and Simone de Beauvoir were among two of the prominent members of this committee.

One of de Beauvoir's first actions after hearing of the case was to publish 'In defense of Djamila Boupacha' in *Le Monde* on 3 June 1960. As a matter of principle and law, de Beauvoir's article indicated that if the French did nothing to prevent Boupacha's trial from going forward without a full inquiry, then the government and entire French nation would be guilty of a collective crime. France, she warned, must live up to its reputation as a just nation. Above all, this case would have to prove to the French in Algeria that they would no longer be allowed to commit such crimes. Justice would dictate that Djamila's case would be postponed until a thorough investigation into the charges she had brought against the state could be undertaken. The first response to de Beauvoir's article was Prime Minister Michel Debré's decision to seize *Le Monde*'s Algerian editions. His next reaction was to claim that the state had undertaken the initial steps of the investigation.

Regardless of the government's actions, other French intellectuals began to come to Boupacha's defence, starting with Laurent Schwartz and Pierre Vidal-Naquet, followed by other intellectuals such as Françoise Sagan. André Philip, a Professor of Political Economy and a former Finance Minister, had perhaps the most damning testimony of the case. In his words:

> But, with the Algerian war, France has permitted practices to spread which reduce us to a level far below that of the Middle Ages. Torture has been used not only to obtain the suspect's admissions, which is already contrary to all the rules of law, but to drag information from him about those who might have participated in his actions. Our present-day inquisitors no longer claim to save the soul of the person concerned by making his body suffer; they seek *to break*

the sense of human responsibility within him, to destroy his personality, so as to lead him to accomplish the most dishonourable of all acts: betrayal. . . .

But our moral reaction is insufficient; we must recognize that *torture is logically implied* in the type of war being fought in Algeria. . . . The only way of acting effectively is then to arrest the families and friends of suspects and make them 'talk'. This was the method of the GPU in the Soviet Union, the Gestapo in Europe, and the specialized military units in Algeria. . . .

The campaign initiated on behalf of Djamila Boupacha derives part of its importance from the fact that her case is the very symbol of that corruption of ends by means which threatens to destroy our country utterly; it is the very honour of France which has become tarnished in the treatment of this girl, it is the values which define France in the eyes of the world that the torturers are destroying.

May their condemnation and Djamila's liberation show that France is not yet totally unfaithful to herself.[23]

Henri Alleg and General Jacques de Bollardière, who resigned from the army after protesting the use of torture in Algeria, also had similar testimonies regarding Boupacha's case, which were all published in the indices of *Djamila Boupacha*. The publicity around Boupacha's loss of virginity certainly galvanized the French public. Yet, if many French intellectuals and other concerned citizens condemned their nation's criminal use of torture as being even worse than that of the Middle Ages, this is not how the extremists and *colons* viewed the case.

While Halimi, de Beauvoir and others galvanized metropolitan French public opinion to act against the atrocities of the colonial regime in Algeria, colonialist hardliners such as Jacques Soustelle and even mainstream French newspapers such as *Rivarol* and *Fraternité-Française* attempted to stem the tide by calling Boupacha's testimony into question.[24] Understanding that, for many, colonialism and torture were now inseparable, some Parisian newspapers such as *Nouveaux jours* joined the chorus by trying to discredit Boupacha's account, and in so doing targeted the gender of her supporters. As Halimi noted, the paper 'lamented that "our charming companions of the weaker sex" were turning so many Pasionarias, that oblivious of their "gentleness and feminine grace", they had treacherously committed themselves to active participation in the nationalist cause'.[25] In other words, by defending a woman who was wrongfully accusing French soldiers of rape, Boupacha's supporters (e.g. Halimi) were being led astray as a 'weaker sex', thereby becoming accomplices to the rebellion itself.

Offensive as some of the French newspapers were, they paled in comparison to the French dailies in Algeria. Not only did the *colon* press attack Boupacha's defenders, they also labelled Boupacha a nationalist terrorist. Moreover, they questioned her virginity and religious propriety. At issue was an admission that Boupacha had made in her testimony to the effect that, as a member of the FLN, she had been willing to hide male members of the organization in her bedroom during searches. The *colon* press took this admission as licence to cast doubt on her virginity. As one publication put it:

> Do not these documents suggest that Djamila Boupacha, that supposedly straitlaced and orthodox Muslim girl, really used her bedroom to entertain men in? If that be so, what are we to make of her complaint against the troops whom she alleges to have outraged her?[26]

Halimi noted her own disgust at reading the *colon* press's representations of Boupacha. Fully aware of how the French Algerian press was trying to call Boupacha's sexual modesty into question and therefore destroy the importance of the question of the loss of her virginity, Halimi concluded that the 'tone of these comments was characteristic of the heated emotional atmosphere surrounding such trials'. Furthermore, Halimi decided that in order for the case to advance, it would have to be moved out of Algeria to metropolitan France.

The case was eventually transferred to France. However, as Halimi attempted to bring the criminals to justice, she was denied even the most basic of legal rights – the right to subpoena witnesses and evidence. Before the case could be concluded, the French-Algerian War ended (18 March 1962) and, on the terms of the Evian Accords, all Muslim political prisoners were released. Boupacha's family was released the following month and she was freed on 21 April. Conveniently, under the terms of the amnesty, not only was she herself free from further prosecution, so were her torturers.

Pierre Vidal-Naquet, understanding what was at stake with the issue of amnesty, wrote in 1963 that the use of torture in Algeria had left an indelible moral stain on the history of twentieth-century France. Like Thucydides's *The Peloponesian War*, Vidal-Naquet hoped that his history of the use of torture during the French-Algerian War would serve as an example for a tragedy that was a global problem.[27] Regrettably, torture had not slipped away with the coming of modernity. Nazi Germany, Fascist Italy, the Soviet Union, Cyprus, Kenya and France in Algeria had all definitively, Vidal-Naquet noted, shattered this illusion. However, one vital connection linked each of these cases: the modern legal and political systems had either been nullified or hijacked to allow torture to become part and parcel of the state's authority. This being the case, citizens had the right to expect that after decolonization, war crimes such as torture would be punished. While Vidal-Naquet acknowledged that amnesty was certainly not a new proposition for nations emerging from conflicts as violent as the French-Algerian War had been, the question of granting amnesty to torturers was entirely unjustifiable. The French state had unquestionably overstepped its moral limits by granting amnesty to the men who had tortured and murdered with impunity in Algeria. The state gave legitimacy to its immoral actions after the fact when it decided to grant amnesty for itself.[28] In short, Vidal-Naquet argued that France had dishonoured itself by setting its crimes committed during decolonization as being outside the purview of the Geneva Conventions or the International Declaration on Human Rights. Since France could no longer prosecute its own criminals, it would be up to the international community to do so. In the absence of this action, France would have to accept 'moral guilt' (as Karl Jaspers had proposed for the Germans following World War II). France, Vidal-Naquet suggested, would have to mark the men who had tortured with some form of national disgrace.[29]

The French state has never made a formal apology for the atrocities it committed during the French-Algerian War. Nor, it should be noted, has the Algerian government (or the FLN) offered a similar apology for its own excesses during decolonization. In fact, one could say that the French state has allowed these crimes to remain under the radar of historical investigations into human rights violations in prisons. Indeed, one of the great ironies is that the very general who controlled the 10th Paratrooper Division in Algeria during the so-called Battle of Algiers, General Jacques Massu, proved Vidal-Naquet wrong. Without denying the use of torture for posterity, Massu embraced his role in the history of torture. Torture would not become a dirty word. There would be no official political trial against the torturers during decolonization, nor would the torturers feel the weight of the moral question. In fact, in 1972, General Massu published *La vrai bataille d'Alger* as his account of the conflict and even justified his decision to torture Muslims and French alike during the war. Torture was authorized by him, Massu stated, because it was 'a cruel necessity'. It was an 'indispensable' means to get the information out of the guilty and their accomplices in order to prevent even more atrocious events from happening.[30] Massu defended his choice of violence as the only means his men had to defeat an even more immoral foe: the Algerian terrorists who murdered without remorse. As 7for Alleg, Massu stated, he was an accomplice to an indescribable barbarity for which the only response was torture.[31] Again, Alleg had sided with the 'rats' and for this torture was not only warranted but an honourable response for the French military.

How Massu, as a leading military commander in Algeria during the war, could write of his desire to use torture as a legitimate weapon against the FLN with no fear of prosecution remains something of a mystery. But Massu is not alone. For example, Jean-Pierre Vittori, one of the soldiers who by his own count had tortured over 250 prisoners, published his own memoir of his days as a torturer, *Confessions d'un professionnel de la torture* (*Confessions of a Professional Torturer*) in 1980. With these and other confessions in mind (General Paul Aussaresses more recently),[32] it would therefore be possible to call what has happened with regard to the torture question 'collective amnesia' – if there were no public admissions by torturers. This is clearly not the case, and it is now necessary to ask other questions. What is it about the history of the French-Algerian War that allowed for the reappearance of torture? Why could a decorated general such as Massu have avoided prosecution after he admitted to crimes against humanity, while France and other nations continue to arrest war criminals in Bosnia and elsewhere today? Finally, and perhaps most importantly, what is it about the colonial question that makes the torture and execution of the innocent (and 'guilty') any less a crime against humanity than the crimes committed by Pétain and his staff during the Vichy era? Could it be, as Pierre Vidal-Naquet and Jean-Paul Sartre once suggested, the question of 'race'? Or is it merely that the use of torture was politicized to keep the status quo, and that this politicization further victimized the victims of torture by making justice inaccessible?

Returning briefly to Foucault, we can also ask another question about state power and torture during colonial incarceration. Is it not reasonable to suggest that, although torture had disappeared as a form of public spectacle officiated over by state authorities, the torture chambers set up by the French in Algeria and in metropolitan France, as a response to decolonization, constitute a far more egregious affront to humanity than the public spectacles of torture during the old regime? Tortures were certainly inhumane before the modern era, but the French state did not, by and large, hide them as it tried to do during the Algerian revolution. In fact, as Alleg noted during his testimony in the Boupacha case, for the representatives of the French state who have protected the torturers, 'the scandal has never been that prisoners should have been tortured but simply that the facts should have leaked out, and all their efforts have been devoted not to stopping the torture but to concealing it always more effectively'.[33] Two questions remain: What is it about the French government's colonial world view in Algeria that encouraged it to go to such ends? And what is it about such a world view that allowed these crimes to go unpunished?

Notes

1. Michel Foucault, *Discipline and Punish: The Birth of the Prison*, trans. Alan Sheridan (New York, Vintage, 1979). In fact, given the revelations concerning the use of torture during the French-Algerian War, Foucault's claim, and subsequent claims he makes about the disappearance of torture in France, are striking to the degree that he seems to be ignorant of one of the central scandals and themes of decolonization. This could in itself be fodder for an interesting investigation of Foucault's position on the 'Algerian question', but I leave it to readers to ponder the significance of Foucault's omissions.

2. See James D. Le Sueur, *Uncivil War: Intellectuals and Identity Politics during the Decolonization of Algeria* (Philadelphia, University of Pennsylvania Press, 2001).

3. Of particular interest in this regard is the book *The Gangrene* [by 7 Algerians living in France at the time of their arrest], translated by Robert Silvers (New York, Lyle Stuart, 1960), which was originally published as *La Gangrène* by Editions de Minuit in 1959. Also see *Les Crimes de l'armée française*, ed. Pierre Vidal-Naquet (Paris, Maspero, 1975); Alec Mellor, *La Torture: son histoire, son abolition, sa réapparition au XXᵉ siècle* (Paris, Mame, 1961); and Pierre Vidal-Naquet, *Torture: Cancer of Democracy, France and Algeria 1954–1962* (Baltimore, Penguin, 1963).

4. During this most infamous massacre of Algerians, the French police systematically rounded up thousands of Algerians and murdered over three hundred by drowning them in the Seine or by shooting them and burying them in mass graves in the Paris region.

5. For an excellent history of torture, see Edward Peters, *Torture: Expanded Edition* (Philadelphia, University of Pennsylvania Press, 1996).

6. *Ibid.*, p. 54.

7. See Le Sueur, *Uncivil War*, Chapter III.

8. Vidal-Naquet, *Torture*, p. 65.

9. *Ibid.*, p. 66.

10. See the text of the Wuillaume Report in appendix to Vidal-Naquet, *Torture*, pp. 169–79.

11. Mouloud Feraoun, *Journal, 1955–1962: Reflections on the French-Algerian War*, ed. James D. Le Sueur (Lincoln, University of Nebraska Press, 2000), p. 89.

12. *Ibid.*, p. 263.

13. *Ibid.*, p. 105.

14. According to Pierre Vidal-Naquet, French editions of *The Question* sold 66,000 copies before it was suppressed and 90,000 as a semi-clandestine publication immediately after suppression in France: Vidal-Naquet, *Torture*, p. 141.

15. Mauriac even attacked Camus for his refusal to sign this joint protest. But Camus's situation here was consistent with the very complex position he maintained throughout the war. For a thorough analysis of Camus's Algerian position, see Le Sueur, *Uncivil War*, Chapter IV.

16. Jean-Paul Sartre, 'A Victory', introduction to Henri Alleg's *The Question* (New York, Braziller, 1958), p. 19.

17. *Ibid.*

18. *Ibid.*, p. 24.

19. *Ibid.*, p. 33.

20. Vidal-Naquet, *Torture*, p. 167.

21. *The Gangrene* (New York, Lyle Stuart, 1960), p. 29.

22. Halimi, *Djamila Boupacha*, p. 28.

23. Cited in *ibid.*, pp. 233–4, 237.

24. Jacques Soustelle, the former Governor General of Algeria, would eventually have to flee France the following year because de Gaulle's government had placed a warrant out for his arrest. For the history of Soustelle's time in exile, see James D. Le Sueur, 'Before the jackal: the international uproar of *Assassination!*', a historical essay accompanying Ben Abro's *Assassination! July 14* (University of Nebraska Press, 2001).

25. Halimi, *Djamila Boupacha*, p. 87.

26. Cited in *ibid.*, p. 88.

27. Vidal-Naquet, *Torture*, p. 155.

28. *Ibid.*, pp. 161–2.

29. *Ibid.*, p. 164.

30. Jacques Massu, *La Vraie Bataille d'Alger* (Paris, Plon, 1972), p. 166.

31. *Ibid.*

32. In May 2001, General Paul Aussaresses published a shocking memoir in which he justified the use of torture during the war and explained how he had personally supervised the illegal execution of numerous Algerians. This former general, along with the other soldiers who served in Algeria, cannot be prosecuted because all have been granted amnesty. See Paul Aussaresses, *Services spéciaux: Algérie 1955–1957* (Paris, Perrin, 2001).

33. Henri Alleg 'Testimony' in Halimi, *Djamila Boupacha*, pp. 205–6.

CHAPTER ELEVEN

The prisonhouse of language: literary production and detention in Kenya

MARY ROSS

Colonial prison writing

In his introduction to *Writers in Prison*,[1] Ioan Davies argues that the reading and theorizing of prison writing begins with a need to understand not just the incarcerated mind but the conditions in a society that enable and promote the prison. Subsequently, the reader of any prison writing must consider the writing and nature of imprisonment as, in Ngũgĩ wa Thiong'o's words, 'a social, political and historical phenomenon'.[2] In 1977 Ngũgĩ wa Thiong'o, the Kenyan novelist and academic, was detained without trial for twelve months for his role in the writing and production of a Gikuyu language play and, in his status as a political prisoner, joined the collective experience of the colonial and postcolonial era penal system in Kenya.

The present penal system in Kenya is a direct descendant of the British colonial era, and the continuing existence of political prisoners illustrates the absence of a liberal correctional, humanitarian and legal state apparatus. The incarceration of political dissidents, practised by the Kenyatta regime from Independence in 1963 until Kenyatta's death in 1978, has grown under the current President, Daniel Arap Moi, as has detention without trial, torture and disappearances. Ngũgĩ's account of detention in Nairobi's Kamiti Maximum Security Prison, *Detained: A Writer's Prison Diary*, can be regarded as a historical phenomenon, part of the canon of Kenyan prison literature which orders and historicizes, records and frames the experience, language and history of incarceration and resistance. It is also an important primary document as Ngũgĩ incorporates pre-literacy records of individual and collective resistance to colonialism into the literary canon, creating a linear, chronological history of armed and literary resistance.

In the decades following Kenya's Independence, almost two dozen autobiographies were published by the East African Publishing House in Nairobi which dealt exclusively with the experience of war and detention during the State of Emergency years in the 1950s. The Land and Freedom Army, widely known as the Mau Mau, waged a war for Independence, and the experience of armed resistance sometimes translated into literary resistance. Massive British military campaigns meant that by 1956 many of the forest fighters had been captured and this was the beginning of the 'pipeline', the term given to one's journey through the various institutions of the British correctional system. The experience of detention was shared by many Kenyan males, in particular male members of Ngũgĩ's ethnic group, the Kikuyu, and this provided much of the material for the post-Independence autobiographies. The production of literature within the scores of detention camps in Kenya, not only of autobiographical material but also news bulletins for inmates and the colonial forces, newspapers, pamphlets and manifestoes – a considerable corpus of literature – is the focus of this discussion.

The context of the 'Mau Mau' detainee

J. M. Kariuki's account of colonial detention, *'Mau Mau' Detainee: The Account by a Kenya African of His Experiences in Detention Camps 1953–1960*,[3] published in 1963, contains a number of references to several 'news services' operating within hard-core camps. Kariuki himself remained a constant problem to colonial authorities through his work as an editor and as a persistent letter-writer to the international political and legal communities. Literacy, or 'having the book', was acknowledged as an important tool for subversion, making Kariuki indispensable to the move-ment as a documenter of the collective struggle and as the founding figure of Kenyan incarceration literature.

A similar situation occurred in Argentina, during the years of the Generals, when a certain number of *Los desaparecidos*[4] were assigned service and intelligence tasks by their captors. At the El Banco and Olimpo secret detention centres in Buenos Aires, daily military ordersheets were produced by disappeared journalists and lawyers, while at the Navy Mechanics School (ESMA) prisoners were forced to work translating articles of national interest supplied by the press and Office of the Ministry of Foreign Affairs. These prisoners also produced news bulletins for broadcast for a national television station and the Argentine External Broadcasting Service.

Likewise, in Long Kesh Prison in County Down, Northern Ireland, some years before the Argentine Generals, Gerry Adams assisted in producing a regular Gaelic language newspaper for his fellow political detainees. Detained under the Northern Ireland (Emergency Provisions) Act, Adams smuggled fiction, articles and political observations out of Long Kesh, which were subsequently published under the pseudonym 'Brownie' in the Belfast Republican newspaper *An Phoblacht*.

These two examples of incarcerated literary production highlight an

important distinction – that between prisoners coerced into literary production, and prisoners writing for fellow detainees. The aims and purposes of these two kinds of incarcerated literature intersect: first, through
an existing political ideology that is disseminated via writing, second,
because of a 'regulatory' role, that is in one sense oppressive yet, in the
Irish situation for example, illuminating.

The following discussion examines the role of Josiah Mwangi Kariuki,
who produced documents for the British Government relating to the
unique Kenyan detention system, while also documenting prisoners'
grievances in letters smuggled out of the camps destined for the International Red Cross and the British Labour politicians, Barbara Castle and
Fenner Brockway. Kariuki's account of numerous official and clandestine
penal publications in 'Mau Mau' Detainee positions him as a unique and
founding figure of Kenyan resistance literature.

'Mau Mau' Detainee is, foremost, an account of Kariuki's detention
experience from 1953 to 1960 and the experience of the pipeline. Unlike
the autobiographies that poured out of the East African Publishing House
following the 1963 publication of 'Mau Mau' Detainee, this was not the
story of a forest freedom fighter but of a unionist and an oath administrator. Following the declaration of a State of Emergency by the Governor,
Sir Evelyn Baring, on 20 October 1952, Kariuki became a member of the
Nakuru branch of the KAU (Kenya African Union). A Protestant Mission-
ary Society secondary education in Uganda had set Kariuki apart from
many of his fellow Kikuyu. Literacy for the 23-year-old was a 'weapon . . .
and the power of reading and writing'[5] would mean a stake in the
political process of Independence.

Kariuki also worked as an administrator of the Oath of Unity which, in
simplified terms, was the precursor to the oath of membership to the
Movement, the Land and Freedom Army. Kariuki's role as an oath
administrator ran parallel to his work with the proscribed KAU, but he
maintains in his discussion of the two movements that 'K.A.U. was a
completely different organisation [to the Movement] but that some . . .
were also members of it'.[6] The first 'sweep' of Nakuru by British security
forces in January 1953 captured Kariuki but the arresting officer 'had long
been a friend of mine . . . and like many others in the Kenya Police he was
sympathetic to our cause'.[7] He was released. However, twelve months
after the declaration of a State of Emergency and the arrest of Jomo
Kenyatta, Kariuki was detained indefinitely under the Emergency Regulations Act by the Nakuru Special Branch of the Kenya Police and
transported to Kowop reception camp in northern central Kenya's Sam-
buru district.

Official and clandestine communications

Kariuki's position as a disseminator of information is an important feature of *'Mau Mau' Detainee*. The author's account of the various news services, and of the oral and written 'publications' within four hard-core camps and one reception camp, verify the existence and importance of a highly developed communication system which included writing, song and oratory. The production of both forms of literature, official and clandestine, within the detention camps was limited by several different factors.

The first and most fundamental factor in literary production during the Emergency was the categorization of the camp. As Mau Mau was regarded as a form of psychological atavism by the British government,[8] suspects were divided into three categories. 'Black' was the colour of the unrepentant and irredeemable terrorist; 'Grey' was for 'heavily infected but not unreclaimable "Mau Mau"'.[9] 'White' was for those who were not 'infected' or had passed through the rehabilitative journey of the pipeline.[10] The category of a reception centre or detention camp dictated the methods of discipline, the security procedures and the rights of prisoners. Consequently, the physical conditions of a hard-core camp made literary production nearly impossible.

The second factor affecting the production of publications was the proximity of the camp to the nation's capital, Nairobi. This is related to the urban machinations of the Movement, access to information and the relative ease of communicating with a detained person in Fort Hall for example, in comparison with the Northern Frontier District where Kenyatta was detained. The third factor was access to writing materials. Although the volume of oral literature that was produced in the camps is partly testament to the circumnavigation of the problem of writing materials, this discussion is concerned with Kariuki's literary limitations. Only bribery, theft and concealment could ensure the supply of pen and paper. There is a direct line here between two points in the history of Kenya's political development – between Kariuki and Ngũgĩ wa Thiong'o who, twenty-five years later, was to meditate in his prison diary on the importance of paper.

The fourth factor, the quality of publishing materials, is closely related to the issue of access. Maina wa Kinyatti, the exiled Kenyan historian and archivist, has published his findings based on archival/archaeological work undertaken in the late 1970s and early 1980s and relating to the existence and location of the LAFA (Land and Freedom Army) archives that were buried for security purposes. Indeed, the instructions of the LAFA Field Marshal, Dedan Kimathi, to conceal the records highlighted the Movement's high regard for the written word.[11] Kinyatti's limited success was not only due to geographical changes, and to the discovery of some of the caches by British Intelligence, but also to the perishable nature of the written records; Kariuki appears to have had access, through bribery, to government-issue paper which, ironically, was durable and came with a letterhead.

The fifth and sixth factors affecting literary production are also linked because the first sometimes meant submission to the other. The nature and length of incarceration determined a detainee's success in his/her commitment to the importance of, in particular, letter writing. Despite his permanent categorization as a 'hard-core', which ensured a long detention period, Kariuki resisted the fruits of collaboration (i.e. screening positions, administrative jobs, early release or reduced labour). His skills of networking and mediating allowed Kariuki to maintain a supply of writing materials from sympathetic warders, without directly collaborating with the British penal administration. Kariuki explains, 'Those of us who resisted "rehabilitation" to the end did so because we considered that by confession we would lose something essential without which we could not live'.[12] Kariuki also accepted that without democratic change – free and fair elections and an end to detention without trial – the outcomes for which he was writing would not be achieved.

The final factor, and certainly the most important, influencing literary production was literacy. Kariuki makes a number of references to 'our own people . . . the illiterates',[13] whom he represented in his letter writing and camp publications, as the grass roots of the LAFA. Measures were taken by detainee committees within a camp to overcome the inability of the majority of detainees to read by having broadsheets read aloud between compounds by an elected reader. Kariuki worked as a translator at Kowop reception camp, receiving the *East African Standard* and *Baraza* newspapers from a sympathetic Luo police constable, and translating these into Kikuyu to be subsequently read out. The detainees who were 'editorial staff' for written publications, were teachers and printers. However, oral news services required only one literate person to obtain the information through old newspapers or documents left carelessly on a District Officer's desk. The word was then carried by prisoners who memorized what they were told.

Through the power of the pen, Kariuki was able to represent the tens of thousands of Kenyans, detained illegally, in the international arena (literally 'writing back' to the British colonial administration). Yet it was his dedication to the written word, more powerful than the spoken language of his jailers, that produced change in the detention camps across Kenya and these words are still read fifty years later. Kariuki's letters to Barbara Castle prompted political debate in Britain, and the Hola Camp enquiry would arguably not have been instigated had Kariuki not documented grievances so thoroughly.

Through an analysis of Kariuki's account of various news services, both oral and written, and publications produced in Kenya's detention camps, it is possible to ascertain the aims and purposes of such services and their 'success rates'. The first news service to be discussed below is interesting in its regional specificity and the combination of oratory and the written word that was employed for dissemination.

Detention camp 'news services' and magazines

Following transferral from Langata screening camp in August 1954 to Manyani, one of the most infamous hard-core camps,[14] Kariuki was subjected to several lengthy periods of solitary confinement as punishment for his continuous breaches of security through his letter smuggling. During his first period of detention at Manyani, Kariuki was involved in the production of various other 'publications', namely the two news services at Manyani: the *Manyani Times* and the *Waya Times*. These operated on two very different levels for the detainees, the first being informative. Kariuki writes:

> The *Manyani Times* was the news that was known to be true and which had been picked up from newspapers by those cleaning in the warders' lines or had been heard on a wireless by someone working near an officer's house.[15]

This service was orally delivered by each detainee who had information to share to compounds within hearing range. Kariuki considered his situation fortunate 'in Compound 13 since we could converse with five other compounds'.[16] The categorization of Manyani and its extreme isolation meant that in every way 'the most important nourishment we had was from the two news services that we operated'.[17]

The second service, the *Waya Times*, was mostly speculative and humorous and delivered in the evening with the *Manyani Times*. It usually included references to the date of Independence, the detainees' immediate release or 'an electoral victory by the British Labour Party in whom we still passionately believed'.[18] As Kariuki concedes, '[m]ost *Waya Times* headlines exhibited gross wishful thinking on the reporter's part'.[19] The speaker's reliability could be verified by his opening sentence. If he quoted from the *Waya Times*, his audience prepared for satire. The use of warders and collaborators as material for the *Waya Times* was an incarcerated twist on the tabloid gossip column and its oral delivery, title considered, can be regarded as a further inversion.

Kariuki was transferred for the second time from Manyani in June 1956, together with 204 other alleged 'ringleaders' to Saiyusi Island, on the eastern shore of Lake Victoria. Saiyusi, another hard-core camp, operated a daily news bulletin named after a local fish, the kamongo. As editor, Kariuki 'had to arrange for the editing of the daily news bulletin, gathered from the usual sources',[20] indicating that the *Kamongo Times* was 'delivered' as a combination of the separate purposes of the *Manyani Times* and the *Waya Times*. As a member of a popularly elected detainee delegation at Saiyusi, Kariuki maintained writing letters and formal letters of complaint for fellow detainees. Following the refusal of detainees to work, Kariuki was again included in a purge of ringleaders at Saiyusi Island and transferred, shackled on a plane flight, to Lodwar in the Northern Frontier District.

By August 1956, detainees had made contact with Jomo Kenyatta, detained north of Lodwar at Lokitaung, through warders transferring between both camps. Kariuki maintains that the detainee organization at Lodwar was the most productive he had been involved in. This was measured in gains from the camp commandant in relation to rations, labour, physical punishment and detainee delegations.

The Lodwar News Service, or *Mukoma Times*, was an oral service organized by detainees which focused on the themes of Sisyphus – because detainees had been forced to work in the construction of the Lodwar Hospital – and the release of Kenyattta. Categorized as a Black camp, access to publishing materials and the extreme isolation from the metropolis limited literary production in Lodwar to internal memorandums and only one letter was successfully smuggled to the Commissioner of Prisons.

The final publication referred to by J. M. Kariuki in *'Mau Mau' Detainee* is the camp magazine published at Athi River rehabilitation centre, *Atiriri*.[21] In October 1957, four years after his arrest, Kariuki was pushed back into the pipeline and transferred from Lodwar to Athi River, around twenty miles south of Nairobi. The purpose of camps such as Athi River was to extract a 'confession' of oath-taking from the detainee; rehabilitation was considered successful when a detainee renounced 'the psychology of Mau Mau'[22] – the Oath of Unity, the legitimacy of Kenyatta as leader and an independent Kenya.

Atiriri was operated by five detainees, distributed free to all detainees and contained a combination of 'official' news and camp news. Following his arrival at Athi River, Kariuki was requested to translate the paper into English by the camp commandant, Rochester. This circumstance is an example of Kariuki writing official and clandestine literature simultaneously, and he clearly articulated his protest at forced collaboration:

> Before I did this, I told them that they should realise that I would only do this work in the spirit of a prisoner doing, under orders, a job which he dislikes. I would merely translate exactly what was written and if I saw a mistake ... I would not alter it but put it down just as it was.[23]

By listing the editor, Benjamin, and his fellow newspaper staff, Kariuki establishes a professionalism in relation to *Atiriri*. Benjamin, he tells the reader, 'resumed his printing and publishing interests'[24] following his release, but also produced skilfully subversive pamphlets while at Athi River; Kariuki describes him as 'a co-operator, but a most subtle one'.[25]

These pamphlets may be termed as prison ephemera – literature which was produced in a particular historical and literary moment but did not survive that time,[26] due to the poor quality of the publishing materials and the nature and length of incarceration. The confiscation, discovery and/or destruction of detention literature and ephemera 'illustrate[s] not only the interpenetration of the idea of space by the significance of writing, but also the impermanence of a writing which is inserted against the superinscribed prison'.[27] The physical evanescence, however, is counteracted by the concrete differences which can be achieved if the letter/note/message reaches its destination. Kariuki's insistence to write himself and his fellow detainees out of their imprisonment survived failed attempts, confiscation and horrific physical and mental brutality to become the first published account of British human rights contraventions in Kenyan detention camps.

Resistance and writing

Jesse Kariuki is a pivotal figure in Kenyan resistance and prison writing, and is evoked by both Ngũgĩ and Maina wa Kinyatti in their prison diaries as a source of strength and endurance. The publication of 'Mau Mau' Detainee in 1963 by Oxford University Press established a canonical moment in Kenyan literature – the literary response to the experience of the prison. The fact that one of the world's oldest universities had published his account also separated Kariuki from the autobiographies that began to pump out of the East Africa Publishing House and Transafrica Literature Bureau; there was distribution in Britain and a positive, if slightly cautionary, foreword by Margery Perham CBE, a well-known liberal. His autobiography, like that of his contemporaries, is testament to the collective struggle of the Kenyan people, Mau Mau and the early vision of the political party, KANU (Kenyan African National Union), but his methods of letter writing and smuggling, of directing his writing to a particular individual, created a tradition of resistance writing and incarceration literature that is attributable directly to Kariuki.

Following his release from the pipeline in 1960, Kariuki resumed his political work, but now with the new Kenyan Africa National Union, the party established to incorporate the various post-Independence lobby groups and political parties. The success of the incorporation of these bodies into KANU was largely due to Kariuki's skill at mediation and leadership. In May 1960, he became Nyeri District Chairman of a KANU steering committee, established to provide, among other aims, a politically healthy party ready for Kenyatta's triumphant return. Kariuki's popular support grew quickly following his release from detention due to the combination of his legendary detainee status and his founding role in the new KANU. In 1961, following his first meeting with Jomo Kenyatta, still under house arrest at his home in Maralal, Kariuki became the future President's chargé d'affaires; he travelled to Ghana establishing positive relations with Kwame Nkrumah and delivered correspondence for Kenyatta in Britain, preparing the political atmosphere for Independence.

Kariuki's narrative concludes before Independence, and with the following caution to the prospective leaders of an Independent Kenya:

> Our leaders must realise that we have put them where they are not to satisfy their ambitions nor so that they can strut about in fine clothes and huge Cadillacs as ambassadors and ministers, but to create a new Kenya.... This will require responsible leadership, hard work, unity and honesty.... Selfish power seekers will have to go.[28]

The decade after Independence in Kenya saw Josiah Kariuki embrace Pan-Africanism and a range of social and legislative issues that Independence had exacerbated, not solved, particularly land consolidation and ex-detainees' rights. Though he continued to work for the new President as his personal secretary, he became MP for Nyandarua North and the leader of the National Youth Service. His popularity and political capabilities continued to grow, yet his successful work for KANU began to expose less diligent politicians and a parliamentary penchant for embezzlement. Fearing his increasing popularity and socialist reform approach, Kenyatta refused to allow Kariuki to address or convene public meetings, a death-knell for a politician.

On Sunday 2 March 1975, Josiah Kariuki was found murdered at Ngong Hills, famous in the European literary imagination as Karen Blixen's vista in *Out of Africa*. 'Who betrayed J. M. Kariuki? Who killed him?' Ngũgĩ asks in 'J.M. – a writer's tribute',[29] and Ngũgĩ proceeds to list other post-Independence murders and disappearances, establishing a pattern of political suppression and intimidation. There are other questions, too: What does the nature of Kariuki's disappearance indicate for writers in Kenya? What has been his literary legacy? These questions are, in part, answered by the existence of Kamiti Maximum Security Prison and Nyayo House, both in Nairobi. Nyayo House,[30] located in the centre of Nairobi, is a government-owned building that houses a clandestine torture centre, referred to by Maina wa Kinyatti and Koigi wa Wamwere in their respective prison accounts.[31] Following a 'reception' at Nyayo House, both 'disappeared' individuals and those with 'legitimate' charges are transferred to Kamiti, where Dedan Kimathi was hanged during the Emergency.

This is where writers, political dissidents and those out of favour with the Moi regime find themselves living the sentence imposed on Kariuki nearly fifty years ago. British modes of punishment were not eradicated with Independence, and have in fact been carefully preserved and enhanced. Kariuki's literary legacy is a large body of Kenyan literature that deals exclusively with the experience of the prison; this corpus of incarceration literature plays an invaluable role in the construction of an alternative political and national ideology similar to that of an armed struggle. It is a tangible record of armed and literary resistance that still resonates long after it was 'written'.

Notes

1. Ioan Davies, *Writers in Prison* (New York, Basil Blackwell, 1990). The title of this chapter is a term used by Davies in *Writers* to express the suppression of free communication, both written and verbal, in a penal situation.

2. Ngũgĩ wa Thiong'o, *Detained: A Writer's Prison Diary* (London, Heinemann, 1981).

3. Josiah Mwangi Kariuki, *'Mau Mau' Detainee: The Account by a Kenya African of His Experiences in Detention Camps 1953–1960* (London, Oxford University Press, 1963).

4. Literally 'the disappeared'.

5. Kariuki, *Detainee*, p. 13.

6. *Ibid.*, p. 28.

7. *Ibid.*, p. 43.

8. A report by a British psychiatrist, Dr J. C. Carothers (*The Psychology of Mau Mau* (Nairobi, Government Printer, 1954)). Carothers's report was a clinical assessment of a political situation which solidified and justified the British government's rehabilitative and reformative approach.

9. Kariuki, *Detainee*, p. 61.

10. *Ibid.* Kariuki notes: 'I never found out whether the inventor of these labels realised the double symbolism inherent in them.'

11. Maina wa Kinyatti's investigative title, *Kenya's Freedom Struggle: The Dedan Kimathi Papers* (London, Zed Press, 1986) reproduces Kimathi's own letters and instructions to document the evolution of the Movement, dictating that each location leader had his own scribe to record the daily proceedings of a platoon.

12. Kariuki, *Detainee*, p. 81.

13. *Ibid.*, p. 68.

14. *Ibid.*, p. 1. Kariuki mentions Manyani in the first paragraph of his acccount; alongside the Hola Camp massacre, '"Manyani", the largest camp, capable of holding up to 30,000 of us, is now a word deeply entrenched in the language of every tribe in Kenya'.

15. Kariuki, *Detainee*, p. 74.

16. *Ibid.*

17. *Ibid.*

18. *Ibid.*

19. *Ibid.*

20. *Ibid.*, p. 101.

21. I have been unsuccessful in finding a translation or reference for this word in either the Kiswahili or Gikuyu languages. It may be a word play on 'Athi River', a common linguistic game amongst Gikuyu speakers, particularly young children, according to Kariuki's explanation of the word 'Mau Mau':

> Kikuyu children when playing and talking together often make puns and anagrams with common words. When I was a child I would say to other children 'Ithi, Ithi' instead of 'Thii Thii' (meaning 'Go, Go'), and 'Mau Mau' instead of 'Uma Uma'.

22. Carothers, *Psychology*.

23. Kariuki, *Detainee*, p. 128.

24. *Ibid.*

25. *Ibid.*, p. 129.

26. See Maina wa Kinyatti, *Kimathi Papers*, for results in the retrieval of LAFA pamphlets, plays and songs. Also Kinyatti, *Thunder from the Mountains: Anthology of Mau Mau Songs* (London, Zed Press, 1980).

27. Davies, *Writers*, p. 65.

28. Kariuki, *Detainee*, p. 181.

29. Ngũgĩ wa Thiong'o, *Writers in Politics* (London, Heinemann, 1981), p. 85.

30. The building is named after the political philosophy of the Moi administration. 'Nyayo',

in Kiswahili, means 'to follow in the footsteps' – after Kenyatta's death in 1978, his political heir, Moi, coined this term to refer to his style of rule that followed not only Kenyatta but also the colonial administration.

31. Koigi wa Wamwere, imprisoned for treason, was published by Zed Books, a London-based publishing house that has continued a tradition of publishing literature smuggled out of Kenya.

CHAPTER TWELVE

Trapped daughters: American Chinatowns and Chinese American women

DI GAN

'Oriental girls'

Is it possible to draw a fine line between the colonized and the oppressed? Current scholarship has generated enough debate on the conceptualization of the terminology associated with 'postcolonial'. For instance, in 'The post-colonial project: critical approaches and problems', Gareth Griffiths laments that in America the concept of postcolonial has shifted from specific references to historic and geographic colonization experience to philosophical and ideological concerns about marginality:

> [T]he diffusion of the term 'post-colonial' in recent accounts to refer to any kind of marginality at all, either directly or by loose association with the interests of other marginalized groups, has tended to leach out its specific political valency and its central, defining concern with the historic reality of colonization.[1]

Griffiths stresses critics' obligation to identify colonization with specific geographical sites and tightly associate the term 'postcolonial' with the 'historic reality of colonization'.[2]

This restriction on the term 'colonization' seems debatable. According to Griffiths's definition, Native Americans are the only 'colonized' ethnic group in postcolonial North America and thus only Native American literature qualifies as a postcolonial discourse; literatures of African American, Hispanic American, Asian American, and other ethnic minorities cannot be considered postcolonial because these people did not experience colonization as indigenous peoples on their native land. The British colonization of North America should also be disqualified as 'colonial' – neither were the colonized Americans indigenous people nor were the thirteen colonies their native land; the colonized Americans should then be more accurately referred to as oppressed immigrants.

In disagreement with Griffiths's definition, Stephen H. Sumida in 'Postcolonialism, nationalism, and the emergence of Asian/Pacific American literatures' points out that since ethnic American literatures 'are often still considered minority ones', for 'peoples of racial minority groups of the United States there has not been a point of liberation from colonialism in the political, *inter*national sense that the British colonies became liberated, gained independence and nationhood'. Postcolonial literature can therefore be defined as literature that expresses a philosophical concern with issues caused by metaphysical colonization.[3] In this sense, a postcolonial approach toward a contemporary American literary text tends to disclose the dynamics of a given narrative (the Western-white-mainstream discourse) and a reconstructed one (various suppressed discourses of minorities). In other words, postcolonial literature acknowledges the necessity of liberating the oppressed/colonized minorities. The postcolonial discourse empowers the powerless, gives voice to the silenced and coordinates the subordinated.

In 'Decolonization, displacement, disidentification', Lisa Lowe further pushes 'the role of colonial narratives to modes of cultural imperialism' which 'cross national boundaries, are in excess of a single nation-state formation, and are complicated by displacement and immigration'. Lowe claims that besides playing a role in historic realities such as the military colonization of the Philippines, the war against the Japanese and the wars in Korea and Vietnam, postcolonial Orientalism has also developed indispensable connections to 'the history of Asian immigration, exclusion, and naturalization'. Hence, the complex dynamics between colonization and immigrant displacement go beyond the border of the colonized nations and manifest themselves through the metaphysical 'oriental otherness' in the colonizer's own country, which in our case is America.[4]

In agreement with Sumida and Lowe, I use the terms 'colonization' and 'postcolonial' with their philosophical and ideological connotations and treat the Chinese American experience as a colonial one. The main purpose of this chapter is to show the connection between historical colonization and its long-lasting, confining power over the individual subject's psyche. I view the Chinatown family and parents as the colonized objects, and the American-born daughter as the self-conscious subject that cognitively tries to define this colonized object. The daughter is both part of the object, the colonized Chinese Other, and simultaneously the self-fashioning subject, the American Self. In other words, she is both the Foucaultian 'director' who dwells in the 'all-seeing central tower' and the inspected/self-inspected inmate captured in the assigned cultural cell.[5] She is unable to fully disconnect herself from the imprisoned/'punished' Other, who is most directly represented by her Chinese immigrant parents.

Colonial Chinatown and its binding label of Chineseness

Similar to the origins of Indian reservations in the nineteenth century and the Japanese internment camps during World War II, the beginnings of Chinatowns in the United States carry undeniable colonial traits. Early

Chinese American experience is characterized by racial hostility, physical violence, political exclusion, economic exploitation and geographic separation and incarceration. Research findings provided in Sucheng Chan's *Asian Americans: An Interpretive History* and Shih-shan Henry Tsai's *The Chinese Experience in America* depict a colonized 'historic reality' of the Chinese American experience.

The most commonly shared sentiment white Americans had towards the early Chinese immigrants was racial hostility. As Sucheng Chan points out, since the Chinese were the earliest Asian immigrants arriving on American soil, they suffered 'the most clearly delineated and long-lived' prejudice. Nineteenth-century Americans looked down on China as a decayed nation bearing shame for her once extraordinary civilization. Accordingly, they viewed her people as 'nothing more than starving masses, beasts of burden, depraved heathens, and opium addicts'.[6] The nineteenth-century American novel, *Almond-eyed: The Great Agitator: A Story of the Day* (1878), explicitly and representatively expresses the white majority's hostility toward the Chinese immigrants:

> The stream of heathen men and women still comes pouring in, filling the places which should be occupied by the Caucasian race, poisoning the moral atmosphere, tainting society, undermining the free institutions of the country, degrading labor, and resisting quietly, but wisely and successfully, all efforts to remove them, or prevent their coming.[7]

White hostility toward the Chinese was expressly linked to physical violence. Numerous riots against Chinese coolies were committed in the western frontier states in the late nineteenth century.

> Chinese were attacked in 34 California communities, harassed or expelled from 9 Washington localities and tormented in 3 Oregon and 4 Nevada towns. Millions of dollars worth of their property was damaged and burned in mining towns in Colorado, Alaska, South Dakota, and elsewhere. Notable atrocities against the Chinese took place in the California towns of Eureka (1885), Redlands (1893), and Chico (1894), and in Juneau, Alaska (1886). But the most serious incidents occurred in Los Angeles, Denver, Rock Springs in Wyoming, on the Snake River, and in Tacoma and Seattle in Washington.[8]

In many cases, white perpetrators of this violence were unpunished or lightly punished,[9] while economic exploitation further aggravated the situation. For instance, a Foreign Miners' Tax, which was first passed in 1850 and re-enacted in 1852, 'was enforced primarily against Chinese, even though in theory it applied to all foreigners'.[10] In 1855, the state legislature of California decided to charge an extra tax of $50 on 'the immigration to this state of persons who cannot become citizens thereof'. In 1862, an act was passed to 'protect free white labor against competition with Chinese coolie labor' by levying a $2.50 monthly 'police tax' on every Chinese.[11]

Political exclusion was the next 'natural' step. On 3 April 1876, hostile partisans organized a mass rally in San Francisco, while the California legislature 'appointed a special committee to investigate the social, moral, and political effects of Chinese immigration'. During the hearing, white witnesses not only attributed the problem of unemployment to the exaggerated number of Chinese immigrants but also accused Chinese labourers of hindering the emigration of better-skilled white European labourers. As a result, Angell's Treaty was signed by both Chinese and American governments, 'mark[ing] the end of the free Chinese immigration'. Consequently, the United States Congress started conceiving its first exclusion law against the Chinese.[12]

In 1882, Senator John F. Miller, Republican of California, submitted a bill to suspend the immigration of both skilled and unskilled Chinese labourers. Slightly revised, this bill was passed by Congress, suspending Chinese labour for ten years. It also listed the strict certifications and identifications required, especially from arriving Chinese, and set penalties for the illegal landing of Chinese labour and for those who could not provide the required documents. At the same time, it demanded that 'State and Federal courts were forbidden to naturalize Chinese'.[13] On 6 May 1882, President Arthur signed the bill into law. As observed by Shih-shan Henry Tsai, the notorious Exclusion Act of 1882 was 'the first of a series of increasingly stringent laws against the Chinese'.[14]

Physical incarceration of the Chinese, as the major feature that later characterized life in Chinatowns, was a direct result of the 1882 Exclusion Act. To prevent illegal Chinese immigration, the United States Immigration Bureau built an immigration station on a small island in San Francisco Bay. Like Ellis Island on the east coast which interrogated millions of European immigrants, Angel Island station functioned as 'the detention quarters for Asiatic immigrants, primarily Chinese, from 1910 to 1940'.[15] The procedure of cross-examining the Chinese arrivals lasted from a few days to a few years. During this time, the detainees were imprisoned in filthy rooms and provided with bad food. Bored and distressed in their seemingly endless waiting, some of them wrote poems on the walls of the detention rooms to express their frustration:

> This is called an island of immortals, but as a matter of fact,
> the mountain wilderness is a prison.[16]

> Everybody says journey to North America is easy and a pleasure,
> But I suffered misery on the ship and worry in the wooden enclosure,
> Several interrogations I have been through, but still feel in chain,
> I sigh for my brethren who are being detained.[17]

These poems not only recorded the actual experience of the detainees but also foreshadowed the future imprisonment they had to face while living in Chinatowns.

Geographical separation was another product of racial hostility. According to the federal census, 'during the ten-year span after the passage of the 1882 Exclusion Act, the Chinese population decreased by a total of 81,973'. Beside this change in numbers, the Chinese population also started retreating from small towns and rural areas to assemble in certain districts of metropolitan cities. As William F. Wu points out in his social-literary studies of the Chinese American experience, the burgeoning of Chinatown was the direct result of the anti-Chinese riots between 1870 and 1890 and of the legalization of residential segregation in 1878. As the Chinese Exclusion Act of 1882 justified and encouraged the white hostility against the Chinese, '[a] period of riots and violence against the Chinese immigrants already in the United States drove them out of rural areas and smaller communities into the larger Chinatowns such as those in San Francisco, Sacramento, and Seattle'.[18]

The autonomous design of the Chinatown was a typical product of the self-survival sentiments shared by many Chinese immigrants in the late nineteenth century. Because of racial prejudice, cultural difference and the language barrier, the Chinese kept themselves away from the hostile white communities and avoided being involved with labour organizations. They opened small family businesses such as laundromats, grocery stores and restaurants, which enabled them to be socially independent. As Tsai concludes, 'They socialized primarily with their kinsmen and rarely participated in local and state affairs. They became an invisible minority.'[19]

Like Native American reservations, Chinatowns function as racial associations that label their residents' Chineseness and signify their Otherness opposite the mainstream American Self. While serving as racial havens that protect their own people, the Chinatown associations also impose social control over their members. Association leaders 'exercised power and acquired prestige not only by virtue of being officers of community organizations but also by serving as communication links – and consequently, as power brokers – between their compatriots and the external world'.[20] From small family associations to big interstate financial associations, many Chinatowns constructed levels of associations to resist the outside oppression.

Racially oppressed, geographically separated and economically exploited, the Chinatown in many ways is 'a resistant, recalcitrant "historical" space' that resembles a colony.[21] In short, it is a space that confines the colonized Other within the colonial Self's design and is simultaneously a resistant region that protects the Other from the colonizer's cultural annihilation.

Four novels

Four of the most recently published novels by Chinese American women writers illustrate the confining features of Chinatowns as well as the binding ties of Chinese American families within the context of colonial incarceration: *Bone* (1994) by Fae Myenne Ng, *Eating Chinese Food Naked*

(1998) by Nei Ng, *Monkey King* (1997) by Patricia Chao, and *Oriental Girls Desire Romance* (1997) by Catherine Liu.

Bone tells the Leng's family stories in San Francisco's Chinatown. Leon, the Chinese American father, explains the racially confining-protecting function of the Chinatown to his wife, 'You are inside Chinatown; it's safe. You don't know. Outside, it's different.'[22] As a result of Leon's teaching, his favourite daughter, Ona, 'never felt comfortable' outside Chinatown. As does a Native American reservation for a Native American, Chinatown nurtures Ona with her own cultural heritage but, at the same time, confines her into her Chineseness and thus separates her from the American majority. She remains a 'Chinese (or Chinatown) daughter', an Other.

Ona's boyfriend, the half-white boy Osvaldo, brings disorder into Ona's Chinatown life. The young lovers' romance is approved by both families until Osvaldo's deceiving parents cheat Leon in their joint family business. Showing no guilt about their actions, Osvaldo's parents are depicted as symbolic colonizer figures conspiring in the repeated colonial episode of white-men-shamelessly-robbing-the-natives-on-the-natives'-own-land. As millions of Chinese immigrants had passively accepted violation and exploitation for decades, Leon's hysterical anger should be read as the ethnically colonized Other's venting of his long-smothered fury against the 'innocent' white (half-white in this case) colonizer.

Tormented between her love for both Leon and Osvaldo, Ona feels stuck: 'In the family, in Chinatown. Ona was the middle girl and she felt stuck in the middle of all the trouble.'[23] Incapable of living a life outside Chinatown, Ona finds no reconciliation for her split identity as the daughter of the colonized Other and the lover of the colonizer Self. As a racial and social association, Chinatown demands Ona's loyalty, which eventually dooms her fatal confinement in the town. By jumping from the highest building in Chinatown, Ona makes herself a Chinatown martyr.

Unlike Ona, who willingly played the role of the Chinatown captive beauty, her two sisters Leila and Nina are frustrated with their clearly labelled Chinatown legacy and yearn to escape. Reflecting on Ona's death, Leila concludes that escape was 'what Ona needed'.[24] In order to move outside of her parents' Chinatown home, Leila takes Nina's advice and rashly gets married in the City Hall. Nina, the youngest of the three, runs away as far as she can and takes a tour guide job in New York. Although moving and travelling seems to ease the tension caused by the imprisonment in Chinatown, both sisters later realize that their attachment to it was too strong to be broken. For example, Leila and Nina decide to choose an Italian restaurant over a Chinese one, hoping to escape the haunting memories associated with Chinatown life. Unconsciously separating/freeing herself from her own Chineseness, Nina comments with a detached outsider's tone that Chinatown is 'too depressing', and that '[t]he food is good . . . but the life's hard down there'.[25] She also tells Leila that she 'hardly ever uses chopsticks anymore. . . . At home she eats her rice on a plate, with a fork.'[26]

However, the sisters' escape from Chinatown is soon deemed unsuccessful when they are recognized by their inescapable label of Chineseness: 'The waiter stood there, the dark plates balanced on his arm. "You two Chinese?" he asked. "No." I let my irritation fill the word. "We are two sisters." '[27]

Leila's answer sounds like an illogical response to the waiter's inquiry about their ethnicity – she chooses to emphasize family links as an alternative to ethnic identity. Just like Chinatown, which is simultaneously a forced space designed by the colonizer and an autonomous region guarded by Chinese American residents against cultural annihilation, the labelling of Chineseness functions both as a label of racial colonization and a cultural signifier that preserves the Chinese heritage. Leon's daughters are not the only ones frustrated with this colonial labelling of Chineseness.

While Leila and Nina are confronted by an outsider American, in *Monkey King,* Sally's Chineseness is imposed by her Chinese immigrant parents. Sally is required to remain a 'Chinese daughter' for her father, who is referred to as an 'incurable Chinese'.[28] Sally's mother also asserts that she 'has old-fashioned Chinese mentality', which demands her to 'be a good daughter, be a good wife. Obedience. Confucian law . . . what her father teaches her'.[29] As a forced given, this Chineseness confuses the American-born daughters, who often view themselves as members no less – if not more – of the large American society than of the segregated Chinatown. They do not share their first-generation immigrant parents' cultural obligation to China and Chineseness, as is shown when Sally's father tries to demand the obedient behaviour of a Chinese daughter, she protests: 'but we are not in China'.[30]

The labelling gaze from others, which keeps reminding these Chinese American daughters of their Chineseness, is one of control, discipline and confinement. No matter how American these daughters feel, they are prohibited from stepping outside of their cultural cell. As Michel Foucault elaborates in *Discipline and Punish: The Birth of the Prison,* the controller (the 'director' or 'supervisor' who dwells in the centre tower), exercises his power by means of visual observation. The gaze he makes on the exposed 'prisoners' (each of whom takes a cell in the prison that surrounds the centre tower) turns them into objects of his 'correct training'.[31]

Moreover, Foucault asserts that '[d]isciplinary punishment has the function of reducing gaps. It must therefore be essentially *corrective*.' Since the daughters' desire to break away from the Chinatown life threatens to widen the gap between them and normalized/colonized Chineseness, this desire must be corrected. The method involved in disciplinary punishment, as Foucault puts it, is 'isomorphic with obligation' and 'is not so much the vengeance of an outraged law as its repetition, its reduplicated insistence'.[32] In other words, the most effective way to correct these daughters is to make them replay the assigned role, which is the unnegotiable Chineseness.

Being imprisoned in Chineseness by such disciplinary gazes, however, does not mean that these daughters can not look back. Foucault makes it clear that, eventually, 'it does not matter who exercises power. Any individual, taken almost at random, can operate the [panopticon] machine.'[33] Hence, these Chinese American daughters can exercise their Americanness by entering the controller-colonizer's 'all-seeing tower'. Their multicultural identity complicates the network of their gazes, for they can both see from the American controller-colonizer's tower and from the colonized Chinese prisoner's cell.

In her postcolonial study, *Woman and Chinese Modernity: The Politics of Reading between West and East*, Rey Chow points out that '"seeing" carries with it the connotation of a demarcation of ontological boundaries between "self" and "other", whether racial, social, or sexual'. Chow defines 'seeing' as 'an instance of the cultural predicament in which the ethnic subject finds herself':

> The most difficult questions surrounding the demarcation of boundaries implied by 'seeing' have to do not with positivistic taxonomic juxtapositions of self-contained identities and traditions in the manner of 'this is you' and 'that is us', but rather, *who is 'seeing' whom, and how?*[34]

Chow highlights the 'power relationship' between the 'subject' and 'object' of the 'culturally overdetermined "eye"'.[35]

Overlapping Foucault and Chow, Edward Said argues in *Orientalism* that one characteristic of colonialism is the non-reciprocal and hierarchic relations between the colonizer and the colonized. In other words, the colonizer identifies himself as the authoritative subject who asserts his right to define the colonized object.[36] For example, identifying with the ethnic Other, the daughter in *Oriental Girls Desire Romance* rejects the Chinese discourse composed and publicized by a white American Self:

> When I returned to the U.S., a book about China, written by an American who had taught English there at about the same time I did, was published. It received a great deal of press and presented a hopelessly naive and idealized portrait of China and the Chineseness, and of teaching as well. This book put me in a darker mood than ever. I thought that no one would ever be able to understand what I had gone through in China.[37]

This misreading of her ethnic background further aggravates the daughter's frustration over her Chineseness. The popularity of this colonial reading (with the white American writer as a recently returned colonizer) signifies the defining power the cultural majority has over minority groups. As the native, the daughter finds her own voice suffocated and suppressed; consequently, she delays her own articulation of the Chinese experience.

However, trained in Western art history and theory at a famous Ivy League school, the daughter also identifies with the American Self who feels at odds with her Chineseness: 'My parents had always held up Chineseness to us as some state of unattainable purity from which we, the Americanized children, had been exiled.'[38] From time to time, she doubted the substantiality of her Chineseness: she called the Chinese 'my supposed people' and 'was afraid that this famous wisdom never really existed at all'. She wondered if the superb Chinese cultural heritage her parents bragged about 'was just a fortune cookie rumor' or 'just a silly fantasy'. China becomes an elusive symbol of the inaccessible past: 'Maybe the past beyond my memory never existed, China never really existed, *I was never really Chinese.*'[39]

Trapped in the dilemma of defining Chineseness either as superior wisdom or as a 'fortune cookie rumor', the heroine found herself caught in two different 'missions':

> I had the distinct feeling that I was on some sort of mission, that I had been programmed to do something in this brave new world by my Chinese ancestor, and that I was failing.[40]

> But I had been sent on a special mission . . . I was trying to figure out what was going on on this planet in order to save everyone – my people, and the people of this place. I was working with others, but I had lost contact with them.[41]

In both statements, she identifies herself with her Chineseness and calls Chinese people her people. However, the nature of the missions differs. For the first mission, she is sent by her Chinese people to 'do something' in America; for the second mission, she feels obliged to free her Chinese people 'on this planet'. While the first mission may indicate her desire to assert her ethnic heritage, the second mission carries out her anxiety to decolonize her suppressed Chineseness. In the end, she reports her confusion: 'I began to lose track of my mission. Chaos and confusion engulfed me.'[42]

Likewise, Leila in *Bone* acknowledges her special position on the threshold. Like the daughter in *Oriental Girls Desire Romance*, although living among the colonized Chinese inmates, Leila has a legitimate membership in the American 'centre tower'.[43] Born and educated in America, Leila could identify with the white American tourists and adapt to their outsider's gaze; being a Chinatown resident and raised by Chinese immigrant parents, she knows the inside story of the Chinatown that is not exposed to the exoticizing voyeur. In other words, Leila's access to the prison cells allows her to see the 'inside story' that a white 'supervisor' can not see:

> From the low seats of the Camaro, I looked out . . . I thought, So this is what Chinatown looks like from inside those dark Greyhound buses; this slow view, these strange color combinations, these narrow streets, this is what tourists come to see. I felt a small lightening up inside, because I knew, no matter what

people saw, no matter how close they looked, our inside story is something entirely different.[44]

The confining ties of the Chinese American home

In *Asian Americans: An Interpretive History*, Chan states that 'the ability to form associations, along with their repeated efforts to resist oppression, enables Asians to carve a place for themselves in a host society that did not welcome them'.[45] If the Chinatown functions as a group of associations that build up ties to strengthen themselves against a hostile society, the Chinese immigrant family, as the smallest association within the Chinatown, provides indispensable ties that bond the family members together against the outside world.

The significant role of family in Chinese culture is also elaborated by Elaine Kim in *Asian American Literature: An Introduction to the Writings and their Social Context*. Kim points out that, in China, family functions as the primary foundation of individual identity:

> Traditionally, an individual's first loyalty was to his kinsmen. Chinese family relationships dominated political and economic activities and served as a primary tool for social control. An individual's reputation was his family's reputation and one's personal affairs could not be strictly one's own.[46]

Just as Sally comments in *Monkey King*, 'Family is fatal but they created you after all',[47] narrators of the selected Chinese American novels have been raised to experience and require a powerful identification with their families.

As discussed earlier, these Chinese American daughters are often eager to break away from the confining Chineseness. They pity their poor, illiterate Chinese immigrant parents and resent the suffocating and miserable Chinatown life.

Applying Chow's 'Who's seeing who?' theory to the daughter–parent relationship in the four selected novels, one may notice that this dynamic shifting of the eye causes unbearable confusion in the subject (the daughter): while the subject's identity, in this case, is defined/shaped by the object (the parent), the object's identity is mutually decided by (the gaze of) the subject. This interdependent identification results in a very unstable psyche for the subject, who takes the double responsibility of both defining the object and letting herself be defined by the to-be-defined object. In other words, a slightly different perspective taken by the subject's eyes may greatly change her own identity. The profound dynamics of the Chinese American family relationship both construct and are constructed by the daughter's gazes.

Depending on the perspective of the subject (the American daughter), different readings of the object (the Chinatown home and the 'Chinese' parents) simultaneously exist and constantly contradict (if not deconstruct) one another.[48] The subject composes a compound identity of the object, based on her own respective interactions with the multiple social, cultural, historical and political elements. To harmonize these conflicting versions of the object into a well-defined perception, the subject forces herself to justify her relationship with each version of the object. She realizes that her need to build and sustain one version of the object usually requires her to deconstruct or sacrifice another version of it. Her need for a clearcut relationship between family and self provokes deeper obsession with the very defining process, while the complexity of cross-cultural gender roles further aggravates her confusion. She feels trapped between different dichotomies and suffers confinement at home, both physically and psychologically.

The parents: how they trap their daughter

In *Eating Chinese Food Naked* Ruby realizes, even as a little girl, that being Chinese is nothing to brag about but, rather, it is something to be ashamed of. She notices that when her father, Franklin, threw garbage into a bag from the American supermarket, he was 'calm', but

> when he used a bag from Chinatown, his face would get tight and his hands quick and angry as he turned the bag inside out so the Chinese lettering didn't show as much. . . . 'So people don't know this is Chinese garbage', he had said.[49]

In 'The gentle way in punishment', Foucault argues that true punishment changes the convict's 'interior tendency' and makes him completely ashamed of himself by making his crime a public shame.[50] Franklin's shame about the Chinese garbage is a result of this kind of punishment. As a rejected immigrant, he is placed on the opposite side and 'punished' by the social majority. Everything that exposes his ethnicity becomes a social outrage.

Chinese American daughters, although not suffering this colonial rejection directly, are the closest witnesses of it. In *Bone*, Leila reads her family's emigrant history from items in her stepfather Leon's suitcase:

> I only had to open the first few to know the story: 'We Don't Want You'.
> A rejection from the army: unfit.
> A job rejection: unskilled.
> An apartment: unavailable.[51]

Growing up in America, Chinese American daughters are keenly aware of their fathers' inferior status in American society. To identify themselves as Americans, these daughters look at their Chinatown fathers with contempt and pity and refuse to associate with their shame and powerlessness. However, raised up in Chinese immigrant homes where the traditional behaviour codes of the 'Three Obedience . . . enjoined a woman to obey her father before marriage, her husband after marriage, and her eldest son after her husband's death',[52] these Chinese American daughters cannot fully neglect the virtue and responsibility of respecting their parents, especially the fathers. The two different gazes the daughter takes form two radically different images of the immigrant father: he is the pitiable, oppressed Other, the weird alien; he is also the honourable, respectable patriarch.

In these four novels, stereotypes of the Chinese American male are apparent; however, these young Chinese American women writers' use of these stereotypes is not an unconscious acceptance of the colonial reading but, instead, a highly conscious strategy to unfold the myth of ethnic caricature. Stereotypical characteristics of the Chinese American male, as these novels indicate, are not merely misrepresentations of the reality. On the contrary, these stereotypical characteristics, be it impotency, childishness or patriarchal dictatorship, reflect the oppressed and quite often distorted psyche of the immigrant Chinese fathers.

In *The History of Sexuality*, Foucault stresses the interchangeable positions of the dominant and the subordinate through 'power and pleasure'. Although power suggests inequality, oppression and suffering, both the dominant and the dominated can experience pleasure and power through sadomasochism. Since both the dominant and the subordinate positions can offer power and pleasure – which are exchangeable – both the one who exercises power and the one who it is exercised upon are able to attain power and pleasure.[53]

Chinese immigrant parents become 'the king and queen of emotional blackmail' to their bewildered daughters.[54] Realizing that most of their hardship and pain are unappreciated and undermined by the colonizers, they demand their daughters to be forever grateful. When Lily tells her other Chinese American friends that 'My dad's a dictator', they simply reply that 'Fathers are like that.'[55] Chinese fathers are supposed to be like that. As the oppressed (by white Americans) and the oppressor (of his family members), Franklin is both the manipulated and manipulative. He transforms his sufferings – as typical for the Chinese American immigrants – into the sacrifices he makes for his family. The immigrant Chinese father's shame becomes the boast and excuse that support his patriarchal reign. Witnessing the hardship of what he has experienced and acknowledging the intensity of his pain his daughters have no heart to defer his demand for sympathy, which he can get from nowhere else but his own family. Hence, although tortured by their resentment of his 'dictatorship', Lily and Ruby feel sorry for their old father and would do everything to please him.

When her father says pitiful things about himself, Ruby still feels sorry for him. She does not know 'why it was so hard to say no to him' and feels furious at herself for letting her father 'win yet again'.[56] Loathing her father's control over her mother, Ruby gathers her courage and decides to take her long home-confined mother out for a vacation. Once the decision is made, however, she feels even more bound by the tie with her father:

> Thinking about her father at home watching TV in the middle of the day made her forget what a tyrant he could be. She felt gentle toward him and worried that he would be lonesome if she and her mother went away to Florida.[57]

The efforts, sometimes even irrational ones, she would take to please him reveal the American-born daughter's immovable wish to undo the ethnic oppression imposed on her immigrant father. However, in order to redeem the father from his colonized experience, the daughter further submits herself to his patriarchy, which captures her in the very law that is represented by the father's colonized Chineseness and is the very thing the daughter tries to break away from. To compensate for her father's colonial suffering, to free her father from his pathetic sense of powerlessness, the freedom-seeking American daughter paradoxically confines herself within her Chinatown home and its patriarchy.

Like the colonized father figure, the image of the immigrant mother is also too confusing and complicated for the daughter to describe. In front of the father, the mother keeps her submissive, masochist image, but in front of the daughter she is a sadist with 'a heart of ice and a dagger for a tongue', 'a nightmare'. The daughter depicts her mother's sadomasochistic strategy: 'my father belittled her ... and screamed at her when he was enraged, but she knew very well how to defend herself against criticism or attack – she played the martyr card'.[58] The 'martyr card' is the sadomasochist power card. Accordingly, the martyred mother can turn into a true sadistic tyrant who enforces masochism onto her daughter:

> I groveled and shivered at her feet like a dog. I thought there were no depths to which I would not sink in order to win her love. If, only once, she could feel sorry for me, I'd be satisfied. I wanted her pity because it seemed like the closest thing to love that she was capable of, at least toward me ... she was obsessed with the sacrifices she had had to make; she wanted to believe that she was a kind of martyr.[59]

Culturally imprisoned, the Chinese immigrant mother's stark, confined and sexless life becomes a haunting inspector that censors even the smallest inclination of hedonism in the American-born daughter's life. For instance, in *Eating Chinese Food Naked*, Ruby feels obliged to stay home with her mother and the very thought of enjoying life outside of the Chinatown home overwhelms her with guilt. Wishing to deliver their mothers from their harshly disciplined, long confined and pleasure-deprived life, the Chinese American daughters only find themselves in the same masochistic trap, which is the sadomasochistic mothers' power domain.

The Chinese American daughters, consequently, become sadomasochistic when submitting themselves to their parents' power; while, to empower themselves as free American women, these daughters have to identify themselves with Western democracy and feminism, and thus subvert the Chinese fathers' patriarchy at home.

In *Bone* Nina watches her two sisters being trapped at their Chinatown home:

> Nina said she watched us. She saw how I was locked into living Mah's and Leon's lives for them. She saw how Ona's need for them destroyed her. Nina said she always felt that by the time it got to be her turn, Mah and Leon acted like they'd given up on the family.[60]

While, in *Oriental Girls Desire Romance*, the daughter realizes that she has to live 'under the spell of the Fat Man and his pale, vengeful Wife':

> They were the ones who never let me forget that they were the ones who loved me. They were the ones who provided for me. They said they were always there for me. They said they knew me best. They told me what my weaknesses were, and then they punished me for them . . . he reminded us that because we were all Chinese, we were in this together. We were a family.[61]

In *Eating Chinese Food Naked*, trapped for years in the 'cramped and stifling' Chinatown apartment above her parents' home, Lily expresses a sense of despair about such imprisonment:

> Someone had to stay at home; she didn't know why it always had to be her. First Van left, and then Ruby, and now even her mother wanted to go. Then it occurred to her that the older she got, the more timid she felt, while her mother seemed to be getting tougher.[62]

Fighting against her parents' influence, while at the same time clinging to their ties, Ruby also feels stuck at the privacy-deprived home. Unconsciously, the homebound daughter develops a fear of any kind of relationship that requires similar ties. A steady sexual relationship or a permanent job scares her. For example, considering it 'dangerous', Ruby dreads the idea of settling down with her boyfriend:

> It felt dangerous to see him while she was living at home – she might be tempted to stay with him; days and weeks and then years would pass without her noticing, and one morning she'd wake up and look out the window and there, surrounding the house, would be the dreaded white picket fence.[63]

She fears for a permanent job. 'The thought of settling down scares her out of her wits.'[64] Working as a temporary, she quits the job as soon as she is offered a permanent position. Likewise, in *Oriental Girls Desire Romance*, the heroine is afraid of taking a permanent job for the same reason. Keeping everything temporary gives her an imagined sense of freedom: 'With all things temporary, I avoided the thought of beginning or doing something for what was to me a terrifying eternity: the rest of my life.'[65]

American? Chinese? Inspector? Inmate? Free? Trapped? At the threshold position, the daughter cannot attain a clearcut definition of herself as well as of her relationship with her parents. She is confused about her Chineseness. Ruby 'envied' the other girls 'who could play at being Chinese' and 'could put it on and take it off as easily as doing up the straps of their shoes in the morning and kicking them off after school'.[66] But for Ruby, her Chineseness is sealed permanently on her. At the Asian Student Union parties, Ruby 'felt everyone knew one another and that they were Chinese in a way she didn't know how to be'.[67] She ended up receiving a reproof for 'trying to act black or white or Puerto Rican'.[68] In *Monkey King*, Sally tries to solve her confusion through play-acting: 'I pretended I am Natalie Wood in *West Side Story*. She is really American, my mother says, only playing the part of a foreigner.'[69]

This deep-rooted confusion gradually leads to neurosis. Ruby's unpredictable crying and wailing in front of Nick, her boyfriend, bear psychotic traits. As a young college graduate, she is restless, unstable, driven between murderous anger and heartbreaking love toward her father, and impulsively jumping in and out of the obsession with her mother. Her ambivalent feelings about home terribly disturb her and prevent her from having a normal romantic relationship with Nick. Likewise, without knowing any normal parent–child relationship, the daughter in *Oriental Girls Desire Romance* believes that she herself is 'crazy':

> When I was a little older, I read every book I could about mental disorders in the young adult section of our public library. I began to think I was crazy. If I was being treated so badly and it was my fault, perhaps I was not simply selfish, incompetent, mean, impatient – that is, flawed in a modest or at least normal way – perhaps I was actually mentally ill.[70]

The daughter feels paralysed by the confusing perceptions imposed by her parents. Having always been taught to love and respect her father, she cannot understand the father's physical abuse. Although trying desperately to see things from her mother's perspective, she finds the imposed perception incomprehensible:

> I believed her. As I reached puberty, I tried even harder to convince myself of it. It took a lot of energy. *I never developed any confidence in my perceptions of the world*, because if I could have believed that she loved me, I could have believed anything. I wanted so badly to give her what she wanted.[71]

By telling her that she knows nothing about China, the father further aggravates the daughter's insecurity about her perceptions. Feeling paralysed by her father's disdain, she delays her writing for years.[72] Suffocated by the stern parents' demands, she 'believed that all other people lived in harmony with themselves and each other', all but herself. Bewildered by her Chinese parents' harshness, she feels that she 'was the only one who existed in a perpetual state of internalized exile'.[73]

Ultimately, the daughter becomes infatuated with the 'normality' of one of her boyfriends: 'Joe ... was so normal ... I had been trapped by my own disbelief, by my desire to get inside that normalcy'.[74] However, she later realizes that her 'visions' and her 'thoughts were getting more and more psychotic':[75]

> I couldn't stop thinking, I couldn't stop not thinking. I couldn't stop feeling that all things were multicolored. Multi, multi-multiple, multicultural, multilateral, multilingual . . . I wished for a kind of amnesia, and I had no tolerance or humility. I want to live outside my life. I knew this kind of desperation meant that I was a little bit crazy, but there was nothing I could do. To top it all off, I wanted time to end.[76]

This 'multi-ness', the very characteristic of her compound identity and the provider of her multi-gazes at her parents, her home and herself, overwhelms the daughter and pushes her to the point of insanity. For her, '[t]he end of each day seemed like a big unbearable blank'. She asks herself: 'How was I going to make any sense of life in this place when I couldn't connect one day with the one that followed or preceded it.'[77] She gets lost in the maze of cultural multi-ness. Likewise, Sally, the daughter in *Monkey King*, lets her mother decide her identity/sanity: 'If my mother admitted it, I really was crazy.'[78] Moreover, Sally also questions other people's normalcy. When in hospital she asks a member of staff: 'What makes you so normal?'[79] Suffering from hallucinations and suicidal impulses, Sally ends up in a psychiatric hospital.

Quite different from older writers within the canon, such as Maxine Hong Kingston, who suggests cultural transcendence, and Amy Tan, who proposes healing through family ties, these younger writers point out the impasse of intercultural self-identification. Contrary to T'sai Yen in *The Woman Warrior*, who wrote the song that 'translated well', Lei in *Bone* 'hated' translating for her Chinese-speaking parents and asserted that 'not everything can be translated'.[80] At the end of *Monkey King*, Sally admitted her inability to 'translate' while recalling her attempted suicide: 'what I'd felt, finally, was failure. . . . It was my doom to be able to see, to feel like this, and not be able to translate.'[81] Likewise, the daughter in *Oriental Girls Desire Romance* 'believe[s] that no one, especially not Americans, could understand us, the Chinese'.[82]

These American-born daughters are captured by the network of power dynamics. Being 'cross-cultural', they take a threshold position in the power-driven American society. Their American identity allows them to enter the 'centre tower'. They see their parents imprisoned in the assigned ethnic cells; on the other hand, the daughters' Chineseness labels them as one of the inmates belonging to that very cultural cell. The power dynamics among the family members, as these novels demonstrate, further destabilizes the daughters' already confused perceptions. Instead of attaining cultural harmonization and racial transcendence, these Chinese American daughters become trapped in the impasse.

Notes

1. Gareth Griffiths, 'The post-colonial project: critical approaches and problems', in Bruce King (ed.), *New National and Post-colonial Literature: An Introduction* (Oxford, Clarendon Press, 1996), p. 167.

2. *Ibid.*

3. Stephen H. Sumida, 'Postcolonialism, nationalism, and the emergence of Asian/Pacific American literatures', in King-Kok Cheung (ed.), *An Interethnic Companion to Asian American Literature* (Cambridge, Cambridge University Press, 1997), p. 274.

4. Lisa Lowe, 'Decolonization, displacement, disidentification', in Deire Lynch and William B. Warner (eds), *Cultural Institutions of the Novel* (Durham, NC, Duke University Press, 1996), p. 120.

5. Michel Foucault, *Discipline and Punish: The Birth of the Prison* (New York, Pantheon Books, 1977), p. 200.

6. Sucheng Chan, *Asian Americans: An Interpretive History* (Boston, Twayne, 1991), p. 45.

7. Quoted from William F. Wu, *The Yellow Peril: Chinese Americans in American Fiction 1850–1940* (Hamden, Archon Books, 1982), p. 32. See Atwell Whitney, *Almond-Eyed: The Great Agitator: A Story of the Day* (San Francisco, A. L. Bancroft, 1878), p. 168.

8. Shih-shan Henry Tsai, *The Chinese Experience in America* (Bloomington and Indianapolis, Indiana University Press, 1986), p. 67.

9. See Chan, *Asian Americans*, Chapter 3, 'Hostility and conflict', for detailed accounts of these riots.

10. *Ibid.*, p. 46.

11. *Ibid.*, p. 54.

12. Tsai, *Chinese Experience*, pp. 56–62.

13. Quoted in *ibid.*, pp. 64–65. See *United States Statutes* 1881–83 (Washington, DC, 1883), vol. XXXII, pp. 58–61.

14. Tsai, *Chinese Experience*, pp. 62–5.

15. *Ibid.*, pp. 99–103.

16. *Ibid.* For the entire collection of written and carved poems, see H. Mark Lai, Genny Lim and Judy Yung, *Island: Poetry and History of Chinese Immigrants on Angel Island 1910–1940* (San Francisco, Hoc Doi, 1980).

17. *Ibid.*

18. Wu, *Yellow Peril*, p. 2.

19. Tsai, *Chinese Experience*, pp. 66–7.

20. Chan, *Asian Americans*, p. 63.

21. Lowe, 'Decolonization, displacement, disidentification', p. 120.

22. Fae Myenne Ng, *Bone* (New York, HarperPerennial, 1993), p. 181.

23. *Ibid.*, p. 139.

24. *Ibid.*, p. 150.

25. *Ibid.*, p. 26–7.

26. *Ibid.*, p. 27.

27. *Ibid.*, p. 36.

28. Patricia Chao, *Monkey King* (New York, HarperCollins, 1997), pp. 149, 190.

29. *Ibid.*, p. 48.

30. *Ibid.*, p. 149.

31. See part three of Foucault, *Discipline and Punish*.

32. *Ibid.*, pp. 179–80.

33. *Ibid.*, p. 202.

34. Rey Chow, *Woman and Chinese Modernity: The Politics of Reading between West and East* (Minneapolis, University of Minnesota Press, 1991), p. 3 (my italics).

35. *Ibid.*

36. Edward Said, *Orientalism* (New York, Pantheon, 1978).

37. Catherine Liu, *Oriental Girls Desire Romance* (New York, Kaya, 1997), p. 143.

38. *Ibid.*, p. 60.

39. *Ibid.*, p. 233 (my italics).

40. *Ibid.*, p. 233.

41. *Ibid.*, p. 291.

42. *Ibid.*

43. Foucault, *Discipline and Punish*, p. 202.

44. Fae Myenne Ng, *Bone*, p. 145.

45. Chan, *Asian Americans*, p. 63.

46. Elaine H. Kim, *Asian American Literature: An Introduction to the Writings and Their Social Context* (Philadelphia, Temple University Press, 1982), p. 102.

47. Chao, *Monkey King*, p. 290.

48. I put the word 'Chinese' in quotation marks because these parents should be more correctly called 'Chinese Americans' instead of 'Chinese'.

49. Mei Ng, *Eating Chinese Food Naked* (New York, Washington Square Press, 1998), p. 126.

50. Foucault, *Discipline and Punish*, p. 104.

51. Fae Myenne Ng, *Bone*, p. 57.

52. Amy Ling, *Between Worlds: Women Writers of Chinese Ancestry* (New York, Pergamon Press, 1990), p. 3.

53. Michel Foucault, *An Introduction. Vol. 1 of the History of Sexuality* (New York, Random, 1980), p. 45.

54. Liu, *Oriental Girls*, p. 131.

55. Mei Ng, *Eating Chinese*, p. 37.

56. *Ibid.*, p. 61.

57. *Ibid.*, p. 71.

58. Liu, *Oriental Girls*, pp. 279, 269.

59. *Ibid.*, p. 279.

60. Fae Myenne Ng, *Bone*, p. 112.

61. Liu, *Oriental Girls*, p. 127.

62. Mei Ng, *Eating Chinese*, p. 98.

63. *Ibid.*, p. 115.

64. *Ibid.*, p. 153.

65. Liu, *Oriental Girls*, p. 283.

66. Mei Ng, *Eating Chinese*, p. 65.

67. *Ibid.*, p. 119.

68. *Ibid.*, p. 65.

69. Chao, *Monkey King*, p. 129.

70. Liu, *Oriental Girls*, p. 151.

71. *Ibid.*, p. 280.

72. *Ibid.*, p. 178.

73. *Ibid.*, p. 257.

74. *Ibid.*, p. 214.

75. *Ibid.*, p. 229.

76. *Ibid.*, pp. 227–8.

77. *Ibid.*, p. 15.

78. Chao, *Monkey King*, p. 29.

79. *Ibid.*, p. 10.

80. Fae Myenne Ng, *Bone*, p. 18.

81. Chao, *Monkey King*, p. 307.

82. Liu, *Oriental Girls*, p. 97.

CHAPTER THIRTEEN

'On England's doorstep': colonialism, nationalism and carceral liminality in Brendan Behan's *Borstal Boy*

JOHN BRANNIGAN

Carceral cartographies

> Each narrow cell in which we dwell
> Is a foul and dark latrine,
> And the fetid breath of living Death
> Chokes up each grated screen,
> And all, but Lust, is turned to dust
> In Humanity's machine.
>   Oscar Wilde, *The Ballad of Reading Gaol*[1]

Wilde's poem draws together much that is emblematic of the literary topography of imprisonment: its humanist extrapolation of the significance for issues of civilization and society of specific instances of confinement, deprivation and punishment, its attention to the architectonics of carceral space and of the body, its intensification of sexual desire, and its sanctification of an imagined community of subaltern delinquents made the scapegoats of humanity's 'sins'.

In its repeated imagery of prisoners looking 'with such a wistful eye / Upon that little tent of blue / Which prisoners call the sky', the poem recapitulates the characteristic ingressive and egressive metaphors which structure the literal and figurative cartographies of the prison. Wilde figures the prison as self, as death, as language, as hell, as huddled community of outcasts, as the demarcated shame of modern society, but without permitting the epistemological reality of imprisonment to slide into abstracted metaphors for the human condition. But the metaphorical economy of incarceration in Wilde's poem works to secure the association of the disciplinary and punitive practices of prison with the domain of 'liberal society', thus establishing the interdependence of incarceration and 'free' society.

The metaphorical capabilities of imprisonment function in a way which, for Wilde, invites liberal critique. But they have other functions too. For Jean Genet, prison was the source of love, for he wrote in *Miracle of the Rose* 'it is the rigors of prison that drive us toward each other in bursts of love without which we could not live'.[2] Genet, like Michel Foucault, conceived of the ambivalence and liminality of the prison as a disciplinary institution, of its role in the production of desire as well as deprivation, of love as much as violation. Victor Brombert in *The Romantic Prison* delineates a particularly Gothic vision of imprisonment, embedded in complex interplay between fantasy and fear, and signifying release as well as constraint.[3] W. B. Carnochan argues indeed that the metaphorical potency of the prison tends rather to prevail over its concrete existence, and even that the 'reality follows rather than precedes metaphor',[4] a notion which resonates through Foucault's explication of the discursive formation of disciplinary power.[5] Literary prisons, whether the subject of fictional, poetic or autobiographical writings, function largely in metaphorical economies in which confinement and punishment inevitably have corporeal manifestations, but have more pertinent symbolic ends.

The symbolic significance of imprisonment is particularly apparent in the literature of Irish nationalism which, since the 1790s, has employed narratives of penal discipline to produce its own mythology of martyrdom, sacrifice, protest and regeneration. This is especially the case in the nationalist testimonies of the nineteenth century: John Mitchel's *Jail Journal*, John Devoy's *Recollections of an Irish Rebel*, Jeremiah O'Donovan Rossa's *Prison Life*, Michael Davitt's *Leaves from a Prison Diary*, Wolfe Tone's *The Autobiography* and Thomas Clarke's *Glimpses of an Irish Felon's Prison Life*.[6] Such narratives work to transform the punishment of nationalist rebellion into the heroic election of sacrifice and to organize the political failure of rebellion into a mythic pantheon of Christlike martyrs. The narratives of Mitchel, Clarke and O'Donovan Rossa, in particular, represented the dark, solitary confines of English prisons as the testing grounds of the spirit and determination of Irish nationalism, while Davitt, Tone and Devoy are concerned more with justifying and explaining the basis for nationalist rebellion in which imprisonment and punishment are merely extensions of the machinery of colonial government. All of these narratives were written either as records or responses to the experience of rebellion and punishment, from Tone's *Autobiography* written in the 1790s, to the narratives of Clarke and Devoy who were instrumental in organizing the nationalist campaigns of the 1880s and of 1916. Common to each of them is the notion that suffering and death are the symbolic rituals through which the national cause will be served and won, that endurance and martyrdom are as essential to revolution as arms and men.

Failure, and indeed the endurance of deprivation and confinement was, by the late nineteenth century, a necessary component in the construction of a sacred myth of heroic struggle, which required its register of executions, deportations, penal colonists and prisoners in order to sanction the violence of the present. Imprisonment and deportation, in the language and iconography of modern cultural nationalism, paradoxically signified the legitimation of the struggle against British imperialism, and the prison thus became a metaphorical projection both of colonial rule and of its limits.

While imprisonment signified endurance and transcendence, the nationalist imagination reserved execution and the rhetoric and imagery of resurrection for the apotheosis of imperial punishment. Thomas Mac-Donagh, for example, executed for his part in the nationalist uprising of 1916, concluded his speech from the dock with an emboldened summons to 'Take me away, and let my blood bedew the sacred soil of Ireland. I die in the certainty that once more the seed will fructify.'[7] The metaphors for 'blood sacrifice' were abundant in the literary construction of the 1916 Rising in particular, drawing upon the ballads and narratives of the nineteenth century to ritualize the foredoomed Rising as yet another glorious failure. The trial reports and speeches from the dock of those who were to be executed, and the prison memoirs of those who endured penal servitude, formed a popular genre of reading.

In the early twentieth century, the iconography of nationalism was deeply indebted to the prison scenario, and particularly to imprisonment as being the inevitable prelude to the rekindling of the flame of rebellion. Nationalist narratives of imprisonment tend to suggest the unequivocal identification of the individual with the nation so that, as Sean Ryder has argued, 'the historical, contingent subject . . . appears to achieve authenticity and completion – its heroic realisation – through identification with the transcendent, impersonal entity known as "the nation"'.[8] This is the 'tradition', or discourse, in which Brendan Behan and his autobiographical novel, *Borstal Boy*, are thoroughly, irretrievably immersed.[9]

Borstal Boy

Borstal Boy appears to conform to the generic conventions of nationalist prison narratives, from the opening scene in which Behan is captured in England (which he compares to the arrest and trial of the Fenian, Thomas Clarke) to the conclusion in which Behan returns to Dublin, which bears striking similarities to John Mitchel's final passage to New York in his *Jail Journal*. At the age of sixteen, Behan was arrested in Liverpool and sentenced to three years borstal detention for carrying explosive charges into England, allegedly to cause explosion either at Cammell Lairds shipyard or a city-centre department store. *Borstal Boy* is the narrative of his experiences in the English carceral system between 1939 and 1941.[10] When a detective voices disgust at Behan's actions: 'You facquing bestud, how would you like to see a woman cut in two by a plate-glass window?', Behan conceives of his desperate ploy as being the only recourse of men engaged in anticolonial war, and the inevitable reply to colonial atrocities

(p. 10). Behan's own part in the IRA bombing campaign against England in 1939 is the silent subtext for his exploration throughout *Borstal Boy* of nationalist ideology and anticolonial struggle. It is rarely mentioned beyond the first scene, but it informs and fuels the identity crisis with which Behan wrestles throughout the narrative.

The novel begins with a scene in which Behan is cast as the tough rebel, defiant of his captors and scornful of England. 'If I'd have had a gun you wouldn't have come through the door so shagging easy', he tells the detectives who arrive to arrest him (p. 9). There follow scenes in which he conforms to the expected role of a Republican prisoner:

> I was brought to the C.I.D. headquarters in Lime Street. In accordance with instructions, I refused to answer questions. I agreed to make a statement, with a view to propaganda for the cause. It would look well at home, too. I often read speeches from the dock, and thought the better of the brave and defiant men that made them so far from friends or dear ones.
>
> 'My name is Brendan Behan. I came over here to fight for the Irish Workers' and Small Farmers' Republic for a full and free life, for my countrymen, North and South, and for the removal of the baneful influence of British Imperialism from Irish affairs. God save Ireland.' (pp. 12–13)

Behan's statement is elaborated further in his speech from the dock of his trial, which is barely tolerated in court and, similar to the accounts of Robert Emmet's speech from the dock, is interrupted by the judge (pp. 143–4).[11] In addressing the court, and constructing himself within the mould of the nationalist martyrs and heroes of previous struggles, Behan advertises his conformity to the conventions of nationalist iconography. 'I was a good volunteer,' he writes, 'captured carrying the struggle to England's doorstep' (p. 13).

As Colbert Kearney argues, what we find in Behan's narrative is that 'the narrator is perpetually posing and examining the pose'.[12] After he has made his statement, he compares himself to the Manchester Martyrs.[13] When he is being searched in prison, he alludes to Tom Clarke's description of prison searches in *Glimpses of an Irish Felon's Prison Life*. Throughout the narrative, Behan intersperses his descriptions and reflections on prison life with the verses from Irish nationalist ballads and songs, seeming to construct his own prison experiences through the echoed voices and cries of nationalist heroes – 'In boyhood's bloom and manhood's pride, / Foredoomed by alien laws, / Some on the scaffold proudly died, / For Ireland's holy cause' (p. 93).

Imprisonment in England seems to validate Behan's self-image as Republican hero, an image which he works frequently to underpin in the narrative through allusion to nationalist culture and heroics. He rarely considers the crime for which he has been imprisoned, and instead imagines imprisonment as a censure of national difference. The prison is for him an extension of colonial rule – he is jailed, it appears, for being an Irish nationalist. His treatment seems to him particularly punitive when he is forbidden to express what he considers to be his national culture. He is excommunicated by the priest from Catholic services, for example, and beaten severely when he shouts nationalist criticism at the priest for colluding with imperialism. For Behan, the prison frequently seems to be the site of fraught colonial struggle, governed by a 'tired old consul, weary from his labours amongst the lesser breeds' (p. 90), and policed by colonial warriors in flight from the impending demise of the empire. Carceral space is thus for Behan the extended instrument of colonial rule, its regimes and strategies calculated to undermine and censure his sense of national identity.

Carceral masculinities

Colonial topographies are strongly gendered and, as Ashis Nandy noted, the consequence of the association of the imperial ruler with masculinity, and the effective 'feminization' of the colonized, is the aggressive assertion of masculinity in anticolonial discourse.[14] Masculinity becomes the absolute gender of the colonial struggle, with the inevitable negation of femininity, and the recapitulation of imperialist terms of conflict. In the prison scenario, this effect is exaggerated even further. The threatened violence of nationalism can only be treated by the systematic application of violence against the body – not just the beatings which Behan receives, but also the deprivation and containment of the body which Foucault observed as the focal point of disciplinary power.

Similarly, when Behan is threatened by anti-Irish intimidation in the prison his instinctive response is to demonstrate his masculine authority through violence. Frantz Fanon argued that the violence of anticolonial struggle was 'a cleansing force', which freed 'the native from his inferiority complex', but at the same time that nationalist violence was the product of the imperialist, 'the bringer of violence into the home and into the mind of the native'.[15] The effect in the colonial struggle is to produce a competitive masculinity, which in terms of violence produces the cyclical rivalry of meeting force with force, atrocity for atrocity. The atrocities at Cork and Balbriggan are thus the justification Behan offers for his attempt to bomb Liverpool.[16] But the competitive masculinity of Behan's nationalism sometimes assumes comic proportions when, for example, he believes he may have lost his girlfriend in Dublin to a fellow Republican who has been sentenced to fourteen years penal servitude which, compared to his own three years borstal detention, somehow makes him less attractive (p. 281). The nationalist call to arms, it seems, is also a call to manliness and virility, and Behan experiences his imprisonment as the necessary authentication of his masculine credentials and also as the sustained attempt by the imperial power to undermine and negate his masculinity.

The power to subject Behan to discipline, to make him passive and submissive, is manifest in the topography of imprisonment. The spatial rigours of imprisonment discipline the body into new habits of walking, sleeping, excretion, communication, reading and thinking. Every aspect of Behan's life as a prisoner is subject to control, not merely because his freedom to move and communicate is at the mercy of lock and key but also because, in the course of the narrative, prisoners are regulated as to when they may defecate, when light permits them to read, when their behaviour controls their rations of food. 'Systems of punishment,' Foucault writes

> are to be situated in a certain 'political economy' of the body: even if they do not make use of violent or bloody punishment, even when they use 'lenient' methods involving confinement or correction, it is always the body that is at issue – the body and its forces, their utility and their docility, their distribution and their submission.[17]

When Behan enters Walton Jail for the first time, he is first placed in a line of other prisoners and abused and beaten by two warders, who pounce on his omission of the word 'sir', and then is stripped of his clothes and made to bathe. These are the routine instruments of carceral discipline. They demand passivity and submission. In his confrontation with the two warders, Behan considers the nationalist mythology which might sustain him and inspire his defiance:

> Young Cuchulainn, after the battle of the ford of Ferdia, on guard at the gap of Ulster, with his enemies ringed around him, held his back to a tree and, supported by it, called on the gods of death and grandeur to hold him up till his last blood flowed. (p. 41)

Behan here draws upon the eighth-century Irish mythological figure, Cuchulainn, and his legendary defiance of his 'ringed enemies', a figure of nationalist heroism who was revived and appropriated in the Rising of 1916 and has been central to nationalist iconography ever since.[18] Yeats figured Cuchulainn in his final play, *The Death of Cuchulain* (1939), as the Nietzschean 'superman', while the leader of the 1916 Rising, Patrick Pearse, had made a sacred cult of the mythic hero as the model of masculine strength and nobility while still at school. Yet, however heroic, the myth of Cuchulainn fails to mean anything to Behan when confronted with the impending violence which British warders will inflict on a Republican prisoner. He submits to the demands of the warders, and surrenders his defiance to the dawning realization of the inflated reputation of martyrdom. 'They could easily kill you,' he reflects at another point in the narrative, 'Who would give a fish's tit about you over here?' (pp. 21–2). This signals a turn in Behan's conception of his role as a nationalist – the symbols and ideology of sacrifice and endurance prove difficult to mobilize when faced with the threat of death.

In the early scenes in *Borstal Boy*, Behan proves all too willing at times to play the rebel hero – when he shouts 'Up the Republic!' in the Assizes in Liverpool, for example – but the limitations of the heroic mask become all too apparent to him. When a fellow Republican prisoner, Callan, in a cell below Behan's, incites him to shout 'Up the Republic' later in Walton Jail, Behan discreetly fakes a defiant shout by whispering down the ventilator and telling Callan that the walls are too thick to hear him shouting. Callan is beaten by the warders for his gesture, while Behan is found reading Mrs Gaskell's *Cranford* on his bed when the warders check his cell (pp. 140–1). Behan is caught between the demands of his Republican fellows to answer the historic call to sacrifice, and the pressures imposed upon him to submit to the disciplinary violence of the prison. He cowers from the opportunity to defy his captors, and instead offers himself up as the ideal subject for reform. Behan's cowardice may be a matter of prudence, strategy or even instinctive preservation, but it also signifies the failure of nationalist imagery of masculinity. In refusing the call to defy the authority of his jailers, he elects for the passivity and malleability which prison requires of him.

However, Behan is not merely the willing dupe of the prison guards. There is a certain seduction taking place, whereby Behan submits the alluring image of a model prisoner to his jailers without relinquishing his capacity for less obtrusive means of resistance. If he recognizes that the effective locus of prison discipline and punishment is the body of the prisoner, he also remembers that the body can also be the locus of resistance. When he is confined to his cell and deprived of food for assaulting another prisoner, he is reminded of the hunger strikes of Republican prisoners of a previous generation, in particular of Terence MacSwiney – 'seventy-eight days and no scoff at all' (p. 95):[19]

> MacSwiney had the eyes of the world on him, and knew that it must be driving these bastards mad from the publicity it was getting. They were up and offering him every conceivable delicacy, chicken, ham, turkey, roast pork, steak, oh for the love of Jesus, give over, me mouth is watering. If Johnston came up and said, 'Here you are, sing two lines of "God Save the King" and I'll give you this piece of round steak,' would I take it? Would I what? Jesus, Mary and Joseph, he'd be a lucky man that I didn't take the hand and all off him. And sing a High Mass, never mind a couple of lines of "God Save the King" for it, aye or for the half of it. (p. 96)

The hunger strike is an effective mode of resistance, Behan knows, because it threatens to remove the only weapon available to prison authorities. A dead prisoner is a martyr, not a warning of the power of punishment, and a hunger strike has the effect of winning the sympathy of the public for the corporeal deprivation which the prisoner is willing to endure for an ideal or principle. However, Behan confesses to being incapable of such sacrifice, and the fact that he compares his own twenty-four-hour fast with MacSwiney's hunger strike, and later with the Irish Famine, reveals the disparity between Behan and the nationalist icons to whom he compares himself.[20] But Behan recognizes in MacSwiney's protest the power of appropriating the weapons of incarceration and turning them into acts of resistance. MacSwiney symbolizes the equivocal relationship between prison and prisoner, between colonizer and colonized, for his protest shows that the power to deprive the body is, as Foucault suggests, 'exercised rather than possessed' (p. 174). It is not the sole preserve of the warders, but can be utilized by those who are dominated too. This is most clearly visible in *Borstal Boy* in the sexual relations between the prisoners.

Transgression and liminality

There are faint intimations of homoerotic desire from an early point in the narrative. When Behan first meets Charlie Millwall, the young sailor remanded for stealing, he admires the line of his neck, and they indulge in a kind of light petting as Behan towels Charlie dry and Charlie puts his hands into Behan's pockets and shirt. There follows a number of subdued courtship rituals in which Behan sings Charlie a love song (p. 24), Charlie bids Behan 'Good night' through the aperture on his cell door (p. 26), and they continue their relationship in the washroom every morning (p. 28). More important is the symbolic conversion of carceral spaces of containment into the sites of sexual desire. Behan and Charlie, along with another inmate, Ginger, are not humiliated by the ritual at Walton Jail of being forced to strip naked in front of each other and bathe. Instead, in a scene which is repeated several times in *Borstal Boy*, the three young men stand admiring each other. The boys are occasionally interrupted by an older man who makes crude homosexual jokes and asks if they want to be helped to bathe, but Behan contrasts the idealized homoeroticism of the boys with the older man's crudity. Desire, it seems, is a more potent force than sexual release and works to transform the spaces of containment and repression into sites of fantasy, perhaps even, as Genet described, of love.

Behan is not so much departing from conventional nationalist representations of relations between men in prison as appropriating and converting a consistent feature of nationalist prison narratives – the celebration of masculine homosociality. In *Jail Journal*, for example, John Mitchel begins to recognize in the course of his sea voyage to Australia a strong camaraderie with his shipmates, which does not manifest itself in overtly erotic terms but finds expression in Mitchel's increasing emphasis on a Carlylean notion of masculine 'greatness'. Mitchel asserts that it is the duty of great men to lead, to carry themselves above the 'subterhuman' lower classes of convicts and fiends, to bear arms nobly and bravely and to raise other men up to follow glorious causes. 'We must openly glorify arms,' he writes, 'until young Irishmen burn to handle them.'[21] However, manhood is also about the capacity to absorb punishment and to endure sacrifice. Thus, Mitchel dismisses suicide as a solution to his misery in captivity because it is unmanly: 'sometimes to suffer manfully is the best thing man can do'.[22] For Thomas Clarke, too, prison is experienced as 'a test of manhood as severe and searching as mortal man could be subject to', which he endures through his intimacy with other 'manly, self-reliant men'.[23]

Nationalist prison narratives tend to emphasize, perhaps defensively, the 'manliness' of their bonds and experiences, the resort to homosocial notions of shared bravery and vigour. In *Borstal Boy*, Behan exaggerates the erotic identification which such notions contain, distinguishing (in a passage omitted from the published novel) between the homoeroticism of 'the youth of healthy muscle and slim-wrought form' and that of 'the powdered pansy'.[24] Effeminacy had no place in Behan's erotic identification with his fellow prisoners (in keeping with Mitchel, Clarke and O'Donovan Rossa) but his relationship with Charlie Millwall threatens to subvert other conventions of nationalist prison narratives besides their celebration of masculine homosociality. Charlie is a common criminal, a thief, while Behan is, in nationalist terms, a political prisoner. Behan's identification with him rather than his IRA comrades offends the distinction made, particularly by Mitchel and Clarke, between the noble, splendid men serving the cause of Irish freedom and what Clarke calls the 'dregs' of English society.[25]

Behan's relationship to Charlie Millwall occupies a muted but central role in the narrative, developing out of sensuous gazes in Part one of *Borstal Boy*, into mutual dependence in Part two, and finally into Charlie's jealousy and resentment of Behan's new friends in Part three. Behan's behaviour alters with every passing stage in their relationship and, when he receives word of Charlie's death as a sailor on board the *Southampton*, he becomes silent, mournful and restless. That Behan and Charlie are homosexual lovers in the narrative is not made explicit, but the imagery and language of homoeroticism need not constitute a dissident sexual identity in order to make transgressive the relationships between the boys. Behan reacts coldly to jokes about sodomy, for example, and rejects identification with a homosexual subculture, yet his depiction of boys bathing naked together in the sea at Hollesley Bay Borstal suggests an idyll of homoerotic love which, in its subtlety and openness, threatens to draw the homosocial into the realm of desire and the erotic and, thus, to disrupt radically the sexual order of incarceration.[26]

When prison becomes the site of homoerotic initiation and the symbolic spaces of punishment are appropriated in acts of desire, the languages and ideologies of imprisonment begin to falter, especially because there is no discernible transgressive practice to be policed or punished. Behan's homoerotic imagery is effective because it is unobtrusive without being secret – it is formed and practised under the watchful, oblivious eyes of the warders, arrogating for itself only those spaces and relationships which carceral discipline permits and fosters.

The homoerotic relationships in *Borstal Boy* are not significant for their sexual transgressiveness, then, but because they cut across the other relationships between the boys. In Behan's case, the fact that he has been suspected of planning to blow up a naval dockyard, and proceeds to have homoerotic relations with a naval rating, emphasizes the transgressive potential of same-sex relations with regard to the homosocial discourses of imperialism and nationalism. While this is hardly a startling revelation about a writer who celebrated Wilde for having it 'both ways',[27] it does perform a more specific and more dynamic function in *Borstal Boy* of radically altering the terms in which Behan conceives of, and relates to, his imprisonment. If prison is experienced at first as the colonial censure of his national identity, the validation of his Republican persona, it becomes instead the condition in which he is compelled to re-imagine his cultural identity in relation to others, specifically those Others he once construed in absolutist terms as opposites. He comes to the realization that he would

> rather be with Charlie and Ginger and Browny in Borstal than with my own comrades and countrymen any place else. It seemed a bit disloyal to me, that I should prefer to be with boys from English cities than with my own country-men and comrades from Ireland's hills and glens. (p. 129)

However ashamed of this disloyalty he may be, it is merely a passing reservation which does not impede his growing sense of fraternity and intimacy with young Englishmen. Behan becomes entangled in an elaborate negotiation of national and sexual identities in which, as Eve Kosofsky Sedgwick argues of Oscar Wilde and Roger Casement, 'the question of the Other of a national, as of a sexual, identity was an irreducibly – and *sometimes* an enablingly – complex one'.[28]

If the communal spaces of prison enable Behan to explore his cultural and sexual identifications with others, the constraints of his own cell prove to be no less enabling. Colbert Kearney has argued that the prison in *Borstal Boy* serves as metaphor for the unfolding and evolving personality of the young Behan: 'the penal institutions bear much the same relationship to *Borstal Boy* as the island does to *Robinson Crusoe*. Beneath the illusion of actuality is a structure which expresses the development of a personality.'[29] The metaphorical relation between Behan and the confined space of his cell, however, pertains neither to insularity nor to coherent identity; rather, I would argue, it pertains to the liminality of both spaces.

As Monika Fludernik argues, the delimiting barriers of the cell – the walls, the door, the window, the body – are 'breachable and permeable boundaries that incorporate a transitional area of interfacing'.[30] Confined to his cell, Behan is also such a transitional space – the median point of imperialist and nationalist discourses, the interface between hermetic inside and expansive outside, the site of translation of writings, noises and gestures from beyond his cell into the language and imagery of his own confinement. This process, of the transformation of the limits of his confinement into figures of his own liminality, is clearly at work when Behan reads. Behan remarks throughout his narrative on the progress and content of his reading, from his stolen glances at the *News of the World* in the washroom in Walton to his intense consumption of novels by Hardy, Mrs Gaskell and Joyce, plays by Shaw, O'Casey and Synge, and an assortment of biographies, histories and memoirs. In part, his reading sustains an important link with Ireland while he languishes in an English jail – hence his enjoyment of Joyce, Synge and O'Casey as well as Robert Lynd and Robert Collis – but reading also enables him to explore his cultural Other, to discover the meanings and representations of 'Englishness' outside of Ireland.

Cultural translation

Reading is Behan's endeavour to metamorphose his surroundings into the desired (and desiring) landscape of the imagination, by which he can simulate the effect of transcendence. He rations his reading over time, saving it up as self-indulgent play. Behan gives himself over to the narratives, reporting his engagement with the characters and plots of the books he reads, but there is also an important process of cultural conversion taking place in his readings. Behan inserts himself into his reading of Thomas Hardy's *Under the Greenwood Tree*, for example. He appropriates a song from Hardy's novel, putting a Christmas carol from the novel to the tune of the 'Famine Song' – as Behan points out, 'my situation being more like Famine than like Christmas' (p. 96). Here Behan clearly signals the necessity of reading one's self into a text, and of making the reading conform to his own situation. In other readings, he resists conforming to the cultural assumptions and identities of that text. Hardy's novel at times becomes allegorical of idyllic English rural life, the tree itself used as a microcosm of this idyll which spawns tribes and families and provides 'healthy exercise ground'.[31] This is also where Fancy, newly wed to Dick Dewy, marks the passing of ancient manners into new ways, and the marriage of Dick and Fancy seems to herald new times, celebrated on this exercise ground. But Behan converts the novel through his own reading, and performance of the text, to new purposes. The ending of Hardy's novel, where Thomas Leaf, whom Behan calls an amadán (Gaelic for fool), tells his 'half-arsed class of a story', finds the tranter speaking of Leaf's wish to join the party:

> 'Poor feller!' said the tranter, turning to Geoffrey.
> 'Suppose we must let en come? His looks are rather against en, and he is terrible silly; but 'a never been in jail, and 'a won't do no harm.'[32]

In Behan's performance of the novel, a different voice speaks out of Hardy's characters:

> 'Let the poor bastard in,' says the Tranter, 'he's a bit silly-looking but I never heard he was in jail.' Sure, if he was itself, there was as good as ever he was in it. (p. 99)

Behan inserts his own voice into Hardy's story, converting Hardy's story of idyllic rural England into a working-class Dubliner's story. He appropriates the power of English symbolic representations, and exerts an ironic manoeuvre in his writing which undermines English cultural power. This move is described by Ashcroft, Griffiths and Tiffin in *The Empire Writes Back* as abrogation and appropriation, that of simultaneously denying privilege to the metropolitan centre while seizing and adapting the language of the centre for the colonized.[33] In this case, the language which Behan translates Hardy's novel into is comic farce. This comic device is also a critical manoeuvre whereby Behan draws attention to the obscene disparity between an idyllic representation of rural England and his situation in prison, between English cultural power, exemplified in the idyllic novel, and Irish rebel culture, exemplified in the Famine Song. This puts Behan back into a situation in which he is affirming Irish national identity as being different from English national identity, and yet at the same time he is showing how English culture is permeable to an Irish rebel. It doesn't exclude or marginalize him: in fact, it allows him to find his own identity, and to add his own voice. The characters in Hardy's novel remind him of his family, 'even their speech when they said "carrel" and "traypsing and rambling about" was like Dublin speech' (p. 81).

That Behan reads into Hardy's novel his cultural identity as a working-class Dubliner, and his situation as a prisoner in an English jail, reveals not only the cultural permeability enacted in the process of reading, but also that there is no 'pure' transcendence for Behan. Reading is rather an extension of that condition of liminality by which Behan shows that prison is not absolute containment either. Just as he can 'resist' the cultural imperatives of Hardy's novel, he can also resist the imposed limitations and constraints of imprisonment. Kearney remarks on the metamorphic qualities of Behan's narrative: 'prison food is often described with a relish normally reserved for more imaginative cuisine, reading a book is made to seem a feast, a mishap to a member of the staff provokes an orgy of pleasure'.[34] This is a consistent feature of Behan's interaction with his surroundings. Both Walton Jail and Hollesley Bay Borstal remind him in different ways of life in Dublin (p. 27, pp. 212–13). The gardens around the borstal prompt him to cite a passage from Brian Merriman's Gaelic poem, 'The Midnight Court', which describes this scene perfectly (pp. 319–20). In part, this feature of Behan's narrative is a conservative conversion of difference into the same – it enables Behan to bolster his sense of 'Irishness' by appropriating the materials of his 'foreign' surroundings, and thus works to foreground the nationalist dialectic of sameness and difference. But, as in Behan's reading of Hardy, it also suggests the permeability of English and Irish cultures to each other, that they can be read in and through each other. In fact, in every instance of Behan's engagement with English culture and landscape, he exhibits that 'exquisitely exacerbated sensitivity' which Sedgwick observes in Wilde, as to 'how by turns porous, brittle, elastic, chafing, embracing, exclusive, murderous, in every way contestable and contested were the membranes of "domestic" national definition signified by the ductile and elusive terms of England, Britain, Ireland'.[35]

Behan complicates the 'simple' narratives of nationalist incarceration as his story unfolds, therefore, after finding himself incapable of identifying with, or mobilizing the resources of what David Lloyd calls 'the monologic desire of cultural nationalism',[36] and after failing to isolate the distinctive characteristics of a national culture required in the ideology of separatist nationalism. In identifying with West Country dialects, Cockney humour or Lancashire bluffness, each of which delineate and reiterate discrete regional stereotypes, Behan resituates his own sense of cultural distinction within a diffusive field of hybridized identities and cultures. At stake in this contrivance is not just his recognition that he shares more in common culturally with a Londoner than with an Irish farmer, but also that he can no longer accommodate the stories he wishes to construct of himself comfortably within the province of Irish nationalism.

In thinking of Wilde, for example, he realizes that his upbringing has inadequately equipped him to conceptualize Wilde's rebelliousness. Behan's mother tells him that Wilde was brought down by sex, just like the Nationalist Party leader, Parnell, but Behan discerns that Wilde's 'fall' was profoundly incompatible with the language and ideology in which Parnell's ruin was explained (pp. 253–5). Similarly, Behan's own embarrassment about his love for English boys is, in part, recognition of the awkward incongruity of his new relationships with the cultural baggage of both colonialism and nationalism. It seems not to fit into the available typology, nor do many of Behan's associations accord with all his friends and overseers, particularly because he learns in the course of his incarceration to cut across class, sexual, religious, political and national boundaries:

> The other fellows might give me a rub about Ireland or about the bombing campaign, and that was seldom enough, and I was never short of an answer, historically informed and obscene, for them. But I was nearer to them than they would ever let Ken be. I had the same rearing as most of them, Dublin, Liverpool, Manchester, Glasgow, London. All our mothers had all done the pawn – pledging on Monday, releasing on Saturday. We all knew the chip shop and the picture house and the fourpenny rush of a Saturday afternoon, and the summer swimming in the canal and being chased along the railway by the cops. But Ken they would never accept. In a way, as the middle and upper class in England spent so much money and energy in maintaining the difference between themselves and the working class, Ken was only getting what his people paid for but, still and all, I couldn't help being sorry for him, for he was more of a foreigner than I, and it's a lonely thing to be a stranger in a strange land. (pp. 241–2)

When Behan explores his interactions with fellow inmates, as he does in this passage, he finds a mess of contradictory, complex subject positions which shift constantly, from defending Irish nationalism to identifying a common culture shared with the English urban working class, and to seeing his own alterity reflected in an English middle-class boy alienated in the borstal. There is no sense of transcendence in any of these subject positions, nor does Behan adopt one over the other in anything but the most contingent fashion, but each rebuts and intersects with the others. Irish nationalism can weaken English imperialist assumptions by being 'historically informed and obscene', by which Behan means that he interrupts colonial myths with terse, 'obscene' reminders of colonial atrocities. So too, the separatist assumptions of Irish nationalism are undermined by the common social history which Behan identifies between Dublin, Liverpool, Glasgow, Manchester and London. Colonialism has forged a common heritage for London and Dublin: an urban industrial and artisan working class which communicates in English and which shares specific forms of cultural expression and entertainment. The heritage is still valid enough so that Behan is closer to the English working-class characters than they are to Ken, the alienated middle-class inmate, but it is not strong enough to cancel the differentiation which Behan's English friends make by unanimously referring to him as 'Paddy'. Behan's residual sense of alienation also enables him, paradoxically, to identify with Ken in a way which seems to be impossible for the other inmates.

Throughout *Borstal Boy*, and increasingly as the narrative progresses, Behan explores and delineates the subaltern positions which become available to him through the enabling metaphors of class, sexuality, politics and religion. Subalternity, as Ranajit Guha suggests in his conception of it as the unspoken, unintegrated residue of nationalism and colonialism, is not equivalent to the subcultural, which is constructed necessarily as a minority culture.[37] It crosses over and speaks from within hegemonic discourses, mobilizing contradictions and weaknesses within such discourses. Behan refuses to formulate a specific, transgressive subjectivity which might encompass and authenticate the various forms of his engagement with subaltern positions. This is particularly evident when he arrives back in Dublin after his release in the conclusion to his narrative, a conclusion which resists resolving his borstal experiences and discoveries into a coherent identity. 'It must be wonderful to be free,' says the immigration officer in Dublin who studies Behan's expulsion order. '"It must," said I, walked down the gangway, past a detective, and got on the train for Dublin' (pp. 378–9). In this final scene of *Borstal Boy*, Behan conceives of his liberty in ironic terms and, in playing intertextually with John Mitchel's exile to New York at the end of *Jail Journal*, Behan situates Dublin as the location of his exile even as he recounts its familiarity.

Conclusion

Borstal Boy concludes ironically, therefore, by suggesting that the carceral condition is not defined by prison walls, and that post-colonial Dublin is as much bound up in the legacy of imperialism as the Six Counties, for which Behan was apparently prepared to bomb Liverpool. The project of 'national liberation', it turns out, is more difficult than it seemed. If Behan's narrative begins by recapitulating the terms in which nationalism imagined colonial incarceration as the necessary and paradoxical condition for producing the symbolic resources of nationalist resurrection, Behan finds that his time in an English prison has exerted an equally paradoxical effect in him, of emancipating him from the psychological binds both of colonial stereotypes and nationalist iconography. His 'emancipation' is, of course, contingent and contradictory, never transcendent, but it begins to delineate what Fanon called the 'new humanism' which would emerge in the wake of anticolonial nationalism. 'After the conflict,' Fanon wrote, 'there is not only the disappearance of colonialism but also the disappearance of the colonized man.'[38]

In moving beyond the weary subject positions which colonial relations bestowed as their legacy, Behan's narrative glimpses the contours of what Andrew Murphy calls an 'ante-colonial' project, which moves beyond the 'simple colonial narrative'.[39] *Borstal Boy* mimics the *anti*colonial discourse of Irish nationalism in Behan's refusal to atone for his attempted atrocity, in justifying his 'mission' through epigrammatic history lessons, and in advertising his struggle in isolation against the brutal, degrading machinery of incarceration. But it deviates considerably from the popular Irish prison narratives in which it is immersed by identifying, culturally and erotically, with Englishmen, and by refusing the call to open defiance. Behan refuses to be consoled or enlightened by the prospect of sacrifice, suffering or martyrdom, and thus chooses to abandon his faith in the redemptive properties of nationalist struggle.

It is the ironic consequence of the penal demand for the malleable subject that produces in Behan his erotic identification with English Otherness, his rejection of the timeworn casts of nationalist martyrology, and his subaltern realignment of the colonial and carceral paradigm. Just as the prison of his captivity becomes for Behan the metamorphic site of his reform, so 'England's doorstep' becomes the metaphor for his discovery of the potentially liberating thresholds of postcolonial relations. As an Irish nationalist captive in an English jail, Behan negotiates what Mary Louise Pratt calls the 'contact zone', in which the fraught struggle between disparate cultures is telescoped into a contested social and symbolic space.[40] Behan's narrative begins, in common with the narratives of Mitchel, Clarke, Devoy, O'Donovan Rossa and others, with the clash of two antithetical cultures – English imperialism and Irish postcolonial nationalism – but it collapses these opposed cultures in the course of exploring his subaltern resistances to both and in identifying the hybrid cultures to which both he and his fellow prisoners belong. Behan discovers in the mobilizing contradictions of postcolonial hybridity the potential to move beyond the 'perceptual prison' of colonialism.[41]

Notes

1. Oscar Wilde [C.3.3.], *The Ballad of Reading Gaol* (London, Leonard Smithers, 1898), p. 27.

2. Jean Genet, *Miracle of the Rose*, trans. Bernard Frechtman (New York, Grove Press, 1966), p. 1.

3. Victor Brombert, *The Romantic Prison: The French Tradition* (Baltimore, Johns Hopkins University Press, 1978).

4. W. B. Carnochan, *Confinement and Flight: An Essay on English Literature of the Eighteenth Century* (Berkeley, University of California Press, 1977), p. 4.

5. Michel Foucault, *Discipline and Punish: The Birth of the Prison*, trans. Alan Sheridan Smith (London, Penguin, 1979).

6. John Mitchel, *Jail Journal* (Washington, DC, Woodstock Books, 1996); John Devoy, *Recollections of an Irish Rebel* (Shannon, Irish University Press, 1969); Jeremiah O'Donovan Rossa, *My Years in English Jails* [*Prison Life*] (Tralee, Anvil Books, 1967); Michael Davitt, *Leaves from a Prison Diary; or, Lectures to a 'Solitary' Audience* (London, Chapman and Hall, 1885); Wolfe Tone, *The Autobiography*, ed. R. Barry O'Brien (London, T. Fisher Unwin, 1893); Thomas J. Clarke, *Glimpses of an Irish Felon's Prison Life* (Dublin, Maunsel and Roberts, 1922).

7. Thomas MacDonagh, quoted in T. D., A. M. and D. B. Sullivan (eds), *Speeches from the Dock* (Dublin, Gill and Macmillan, 1968), p. 340.

8. Sean Ryder, 'Male autobiography and Irish cultural nationalism: John Mitchel and James Clarence Mangan', *Irish Review*, 13 (Winter 1992/93): 70.

9. Brendan Behan, *Borstal Boy* (London, Corgi, 1961; first published 1958). All page references to *Borstal Boy* are subsequently cited in parentheses.

10. Behan joined the Irish Republican Army (IRA) in 1937, at the age of fourteen, having been a member of its youth organization, the Fianna Eireann. The IRA at this time was a faction of the Irish Volunteer Movement, which had fought for and negotiated the independence of the twenty-six 'southern' counties of the island of Ireland from British rule. Its members continued to fight for the six 'northern' counties still under British rule and, in 1939, launched a bombing campaign in England, the aim of which was to terrorize the British government into ceding Northern Ireland to the Irish Free State. It is, however, unclear as to whether Behan was ordered to carry explosives into England on the occasion described in *Borstal Boy*. He may have acted on his own initiative. See Ulick O'Connor, *Brendan Behan* (London, Abacus, 1993) and Michael O'Sullivan, *Brendan Behan: A Life* (Dublin, Blackwater Press, 1997). Throughout *Borstal Boy* Behan's republicanism is of a peculiarly aestheticized and romantic kind, which is constructed more often through songs, ballads and literary references than through political arguments or debate. The IRA were, at the time, supposed to be fighting for the liberation of the northern six counties of Ireland, but Behan refers to Northern Ireland hardly at all. The consequence is that Behan's republicanism appears to be anachronistic, similar to that of his caricature, Monsewer, in *The Hostage*, who wanders around an IRA safe house in the 1950s believing that the war of independence is still being fought.

11. Robert Emmet's speech from the dock is quoted in Sullivan *et al.*, *Speeches from the Dock*, pp. 31–44. Behan was well-versed in republican speeches and, as a young child, could recite every word from Emmet's famous speech from 1803. One of his favourite plays was H. C. Mangan's *Robert Emmet: A History Play in Three Acts* (Dublin, Gill and Son, 1904), which was performed at the Queen's Theatre in Dublin with Behan's uncle, P. J. Bourke, in the lead role. Mangan's play emphasizes the Republican ideology of martyrdom and sacrifice, with Emmet declaring that 'The hope that has lived for centuries can be crushed only by the extermination of our people' (p. 7), and it also justifies nationalist struggle on the basis of a distinct racial mentality: 'God placed our islands and our souls apart. We do not *think* as they do' (*ibid.*).

12. Colbert Kearney, 'Borstal boy: a portrait of the artist as a young prisoner', in E. H. Mikhail (ed.), *The Art of Brendan Behan* (New York, Barnes and Noble, 1979), p. 108.

13. The Manchester Martyrs were William O'Meara Allen, Michael Larkin and William O'Brien. They were hanged for their part in the murder of a police sergeant who was shot in a bid by the Fenians (a nationalist insurrectionary movement) to rescue two Fenian prisoners in 1867. The hangings provoked a wave of popular support for the Fenian cause in Ireland.

14. Ashis Nandy, *The Intimate Enemy: Loss and Recovery of Self under Colonialism* (Delhi, Oxford University Press, 1998). See particularly Nandy's first essay, 'The psychology of colonialism', pp. 1–63.

15. Frantz Fanon, *The Wretched of the Earth*, trans. Constance Farrington (London, Penguin, 1967), pp. 74, 29.

16. Behan is referring to the reprisal attacks by British police auxiliaries in 1920 on Cork and Balbriggan, after Irish Volunteers had successfully ambushed British forces. These reprisals were largely characterized by undisciplined looting, burning and destruction of property. In Cork, much of the city centre was burned to the ground while police auxiliaries obstructed fire-fighters from attending the scene.

17. Foucault, *Discipline and Punish*, p. 25.

18. Patrick Pearse, the leader of the 1916 Rising, in particular was renowned for the cult of Cuchulainn which he fostered while at school, St Enda's, in Dublin, but W. B. Yeats, Lady Gregory and others contributed to the revival of the mythological figure, too, partly in publishing the ancient stories and myths of Ireland in collected volumes, but also in theatre productions.

19. MacSwiney was the most renowned of the Irish prisoners on hunger strike during the war of independence against Britain (1919–21). He died in Brixton Jail, London, on 25 October 1920, after a hunger strike which lasted 74 days. He had been elected Lord Mayor of Cork as a nationalist candidate earlier in 1920. The hunger strike as used by nationalist prisoners in the war of independence is thought to have derived from suffragette tactics in England. It has since become a powerful weapon for protest for nationalists in Ireland, not so much in winning concessions from governments as winning popular sympathy and support.

20. The disparity functions to enable Behan to contextualize his lonely struggle against imperialism, and the comparatively lenient ways in which he is treated in British prisons, in relation to the martyr figures of nationalist history. The comparison tends to reduce Behan's occasional encounter with official disapproval, beatings and short periods of deprivation of privileges to insignificance. The effect is almost comic in suggesting both that British imperialism now treats a potential terrorist as if he has stolen a watch, and that Behan's republicanism falls pathetically short of the nationalist ideal.

21. Mitchel, *Jail Journal*, p. 52.

22. *Ibid.*, p. 61.

23. Clarke, *Glimpses*, p. 13.

24. Quoted in O'Sullivan, *Brendan Behan*, p. 69.

25. Clarke, *Glimpses*, p. 41.

26. On the potential transgression of drawing the homosocial into the homoerotic, see Eve Kosofsky Sedgwick, *Between Men: English Literature and Male Homosocial Desire* (New York, Columbia University Press, 1985) and *Epistemology of the Closet* (Hemel Hempstead, Harvester Wheatsheaf, 1991).

27. See Brendan Behan, 'Oscar Wilde', *Poems and a Play in Irish* (Oldcastle, The Gallery Press, 1981).

28. Eve Kosofsky Sedgwick, 'Nationalisms and sexualities', in *Tendencies* (London, Routledge, 1994), p. 152.

29. Kearney, 'Borstal boy', p. 108.

30. Monika Fludernik, 'Carceral topography: spatiality, liminality and corporality in the literary prison', *Textual Practice*, vol. 13, no. 1 (Spring 1999): 64.

31. Thomas Hardy, *Under the Greenwood Tree* (London, Penguin, 1994), p. 216.

32. *Ibid.*, p. 212.

33. Bill Ashcroft, Gareth Griffiths and Helen Tiffin, *The Empire Writes Back: Theory and Practice in Post-colonial Literatures* (London, Routledge, 1989), p. 38.

34. Kearney, 'Borstal boy', p. 115.

35. Sedgwick, 'Nationalisms and sexualities', p. 151.

36. David Lloyd, *Anomalous States: Irish Writing and the Post-Colonial Moment* (Dublin, Lilliput Press, 1993), p. 89.

37. Ranajit Guha, 'On some aspects of the historiography of colonial India', in *Subaltern Studies I: Writings on South Asian History and Society* (Delhi, Oxford University Press, 1994), pp. 1–8.

38. Fanon, *The Wretched of the Earth*, p. 198.

39. Andrew Murphy, 'Ireland and ante/anti-colonial theory', *Irish Studies Review*, vol. 7, no. 2, (August 1999): 160.

40. Mary Louise Pratt, *Imperial Eyes: Travel Writing and Transculturation* (London, Routledge, 1992), p. 4.

41. 'Perceptual prison' is a term used to describe the vicious circle of colonial stereotypes and neo-colonial behaviour by Richard Ned Lebow, *White Britain, Black Ireland: The Influence of Stereotypes on Colonial Policy* (Philadelphia, Institute for the Study of Human Issues, 1976).

CHAPTER FOURTEEN

Apartheid prison narratives, the Truth and Reconciliation Commission and the construction of national (traumatic) memory

SHANE GRAHAM

Truth and testimony

Captain Jeffrey Benzien of the South African Police Service applied to the Truth and Reconciliation Commission (TRC) for amnesty for his actions as a member of the so-called Terrorist Detection Unit from 1986 to 1990. Benzien (still an officer in the police force at the time of the hearings) was notorious throughout the country as a torture specialist, and he confessed in his amnesty application to having regularly practiced the 'wet bag' suffocation technique. Several of his former victims opposed the applica- tion, and were given the opportunity to cross-examine Benzien at his amnesty hearing in July of 1997.

The scenes that unfolded over three days of hearings were high drama. One of the torture victims, African National Congress (ANC) activist and now Member of Parliament Tony Yengeni, insisted that Benzien physically demonstrate the wet bag technique with a pillowcase and a volunteer from the audience: 'As [Benzien] explains it to me, I can hear his explanation, but I would want to be given the opportunity by the Commission to see what he did to me, with my own eyes.'[1] Later, Benzien was cross-examined by another former victim, Ashley Forbes, with whom the policeman remembered developing a 'very good rapport'. The dia- logue reads like a Harold Pinter play: Benzien recalls taking Forbes out for Kentucky Fried Chicken and walks in the park, while Forbes responds with further questions about electric shocks administered to his rectum. All of the former victims repeatedly charged Benzien with using additional torture methods, such as electric shocks; Benzien either denied these allegations outright, or claimed not to remember the events but 'concedes yes' when asked about them. On the second day of the hearings, Benzien's counsel presented a statement from his psychiatrist declaring that 'because of the trauma experienced by my client, and all the various experiences, there was a psychological block and therefore he cannot remember certain incidents'.

Benzien's hearing, which made the front page of newspapers internationally, was a particularly dramatic and well-publicized case, but it is only one of dozens of hearings by the TRC that generated gripping testimonials to the violence against political detainees and prisoners during the apartheid era, when security police were given virtually boundless powers. These heavily publicized hearings helped awaken many of the beneficiaries of apartheid to the extreme abuses of the previous regime, but little of the evidence given at these hearings came as a surprise to non-white South Africans, who faced those abuses every day, or to whites who had struggled against the system and incurred its wrath. Nor did the TRC's findings surprise many observers abroad who had followed political events in the country. Beginning in the early 1960s, with the state's violent crackdown on all opposition to apartheid policy, vivid descriptions of mental and physical torture were widely available outside South Africa through books, pamphlets, newspaper accounts and films, though such information was routinely censored inside the country.

The TRC Amnesty and Human Rights Violation hearings constitute 'testimony' in a psychological as well as a legalistic sense. Some of the survivors who testified at these hearings have reported feeling a sense of closure and a readiness to begin the healing process after testifying before the Commission and the world (though others, it is important to note, experienced no such catharsis and remain deeply dissatisfied with the amnesty process). More broadly, these survivors entered their stories into the official record, thereby challenging and helping to rewrite the master narratives of separate development, white supremacy and the paternalistic apartheid state. What is clear in the light of the TRC is that South African prison memoirs and autobiographies are always testimonies to individual and collective traumas. In other words, they are attempts to represent what are essentially unrepresentable events, and to piece together narratives out of the fragments, gaps and silences of memory. This process is not merely therapeutic; it also constitutes a highly political act, a blow struck against a regime that systematically inflicted trauma to silence its opponents. But as Benzien's amnesty hearing showed, the TRC also reveals the difficulty of constructing narratives out of the erasures, silences and conflicting versions of traumatic collective memory. The value of these memoirs and hearings, considered together, is that they demolish the self-justifying narrative told by the architects of apartheid and replace it, not with another monolithic narrative, but with a multiplicity of stories, memories and perspectives.

The detention memoir as a history of trauma

Following the massacre at Sharpeville in March of 1960, where South African police fired on unarmed protestors, killing sixty-seven and wounding 186, the government called a state of emergency and detained thousands of people without trial under the Public Safety Act. Soon after, South African legislators began writing a series of 'security' laws giving the state broad powers to detain and prosecute political dissidents without declaring martial law. Several of these laws gave the security police almost unlimited powers to detain opponents of apartheid on the mere suspicion of being a 'saboteur' or a 'Communist', or to detain potential witnesses in political trials. The '90-day law' of 1963, the Terrorism Act of 1967 and the Internal Security Act of 1982 permitted police to detain suspects and witnesses incommunicado in solitary confinement without trial for virtually indefinite periods – in effect, giving police a licence to torture detainees. All of the nominally independent 'homelands' passed similar security legislation. Between January 1963 and June 1988, it is estimated that 21,863 persons were detained under these security laws, many of whom were never charged with any crime. Between 1963 and 1990, at least seventy-three people died in detention, not including those abducted and killed by police outside the aegis of the security laws.[2] Not all political detainees were subject to physical abuse: white prisoners were much less likely than blacks to be physically tortured, and women less likely than men to be beaten, burned or shocked[3] (though other, special forms of cruelty were frequently in reserve for women detainees); high-profile prisoners such as Winnie Mandela were also usually spared physical violence. But virtually all political detainees were subjected to psychological torture of some sort, especially long-term solitary confinement. These forms of mental abuse inflict on the survivor a condition similar in its symptoms to that of post-traumatic stress disorder (PTSD).

In his discussion of trauma and war neuroses or 'shell shock' in *Beyond the Pleasure Principle*, Freud attributes trauma to 'fright', a *surprising* event that the witness isn't prepared for and is unable to assimilate into consciousness. The traumatic experience is inaccessible to memory, can only be repeated *literally*, and is continually re-enacted through dreams, nightmares and hallucinations, or obsessive-compulsive behaviour. As Cathy Caruth explains, the pathology of trauma consists in '*the structure of its experience* or reception: the event is not assimilated or experienced fully at the time, but only belatedly, in its repeated *possession* of the one who experiences it'.[4] The traumatic event cannot be narrativized, and the subjective experience of time is disrupted. Likewise, the event cannot be rendered into language – as Dori Laub puts it, the survivor gives her testimony from the midst of a *silence*[5] – and conscious signification is thus also disrupted.

Freud's paradigm of the frightening traumatic accident seems in some ways the exact opposite of the experience of solitary confinement – rather than happening all of a sudden before the victim can respond, the event of confinement stretches with agonizing monotony over many weeks and months. But such prolonged confinement produces disruptions in the prisoner's sense of time, language and meaning-production, in ways resembling the symptoms of trauma. Like the traumatic accident, solitary confinement becomes an event which cannot be comprehended or represented.

Two of the earliest victims of the solitary confinement provisions of the 90-day law were Albie Sachs, a white attorney, and Ruth First, a white journalist. They were detained separately in 1963 for their connections with and sympathies for the ANC, which had been banned since 1960. Both report being kept in tiny cells for 23 hours or more per day – Sachs was detained for 168 days, First for 117 days – with no reading material other than a bible and nothing to do. Even mundane acts, such as using the toilet, become prolonged rituals designed to kill time. Sachs spends several paragraphs of his *Jail Diary* describing his excitement at success-fully smuggling a comb into his cell, because he can pass a whole afternoon cleaning the grime from between its teeth.

Neither Sachs nor First are entirely deprived of the means of telling time. From his cell at the Maitland Police Station, Sachs can hear the chimes from a nearby church bell, and First, surprisingly, is allowed to keep her watch. Yet the ability to measure time's passing is a curse as much as it is a blessing. Sachs, for instance, is reminded by the church bells every fifteen minutes that only fifteen minutes have passed:

> It is two o'clock now, I hear the chimes. My last train of thought was quite absorbing, I did not count time as it passed. That is the nearest I can come to happiness – not to be aware of time. What was it that so occupied me? I cannot remember now.[6]

The constant memory lapses Sachs experiences are a common effect of prolonged isolation, and result in a feeling of being unstuck in time: 'As the days pass it becomes increasingly difficult for me to think coherently about any subject. I find it easier to make up situations belonging to the future than to recollect with clarity past happenings.'[7] After weeks of isolation and inactivity, the narrativization of memory gives way to the timelessness of fantasy – there has been, as Caruth says, 'a break in the mind's experience of time'.[8]

First describes similar disruptions in her sense of time. In her memoir *117 Days*, she writes:

> I still had my watch. I glued my eyes to the small hand and tried to *see* the passage of time. Surely if I looked hard enough, unblinking, I would see the minute hand move? If I could see time passing it would travel faster, surely. I glared at the hand; it moved as I stared at it, but I did not see the movement. . . . Like sand dribbling through an hour-glass the passage of time became a

physical act dribbling through my consciousness. It seemed I had to push time on for it to move at all, for in my cell it had lost its own momentum.

While time was passing it crawled. Yet when it had passed it had flown out of all remembrance. When I thought back I could not recall how previous days had passed, or what I had done in the weeks gone by. . . . What I had endured now became rapidly buried in part oblivion, like any unpleasant and humiliating experience.[9]

Like Sachs, First begins to lose the ability to impose order and narrative structure on her experience. As with memories of a great trauma, her experience in solitary confinement is 'buried in part oblivion'.

Emma Mashinini's description in her autobiography *Strikes Have Followed Me All My Life* of her period of detention reveals a similar difficulty narrating the past. Mashinini, a black trade union organizer, is detained by security police for over five months in 1981–2 under Section 6 of the Terrorism Act. Partly because she has health problems and partly because she is a well-known figure whose arrest has attracted international protest, Mashinini is never physically assaulted during her detention, but her treatment at Pretoria Central Prison and at Jeppe Police Station is nevertheless cruel and the conditions inhumane. After months in solitary confinement she finds she is unable to remember the name of her youngest daughter:

I could see [her] face and I wanted to call her by her name. I struggled to call out the name, the name I always called her, and I just could not recall what the name was. . . . I'd try to sleep on it, wake up. I'd go without eating, because this pain of not being able to remember the name of my daughter was the greatest I've ever had.

Like Sachs and First, Mashinini begins to question her own identity: 'I didn't think I knew myself any longer. There was no mirror. It's odd what happens when you don't see yourself in a mirror for such a long time. You don't recognise yourself. You think, who am I?'[10]

Mashinini's autobiography performs what Ingrid de Kok calls the 'elegiac function' of art. De Kok borrows this notion from Peter Sacks, in whose view 'the imagination operates most powerfully within the spaces of absence, loss, and figuration, providing a dialectic between language and the grieving mind'. De Kok writes that 'the central drama in elegiac construction is thus the disjunctive process of memory, its traces and asymmetrical rhythms. Loss, suffering, and shame are revisited, and their meanings revised.'[11] The elegiac function of prison literature, then, attempts to recover or reconstitute the prisoner's sense of his or her own identity, which the prison is designed to destroy.

Through the chapters of her autobiography dedicated to her experiences in detention and recovery, Mashinini is revisiting her shame (of forgetting her daughter's name, of being forced to live like an animal, of occasionally breaking down under interrogation) and revising it within the larger context of her life and her struggles against injustice. She is also trying to reconstruct the past from the shards and silences of her traumatic memory, especially in the days following her release after more than five months in solitary confinement. She feels fine at first, but later that evening anxieties begin to possess her:

> At night the cars driving back and forth seemed to me now to be interrogators. Every time there was a car I was terrified, and thought that they were coming back to collect me. These people know what they do when they lock you up. You torture yourself.[12]

She spends a few weeks in a special clinic in Denmark for torture victims, then returns to Johannesburg and goes back to work organizing the union. She continues to suffer from serious memory lapses, however. One day, when she 'wasn't herself', the car breaks down on the road from Soweto to Johannesburg. Her husband goes to find a tow truck and, when he comes back, Emma is gone:

> I don't remember anything of what happened. I just remember feeling vaguely that I was walking back to Soweto [many kilometres away]. . . . I must have got tired along the way, and I sat somewhere on the sidewalk. I was very tired and I didn't know what was going on.[13]

Her husband's cousin happens to pass by and see her, and eventually takes her to the hospital.

Mashinini's symptoms are a textbook example of traumatic disorders: the latency of the disorder for weeks before her breakdown (what Freud calls the 'incubation period'), then the possession of her consciousness by the past, and her inability to recall the moments she is nevertheless forced to relive. As Laub says:

> Trauma survivors live not with memories of the past, but with an event that could not and did not proceed through to its completion, has no ending, attained no closure, and therefore, as far as its survivors are concerned, continues into the present and is current in every respect.[14]

What is needed to attain closure, Laub says, and to avoid the unconscious return and re-enactment of the traumatic event, is a testimony. For Mashinini, this autobiography seems to serve that purpose by breaking the silence: 'For a long time I didn't talk to my family about my prison experiences. . . . This book will serve as a living memory of the evil of the apartheid regime. It is an opportunity for me to speak to my children.'[15] Mashinini feels compelled to testify to the horrors of her detention, just as Laub explains that Holocaust survivors feel the need to bear witness to their loss. According to Laub, testimony is a process of 'constructing a narrative, of reconstructing a history and essentially, of *re-externalizing the event*'.[16] This re-externalization allows the survivor to reify and affirm the reality of the event and thereby gain some degree of mastery over it, rather than letting the memories possess him or her.

As potentially useful as Caruth's, Laub's and Felman's formulations of trauma are, however, they tend to downplay the most significant aspect of these testimonies to imprisonment under apartheid: the highly charged *political* nature of these texts. Here, the Freudian understanding of trauma as resulting from an accident begins to fail us. There is nothing accidental nor incidental about the trauma inflicted by security police in South African gaols and prisons; rather, the apartheid state used physical and psychological torture *deliberately* and *systematically* as a tool for destroying resistance.

Perhaps a more applicable model for understanding the resulting trauma is that offered by Kali Tal in *Worlds of Hurt*, a work which 'moves back and forth between the effects of trauma upon individual survivors and the manner in which that trauma is reflected and revised in the larger, collective political and cultural world'. One of the 'strategies for cultural coping' that Tal describes is *mythologization,* or 'reducing a traumatic event to a set of standardized narratives (twice- and thrice-told tales that come to represent "the story" of the trauma) turning it from a frightening and uncontrollable event into a contained and predictable narrative'.[17] In South Africa under apartheid, certain 'standardized narratives' were offered by the police as explanations for deaths in detention: he hung himself; he hit his head trying to escape; he died of natural causes. When irrefutable proof of torture by police did occasionally surface, it was dismissed as an isolated incident attributable to the chosen scapegoats, 'a few bad apples'. Applying Tal's formulation to the situation in South Africa, then, the testimonies of torture survivors are not merely attempts to come to terms with their individual trauma: they constitute challenges to the 'mythologization' of torture and violence by the apartheid regime, and efforts to change the status quo.

This formulation parallels in important respects Barbara Harlow's reading of First's *117 Days* and other memoirs from political prisoners. Harlow suggests that these narratives 'are actively engaged in a redefinition of the self and the individual in terms of a collective enterprise and struggle'.[18] Like Tal, she regards the texts themselves as engaging in a battle to control the representation of the apartheid state and the resistance movement:

> In prison her state interrogators demand that Ruth First contribute to a punitive narrative that will be deployed in order to incarcerate for life the Rivonia activists. . . . Her intellectual contest with her interrogators must prevent that history from being written and carried out.[19]

Under physical and psychological torture, the detainees sometimes lose the initial battle with the police, and are forced to make a statement implicating themselves or others. The political stakes behind publishing their memoirs are thus all the greater as they attempt to regain control over the terms of representation.

The idea that interrogation under torture is a kind of contest or battle becomes especially clear in narratives of physical torture, which often illustrate the dynamic that Michel Foucault describes in *Discipline and Punish*. It is important to note that in Part One of his book Foucault discusses judicial practice common in western Europe before the penal reforms that began at the end of the eighteenth century. According to Foucault, such grossly physical and spectacular practices as torture and ritual executions were gradually phased out in favour of more subtle and internalized systems of control that depend on perpetual discipline and surveillance. The school, the prison and the workplace were all reconfigured along models such as Jeremy Bentham's panopticon, to create subjects who are, in a sense, self-policing. But one of Foucault's more troubling omissions is the fact that the very governments that began to frown on torture and public execution within Europe's borders continued to use such tactics systematically in colonies throughout the world, well into Foucault's lifetime. Indeed, this appeared to be a distinguishing attribute of colonial occupations everywhere in the twentieth century: modern surveillance apparatus and intelligence-gathering technologies operated in tandem with the most barbaric of practices involving kidnapping, assault, torture and murder, all with the aim of controlling the population of the colonized territory.

Despite Foucault's shortsightedness in this regard, his description of the psychological dynamic between torturer and victim is revealing in relation to South African prison narratives. Torture under interrogation, Foucault argues, is intended not to extract the 'truth' from the victim, but to force the victim to participate in creating the 'truth' of the sovereign's absolute power:

> Beneath an apparently determined, impatient search for truth, one finds in classical torture the regulated mechanism of an ordeal: a physical challenge that must define the truth. . . . The search for truth through judicial torture was certainly a way of obtaining evidence . . . but it was also the battle, and this victory of one adversary over the other, that 'produced' truth according to a ritual. In torture employed to extract a confession, there was an element of the investigation; there also was an element of the duel.[20]

Elaine Scarry makes a similar point in *The Body in Pain*. She argues that the goal of interrogation through torture is to destroy the voice of the other, and to extract a confession that serves as a physical signifier of that destruction and subjugation:

> the confession that can be carried away on a piece of paper or on a tape is only the most concrete exhibition of the torturer's attempt to induce sounds so that they can then be broken off from their speaker so that they can then be taken off and made the property of the regime.[21]

For both Foucault and Scarry, the confession extracted through torture is useful not only (and sometimes not at all) for its value to detectives and prosecutors, but primarily for its acknowledgment of the state's power over the prisoner's body.

And Night Fell, by Molefe Pheto, illustrates the aptness of Foucault's and Scarry's formulations. Pheto describes being repeatedly beaten and tortured by security police while in detention in 1975 under the Terrorism Act: 'I knew then that I had received the worst beating because I did not yell or beg for mercy. I was told that my attitude was interpreted as resistance.'[22] After he complains to the magistrate, the police stop assaulting him in ways that leave physical evidence, but instead force him to stand for three days and nights without end. When he finally collapses from the strain and exhaustion, he agrees to sign a statement that he had received guerilla training from communists abroad, among other charges. But the interrogators insist on knowing 'the truth', to which Pheto responds: 'the truth is that I do not know what has happened to the missing pages of my passport! I don't know any of the Coloured people except Clarence Hamilton, and I am not a Communist. That is all!'[23] Nevertheless, the police ask him a moment later to sign a statement that he tried to help the coloureds, who are accused of being guerilla soldiers, and that he knew about military training. Clearly this statement is not needed for its judicial value – indeed, when Pheto is finally brought to trial after 281 days in detention, the prosecutor's case falls apart for lack of evidence. Perhaps the statement was useful to the security police, who could have shown it to other detainees to convince them that their 'comrade' had betrayed them. But the confession seems important primarily for its symbolic value: it signifies the submission of a stubborn prisoner who refused to cry out in recognition of the state's power over him. The written statement is the physical signifier of the silencing of Pheto's oppositional voice, and of his coerced consent to be dominated by their power.

The apartheid state's strategy of systematically inflicting trauma on its victims in order to silence them and win their submission, however, frequently backfires. It is true that physical torture and solitary confinement can shatter a person entirely. But it is also true that the survivor of trauma is compelled to continually relive the event, often unconsciously, until he or she is able to narrativize it and thus give it closure. In suggesting that testimony, whether written or performed, can provide this closure, I wish neither to romanticize the plight of the torture victim, nor to minimize his or her suffering. Breyten Breytenbach warns that after long-term isolation, 'parts of you are destroyed and these parts will never again be revived. You are altered in your most intimate ways exactly because all objectivity is taken away from you.'[24] But Breytenbach, like so many other political prisoners, continued to speak out against apartheid from exile after his release, not least by publishing his memoir *The True Confessions of an Albino Terrorist*. He writes:

> The document itself took shape from the obsessive urge I experienced during the first weeks and months of my release to talk talk talk, to tell my story and

all the other stories ... it had to become the reflection of a search for what really happened, and for the identity of the narrator.[25]

Breytenbach, Pheto, and the others are each engaging in the ongoing process of testifying to a personal trauma. But they are also committing an act of resistance and participating in the struggle against apartheid, by testifying publicly to the government's abuses. It is precisely this compulsion to testify, to revisit the stories in an attempt to excavate the truth, that lies at the heart of the TRC's project.

The Truth and Reconciliation Commission

Many of the witnesses who testified at the TRC Human Rights Violation, Amnesty and Special Hearings had told their stories many times before. For example, in 1982 Indres Naidoo published his story *Robben Island: Ten Years as a Political Prisoner in South Africa's Most Notorious Penitentiary*, as told to Albie Sachs (recently reprinted under the title *Island in Chains*). And Naidoo's sister Shanti, who was detained in 1969 as a witness in the famous 'Trial of the 22', testified at the trial that she had been subjected to torture by security police and kept in solitary confinement for six months. But at the Special Hearings on Prisons in July of 1997, Indres, Shanti and three of their siblings – Prema, Murthi and Ramnie, all of whom were detained at various times – were able to enter their stories into an official chronicle of the apartheid years, and to resituate their experience within the context of the collective struggle.

At the hearing, presided over by Hugh Lewin (himself the author of a well-known prison memoir), Indres was the first to testify:

> You see five of us here and as Hugh Lewin said it's not only the five of us but in fact our parents and our grandparents, our whole family has actually been involved in the struggle for well over a century.

He then recited a brief history of his family's involvement in the freedom movement, up to his own decision to take up arms in 1961. After his brothers and sisters had spoken, Indres added, 'Prema's eldest son who in fact is the fourth generation in the family was detained in [1987]. . . . Even the fourth generation have been fully in the struggle.'[26]

This process of documenting and vindicating the roles of individuals in the struggle against apartheid was one of the key functions of the TRC, and reveals the extent to which the individual narratives of imprisonment and torture were always part of a larger, collective trauma and resistance. Another important function of the TRC was to unearth previously repressed or contested information and provide a sense of closure, both for victims and for the nation as a whole. The TRC frequently provided such closure for individual survivors of apartheid's violence. Many of the requests for reparation asked the Commission to find the bodies of family members for proper burial. One woman requested that her husband's hand, kept in a jar by police, be turned over to her for burial. Lucas Sikwepere, who was shot and lost his eyesight during a police raid on the Cape Flats townships says that

> I feel what . . . has brought my sight back . . . is to come back here and tell the story. But I feel what has been making me sick all the time is the fact that I couldn't tell my story. But now I – it feels like I got my sight back by coming here and telling you the story.[27]

The architects of the TRC hoped that a corresponding sense of closure would occur at the national collective level. Indeed, the Commission's very title was premised on the notion that reconciliation would occur only after the truths of the nation's history had been made public. As Archbishop Tutu, chairperson of the TRC, wrote in his foreword to the final report:

> Having looked the beast of the past in the eye, having asked and received forgiveness and having made amends, let us shut the door on the past – not in order to forget it but in order not to allow it to imprison us.[28]

The task of the TRC, then, was to forge a narrative, including at least a tentative conclusion, out of the memories of apartheid's survivors.

Not everyone was satisfied with the TRC process, however. Many white leaders refused to testify before the Commission, and many who did – former state President F. W. de Klerk, for example – downplayed or denied their knowledge of and responsibility for abuses and were thus accused of insincerity or disingenuousness. Moreover, while many victims of state violence felt a sense of closure after their testimonies, many remained deeply dissatisfied and continued to seek other avenues for bearing witness to apartheid, such as the Khulumani Support Group, which re-enacted on stage the human rights abuses about which the members of the group testified at the TRC. Captain Benzien's amnesty hearing likewise revealed the gaps and seams of the TRC's burgeoning narrative: the hearing quickly boiled down to a battle of memories, illustrating what happens when recollections of an event not only differ, but conflict with or contradict one another. The presence of the torturer and his victims together in the hearing chamber, each giving their own testimony to their own trauma, appeared to throw the process of testimony (and by extension the project of constructing a national memory) into crisis.

From the beginning, Benzien's explanations of his activities displayed a complicated and seemingly contradictory logic. For example, to the family of Ashley Kriel, an ANC militant whom he shot and killed during an arrest, he said: 'Although I deny that I killed him unlawfully and wrongfully, he did however die as a result of an action on my part and for that I apologise.'[29] His testimony was a confusing assembly of old right-wing nationalist rhetoric and the new rhetoric of reconciliation and racial harmony. He told the committee, 'As Director Kruse mentioned, "Jeff, we are all now on the same side." . . . It is now reconciliation, forgive and forget at its best.' In the amnesty application, on the other hand, he wrote that his political motive was 'the averting of the onslaught from the ANC/SACP [South African Communist Party] alliance which was aimed at overthrowing the previous government by violent means and destroying the constitutional dispensation'. This complicated logic of then-and-now legality led Benzien to make numerous paradoxical statements, as when Tony Yengeni asked him if he believed the wet bag and other torture methods were lawful: 'I was engaged in a lawful activity, using unlawful, unconstitutional methods, yes Sir.'

Not only did Benzien's testimony contain these apparent contradictions within itself, it was also often at odds with the testimony of his former victims. Several of those victims opposed his amnesty application because they were not satisfied that he disclosed the full truth. Much of the cross-examination by Ashley Forbes consisted of contradictory memories of Forbes's detention. Forbes, who was detained on 16 April, insisted that he was routinely tortured on the 16th of every month thereafter, but Benzien denied torturing him after the first week:

> *Mr Benzien*: I took you on investigation to the Eastern Cape . . . you said it was the most Kentucky Fried Chicken you have ever eaten. Either after that or prior to that, we attempted to go to the Western Transvaal where you were going to do some pointing out [of ANC hideouts]. Could you remember the time that you had seen snow for the first time? Can you remember what happened in the snow? . . . Your trip to Colesberg, where you braaied [barbecued] with me that night and with the rest of the Unit? Therefore Mr Forbes, in the spirit of honesty and reconciliation, I am sure you are making a mistake about the 16th of every month. . . .
>
> *Mr Forbes*: Mr Benzien, maybe I will take you through the next time that I was assaulted and I will just see if there are aspects of that torture that you may remember. For example, on the second occasion do you remember that I was wrapped in the carpet?

Others of Benzien's former victims also had different memories of their interrogation. For instance, Gary Kruse grew frustrated at what he called Benzien's 'very selective truth':

> You seem to remember very flimsy things like Kentucky [Fried Chicken] and things which I would have thought you had forgotten, but things which stand out more permanently in terms of our interrogation and our experience, you don't seem to remember.

Benzien claimed his memory lapse was so severe that he could remember the names of only seven of his former victims: Of the other names, 'I have forgotten them, therefore I also apply [for amnesty] for the cases I cannot remember.'

Assuming the victims' own memories of their torture are accurate, there are two likely explanations for Benzien's alleged memory lapses: he could have been shamming, denying some crimes for fear the Committee would reject his amnesty application (though full disclosure is one of the conditions of amnesty), or lying to cover for his colleagues who had not applied for amnesty. The other explanation is the one offered by Benzien's counsel and by a psychiatrist who later testified on Benzien's behalf: he himself had been traumatized by his own actions. Dr Ria Kotze diagnosed Benzien as having post-traumatic stress disorder, with symptoms including auditory hallucinations and memory loss. She told the TRC that during his time with the Security Branch 'he was torn by his belief that he was saving the lives of the public . . . and the disgust that he felt in the measures he had to take. . . . These thoughts tore him apart and destroyed his self-respect.'[30] During the hearing, as he was being questioned by Tony Yengeni, he had a momentary breakdown. Describing the torments his family faced because of his reputation as a policeman, he said, 'Yes, Mr Yengeni, I did terrible things, I did terrible things to members of the ANC, but as God as my witness, believe me, I have also suffered. I may not call myself a victim of Apartheid but, yes sir, I have also been a victim.'

While I share many of the reservations of those who opposed Benzien's (ultimately successful) amnesty application,[31] it is not my purpose here to judge whether or not Benzien was lying about the events he claimed not to remember. I refer to his hearing simply to demonstrate the extreme difficulties inherent in the TRC's task of forging an official national memory. If the act of interrogation resembles the duel/ordeal that Foucault describes, the narration of that encounter at the hearing repeats the duel, as in Benzien's cross-examination by another former victim, Peter Jacobs. Benzien had already conceded that 'the torture of Mr Jacobs was robust and very long', but his memories of the details were fuzzy:

> *Mr Jacobs*: [Y]ou put the [electric shocks] up my rectum and in my ear. So how is it possible that you were doing that alone, throughout the past two days you were saying you were doing that alone?
> *Mr Benzien*: I said on most of the occasions with the wet bag method I could do it alone. I have already conceded that with your interrogation, it took longer. I could remember I think it is Johan Kotze, you mention Nortje. . . .
> *Mr Jacobs*: Can you then explain to us . . . why you haven't mentioned his name? Because I remember he was the one, Kotze was there, putting the electric shocks on. I remember his voice saying should I do it here or there, where should I put it? And then you held the bag down and then Nortje was shouting the questions down my ear. Now how come you don't remember him and I was supposedly your first victim?

Much of the hearing went on like this, with the victims certain of the most minute details of the torture and unable to comprehend how Benzien could have forgotten them.

Unlike the classic case of post-traumatic stress disorder, these torture victims did have conscious memories of the traumatic event, but they were no less possessed by the past. Like the amnesiac victims, they felt compelled to return to the trauma, to testify to and thereby re-externalize the event, and to affirm its reality. They were already able to describe the external details of the event; what had not been assimilated into a comprehensible narrative was the destruction of language and consciousness itself under the extreme pain of torture. Thus, although Yengeni remembered all too well what Benzien and his team did to him all those years ago, he wanted to see it physically re-enacted ('I also want to see it with my own eyes what he did to me'). Most of his questions were aimed at understanding the reality of his torture: he wanted Benzien to describe the physical reaction of prisoners to the wet bag, asking 'at what point do you release the bag to give the person who is tortured, more air? Is there something – are you counting time or is there something that you feel and then you release the bag?' In the terror and suffocation of the wet bag torture, Yengeni experienced a disruption in his sense of time, the very foundation of consciousness and memory. He hoped to elicit from Benzien's testimony something that could help him fill in the moments he had lost.

The cross-examination by Benzien's former victims thus became a forum for personal testimony – they had an opportunity to narrativize their experience and re-externalize the source of trauma. The ritual of the public testimony re-enacted and thereby negated (one hopes) the ritual of torture. But Benzien's hearing seemed to offer little therapeutic release for his victims. Indeed, the experience of giving testimony seemed to repeat the trauma for at least one of those victims: Benzien publicly shamed Tony Yengeni by asking if he remembered 'that within thirty minutes you betrayed Jennifer Schreiner? Do you remember pointing out Bongani Jonas to us?'

As Laub explains, testimony requires an Other, not only to hear the story but to comprehend it and affirm its reality. In Benzien's case, however, the presence of the torturer himself, denying the victim's claims and reminding him of his humiliation, threw that reality into doubt and the whole process of testimony into a crisis. This crisis extended to the larger project of constructing a national testimony: Peter Jacobs seemed to speak for most, if not all, of the victims at the hearing when he said, 'It would be in the national interest for us to support an application for amnesty if the whole truth is told, not just a part of the truth'. Since none of the victims was convinced that the 'full truth' had emerged from this hearing, the implication is that amnesty and reconciliation were unacceptable, perhaps even impossible.

Conclusion

If Benzien's hearing marks a rupture or failure in the TRC project of discovering Truth and achieving Reconciliation, I believe this failure lies not within the TRC *per se* but is intrinsic to the whole country's process of reconstructing a national history, a national memory and a national identity. Since the first Dutch settlement of the Cape in the seventeenth century, South Africa's official history has been exclusionary and selective. Textbooks and museums showed the glorious Afrikaner past – the Voortrekker pioneers setting off into the interior in their wagon trains, fending off the Black Peril. What have been excluded from this narrative, of course, are the histories of the majority of people in South Africa – histories of trauma, violence, displacement, disenfranchisement and struggle. Now the nation is rewriting the textbooks and constructing a new national history, one that incorporates the trauma of apartheid into a narrative of reconciliation. One task of the TRC was to document and collect the various memories but, as the Benzien hearing showed, sometimes these memories were incompatible or contradictory.

Perhaps it would have been a mistake, however, to insist that the TRC produce a unified and totalizing narrative of the apartheid past. Steven Robins warns that in Truth Commissions in other parts of the world, and indeed in historiographical representation in general, 'embodied personal memories of trauma are often erased and rewritten in the name of nationalism. The recasting of personal memory as nationalist narrative reconfigures and erases the fragmented character and silences of embodied experiences of violence.'[32] It is important to read apartheid-era prison memoirs and TRC testimonies as part of a collective struggle against apartheid rather than as isolated accounts. But Robins reminds us of the danger of reading them *only* as parts of a totalizing narrative, especially when that narrative is employed to justify the new ruling regime. Similarly, Ingrid de Kok advises South Africa to resist the impulse to provide a 'grand concluding narrative' to the TRC. 'It is in the multiplicity of partial versions and experiences, composed and recomposed within sight of each other, that truth "as a thing of this world", in Foucault's phrase, will emerge.'[33] This is not to say that we must accept the perpetrator's and the victim's views as equally valid. Nor must we abandon the search for truth, or fatalistically embrace ambiguity. But de Kok's warning does suggest that we must tolerate some ambiguity and contradiction at the level of individual cases, while looking for the larger patterns of truth revealed in the TRC's findings.

Archbishop Tutu seems to agree with de Kok, referring to the past as a 'jigsaw puzzle' of which the TRC is only a single piece, and alluding to the TRC search 'for the clues that lead, endlessly, to a truth that will, in the very nature of things, never be fully revealed'.[34] Bearing witness to a trauma is never a one-time event, after which the survivor achieves immediate closure and mastery over the past. Rather, testimony, like the construction of a national memory, is an ongoing process of telling and retelling, of narrativizing and revising. The TRC, like the memoirs and autobiographies that document apartheid's violence, played a crucial role in that process by documenting a multiplicity of stories and perspectives. But it cannot and should not be regarded as providing a monolithic, totalizing and eternal Truth. Instead, these transcripts, reports, and books provide a foundation for the ongoing project of telling and revising the history of South Africa.

Notes

I give special thanks to Jessica Baldanzi, Eva Cherniavsky, Christie Fox and Natasha Vaubel for their careful readings, keen insights and apt suggestions on this chapter through several evolutions. Nevertheless, I am solely to blame for any and all shortcomings.

1. Truth and Reconciliation Commission Amnesty Hearing. Jeffery T. Benzien. Johannesburg, 14–16 July 1997. http://www.truth.org.za

2. Max Coleman (ed.), *A Crime Against Humanity: Analyzing the Repression of the Apartheid State* (Johannesburg/Bellville, HRC/Mayibuye Books, 1998), pp. 48, 59.

3. Don Foster, Dennis Davis and Diane Sadler, *Detention and Torture in South Africa: Psychological, Legal and Historical Studies* (New York, St. Martin's Press, 1987).

4. Cathy Caruth (ed.), *Trauma: Explorations in Memory* (Baltimore, Johns Hopkins University Press, 1995), p. 4.

5. Dori Laub, 'Bearing witness, or the vicissitudes of listening', in Shoshana Felman and Dori Laub (eds), *Testimony: Crises of Witnessing in Literature, Psychoanalysis* and *History* (New York, Routledge, 1992), p. 60.

6. Albie Sachs, *Jail Diary of Albie Sachs* (London, Sphere, 1966), p. 62.

7. *Ibid.*, p. 114.

8. Cathy Caruth, *Unclaimed Experience: Trauma, Narrative, and History* (Baltimore, Johns Hopkins University Press, 1996), p. 61 (emphasis mine).

9. Ruth First, *117 Days* (New York, Monthly Review, 1965), pp. 80–1.

10. Emma Mashinini, *Strikes Have Followed Me All My Life* (New York, Routledge, 1991), pp. 86–7.

11. Ingrid de Kok, 'Cracked heirlooms: memory on exhibition', in Sarah Nuttall and Carli Coetzee (eds), *Negotiating the Past: The Making of Memory in South Africa* (Cape Town, Oxford University Press, 1998), p. 62.

12. Mashinini, *Strikes Have Followed Me*, p. 90.

13. *Ibid.*, p. 108.

14. Laub, 'Bearing witness,' p. 69.

15. Mashinini, *Strikes Have Followed Me*, p. 110.

16. Laub, 'Bearing witness,' p. 69 (emphasis his).

17. Kali Tal, *Worlds of Hurt: Reading the Literatures of Trauma* (Cambridge, Cambridge University Press, 1996), pp. 5–6.

18. Barbara Harlow, *Resistance Literature* (New York, Methuen, 1987), p. 120.

19. Barbara Harlow, *Barred: Women, Writing, and Political Detention* (Hanover, NH, Wesleyan University Press, 1992), p. 149.

20. Michel Foucault, *Discipline and Punish: The Birth of the Prison*, trans. Alan Sheridan (New York, Vintage, 1977), p. 41.

21. Elaine Scarry, *The Body in Pain* (New York, Oxford University Press, 1985), p. 49.

22. Molefe Pheto, *And Night Fell: Memoirs of a Political Prisoner in South Africa* (Ibadan, Heinemann, 1983), p. 106.

23. Pheto, *And Night Fell*, pp. 132–3.

24. Breyten Breytenbach, *The True Confessions of an Albino Terrorist* (New York, McGraw-Hill, 1983), p. 163.

25. *Ibid.*, p. 452.

26. TRC Special Hearings – Prisons. Murthi Naidoo/Indres Naidoo/Prema Naidoo/Ramnie Naidoo/Shanthie [sic] Naidoo. Johannesburg, 21 July 1997. Case JB04506.
www.truth.org.za

27. TRC Human Rights Violation Hearing. Lucas Baba Sikwepere. Cape Town, 25 April 1996. Case CT/00508.
www.truth.org.za

28. Desmond M. Tutu, 'Foreword by chairperson', in *Truth and Reconciliation Commission of South Africa Report* (London, Macmillan, 1998), p. 22.

29. TRC Amnesty Hearing, Jeff Benzien.

30. South African Press Association, 'Police torturer despises himself, TRC told' (20 October 1997).

31. Other recent amnesty decisions have proven even more troubling. For example, in its decision regarding ten former security policemen for their roles in the torture and murder of Stanza Bopape in June 1988, the TRC wrote that it was left 'with the uneasy feeling that [the applicants] may be protecting themselves by playing down their culpability' regarding the degree of violence they used on Bopape. Despite these suspicions that the policemen were not providing full disclosure, the committee granted them amnesty – a finding that threatened the credibility of the entire TRC process. Piers Pigou, 'Lid not lifted on Bopape cover-up', *Mail & Guardian* (Johannesburg, 28 April 2000), p. 8.

32. Steven Robins, 'Silence in my father's house: memory, nationalism, and narratives of the body', in Sarah Nuttall and Carli Coetzee (eds), *Negotiating the Past: The Making of Memory in South Africa* (Cape Town, Oxford University Press, 1998), p. 123.

33. de Kok, 'Cracked heirlooms', p. 61.

34. Tutu, 'Foreword', p. 4.

CHAPTER FIFTEEN

Conclusion

GRAEME HARPER

Were it the case that this has been a study of a long-past phenomenon, this conclusion could set out boldly to reiterate our disgust at the conditions of our barbarous past, note the interesting economic, social and cultural conditions under which they occurred, marvel a little at the fortitude of some and the lack of moral integrity in others, and sum up the experience as one the world should never, on its own oath, repeat.

The fact is, however, the condition has only altered – it has not disappeared. If in the recent narratives of Kosovo, Tibet, Angola, Fiji, Sierra Leone, Kurdistan, East Timor and so on and on we find something to whet our Western appetites for observing the turmoil of one political or cultural system trying to dominate another, we equally find within these often televised events colonial carceral conditions which trek back through the entire history of the rise of our own modernity.

If we hear that Indian Ocean islanders have been evicted by Britain in order for it to build a military base, or that the Australian Prime Minister refuses to apologize to the indigenous population for the white land appropriations of the past, or that US and Cuban authorities debate the future of a Cuban boy, each arguing he is 'best off' in a country as forward thinking as their own, then the emotive, dispositional and behavioural context of colonial incarceration hardly needs its material prisons, its bricks and mortar, to remind us that it still exists.

It would, likewise, be inaccurate to treat all this carceral currency as simply an ongoing trade in holistic human history. The individual stories, the stories of people caught in the prisons of colonialism, are as constantly contiguous to our modern Western lives as they are harrowing – though the world's media hardly maintains a stream of reportage to match the frequency of these instances.

'[T]he imagery of Africa, as reflected in the media and by which public perceptions are formed, is indubitably dominated by the other, the historical factor,' writes Nadine Gordimer:

> I call it the Heart of Darkness syndrome. The Europeans, the North Americans, the Japanese, Chinese, others – with the exception, perhaps of the Latin American countries – all still conceptualise Africa as alienated from their own particular human condition; the Dark Continent. This leads them, the non-

Africans, to an incredible distortion of the sense of values they claim, and which they believe has been and continues to be their dutiful gift to Africa's darkness.[1]

Nadine Gordimer's reference to 'an incredible distortion of the sense of values' reflects exactly the point the writers in *Colonial and Postcolonial Incarceration* are making. It is the sense of values, the dispositional history of interaction between one human being and another, the behavioural context behind the creation of political systems and cultural hierarchies, the intentions, meanings, feelings and reasons which underpin social and economic relations, which feed the colonial carceral.

Were this carceral no more than its bricks and mortar appearance, much of this could be discarded. We could go around dismantling such colonial prisons and creating from them, no doubt, bespoke homes with quaint historical pasts, neat tourist attractions, complete with souvenirs and suitably weather-worn carceral maps, a garden wall with a nice brass plaque. But, as this book has shown, this would not dismantle such a carceral, any more than declaring the end of the Age of Imperialism (taken to be some time between the mid-nineteenth century and the end of the First World War, by most accounts) ended imperialism.

The true prison, writes Ken Saro-Wiwa, poet, novelist and outspoken opposer of Nigeria's successive military governments, executed in Nigeria in 1995:

> It is the lies that have been drummed
> Into your ears for a generation
> It is the security agent running amok
> Executing callous calamitous orders
> In exchange for a wretched meal a day
> The magistrate writing into her book
> A punishment she knows is undeserved
> The moral decrepitude
> The mental ineptitude
> The meat of dictators
> Cowardice masking as obedience
> Lurking in our denigrated souls
> It is fear damping trousers
> That we dare not wash
> It is this
> It is this
> It is this
> Dear friend, turns our free world
> Into a dreary prison.[2]

Is there, after all, a truly *post*colonial world? The word postcolonial has currency because we use it to declare a state of intellectual engagement with seeing the end of colonialism, with the repudiation of imperialism.

However, like the argument that postmodernism is merely a later stage of a still existent modernism, so the argument that there is anything 'post' the colonial enterprise too often relies on an intellectual belief in an already changed or, more often, a contemporary 'more-advanced' state of affairs. Common-sense observation records that this is simply not the case. The colonial carceral can only be considered *post*, not because of 'advance' but by alteration; not because of actuality but only (and we surely can say this is the case) because of a widening commitment to the desire to see such things left in the past.

Duncan Forrest, writing in *A Glimpse of Hell: Reports on Torture Worldwide*, records:

> A Turkish Kurd told me how he had been put in a sack with wild cats and the sack then beaten to make the cats bite and scratch. This seemed so unlikely that it would have been dismissed out of hand had not a previous resident in the area provided strong evidence that it was a common torture in that particular police station at about the time of the subject's detention.[3]

A slave in shackles? An indigenous American forcibly relocated to a barren reservation hundreds of miles away from his spiritual home? An Algerian woman tormented for wearing traditional Muslim dress? An indigenous Australian dying in a police cell, without explanation? An Albanian family killed for remaining in their ancestral home? When all is said and done, how unusual really is a man imprisoned in a bag of cats?

Surely, hardly much more than another incident in the history of colonial incarceration.

Notes

1. Nadine Gordimer, 'Read all about it: the way they see us', in Liam Browne and Graeme Harper (eds), *Touchpaper Contemporary Pamphlets*, no. 1 (London, Waterstones/Arts Council of England, 2000).

2. Ken Saro-Wiwa, 'The true prison', in Siobhan Dowd (ed.), *This Prison Where I Live* (London, Cassell, 1996), p. 82.

3. Duncan Forrest, Bernard Knight and Morris Tidball-Binz, 'The documentation of torture', in Duncan Forrest (ed.), *A Glimpse of Hell: Reports on Torture Worldwide* (London, Cassell, 1996), p. 176.

Selected bibliography

A Relation Strange and True, of a Ship of Bristol named the Jacob, of 120 tunnes, which was about the end of Octob. last 1621 taken by the Turkish pirats of Argier. And how within five dayes after, foure English youths did valiantly overcome 13 of the said Turks, and brought the ship to S. Lucas in Spaine, where they sold nine of the Turks for gally-slaves (London, 1622).

A True and Perfect Account of the Examination, Confession, and Execution of Joan Perry and her two sons . . . for the supposed murder of Wm. Harrison [incl.] Mr. Harrison's own account, how he was conveyed into Turkey, and there made a slave for above two years . . . how he made his escape (London, 1676).

Adams, Steve L. and Harper, George Mills (eds), 'The manuscript of "Leo Africanus"', *Yeats Annual*, vol. 1 (1982): 3–47.

Alexander, Meena, *The Shock of Arrival: Reflections on Postcolonial Experience* (Boston, South End Press, 1996).

Alleg, Henri, *The Question.* Introduction by Jean-Paul Sartre (New York, George Braziller, 1958).

Anonymous, *An Account of the Rise, Progress and Termination of the Malignant Fever Lately Prevalent in Philadelphia* (Philadelphia, Benjamin Johnson, 1793).

Anonymous, *An Earnest Call Occasioned by the Alarming Pestilential Contagion, Addressed to the Inhabitants of Philadelphia* (Philadelphia, Jones, Hoff & Derrick, 1793).

Anonymous, *Observations on Doctor Mackrill's History of the Yellow Fever* (Baltimore, John Haynes, 1796).

Anstey, Roger, *The Atlantic Slave Trade and British Abolition, 1760–1810* (London, Macmillan, 1975).

Arch, Stephen Carl, *Authorizing the Past: The Rhetoric of History in Seventeenth-Century New England* (Dekalb, Northern Illinois University Press, 1994).

Armstrong, Nancy, *Desire and Domestic Fiction: A Political History of the Novel* (New York, Oxford University Press, 1987).

Arnaud, Georges and Vergès, Jacques, *Pour Djamila Bouhired* (Paris, Minuit, 1957).

Ashcroft, Bill, Griffiths, Gareth and Tiffin, Helen, *The Empire Writes Back: Theory and Practice in Post-colonial Literatures* (London, Routledge, 1989).

Asmal, Kader, Asmal, Louise and Roberts, Ronald Suresh, *Reconciliation Through Truth: A Reckoning of Apartheid's Criminal Governance* (Cape Town, David Philip, 1997).

Aussaresses, Paul, *Services spéciaux: Algérie 1955–1957* (Paris, Perrin, 2001).

Ballard, J. G., *The Drowned World* (New York, Berkley, 1962).

Ballard, J. G., *The Wind from Nowhere* (New York, Berkley, 1962).

Ballard, J. G., *The Burning World* (New York, Berkley, 1964).

Ballard, J. G., *The Drought* (London, Cape, 1965).

Ballard, J. G., *The Crystal World* (New York, Farrar, Straus & Giroux, 1966).

Ballard, J. G., *The Atrocity Exhibition* (London, Cape, 1970; revised, with annotations by Ballard, San Francisco, Re/Search, 1990).

Ballard, J. G., *Crash* (London, Cape, 1973).

Ballard, J. G., *Concrete Island* (London, Cape, 1974).

Ballard, J. G., *High Rise* (London, Cape, 1975).

Ballard, J. G., *The Best Short Stories of J. G. Ballard* (New York, Holt, Rinehart & Winston, 1978).

Ballard, J. G., *The Unlimited Dream Company* (London, Cape, 1979).

Ballard, J. G., *Hello America* (London, Cape, 1981).

Ballard, J. G., *Myths of the Near Future* (London, Cape, 1982).

Ballard, J. G., *War Fever* (1984; reissued Collins, 1990).

Ballard, J. G., *Empire of the Sun* (London, Gollancz, 1987).

Ballard, J. G., *The Kindness of Women* (New York, Farrar, Straus & Giroux, 1991).

Ballard, J. G., *Rushing to Paradise* (New York, Picador, 1994).

Ballard, J. G., 'Desperate Humours', in *A User's Guide to the Millennium: Essays and Reviews* (New York, Picador, 1996).

Barker, Francis, Hulme, Peter and Iversen, Margaret (eds), *Cannibalism and the Colonial World* (Cambridge, Cambridge University Press, 1998).

Bartels, Emily, 'Making more of the Moor: Aaron, Othello, and Renaissance refashionings of race', *Shakespeare Quarterly*, vol. 41, no. 4 (1990): 433–54.

Bartels, Emily, 'Othello and Africa: postcolonialism reconsidered', *William and Mary Quarterly*, 3rd series, vol. 54, no. 1 (1997): 45–64.

Barton, Benjamin, Letters to Thomas Pennant, 26 March and 11 April 1794, Benjamin Barton Papers (1790–1794), American Philosophical Society, Philadelphia, Pennsylvania.

Barton, Benjamin, Benjamin Barton Papers, November 1793–February 1794, Medical Box, American Philosophical Society, Philadelphia, Pennsylvania.

Bartram, Moses, Letter to Isaac Bartram, 3 October 1793, Miscellaneous Manuscript Collection, American Philosophical Society, Philadelphia, Pennsylvania.

Behan, Brendan, *Borstal Boy* (London, Corgi, 1961; first published 1958).

Behan, Brendan, 'Oscar Wilde', in *Poems and a Play in Irish* (Oldcastle, Ireland, The Gallery Press, 1981).

Bénichou, François, 'Amin Maalouf: "Ma patrie, c'est l'écriture"', *Magazine littéraire*, vol. 359 (1997): 114–15.

Bercovitch, Sacvan, *The American Jeremiad* (Madison, University of Wisconsin Press, 1978).

Berkhofer, Robert F., Jr, *The White Man's Indian: Images of the American Indian from Columbus to the Present* (New York, Knopf, 1978).

Bhabha, Homi K., *Nation and Narration* (London, Routledge, 1990).

Bhabha, Homi K., *The Location of Culture* (London, Routledge, 1994).

Biggs, Chester M., Jr, *Behind the Barbed Wire: Memoir of a World War II U.S. Marine*

Captured in North China in 1941 and Imprisoned by the Japanese until 1945 (London, McFarland, 1995).

Blackburn, Robin, *The Making of New World Slavery from the Baroque to the Modern, 1492–1800* (London, Verso, 1997).

Blackburn, Robin, *The Overthrow of Colonial Slavery, 1776–1848* (London, Verso, 1988).

Blake, John, 'Yellow fever in eighteenth century America', *Bulletin for the New York Academy of Medicine*, 2nd series, vol. 44 (1968): 673–86.

Bonga, Dieuwke Wendelaar, *Eight Prison Camps: A Dutch Family in Japanese Java*. Monographs in International Studies, Southeast Asia Series, no. 98 (Athens, OH, Ohio University for International Studies, 1996).

Bonyhady, Tim, *Images in Opposition: Australian Landscape Painting 1801–1890* (Melbourne, Oxford University Press, 1985).

Bosman, Herman Charles, *Cold Stone Jug* (Cape Town, Human & Rousseau, 1969).

Boulle, Pierre, *The Bridge over the River Kwai*, trans. Xan Fielding (New York, Time, 1954).

Bovill, E. W., *The Niger Explored* (London, Oxford University Press, 1968).

Bradsher, Earl L., *Mathew Carey: Editor, Author and Publisher; A Study in America's Literary Development* (New York, AMS, 1966).

Brahimi, Denise, 'Mungo Park en Afrique, ou l'explorateur exploré', *Dix-huitième siècle*, no. 22 (1990): 149–58.

Brannigan, John, 'An historical accident: national identity in the writings of Brendan Behan', *Irish Studies Review*, 13 (Winter 1995/96).

Brannigan, John, 'Historically informed and obscene: Brendan Behan and the politics of comedy', *Imprimatur*, 2, 1/2 (Autumn 1996).

Brent, Peter, *Black Nile: Mungo Park and the Search for the Niger* (London, Gordon Cremonesi, 1977).

Breytenbach, Breyten, *The True Confessions of an Albino Terrorist* (New York, McGraw-Hill, 1983).

Brombert, Victor, *The Romantic Prison: The French Tradition* (Baltimore, Johns Hopkins University Press, 1978).

Brooks, Francis, *Barbarian Cruelty. Being a True History of the Distressed Condition of the Christian Captives under the Tyranny of Mully Ishmael Emperor of Morocco, and King of Fez and Macqueness in Barbary. In which is likewise given a particular Account of his late Wars with the Algerines. The manner of his Pirates taking the Christians and Others. A Description of his Castles and Guards, and the Places where he keeps his Women, his Slaves and Negroes. With a particular Relation of the dangerous Escape of the Author, and two English Men more from thence, after a miserable Slavery of ten Years* (London, 1693).

Brown, Charles Brockden, *Arthur Mervyn; or, Memoirs of the Year 1793* (New York, Holt, 1962).

Brown, Charles Brockden, *Ormond; or, the Secret Witness* (New York, Hafner, 1937).

Brown, Dona, *Inventing New England: Regional Tourism in the Nineteenth Century* (Washington, DC, Smithsonian Institution Press, 1995).

Brown, Jeremiah, Letter to Levi Hollingsworth, Philadelphia, September 9, 1793,

Hollingsworth Family Collection, Historical Society of Pennsylvania, Philadelphia, Pennsylvania.

Brown, Samuel, *A Treatise on the Nature, Origin and Progress of the Yellow Fever* (Boston, Manning and Loring, 1800).

Browne, Abraham, 'A Book of Remembrance of God's Provydences towards me, A. B., throughout the cours of my Life, written for my own medytacion in New Engl.' Manuscript. Massachusetts Historical Society. [The portion of this biographical narrative describing Browne's captivity in Sale is printed as part of an article titled 'Abraham Browne's captivity by the Barbary pirates, 1655', in Stephen T. Riley (ed.), *Seafaring in Colonial Massachusetts* (Boston, Colonial Society of Massachusetts, 1980).]

Brutus, Dennis, *A Simple Lust: Collected Poems of South African Jail and Exile including Letters to Martha* (Oxford, Heinemann, 1973).

Bull, Josiah, *John Newton an Autobiography and Narrative* (1849).

Burnham, Michelle, 'Between England and America: captivity, sympathy, and the sentimental novel', in Deidre Lynch and William B. Warner (eds), *Cultural Institutions of the Novel* (Durham, NC, Duke University Press, 1996), pp. 47–72.

Burnham, Michelle, *Captivity and Sentiment: Cultural Exchange in American Literature, 1682–1861* (Hanover, NH, University Press of New England, 1997).

Burton, Jonathan, '"A most wily bird": Leo Africanus, *Othello* and the trafficking in Difference', in Ania Loomba, *Gender, Race, Renaissance Drama* (New York, St Martin's Press, 1989, pp. 43–63.

Caldwell, Charles, *A Semi-Annual Oration, on the Origin of Pestilential Diseases, Delivered before the Academy of Medicine of Philadelphia, on the 17th Day of December, 1798* (Philadelphia, Samuel Bradford, 1799).

Caldwell, Charles, *An Anniversary Oration on the Subject of Quarantines, Delivered to the Philadelphia Medical Society, on the 21st of January, 1807* (Philadelphia, Fry and Kammerer, 1807).

Caldwell, Charles, *Autobiography of Charles Caldwell, M.D.*, preface, notes and appendix by Harriot W. Warner (Philadelphia, Lippincott, Grambo, 1855).

Calloway, Colin, *North Country Captives: Narratives of Indian Captivity from Vermont and New Hampshire* (Hanover, University Press of New England, 1992).

Carey, Mathew, *A Short Account of the Malignant Fever Lately Prevalent in Philadelphia* (Philadelphia, Mathew Carey, 1793).

Carey, Mathew, *Address of M. Carey to the Public* (Philadelphia, Mathew Carey, 1794).

Carnochan, W. B., *Confinement and Flight: An Essay on English Literature of the Eighteenth Century* (Berkeley, University of California Press, 1977).

Carothers, J. C., *The Psychology of Mau Mau* (Nairobi, Government Printer, 1954).

Carr, Julie, 'Unsettling settlement: re-reading the legends of the White Women of Gippsland', Unpublished PhD thesis (La Trobe University, 1998).

Carroll, Lorrayne, '"My outward man": The curious case of Hannah Swarton', *Early American Literature*, vol. 31, no. 1 (1996).

Carson, Andrew D., *My Time in Hell: Memoir of an American Soldier Imprisoned by the Japanese in World War II* (London, McFarland, 1997).

Carter, Norman, *G-String Jesters* (Sydney, Currawong, 1966).

Carter, Sarah, *Capturing Women: The Manipulation of Cultural Imagery in Canada's Prairie West* (Montreal, McGill-Queens University Press, 1997).

Caruth, Cathy, 'Traumatic departures: survival and history in Freud', in Charles B. Strozier and Michael Flynn (eds), *Trauma and Self* (Lantham, MD, Rowan and Littlefield, 1996).

Castiglia, Christopher, *Bound and Determined: Captivity, Culture-Crossing, and White Womanhood from Mary Rowlandson to Patty Hearst* (Chicago, University of Chicago Press, 1996).

Cecil, Richard, *Memoirs of Him* (London, 1808).

Chan, Sucheng, *Asian Americans: An Interpretive History* (Boston, Twayne, 1991).

Chao, Patricia, *Monkey King* (New York, HarperCollins, 1997).

Chau, Phan Boi, 'Nguc Trung Thu', in Christopher Jenkins, Tran Khanh Tuyet and Huynh Sanh-Thong (trans.), David G. Marr (ed.), *Reflections from Captivity* (Athens, OH, Ohio University Press, 1978).

Chow, Rey, *Woman and Chinese Modernity: The Politics of Reading between West and East* (Minneapolis, University of Minnesota Press, 1991).

Chukwudi Eze, Emmanuel (ed.), *Race and the Enlightenment: A Reader* (London, Blackwell, 1997).

Clark, Steve (ed.), *Travel Writing and Empire: Postcolonial Theory in Transit* (London, Zed, 1999).

Clarke, Thomas J., *Glimpses of an Irish Felon's Prison Life* (Dublin, Maunsel and Roberts, 1922).

Clavel, James, *King Rat* (New York, Dell, 1958).

Coast, John, *Railroad of Death* (London, Hyperion, 1946).

Cohen, Ed, *Talk on the Wilde Side: Toward a Genealogy of a Discourse on Male Sexualities* (London, Routledge, 1993).

Cole, Chery L, 'Chinese exclusion: the capitalist perspective of the *Sacramento Union*, 1850–1882', *California History*, vol. 57, no. 1 (1978): 23.

Coleman, Max (ed.), *A Crime Against Humanity: Analyzing the Repression of the Apartheid State* (Johannesburg/Bellville, HRC/Mayibuye Books, 1998).

Colley, Linda, *Britons: Forging the Nation, 1707–1837* (New Haven, Yale University Press, 1992).

Coxere, Edward, *A Relation of the Several Adventures by Sea with the Dangers, difficulties and Hardships I Met for Several years/as also the Deliverances and Escapes through them for which I Have Cause to Give the Glory to God/ For Ever.* Manuscript. Printed as *Adventures by Sea of Edward Coxere*, ed. E. H. W. Meyerstein (Oxford, Clarendon Press, 1945).

Cronin, Jeremy, *Inside and Out* (Cape Town, David Philip, 1999).

Crow, Hugh, *Memoirs of the Late Captain Hugh Crow of Liverpool* (London, Frank Cass, 1970).

D'Amico, Jack, *The Moor in English Renaissance Drama* (Tampa, University of South Florida Press, 1991).

Dabydeen, David (ed.), *The Black Presence in English Literature* (Manchester, Manchester University Press, 1985).

Darian-Smith, Kate (ed.), *Captive Lives: Australian Captivity Narratives* (Working

Papers in Australian Studies 85, 86, 87, London, Sir Robert Menzies Centre for Australian Studies, 1993).

Davies, Ioan, *Writers in Prison* (New York, Basil Blackwell, 1990).

Davitt, Michael, *Leaves from a Prison Diary; or, Lectures to a 'Solitary' Audience* (London, Chapman and Hall, 1885).

de Beauvoir, Simone and Halimi, Gisèle, *Djamila Boupacha*. Introduction by Simone de Beauvoir (New York, Macmillan, 1962).

de Peyster, John, Letter to Charles Willson Peale, 2 October 1793, Peale–Sellers Papers, American Philosophical Society, Philadelphia, Pennsylvania.

Deane, James, 'A Further Narrative of James Deane and others', in William Okeley, *Eben-ezer: or, a Small Monument of Great Mercy Appearing in the Miraculous Deliverance of William Okeley, John Anthony, William Adams, John Jephs, John – Carpenter, From the Miserable Slavery of Algiers*, 2nd edition (London, 1684), pp. 86–100.

Derounian-Stodola, Kathryn Z. and Levernier, James A., *The Indian Captivity Narrative, 1550–1900* (New York, Twayne, 1993).

Devoy, John, *Recollections of an Irish Rebel* (Shannon, Ireland, Irish University Press, 1969).

Dew, Gwen, *Prisoner of the Japs* (New York, Alfred A. Knopf, 1943).

Dikobé wa mogale, *Prison Poems* (Johannesburg, Ad. Donker, 1992).

Dixon, Robert, *Writing the Colonial Adventure: Race, Gender and Nation in Anglo-Australian Popular Fiction 1875–1914* (Oakleigh, Melbourne, Cambridge University Press, 1995).

Dlamini, Moses, *Hell-Hole Robben Island: Reminiscences of a Political Prisoner in South Africa* (Trenton, NJ, Africa World Press, 1984).

Donnan, Elizabeth (ed.), *Documents Illustrative of the History of the Slave Trade to America, vol. II* (Washington, DC, Carnegie Institution, 1931).

Duffy, John, *Epidemics in Colonial America* (Baton Rouge, Louisiana State University Press, 1953).

Dunn, Thomas, *Equality of Rich and Poor* (Philadelphia, Dobson, 1793).

Ebersole, Gary, *Captured by Texts: Puritan to Postmodern Images of Indian Captivity* (Charlottesville, University Press of Virginia, 1995).

Elliot, Adam, *A Modest Vindication of Titus Oates the Salamanca-Doctor from Perjury: Or an Essay to Demonstrate Him only Forsworn in several Instances* (London, 1682).

Equiano, Olaudah, *The Interesting Narrative and Other Writings* (1789), ed. Vincent Carretta (London, Penguin, 1995).

Faery, Rebecca Blevins, *Cartographies of Desire: Captivity, Race, and Sex in the Shaping of an American Nation* (Norman, University of Oklahoma Press, 1999).

Falk, Stanley L., *Bataan: The March of Death* (New York, W. W. Norton, 1962).

Fanon, Frantz, *The Wretched of the Earth*, trans. Constance Farrington (New York, Grove Press, 1963; Harmondsworth, Penguin, 1967).

Fehrenbach, T. R., *Lone Star: A History of Texas and the Texans* (New York, Wings Books, 1968).

Feraoun, Mouloud, *Journal, 1955–1962: Reflections on the French-Algerian War*, ed. James D. Le Sueur (Lincoln, University of Nebraska Press, 2000).

Ferguson, Robert, '"We hold these truths": strategies of control in the literature of the Founders,' in Sacvan Bercovitch (ed.), *Reconstructing American History* (Cambridge, MA, Harvard University Press, 1986).

Ferro, Marc, *Colonization: A Global History* (London, Routledge, 1997).

First, Ruth, *117 Days* (New York, Monthly Review, 1965).

Fitzpatrick, Tara, 'The figure of captivity: the cultural work of the Puritan captivity narrative', *American Literary History*, vol. 3 (1991).

Fludernik, Monika, 'Carceral topography: spatiality, liminality and corporality in the literary prison', *Textual Practice*, vol. 13, no. 1 (Spring 1999).

Folwell, Richard, *Short History of the Yellow Fever That Lately Broke out in the City of Philadelphia in July 1797* (Philadelphia, Richard Folwell, 1799).

Foster, Don, Davis, Dennis and Sadler, Diane, *Detention and Torture in South Africa: Psychological, Legal and Historical Studies* (New York, St. Martin's Press, 1987).

Foucault, Michel, *The History of Sexuality, vol. 1, An Introduction* (New York, Random, 1980).

Foucault, Michel, *Discipline and Punish: The Birth of the Prison*, trans. Alan Sheridan (New York, Pantheon, 1977; New York, Vintage, 1979; 2nd edition 1995; London, Penguin, 1979).

Foucault, Michel, *The Order of Things* (London, Routledge, 1994).

Fox, John, 'The woorthie enterprise of John Foxe, in delivering 266. Christians out of the captivitie of the Turkes at Alexandria', in Richard Hakluyt, *The Principall Navigations, Voiages, and Discoveries of the English Nation* (London, 1589), pp. 131–56. [Another version of this narrative appeared as Anthony Munday, *The Admirable Deliverance of 266 Christians by John Reynard Englishman from the captivitie of the Turkes, who had been Gally slaves many yeares in Alexandria* (London, 1608).]

Freneau, Philip, *Letters on Various and Interesting Subjects* (New York, Scholars' Facsimiles, 1943).

Freneau, Philip, *The Poems of Philip Freneau: Poet of the American Revolution*, ed. Fred Lewis Pattee, 3 vols (New York, Russell, 1963).

Freneau, Philip, *The Prose of Philip Freneau*, ed. Philip Marshall (New Brunswick, Scarecrow, 1955).

Fugard, Athol, Kani, John and Ntshona, Winston, 'The Island', *Statements* (New York, Theatre Communications Group, 1986), pp. 45–77.

Gee, Joshua, printed as the *Narrative of Joshua Gee of Boston, Mass., while he was captive in Algeria of the Barbary States, 1680–1687*, ed. Albert C. Bates. Manuscript. Wadsworth Atheneum (Hartford, 1943).

Gelder, Ken and Jacobs, Jane, *Uncanny Australia: Sacredness and Identity in a Postcolonial Nation* (Melbourne, Melbourne University Press, 1998).

Genet, Jean, *Miracle of the Rose*, trans. Bernard Frechtman (New York, Grove Press, 1966).

Genet, Jean, *The Thief's Journal* (Harmondsworth, Penguin, 1971).

Gibbs, Harry, 'Foreword', in M. A. Stephenson and Suri Ratnapala (eds), *Mabo: A Judicial Revolution – The Aboriginal Land Rights Decision and Its Impact on Australian Law* (St Lucia, University of Queensland Press, 1993).

Goddard, James and Pringle, David (eds), *J. G. Ballard: The First Twenty Years* (Hayes, Barn's Head Books, 1976).

Gordimer, Nadine, 'Read all about it: the way they see us', in Liam Browne and Graeme Harper (eds), *Touchpaper Contemporary Pamphlets*, No. 1 (London, Waterstones/Arts Council of England, 2000).

Gordon, Ernest, *Through the Valley of the Kwai* (New York, Harper, 1962).

Graham, Colin, 'Liminal spaces: post-colonial theories and Irish culture', *Irish Review*, 16, Autumn/Winter (1994).

Greenblatt, Stephen, *Marvelous Possessions: The Wonder of the New World* (Chicago, University of Chicago Press, 1991).

Griffiths, Gareth, 'The post-colonial project: critical approaches and problems', in Bruce King (ed.), *New National and Post-colonial Literature: An Introduction* (Oxford, Clarendon Press, 1996).

Griffiths, Tom, *Hunters and Collectors* (Melbourne, Cambridge University Press, 1996).

Grosz-Ngaté, Maria, 'Power and knowledge: the representation of the Mande world in the works of Park, Caillié, Monteil, and Delafosse', *Cahiers d'études africaines*, vol. 28, no. 3–4 (1988): 485–511.

Guha, Ranajit, 'On some aspects of the historiography of colonial India', *Subaltern Studies I: Writings on South Asian History and Society* (Delhi, Oxford University Press, 1994).

Hacker, Margaret S., *Cynthia Ann Parker: The Life and the Legend* (El Paso, Texas Western Press, 1990).

Hage, Renée Boulos, 'Nouveauté du roman d'Amin Maalouf', *Francographies*, vol. 2 (1995): 23–30.

Hall, Kim F., *Things of Darkness: Economies of Race and Gender in Early Modern England* (New York and London, Cornell University Press, 1995).

Hardy, Thomas, *Under the Greenwood Tree* (London, Penguin, 1994).

Harlow, Barbara, *Resistance Literature* (New York, Methuen, 1987).

Harlow, Barbara, *Barred: Women, Writing and Political Detention* (Hanover, NH, Wesleyan University Press, 1992).

Harris, Caroline, *History of the Captivity and Providential Release Therefrom of Mrs. Caroline Harris, Wife of the Late Mr. Richard Harris, of Franklin County . . . New-York, who, with Mrs. Clarissa Plummer, Wife of Mr. James Plummer, Were, in the Spring of 1835 (with their Unfortunate Husbands) Taken Prisoner by the Camanche Tribe of Indians, while Emigrating from said Franklin County (N.Y.) to Texas . . .* (New York, Perry and Cooke, 1838).

Harris, Cheryl I., 'Whiteness as property', *Harvard Law Review*, vol. 106, no. 8 (1993): 1709–91.

Hartman, James D., *Providence Tales and the Birth of American Literature* (Baltimore, Johns Hopkins University Press, 1999).

Hasleton, Richard, *Strange and Wonderfull Things Happened to Richard Hasleton, borne at Braintree in Essex, in his ten yeares travailes in many forraine countries. Penned as he delivered it from his own mouth* (London, 1595).

Healy, Chris, *From the Ruins of Colonialism: History as Social Memory* (Oakleigh, Melbourne, Cambridge University Press, 1997).

Helmuth, Jutus Henry Christian, *A Short Account of the Yellow Fever in Philadelphia for the Reflecting Christian* (Philadelphia, Jones, Hoff & Derrick, 1974).

Herman, Judith L., *Trauma and Recovery* (New York, HarperCollins, 1992).

Hillen, Ernest, *The Way of a Boy: A Memoir of Java* (New York, Penguin, 1993).

Hindmarsh, David, *John Newton and the Evangelical Tradition between the Conversions of Wesley and Wilberforce* (Oxford, Clarendon Press, 1996).

History of the Captivity and Providential Release Therefrom of Mrs. Caroline Harris (New York: Perry and Cooke Publishers, 1838).

Hodge, Bob and Mishra, Vijay (eds), *Dark Side of the Dream: Australian Literature and the Postcolonial Mind* (Sydney, Allen & Unwin, 1991).

Hollingsworth, Levi, Letters received September and October, 1793 (Hollingsworth Family Collection at the Historical Society of Pennsylvania, Philadelphia).

Hulme, Keri, *The Bone People* (London, Hodder & Stoughton, 1984).

Hulme, Peter, *Colonial Encounters: Europe and the Native Caribbean, 1492–1797* (London, Methuen, 1986).

Ishihara, S., *The Japan That Can Say No* (New York, Simon & Schuster, 1991).

Jacobs, Harriet, *Incidents in the Life of a Slave Girl*. Introduction by Valerie Smith (New York, Oxford University Press, 1988; first published 1861).

Janoff-Bulman, Ronnie, *Shattered Assumptions: Towards a Psychology of Trauma* (New York, Free Press, 1992).

Johnson, Richard, *et al.*, 'The casting away of the *Toby* near Cape Espartel, without the strait of Gibraltar on the coast of Barbary, 1593', in Richard Hakluyt, *The Principal Navigations, Voyages, and Discoveries of the English Nation*, 2nd edition (London, 1598–1600).

Johnson, Rosalind R., 'African presence in Shakespearean drama: parallels between Othello and the historical Leo Africanus', *Journal of African Civilizations*, vol. 7, no. 2 (1985): 276–87.

Johnson, Rosalind R., 'Parallels between Othello and the historical Leo Africanus', *Bim*, vol. 18, no. 70 (1986): 9–34.

Jones, Eldred, *The Elizabethans and Africa* (Charlottesville, University of Virginia Press, for the Folger Shakespeare Library, 1968).

Jones, Luther (ed.), *A Geographical Histories of Africa Written in Arabic and Italian by John Leo, a Moor Born in Granada Brought up in Barbarie*, trans. and collected by John Pory (Pittsburgh, Jones's Research and Publishing Company, 1994).

Kadiba, John, 'Growing up in Mailu', in Ulli Beier (ed.), *Black Writing from New Guinea* (St Lucia, University of Queensland Press, 1973).

Kariuki, Josiah Mwangi, *'Mau Mau' Detainee: The Account by a Kenya African of His Experiences in Detention Camps 1953–1960* (London, Oxford University Press, 1963).

Kathrada, Ahmed, *Letters from Robben Island* (Cape Town/E. Lansing, Mayibuye/MSU Press, 1999).

Kearney, Colbert, 'Borstal boy: a portrait of the artist as a young prisoner', in E. H. Mikhail (ed.), *The Art of Brendan Behan* (New York, Barnes and Noble, 1979).

Keith, Agnes Newton, *Three Came Home*. Introduction by Carl Mydans (New York, Time, 1965).

Keon-Cohen, B. A., 'Some problems of proof: the admissibility of traditional evidence', in M. A. Stephenson and Suri Ratnapala (eds), *Mabo: A Judicial*

Revolution – The Aboriginal Land Rights Decision and Its Impact on Australian Law (St Lucia, University of Queensland Press, 1993).

Kerr, E. Bartlett, *Surrender and Survival: The Experience of American POWs in the Pacific 1941–1945* (New York, William Morrow & Co., 1985).

Kim, Elaine H., *Asian American Literature: An Introduction to the Writings and Their Social Context* (Philadelphia, Temple University Press, 1982).

Kinvig, Clifford, *Death Railway*. Ballantine's Illustrated History of the Violent Century, no. 3 (New York, Ballantine, 1973).

Kirkland, Richard, 'Rhetoric and (mis)recognitions: reading Casement', *Irish Studies Review*, vol. 7, no. 2 (August 1999).

Knight, Francis, *A Relation of Seven Yeares Slaverie Under the Turkes of Argeire, suffered by an English Captive Merchant. Wherein is also conteined all memorable Passages, Fights, and Accidents, which happined in that Citie, and at Sea with their Shippes and Gallies during that time. Together with a description of the sufferings of the miserable captives under that mercilesse tyrannie* (London, 1640).

Kolodny, Annette, *The Lay of the Land: Metaphor as Experience and History in American Life and Letters* (Chapel Hill, University of North Carolina Press, 1975).

Kolodny, Annette, *The Land Before Her: Fantasy and Experience of the American Frontiers, 1630–1860* (Chapel Hill, University of North Carolina Press, 1984).

Krog, Antjie, *Country of My Skull* (Johannesburg, Random House, 1998).

La Guma, Alex, *The Stone Country* (Berlin, Seven Seas, 1967).

Lai, H. Mark, Lim, Genny and Yung, Judy, *Island: Poetry and History of Chinese Immigrants on Angel Island 1910–1940* (San Francisco, Hoc Doi, 1980).

Langford, Paul, *A Polite and Commercial People: England 1727–1783* (Oxford, Oxford University Press, 1992).

Lathrop, John, *A Sermon Preached at the Church in Brattle-Street, Boston, Thursday, September 27, 1798* (Boston, T. & J. Swords, 1798).

Le Sueur, James D., 'Before the Jackal: the international uproar over *Assassination!*' Historical essay accompanying *Assassination! July 14* (Lincoln, Nebraska, 2001).

Le Sueur, James D., *Uncivil War: Intellectuals and Identity Politics during the Decolonization of Algeria* (Philadelphia, University of Pennsylvania Press, 2001).

Leary, Timothy, *Jail Notes* (London, New English Library, 1972).

Lebow, Richard Ned, *White Britain, Black Ireland: The Influence of Stereotypes on Colonial Policy* (Philadelphia, Institute for the Study of Human Issues, 1976).

Lempriere, William, *A tour from Gibraltar to Tangier, Salee, Mogodore, Santa Cruz, Tarudant, and thence over Mount Atlas to Morocco*, 3rd edition (London, 1804).

Levernier, James, 'The captivity narrative as regional, military, and ethnic history', *Research Studies*, vol. 45 (1977): 30–7.

Levin, Carole, 'Backgrounds and echoes of *Othello*: from Leo Africanus to Ignatius Sancho', *Lamar Journal of the Humanities*, vol. 22, no. 2 (1996): 45–68.

Lewin, Hugh, *Bandiet: Seven Years in a South African Prison* (Cape Town, David Philip, 1981).

Ling, Amy, *Between Worlds: Women Writers of Chinese Ancestry* (New York, Pergamon Press, 1990).

Liu, Catherine, *Oriental Girls Desire Romance* (New York, Kaya, 1997).

Lloyd, David, *Anomalous States: Irish Writing and the Post-Colonial Moment* (Dublin, Lilliput Press, 1993).

Loomba, Ania, *Gender, Race, Renaissance Drama* (New York, St Martin's Press, 1989).

Loomba, Ania and Orkin, Martin (eds), *Post-Colonial Shakespeares* (London and New York, Routledge, 1998).

Lovejoy, Paul E., *Transformations in Slavery: A History of Slavery in Africa* (Cambridge, Cambridge University Press, 1983).

Lovesey, Oliver, 'Chained letters: African prison diaries and "national allegory"', *Research in African Literatures*, vol. 26, no. 4 (1995): 31–45.

Lowe, Lisa, 'Decolonization, displacement, disidentification', in Deidre Lynch and William B. Warner (eds), *Cultural Institutions of the Novel* (Durham, NC, Duke University Press, 1996).

Lumiere, Cornel, *Kura!* (Brisbane, Jacaranda Press, 1966).

Lupton, Kenneth, *Mungo Park: The African Traveler* (Oxford, Oxford University Press, 1979).

Maalouf, Amin, *Leo Africanus*, trans. Peter Sluglett (Lanham, MD, New Amsterdam Books, 1992).

Mackrill, Joseph, *The History of the Yellow Fever* ... (Baltimore, John Haynes, 1796).

Magliola, Robert, *Derrida on the Mend* (West Lafayette, IN, Purdue University Press, 1984).

Maina wa Kinyatti, *Kenya's Freedom Struggle: The Dedan Kimathi Papers* (London, Zed Press, 1986).

Maina wa, Kinyatti, *Thunder from the Mountains: An Anthology of Mau Mau Songs* (London, Zed Press, 1980).

Makhoere, Caesarina Kona, *No Child's Play: In Prison under Apartheid* (London, Women's Press, 1988).

Mamdani, Mahmood, 'Reconciliation without justice', *Southern African Review of Books* (November/December 1996).

Mangan, H. C., *Robert Emmet: A History Play in Three Acts* (Dublin, Gill and Son, 1904).

Manning, Patrick, *Slavery and African Life: Occidental, Oriental and African Slave Traders* (Cambridge, Cambridge University Press, 1990).

Maponya, Maishe, 'Gangsters', in *Doing Plays for a Change* (Johannesburg, Witwatersrand University Press, 1995), pp. 74–111.

Maran, Rita, *Torture: The Role of Ideology in the French-Algerian War* (New York, Praeger, 1989).

Mashinini, Emma, *Strikes Have Followed Me All My Life* (New York, Routledge, 1991).

Mason, John Mitchell, *A Sermon, Preached September 20th, 1793; A Day Set Apart, in the City of New-York, for the Public Fasting, Humiliation and Prayer, on Account of a Malignant and Mortal Fever Prevailing in the City of Philadelphia* (New York, Loudons, 1793).

Massu, Jacques, *La Vrai Bataille d'Alger* (Paris, Plon, 1971).

Mauer, Marc, 'The international use of incarceration', *Prison Journal*, vol. 75, no. 1 (March 1995): 113–17.

Mellor, Alec, *Je dénonce la torture!* (Paris, Mame, 1972).

Mellor, Alec, *La Torture: son histoire, son abolition, sa réapparition au XXᵉ siècle* (Paris, Meme, 1961).

Middleton, Henry, 'The sixth Voyage, set forth by the East-Indian Company in three Shippes; the *Trades Increase*, of one thousand Tunnes, and in her the Generall Sir Henry Middleton, Admirall; the *Pepper-Corne* of two hundred and fiftie, Vice-Admirall, the Captaine Nicholas Dounton: and the *Darling* of ninetie. The Barke *Samuel* Followed as a Victualler of burthen one hundred and eightie', in Samuel Purchas, *Purchas his Pilgrimes* (London, 1625), pp. 247–66. Reprinted as 'An Account of the Captivity of Sir Henry Middleton By the Turks at Moka, or Mokha; and of his journey from thence, with thirty four Englishmen more, to the Basha at Zenan, or Sanaa: With a Description of the Country, and a Journal of their Travels to that City, and back again', in Jean de Laroque, *A Voyage to Arabia Foelix through the Eastern Ocean and the streights of the Red-Sea, being the first made by the French in the years 1708, 1709, and 1710 . . . To which is added an account of the captivity of Sir Henry Middleton at Mokha, by the Turks, in the year 1612* (London, 1732).

Miller, Joseph, *Way of Death: Merchant Capitalism and the Angolan Slave Trade* (London, Curry, 1988).

Miller, Samuel, *A Sermon, Delivered February 5, 1799; Recommended by the Clergy of the City of New York . . . on Account of the Removal of a Malignant and Mortal Disease . . .* (New York, George Forman, 1799).

Mitchel, John, *Jail Journal* (Washington, DC, Woodstock Books, 1996).

Modisane, William, 'The dignity of begging', in Peggy Rutherfoord (ed.), *Darkness and Light: An Anthology of African Writing* (London, Faith, 1958).

Morgan, Sharon, *Land Settlement in Early Tasmania: Creating an Antipodean England* (Cambridge, Cambridge University Press, 1992).

Murphy, Andrew, 'Ireland and ante/anti-colonial theory', *Irish Studies Review*, vol. 7, no. 2, (August 1999).

Naidoo, Indres, and as told to Albie Sachs, *Robben Island: Ten Years as a Political Prisoner in South Africa's Most Notorious Penitentiary* (First Vintage edition; New York, Vintage, 1982).

Naipaul, V. S., *The Enigma of Arrival* (London, Penguin, 1987).

Namias, June, *White Captives: Gender and Ethnicity on the American Frontier* (Chapel Hill, University of North Carolina Press, 1993).

Nandy, Ashis, *The Intimate Enemy: Loss and Recovery of Self under Colonialism* (Delhi, Oxford University Press, 1998).

Narrative of the Captivity and Extreme Sufferings of Mrs. Clarissa Plummer (New York, Perry & Cooke, 1838).

Narrative of the Capture and Subsequent Sufferings of Mrs. Rachel Plummer: During a Captivity of Twenty-one Months Among The Comanche Indians; With a Sketch of Their Manners, Customs, Laws, &c., &c., with Short Description of the Country Over Which She Traveled Whilst With the Indians. Written by Herself (Waco, Texan Press, 1968).

Narrative of the Capture, Sufferings, and Miraculous Escape of Mrs. Eliza Fraser (New York, Charles Webb & Sons, 1837).

Nederveen, Pieterse, J. P., *White on Black: Images of Africa and Blacks in Western Popular Culture* (New Haven, Yale University Press, 1992).

Newcomb, W. W., Jr, *Indians of Texas: From Prehistoric to Modern Times* (Austin, University of Texas Press, 1961).

Newes from Sally: Of a Strange Delivery of Foure English Captives from the Slavery of the Turkes (London, 1642).

Newton, John, *Letters to a Wife* (Philadelphia, William Young, 1797).

Newton, John, *The Journal of a Slave Trader*, ed. Bernard Martin and Martin Spurrell (London, Epworth Press, 1962).

Newton, John, *The Life of John Newton, Written by Himself with a Continuation by the Reverend Richard Cecil* (Edinburgh, Johnstone & Hunter, 1855).

Ng, Fae Myenne, *Bone* (New York, HarperPerennial, 1993).

Ng, Mei, *Eating Chinese Food Naked* (New York, Washington Square Press, 1998).

Ngũgĩ wa Thiong'o, *Detained: A Writer's Prison Diary* (London, Heinemann, 1981).

Ngũgĩ wa Thiong'o, *Writers in Politics* (London, Heinemann, 1981).

Ngũgĩ wa Thiong'o, *Decolonising the Mind: The Politics of Language in African Literature* (London, James Currey, 1986).

Nitobe, Inazo, *Bushido: The Soul of Japan* (New York, G. P. Putnam, 1905; rpt, Tokyo, Charles E. Tuttle, 1969).

Nordin, Carl S., *We Were Next to Nothing: An American POW's Account of Japanese Prison Camps and Deliverance in World War II* (London, McFarland, 1997).

Nuttall, Sarah and Coetzee, Carli (eds), *Negotiating the Past: The Making of Memory in South Africa* (Cape Town, Oxford University Press, 1998).

O'Connor, Ulick, *Brendan Behan* (London, Abacus, 1993).

O'Donovan Rossa, Jeremiah, *My Years in English Jails* (Tralee, Ireland, Anvil Books, 1967).

O'Sullivan, Michael, *Brendan Behan: A Life* (Dublin, Blackwater Press, 1997).

Okeley, William, *Eben-ezer: or, a Small Monument of Great Mercy Appearing in the Miraculous Deliverance of William Okeley, John Anthony, William Adams, John Jephs, John – Carpenter, From the Miserable Slavery of Algiers, with the wonderful Means of their Escape in a Boat of Canvas; the great Distress, and utmost Extremities which they endured at Sea for Six Days and Nights; their safe Arrival at Mayork: With several Matters of Remarque during their long Captivity, and the following Providences of God which brought them safe to England* (London, 1675).

Pagden, Anthony, *European Encounters with the New World: From Renaissance to Romanticism* (New Haven, Yale University Press, 1993).

Park, Mungo, Review of *The Journal of a Mission to the Interior of Africa, in the Year 1805, By Mungo Park, Quarterly Review*, vol. 13 (April 1815): 120–51.

Park, Mungo, *Travels in the Interior Districts of Africa* (New York, Arno Press, 1971).

Parker, James W., *Narrative of the Perilous Adventures, Miraculous Escapes and Sufferings of Rev. James W. Parker, During a Frontier Residence in Texas, of Fifteen years; with an impartial geographical description of the climate, soil, timber, water. etc. etc. of Texas; written by himself. To which is appended a Narrative of the Capture and Subsequent Sufferings of Mrs. Rachel Plummer during a captivity of twenty-one months among the Comanche Indians, with a sketch of their manners, customs, laws etc. with a short description of the country over which she traveled whilst with the Indians. Written by Herself* (Louisville, KY, Morning Courier Office, 1844).

Patterson, Orlando, *Slavery and Social Death: A Comparative Study* (Cambridge, MA, Harvard University Press, 1982).

Pearce, Roy Harvey, 'The significance of the captivity narrative', *American Literature*, vol. 19 (1948).

Peters, Edward, *Torture: Expanded Edition* (Philadelphia, University of Pennsylvania Press, 1996).

Phelps, Thomas, *A true account of the captivity of Thomas Phelps, at Machaness in Barbary, and of his strange escape in Company of Edmund Baxter and others, as also of the burning two of the greatest pirat-ships belonging to that kingdom, in the River of Mamora; upon the thirteenth day of June 1685* (London, 1685).

Pheto, Molefe, *And Night Fell: Memoirs of a Political Prisoner in South Africa* (Ibadan, Heinemann, 1983).

Phillips, Caryl, *A State of Independence* (New York, Vintage, 1995).

Pitts, Joseph, *A True and Faithful Account of the Religion and Manners of the Mohammetans. In which is a particular Relation of their Pilgrimage to Mecca, The place of Mohammet's birth; And a description of Medina, and of his Tomb there. As likewise of Algier, and the Country adjacent: And of Alexandria, Grand-Cairo, &c. With an Account of the Author's being taken Captive, the Turks Cruelty to him, and of his Escape. In which are many things never Publish'd by any Historian before* (Exeter, 1704).

Porter, Roy (ed.), *Rewriting the Self: Stories from the Renaissance to the Present* (London, Routledge, 1997).

Powell, J. M., *Bring out Your Dead: The Great Plague of Yellow Fever in Philadelphia in 1793* (Philadelphia, University of Pennsylvania Press, 1949).

Pratt, Mary Louise, *Imperial Eyes: Travel Writing and Transculturation* (London, Routledge, 1992).

Priestley, Philip (ed.), *Jail Journeys: The English Prison Experience since 1918* (London, Routledge, 1989).

Rachael Plummer's Narrative of Twenty-one Months Servitude as a Prisoner among the Commanchee Indians. Introduction by William S. Reese (Houston, Telegraph Power Press, 1838; Austin, Jenkins Publishing Company, 1977).

Rawlins, John, *The Famous and Wonderfull Recovery of a Ship of Bristoll, called the Exchange, From the Turkish Pirates of Argier. With the Unmatchable attempts and good successe of John Rawlins, Pilot in her, and other slaves; who in the end wiuth the slaughter of about 40 of the Turkes and Moores, brought the Ship into Plimouth the 13 of February last; with the Captaine a Renegado and 5 Turkes more, besides the resemption of 24 men, and one boy, from Turkish slaverie* (London, 1622).

Reed, Evelyn, *Woman's Evolution* (New York, Pathfinder Press, 1975).

Reese, William S., Introduction in *Rachael Plummer's Narrative of Twenty-one Months Servitude as a Prisoner among the Commanchee Indians* (Austin, Jenkins, 1977).

Reynolds, John, *Launceston: History of An Australian City* (Melbourne, Macmillan/Adult Education Board of Tasmania, 1969).

Roberts, Richard L., *Warriors, Merchants, and Slaves: The State and the Economy in the Middle Niger Valley, 1700–1914* (Stanford, Stanford University Press, 1987).

Roberts, Sheila, 'South African prison literature', *Ariel*, vol. 16, no. 2 (1985): 61–73.

Rogal, Samuel J., 'Mungo Park: physician-traveler to Africa', *Exploration: Journal of the MLA Special Session on the Literature of Exploration and Travel*, vol. 7 (1979): 29–42.

Rowlandson, Mary White, *A True History of the Captivity and Restoration of Mrs Mary Rowlanson* (New York, Garland, 1977; first published 1682).

Rush, Benjamin, *A Second Address to the Citizens of Philadelphia* (Philadelphia, printed by Budd and Bartram for Thomas Dobson, 1799).

Rush, Benjamin, *An Account of the Bilious Remitting Fever in Philadelphia ...* (Philadelphia, Dobson, 1794).

Rushdie, Salman, *Midnight's Children* (London, Picador, 1982).

Ryan, Lyndall, *The Aboriginal Tasmanians*, 2nd edition (St Leonards, NSW, Allen & Unwin, 1996).

Ryder, Sean, 'Male autobiography and Irish cultural nationalism: John Mitchel and James Clarence Mangan', *Irish Review*, vol. 13 (Winter 1992/93).

S[mith], T[homas], *The Adventures of (Mr. T. S.) An English Merchant, Taken Prisoner by the Turks of Argiers and carried into the Inland Countries of Africa: With a Description of the Kingdom of Argiers, of all the Towns and Places of Note thereabouts. Whereunto is added a Relation of the Chief Commodities of the Countrey, and of the Actions and Manners of the People. Written first by the Author, and fitted for the Publick view by A. Roberts. Whereunto is annex'd an Observation of the Tide, and how to turn a Ship out of the Straights Mouth the Wind being Westerly; By Richard Norris* (London, 1670).

Sachs, Albie, *Jail Diary* (London, Sphere, 1966).

Said, Edward, *Orientalism* (New York, Pantheon, 1978).

Sardar, Ziauddin, *Orientalism* (Philadelphia, Open University Press, 1999).

Saunders, A. C. de C. M., *A Social History of Black Slaves and Freedmen in Portugal, 1441–1555* (Cambridge, Cambridge University Press, 1982).

Saunders, Thomas, *A true discription and breefe discourse, of a most lamentable voiage, made lately to Tripolie in Barbarie, in a ship named the Jesus: wherein is not only shewed the great miserie, that then happened the aucthor hereof and his whole companie, as well the marchants as the marriners in that voiage, according to the curssed custome of those barbarous and cruell tyrants, in their terrible usage of Christian captives: but also, the great unfaithfulnesse of those heathnish infidels, in not regarding their promise. Together, with the most wonderfull judgement of God, upon the king of Tripolie and his sonne, and a great number of his people, being all the tormentors of those English captives* (London, 1587).

Schaffer, Kay, *In the Wake of First Contact: The Eliza Fraser Stories* (Melbourne, Cambridge University Press, 1995/6).

Schalkwyk, David, 'Confession and solidarity in the prison writing of Breyten Breytenbach and Jeremy Cronin', *Research in African Literature*, vol. 25, no. 1 (1994): 23–45.

Schreiner, Barbara (ed.), *A Snake with Ice Water: Prison Writings by South African Women* (Johannesburg, Congress of South African Writers, 1992).

Schwarz, Suzanne (ed.), *Slave Captain: The Career of James Irving in the Liverpool Slave Trade* (Wrexham, Bridge Books, 1995).

Searle, Ronald, *Hello – Where Did All the People Go?* (New York, Stephen Crane Press, 1968).

Searle, Ronald, *The Situation Is Hopeless* (New York, Viking, 1980).

Searle, Ronald, *Ronald Searle in Perspective* (New York, Atlantic Monthly, 1983).

Sedgwick, Eve Kosofsky, *Between Men: English Literature and Male Homosocial Desire* (New York, Columbia University Press, 1985).

Sedgwick, Eve Kosofsky, *Epistemology of the Closet* (Hemel Hempstead, Harvester Wheatsheaf, 1991).

Sedgwick, Eve Kosofsky, 'Nationalisms and sexualities', in *Tendencies* (London, Routledge, 1994).

Seligman, Adam, *The Idea of a Civil Society* (Princeton, Princeton University Press, 1992).

Sellin, Thorstein, 'Culture conflict and crime', in Stuart H. Traub and Craig B. Little (eds), *Theories of Deviance* (New York, Peacock, 1975).

Selvon, Sam, *The Lonely Londoners* (New York, Longman, 1997).

Shryock, Richard H., *The Yellow Fever Epidemics, 1793–1805* (New York, New York University Press, 1952).

Silvers, Robert (trans.), *The Gangrene* (New York, Lyle Stuart, 1960).

Simon, Pierre-Henri, *Contre la torture* (Paris, Seuil, 1957).

Slemon, Stephen, 'The scramble for post-colonialism', in Bill Ashcroft, Gareth Griffiths and Helen Tiffin, *The Post-colonial Studies Reader* (London, Routledge, 1995).

Slotkin, Richard, *Regeneration through Violence: Mythology of the American Frontier, 1600–1860* (Middletown, CT, Wesleyan University Press, 1973).

Smith, Adam, *The Theory of Moral Sentiments*, ed. D. D. Raphael and A. L. Macfie (Oxford, Oxford University Press, 1976).

Smith, Adam, *The Wealth of Nations*, ed. Kathryn Sutherland (Oxford, Oxford University Press, 1993).

Snader, Joe, 'The oriental captivity narrative and early English fiction', *Eighteenth-Century Fiction*, vol. 9, no. 3 (1997): 267–98.

Soyinka, Wole, *The Man Died: Prison Notes of Wole Soyinka* (London: Rex Collings, 1972).

Spivak, Gayatri, *In Other Words: Essays in Cultural Politics* (New York, Methuen, 1988).

Spivak, Gayatri, 'Three women's texts and the discourse of imperialism', *Critical Inquiry*, vol. 12 (1985): 243–61.

Spratt, Devereux, 'The Capture of a Protestant Divine, by an Algerine Corsair, in the Seventeenth Century', in T. A. B. Spratt, *Travels and Researches in Crete*, 2 vols (1865); (reprinted Amsterdam, Adolf M. Hakkert, 1984), vol. 1, pp. 384–7.

Stallybrass, Peter, 'Patriarchal territories: the body enclosed', in M. W. Ferguson, M. Quilligan and N. Vickers (eds), *Rewriting the Renaissance: The Discourse of Sexual Difference in Early Modern Europe* (Chicago, University of Chicago Press, 1986).

Stern, Madeline B, *Imprints on History: Book Publisher and American Frontiers* (Bloomington, Indiana University Press, 1956).

Suleri, Sara, *The Rhetoric of English India* (Chicago, Chicago University Press, 1992).

Sullivan, T. D., A. M. and D. B. (eds), *Speeches from the Dock* (Dublin, Gill and Macmillan, 1968).

Sumida, Stephen H., 'Postcolonialism, nationalism, and the emergence of Asian/ Pacific American literatures', in King-Kok Cheung (ed.), *An Interethnic Companion to Asian American Literature* (Cambridge, Cambridge University Press, 1997).

Tambling, Jeremy, *Confession: Sexuality, Sin, the Subject* (Manchester, Manchester University Press, 1990).

Tan, Amy, *The Joy Luck Club* (New York, Ivy Books, 1989).

Tanaka, Yuki, *Hidden Horrors: Japanese War Crimes in World War II* (Boulder, CO, Westview Press, 1996).

Taylor, Jane and Jarry, Alfred, *Ubu and the Truth Commission* (Cape Town, University of Cape Town Press, 1998).

The Tasmanian Mail: A Weekly Journal of Politics, Literature, Science, Agriculture, News and Notes for Tasmania (Hobart, Hobart Mercury Office 1893–94 etc.).

Thrower, Mrs W. I. (Marian Teresa or Mary Theresa), *Younâh! A Tasmanian Aboriginal Romance of the Cataract Gorge* (Hobart, The Mercury Office, 1894).

Toer, Pramoedya Ananta, 'Transportation', in Siobhan Dowd (ed.), *This Prison Where I Live: The PEN Anthology of Imprisoned Writers* (London, Cassell, 1996).

Tone, Wolfe, *The Autobiography*, ed. R. Barry O'Brien (London, T. Fisher Unwin, 1893).

Tsai, Shih-shan Henry, *The Chinese Experience in America* (Bloomington and Indianapolis, Indiana University Press, 1986).

Turner Strong, Pauline, *Captive Slaves, Captivating Others: The Politics and Poetics of Colonial American Captivity Narratives* (Boulder, CO: Westview Press, 1999).

Tuwhare, Hone, 'Lament', in Vincent O'Sullivan (ed.), *An Anthology of Twentieth Century New Zealand Poetry* (Wellington, Oxford University Press, 1976).

van der Post, Laurens, *A Bar of Shadow* (Hyde Park, NY, Hyde Park Free Library, 1956).

VanDerBeets, Richard, 'A surfeit of style: the Indian captivity narrative as penny dreadful', *Research Studies*, vol. 39, no. 4 (1971).

VanDerBeets, Richard, *The Indian Captivity Narrative: An American Genre* (Lantham, MD, University Press of America, 1984).

Vaughan, Alden T. and Clark, Edward W. (eds), *Puritans among the Indians: Accounts of Captivity and Redemption, 1676–1724* (Cambridge, MA, Harvard University Press, 1981).

Verheyen, Gunther, '"Faire vivre les gens ensemble". Un entretien avec Amin Maalouf', *Französisch heute*, vol. 1 (1996): 36–8.

Vidal-Naquet, Pierre, *Torture: Cancer of Democracy, France and Algeria 1954–1962* (Baltimore, Penguin, 1963).

Vidal-Naquet, Pierre (ed.), *Les Crimes de l'armée française* (Paris, Maspero, 1975).

Vidal-Naquet, Pierre, *L'Affaire Audin* (Paris, Minuit, 1989).

Villa-Vicencio, Charles and Verwoerd, Wilhelm, *Looking back, Reaching Forward: Reflections on the Truth and Reconciliation Commission of South Africa* (Cape Town, University of Cape Town Press/Zed Books, 2000).

Vittori, Jean-Pierre, *Confessions d'un professionnel de la torture: la guerre d'Algérie.* (Paris, Ramsay, 1980).

Wadsworth, James, *The English Spanish Pilgrime, or a new discoverie of Spanish popery and jesuitical strategems* (London, 1630).

Washburn, Wilcomb E., 'Introduction', in Alden T. Vaughan (ed.), *Narratives of North American Indian Captivity: A Selective Bibliography* (New York, Garland, 1983).

Webbe, Edward, *The Rare and most wonderful thinges which Edward Webbe an Englishman borne, hathe seene and passed in his troublesome travailes, in the Cities of Jerusalem, Dammasko, Bethelem and Galely: and in the Landes of Jewrie, Egipt, G[r]ecia, Russia, and in the Land of Prester John. Wherein is set foorth his extreme slaverie sustained many yeres togither, in the Gallies and wars of the Great Turk against the Landes of Persia, Tartaria, Spaine, and Portugall, with the manner of his releasement, and coming into Englande in May last* (London, 1590).

Webster, Noah, *A Collection of Papers on the Subject of Bilious Fevers* (New York, Hopkins, Webb and Co., 1796).

Weigley, Russell (ed.), *Philadelphia: A 300-year History* (New York, W. W. Norton, 1982).

White, Peter (ed.), *Benjamin Tompson, Colonial Bard: A Critical Edition* (University Park, Pennsylvania State University Press, 1980).

Whitehead, John, 'John Whitehead his relation of Barbary'. Ms. Sloane 90. British Library.

Whitney, Atwell, *Almond-eyed: The Great Agitator: A Story of the Day* (San Francisco, A. L. Bancroft, 1878).

Whitney, Lois, 'Did Shakespeare know Leo Africanus?', *PMLA*, vol. 37 (1922): 470–83.

Wideman, John Edgar, 'Fever', in *Fever: Twelve Stories* (New York, Holt, 1989).

Wilde, Oscar, [C.3.3.] *The Ballad of Reading Gaol* (London, Leonard Smithers, 1898).

Williams, Eric, *Capitalism and Slavery* (London, Andre Deutsch, 1964).

Wilson, James, *The Earth Shall Weep: A History of Native America* (London, Picador, 1998).

Wilson, Kathleen, *The Sense of the People: Politics, Culture and Imperialism in England, 1715–1785* (Cambridge, Cambridge University Press, 1995).

Woodward, Theodore E., 'Yellow fever: from colonial Philadelphia and Baltimore to the mid-twentieth century', Zigerist Supplement to the *Bulletin of the History of Medicine* (1980).

Wordsworth, William, *The Prelude* (London, Penguin Classics, 1986).

Wu, William F., *The Yellow Peril: Chinese Americans in American Fiction 1850–1940* (Hamden, Archon Books, 1982).

Yeats, W. B., *Collected Plays* (London, Macmillan, 1952).

Zwelonke, D. M., *Robben Island* (Oxford, Heinemann, 1973).

Index